Deploying Microsoft® Exchange Server 5.5

Microsoft Press

PUBLISHED BY
Microsoft Press
A Division of Microsoft Corporation
One Microsoft Way
Redmond, Washington 98052-6399

Library of Congress Cataloging-in-Publication Data
Deploying Microsoft Exchange Server 5.5 / Microsoft Corporation.
     p. cm.
   Includes index.
   ISBN 0-7356-0529-7
   1. Microsoft Exchange server 2. Client / server computing.
 I. Microsoft Corporation.
 QA76.9.C55D45 1998
 005.7'13769--dc21   98-22195
                                         CIP

Printed and bound in the United States of America.

1 2 3 4 5 6 7 8 9 QMQM 3 2 1 0 9 8

Distributed in Canada by ITP Nelson, a division of Thomson Canada Limited.

A CIP catalogue record for this book is available from the British Library.

Microsoft Press books are available through booksellers and distributors worldwide. For further information about international editions, contact your local Microsoft Corporation office or contact Microsoft Press International directly at fax (425) 936-7329. Visit our Web site at mspress.microsoft.com.

Acquisitions Editor: Anne Hamilton
Project Editor: Maureen Williams Zimmerman

Thank you to all the field consultants and support engineers who contributed their time, expertise, and wealth of experience to make this book possible.

Enterprise Services—Americas
Brian Boruff

Microsoft TechNet
Tim McBride

Editorial
Bob Haynie, Thomas Hoffman, Michael Ohata

Contributing Consultants and Engineers
Michael Aday, John Akers, Michael Armijo, Dan Bloch, Paul Bowden, Jason Brandt, Greg Dodge, Mark Garcia, Matt Finger, Garth Keesler, Stanley Lum, Patrick McFarland, Jeff Newfeld, Peter Nilsson, Perry Owen, Joseph Pagano, Laura Payne, Peter Rakoczy, Bill Skilton, Constantine Vaduva, Martin Thall, Maureen Tracy Venti, Zev Yanovich, Bill Zentmayer

Contributing Groups
Exchange Connectivity Competency Center (EC3), Microsoft Consulting Services New Jersey, Premier Support Team West,

Technical Review
Rabih Andari, Tim Ball, Joanne Bromwell, Jana Field, Jack Huffman, Kristina Marx, Mark van der Merwe, Dian Murray, Marc Stanton, Sameer Patel, Allan Risk, Paul Sockwell, Thomas Spencer

Copy Editing, Graphics Design, and Production
Enterprise Service Assets User Education team

Indexer
Richard S. Shrout

Project Editor
Maureen Zimmerman

Contents

Part 4: Deploying Microsoft Exchange

Introduction

Welcome to *Deploying Microsoft Exchange Server 5.5—Best Practices from Microsoft Consulting Services*, the first in the *Notes from the Field* series. Designed for information technology (IT) and information systems (IS) professionals, this book condenses and organizes the broad expertise of field consultants and support engineers, and offers you the benefit of their real-world experiences.

You should use this book as a supplement to the Microsoft Exchange Server 5.5 product documentation and the *Microsoft Exchange Server 5.5 Resource Guide* in the *Microsoft BackOffice Resource Kit, Second Edition.* The resource guide contains a wealth of information, ranging from high level (Exchange Server architecture) to fine detail (addressing and routing, and a discussion on Collaboration Data Objects—CDO—and the Exchange Forms Designer). The resource guide is the encyclopedia of Exchange, and the book you are reading now often refers you to it for general and background information.

No single book can cover every implementation and maintenance topic for a product as complex as Exchange Server. In fact, this book focuses tightly on planning the rollout, designing the messaging system, understanding coexistence and migration scenarios, and deploying Microsoft Outlook clients and Exchange servers. It does not discuss setting up Exchange for Microsoft Cluster Server, Outlook Web Access, Exchange Event Service scripting, or chat services. Nor does it go into great detail on all the built-in connectivity services. *Deploying Microsoft Exchange Server 5.5* offers practical guidelines and steps to get your system up and running. A companion book, *Managing and Maintaining Microsoft Exchanger Server 5.5*, will deal with optimizing and supporting the Exchange messaging system.

What's in This Book

There are four parts, each with several chapters.

Part 1: Planning For Exchange

Is it possible to exaggerate the importance of planning an Exchange deployment? Most consultants don't think so. This section covers gathering information, specifying the functionality you need, conducting a gap analysis, and setting up a test environment. To create a plan, you thoroughly document the existing network infrastructure and identify what messaging functionality your organization needs. Then you gather and organize this information and use it to build a test configuration in which you systematically evaluate the proposed production environment.

Part 2: Guide to Building the Microsoft Exchange Backbone

Part 2 begins with an overview of site topology and designing the Exchange backbone, then drills down into client and service bandwidth requirements and how to calculate server placement. The front half of the section covers the messaging system's logical design, public folders, and how to configure the message transfer agent (MTA) for slow links. The second half goes into more advanced aspects of backbone design: security design and implementation, connector choices, directory replication, and background traffic.

Part 3: Coexistence and Migration Scenarios

In many cases, rolling out Exchange Server involves integration with legacy messaging systems. This section starts by discussing Lotus Notes and Lotus cc:Mail, providing hands-on, practical information you can use to integrate these systems with—and eventually migrate to—Exchange. It then goes on to cover integration with Microsoft Mail for PC Networks, Fisher EMC2/TAO—SNADS, and AppleTalk/Quarterdeck/StarNine mail systems.

Part 4: Deploying Microsoft Exchange

An Exchange deployment is a complicated process, and when it's time to roll out servers and clients a simple documentation review does not tell you everything you need to know. This section provides an audit template you can use to make sure that all the design work you completed back in Part 1 has made it into the deployment package. Next there is an overview of the deployment principles and planning involved in rolling out Microsoft Outlook clients, followed by instructions for implementing an unattended installation of Outlook clients, Exchange servers, and connectors. Chapter 17 wraps things up with a brief explanation of how to use Active Directory Service Interfaces (ADSI) to create a Microsoft Windows NT Server domain account and an Exchange mailbox, then associate them—all from a simple Web form.

Additional Information

Appendix A details how to configure Windows NT Server and Exchange Server to implement the Dynamic RAS Connector over TCP/IP. Appendix B explains how to configure ShivaRemote 3.59 for use with Exchange. Appendix C lists references and resources, including support offerings, Web sites, white papers, and Microsoft Technical Support Knowledge Base articles on Exchange Server and *upgrading* to Exchange 5.5.

The last thing in the book may be the first thing you'll want to take advantage of: a time-limited Microsoft TechNet sample CD-ROM that includes a representative selection of one issue's contents *and* the sample code files mentioned in Chapter 17. For a book such as this one, drawn from first-hand accounts and experience, TechNet is the obvious companion piece: it is *the* support resource for professionals in the trenches. Each month, it provides subscribing IT professionals with in-depth information on evaluating, deploying, managing, and supporting Microsoft products and technologies.

Conventions Used

Convention	Description
ALL CAPITALS	Acronyms, filenames, and names of commands.
bold	Menus and menu commands, command buttons, property page and dialog box titles and options, command-line commands, options, and portions of syntax that must be typed exactly as shown.
Initial Capitals	Names of applications, programs, servers, windows, directories, and paths.
Italic	Information you have to enter, first occurrences of special terms, and book titles. Used also for emphasis as dictated by context.
`monospace type`	Sample command lines, program code, and program output.
Q123456, Title: XGEN: How to Deploy Microsoft Exchange Server 5.5	Knowledge Base article titles. Search for them on Microsoft TechNet or at http://support.microsoft.com/support/a.asp?M=F using the "Q" number (no spaces).

C H A P T E R   1

Gathering Information

Planning, developing, and deploying a Microsoft Exchange Server version 5.5 messaging solution is a complex undertaking. It is best approached systematically, with an understanding of the phases entailed in the overall project, an efficient distribution of tasks and responsibilities, and all appropriate planning completed at each phase. This section details information you need to plan a deployment.

Define the Project Team and Project Structure

Large-scale Microsoft Exchange Server deployments are complex, making it necessary to divide project tasks by functional areas. In addition, team members should be trained on both Microsoft Windows NT Server and Microsoft Exchange Server so that everyone has the same technical proficiency and understands the implications of adding functionality.

Training for both courses is available at:

- Microsoft Authorized Training Centers (ATECs), which offer courses on Windows NT Server. More information is available at http://www.microsoft.com/Train_Cert/train/atec.htm.

- Specialized training centers authorized by Microsoft Product Support Services, which provide a 10-day Exchange support course.

An Exchange deployment team typically includes these roles and groups:

Role	Responsibility
Product Manager	Sets objectives.
	Manages external relationships.
	Sets the budget.
Program Manager	Has overall responsibility for Exchange network design and implementation.
	Specifies Exchange messaging system functional requirements.
Microsoft Exchange Engineering	Determines technical configuration of all Exchange server components.
Testing/QA	Ensures Exchange messaging system conformance to functional requirements and corporate standards.
Operations Development	Develops procedures, policies, and programs that monitor, control, and backup the Exchange network.
Technical Consulting, (third-level technical support)	Provides consulting services and problem resolution for internal business units.
Training Development	Develops training materials and documentation for users and technical support personnel.
Rollout Planning	Determines the most efficient way to roll out Exchange servers and accompanying Windows NT Servers.
	Minimizes deployment costs.
	Promotes efficient implementation.
Migration Planning	Determines the work needed to migrate from an existing messaging system to Exchange. (This may include porting mail-enabled applications and translating existing user data.)
Implementation Management	Manages the implementation of the Exchange Server and associated components.
End User Technical Support	Provides user technical support of Exchange-related problems and questions.
Messaging Transport Operations	Maintains, operates, monitors, and repairs the Exchange environment (after installation).
ID Administration	Maintains the Exchange user database.

Role	Responsibility
Marketing and Customer Relations	Develops and carries out the Exchange rollout marketing program, including product demonstrations, newsletters, and pilot site coordination.
	Acts as a client advocate in design meetings.
Financial Control	Monitors financial aspects of the project.
	Tracks expenses against budget allocations.

Define the Project Structure

Defining the project structure involves:

- Identifying high-level risks and developing mitigation strategies.
- Building the test lab and developing procedures.
- Defining a communications strategy.

Assess and Mitigate Risks

Although risk assessment and mitigation are started during the envisioning phase, it's important to reassess risks periodically so new ones (perhaps arising out of the completion of a project task or phase) don't delay or derail the project. Use the table below to assess risks identifiable in the planning stage. The risk level is the probability that the problem will occur.

Item	Description	Current status	Risk level
Messaging team	Defined roles and responsibilities		
Project plan	Defined milestone-driven project plan		
Business requirements	Clearly defined business requirements		
Project communication	Process to communicate the status of the project to customers		

Risk assessments for other areas are discussed in these sections:

- Infrastructure requirements
- Exchange-specific planning
- Coexistence and migration issues
- Deployment planning
- Operations and systems management issues
- Technical support

Communicate with Team and Customers

Communicating progress to team members and potential users is vital to coordinating project activity and establishing appropriate expectations. A guiding principle in describing software deployments to end users is: *under-promise and over-deliver.*

Whenever possible, use media accessible to all parties—such as e-mail, web pages, corporate publications, or public folders—so they can review information easily. Schedule project meetings judiciously, invite only those who have something to contribute, and circulate an agenda in advance.

Demonstrations can instill confidence in end users if hardware and software have been thoroughly tested. When ready, focus the demo on how using the product results in increased efficiency and productivity, and how end users will benefit.

Gather Information

Information needed to make design decisions includes:

- Organizational structure and locations
- Current network infrastructure
- Current messaging and directory infrastructure
- Current desktop environment
- Functional requirements
- Desired end state

See the last section of this chapter, "Messaging Environment Checklist," for a full list of all the information you must gather.

Organizational Structure and Locations

Information on where users are physically located can help determine possible server locations and predict the flow of messages across the network. The physical location of business units is important because most electronic communication stays within business units of an enterprise. The areas that need investigation are:

- Geographic locations
- Sites at each location
- Business units at each site
- Site-specific information:
    - Address
    - Contact name, with telephone/fax/e-mail numbers
    - Total number of employees
    - Total number of mail service users
    - Number of local users
    - Number of remote users
    - Number of desktops
    - Number of workstations per configuration (For example: 600 on 386s, 700 on 486s, 60 on Macintoshes)

Current Network Infrastructure

The current connectivity between physical locations and network services can impose constraints on the new Exchange network, so it should be studied carefully.

Focus on:

- Physical network topology
- Protocol management
- Host name resolution services
- Windows NT Server domain structure
- Remote access
- Network operations/performance management

After this information has been gathered, assess and rate the risks in these areas:

Item	Description	Current status	Risk level
Microsoft Windows NT Server domain plan	Microsoft Exchange relying on Windows NT security for access to user mailbox		
Protocol assignment	Services in place to reliably assign protocol addresses		
Host name resolution	Services to allow clients to locate host servers across the network; may include Windows Internet Naming Service (WINS) and Domain Name System (DNS)		
Physical network	Reliable connectivity between network points		
Remote access	Dial-up Point-to-Point Protocol (PPP) services		
Machine naming standards	Definition of machine naming standards to avoid conflicts		
Logon ID standards	Naming standards for logon Ids		

Physical Network Topology

Understanding the physical network that Exchange Server will use is critical to the design of the routing topology, server placement, and choice of site connector. Two areas are particularly important:

- **Bandwidth**—Bandwidth available to branch offices helps determine whether a server should be located at that facility. If a very slow and highly used link serves that office, an onsite server might be an appropriate technical decision.

- **Backbone topology**—Backbone topology helps determine if fault-tolerant routes can be established.

Document network topology by describing:

- Router locations
- Line speeds between routers
- Average use of links
- Redundancy (dial backup in place)
- Remote dial-in points-of-presence
- Protocols supported on the links
- Reliability and service levels of links

Protocol Address Management

Network protocols provide connectivity between the workstation and the server. The most common protocol in use for client server computing is Transport Control Protocol/Internet Protocol (TCP/IP). Messaging services must be in place to assign addresses to workstations, especially for machines that regularly connect to different network segments. Gather information on management technology and server location.

Host Name Resolution Service

Name resolution service allows workstations to connect to servers. Microsoft Exchange running on Microsoft Windows NT 4.0 needs to have WINS installed, in which case you must document the existing WINS environment to ensure it will cover all the workstations and servers involved in the deployment. Information needed:

- Location of existing WINS servers
- WINS replication topology
- WINS node type used

Microsoft Windows NT Server Domain Structure

Exchange Server relies on Windows NT for authentication, so any existing Windows NT Server domain structures must be documented to determine if they will provide coverage for the planned Exchange users. Information needed:

- Existing account domains
- Existing resource domains
- Existing trust relationships

Remote Access

Many Exchange Server users will access the system by dialing in, so existing remote access systems must be identified and evaluated. Information needed:

- Remote access points
- Number of modems
- Current restrictions
- Compatibility with Microsoft remote networking

Network Operations and Performance Management

Exchange Server relies on network services and will be affected by any outages or network-related problems. Therefore, it is important to document current processes for network monitoring and performance management. You should also note the reliability of network links, and any service level agreements for availability.

Current Messaging and Directory Infrastructure

Provide information on other messaging systems with which Exchange Server must coexist during the migration phase. To determine how to connect to other systems and how to migrate users, perform a detailed audit of the existing system. Information needed:

- Messaging topology
- Address naming conventions

Messaging Topology

To assist with planning the Exchange Server site topology and migration plan, document the existing electronic mail network. Information needed:

- Mailbox locations
- MTA locations and mailboxes to which they connect
- Number of users on each mailbox
- Connections to other systems
- Directory synchronization services and agents

Address Naming Conventions

Understanding existing mail address naming conventions helps to define strategies for proxy generation with Exchange Server. Document the current messaging system structure. Information needed:

- Microsoft Mail naming conventions
  - Organization name
  - Site name
  - Server name
  - Mailbox alias name
  - Postoffice first name
  - Postoffice last name
  - Postoffice display name
  - X.400 address
  - Simple mail transfer protocol (SMTP) address
  - Microsoft Mail address
  - Connector names
  - Monitor names
  - Container names
  - Distribution list names
  - Public folder names
  - Custom recipient name
- cc:Mail
- X.400 naming conventions:

Item	Issues	Finding
Surname	How are duplicate names handled?	
Given name		
Initials	Are full initials used or just the middle initial?	
Common name	Is a common name used? What is it?	
Generation qualifiers	Are they used?	
DDA	Is DDA used? What information is contained in the DDA?	

- Internet (SMTP) naming conventions:

Item	Issues	Finding
Domain name	What is the domain name?	
Alias name	How are alias tables maintained?	

External Connectivity

To plan the external connection points for Exchange Server, document existing connection points and their types. Information needed:

- X.400
- Internet/SMTP
- Fax
- SNADS
- PROFS

Backbone

Most corporations use point-to-point connectivity between messaging systems and use a dedicated gateway to separate them. There are also cases where one system acts as a switch to allow connectivity to a third system.

In other cases, a common backbone of a certain message type (often SMTP or X.400) is created, requiring other systems to translate their messages to the common format before they can be sent to another system. Either way, use diagrams to show how messages are routed between internal systems and identify the systems that act as switches.

Use the below table for X.400 backbone systems.

Item	Issues	Finding
Message transfer agent (MTA) vendor	The MTA process is one of the most complex pieces of Exchange. It is extremely important to verify that conformance testing between this MTA and Exchange has been done.	
Standard compliance	Which standard does the MTA follow (1984 or 1988)?	

Item	Issues	Finding
Supported protocols	Does this MTA support Open Systems Interconnection (OSI) and/or Transmission Control Protocol (TCP)?	
What is the name of the MTA?	Who is the vendor?	
Which encoded information types are supported?	Exchange supports IA5, German IA5, Norwegian IA5, Swedish IA5, T61, ISO6937, and 8859 Latin1.	
What is the private management domain (PRMD)?		
What is the organization name?		
Does the company use organizational unit OU routing?	Do they use organizational-based routing? Identify the various organizations and organizational units.	
Is the X.400 backbone system used for auto forwarding or distribution list expansion?		
Is the MTA under maintenance?	Can they get support for it? Are patches available?	
Mail exchangers vendor	Which hardware platform is used for the mail exchangers?	
Version of sendmail	A number of versions of sendmail are available.	
Is uuencode or Multipurpose Internet Mail Extensions (MIME) supported?		
DNS servers	What are the addresses of the DNS servers? Is DNS used?	
Is there a firewall or smart host?	Is all mail forwarded to the firewall/smart host for security reasons?	
Who administers the Mail Exchange Records (MXs)?		
Is the SMTP backbone system used for auto forwarding or distribution list expansion?		
What is the process for adding additional DNS entries?		

Directory Synchronization

A key issue for companies with different messaging systems is keeping the directories of each system up to date during migration. When integrating Exchange into an existing infrastructure or adding another infrastructure, it is crucial to document the current process for synchronizing the various mail systems directories.

Document the directory synchronization issues by explaining the:

- Process currently used within each of the currently installed messaging systems.
- Process currently used between the various messaging systems.
- Fields that are currently part of the mailbox information (for example, phone number and organization).
- Source of the data (for example, feeds from other databases).
- The stability and accuracy of the current system.

Technical Support

During the migration period, technical support may find it hard to keep up with demand as users become familiar with the new environment. To lessen the strain on support, determine whether the current system can handle the load during the migration by examining the current technical support organization in the following areas:

- Current problem resolution process. (Does helpdesk or a local network administrator handle the first report of trouble? What is the escalation procedure?)
- Current excess capacity in the system.
- Training levels of technical support staff.

Operations

The operations group is responsible for the health of the messaging system. Many customers redesign their messaging operations environment when they deploy Exchange. To gauge the need for an overhaul, study these areas:

- Current operations processes for detecting and repairing outages
- Current monitoring systems in use
- Training levels of operations staff

Training

Training provides users, administrators, and operators with information on how to work effectively with the system. The training curriculum should focus on what the new system can do and on improving the performance of users to reduce their reliance on support. Document current training procedures in these areas:

- Delivery methods (classes, videos, etc.) to users, administrators, and operators.
- Expertise of those conducting training.

Assess Network Infrastructure Risks

Use this table:

Item	Description	Current status	Risk level
Server placement	The physical location of the Exchange servers		
Site topology	The logical grouping of Exchange servers		
Connection topology	How the sites will be interconnected		
External connectivity	How Exchange will communicate with external systems such as SMTP and X.400		
Naming standards	Standard values for the critical name spaces: organization, site, server, and domain		
Disaster recovery	Backup and restore processes		
Directory replication topology	Definition of how the Exchange directory will be replicated between sites		
Public folder replication	Definition of how public folders will be replicated		
Administrative model	Definition of how administrative responsibilities will be distributed or centralized		

(continued)

Item	Description	Current status	Risk level
Alternate client access	Definition of how or whether Post Office Protocol version 3 (POP3), IMAP4, or Web clients will be supported		
Server sizing	Definition of size and configuration of Exchange servers		
Security	Definition of what level of security will be supported		

Current Desktop Environment

Deploying Microsoft Exchange clients to individual desktops can be one of the most time-consuming tasks. One way to improve deployment is to estimate the percentages of each type of configuration and identify profiles of all user types for the enterprise messaging system. Information needed:

- Desktop platforms
- Operating systems
- Network redirector
- Protocols
- Desktop or portable system

Functional Requirements

Ask users what kind of functionality they would like out of the new messaging system for ideas that you'll use in designing the functional specification. The list should contain only *what* function is desired, not *how* it should be accomplished. Typically, this is a combination of functions provided by the current system and new functions available from Microsoft Exchange Server 5.5. This list should be continually updated and prioritized by the project team or a specific group within the team.

Administrative Functionality

As a starting point, examine the administrative process in place for the current mail system in these areas:

- Mailbox administration
- Network ID administration
- Server backup and restoration features

User Functionality

To determine user requirements, document features currently available, such as:

- Remote connectivity
- Add-on functions
- Calendar and scheduling

Additional Risk Assessment

Assess risks in the areas of deployment, training, and administration in the areas outlined below.

Item	Description	Current status	Risk
Server deployment	Plans and procedures for deploying servers		
Client deployment	Plans and procedures for deploying clients; include road warriors and home machines		
Site administrator training	Appropriate training for site administration personnel		
User training	Training class and/or materials for users		
Failure monitoring	Systems to alert operations that a network failure has occurred		
Performance trending	Systems to monitor ongoing system performance		
Service pack and upgrades	Systems to allow easy distribution of service packs and upgrades		
Deployment team support	Escalation support for the server and client deployment teams		
User help desk support	First- and second-line user support personnel trained and in place		
Backbone support	Operational support personnel trained and in place		

Desired End State

The information-gathering step is to expand the conceptual design (created during the envisioning phase) by graphically showing the messaging system end state, defined as the desired product of an architecture. This diagram includes end-state Exchange Server locations and shows the interaction of external messaging systems and interactions with other data sources for directory synchronization.

Messaging Environment Checklist

Activity	Issue	Finding
Identifying geographic location and business unit data		
Site data	Address	
	Contact name, with telephone/fax/e-mail numbers	
	Total number of employees	
	Total number of mail service users	
	Number of local users	
	Number of remote users	
	Number of desktops	
	Number of workstations by configuration (For example, 600 on 386s, 700 on 486s, 60 on Macintoshes)	
Documenting the current network environment		
Messaging system environment	High-level system structure	
	E-form features	
	Microsoft Mail address naming conventions	
	X.400 address naming conventions	
	Internet address naming conventions	
	Windows NT–related address naming conventions	

Activity	Issue	Finding
Messaging services	Current Windows NT Server domain model	
	Physical location of the account domain servers	
	Member servers in the account domains	
	Resource domains	
	Domain server locations—primary domain controllers (PDCs) and backup domain controllers (BDCs)—in each resource domain	
	Trust relationships between resource and account domains	
	Current Windows NT Server implementation	
	Windows NT profile	
	Microsoft Mail postoffices	
	Microsoft Mail message transfer agents	
	Microsoft Mail dispatch agents	
	Microsoft Mail gateways	
	Migration from an Exchange-supported mail system	
Messaging backbones	Protocol technology used between the various mail systems	
	Message switches that are used to transfer mail between systems	
	Proprietary backbone Interfaces	
	Proprietary backbone functions	
	X.400 backbones	
	SMTP backbones	

(continued)

Activity	Issue	Finding
Directory synchronization	Mixed directory structure (several mail systems)	
	Current messaging directory processes	
	Directories managed by an external group	
	Extent of the directory and management area	
	Extent of directory management required	
	Update distribution frequency	
	Microsoft Mail systems	
	Current directory synchronization method	
Connectivity issues	High-level WAN structure (diagram)	
	Detailed WAN structure (zoom-view diagram for each WAN section)	
	WAN connectivity	
	Bandwidth	
	Availability	
	Bridge and router hardware and software currently in use	
	Bridge and router configuration	
	WAN link types and speeds	
	Network redundancy	
	Site-specific network availability requirements	
	Planned WAN changes	
	WAN change process	
	Segment-specific bandwidth usage	

Activity	Issue	Finding
	Protocols used on each WAN segment	
	Customer plans for WAN protocol standardization	
	Percentage of the current usage consumed by the current workstation and server messaging platforms	
	Number of messaging users who access the WAN from each site/segment	
	Local area network (LAN) architecture	
	LAN topology at each site	
	LAN segment distribution	
	Protocols are used at each site	
	Areas specifically designed for high traffic	
	Type of planned LAN changes	
	Schedule of planned LAN changes	
	LAN usage	
	Protocols used on LAN segments	
	Protocol bridging	
	Protocol filtering	
	Type of planned LAN standardization	
	Schedule of planned LAN standardization	
	Network connectors (gateways)	
	Which gateways (if any) are used	
	Connectivity options of internal and external systems	
	Gateway alternatives available from third parties	

(continued)

Activity	Issue	Finding
	X.400 configuration	
	Company's administrative management domain (ADMD)	
	Whether the MTA supports the OSI or TCP protocol	
	Multiple links (multinational organizations)	
	X.400 transport	
	Internet connectivity	
	Fax connectivity	
	Coexistence methods	
	Upgrade path to a supported solution	
Documenting the current desktop environment		
User profiles	Local users	
	Remote users	
	Power users	
	International user	
User scenarios	Who uses the mail system	
	What they use the mail system for	
	When they use the mail system versus other forms of communication	
	Where they retrieve mail from	
	Why they use e-mail versus other means of communications	
	How often they use the mail system (high-, medium-, or low-use categories)	
	Whether the mail system is primarily a memo-based messaging tool	

Activity	Issue	Finding
	Whether messaging uses system attachments	
	Which groups communicate with one another	
	When and how often groups are used	
	What users like most (and least) about the current system	
	New feature or capability users would want	
	What level of security users need for their data	
Desktop software	Desktop operating systems	
	Proprietary application configurations	
	Current standard configurations	
	Version	
	Percentage of users on each application	
	Process for selecting which type of applications reside on the workstation versus which ones reside on the server	
	Mail-enabled applications	
	Feasibility of the level of support available for Messaging Application Programming Interface (MAPI) 1.0	
	Multiple redirectors	
	Current standard configurations	
	Version	
	Percentage of users on each operating system	
	Process for selecting which type of applications reside on the workstation versus which ones reside on the server	

(continued)

Activity	Issue	Finding
	Mail-enabled applications	
	Feasibility of the level of support available for MAPI 1.0	
	Multiple redirectors	
	Network drivers	
	The redirector (network shell) being used	
	Whether the redirector supports remote procedure calls (RPCs)	
	Whether redirector is on the list of supported network clients	
	All the protocol stacks	
	Up-to-date list of supported TCP/IP stacks	
	Which business units use which protocol	
	Installation procedures	
	Process for modifying installation procedures	
	Whether the process includes any tools to facilitate distribution of additional packages	
	Patches	
Desktop hardware	Creation of a hardware profile	
	Creation of a representative sample of desktop configurations	
	Disk management	
	Disk space available on workstations	
	Logical partitioning of drives	
	Shared application environments	

Activity	Issue	Finding
	Current attitude about local versus network applications	
	Standard directory structure used in new application installations	
	Remote user patterns (terminal emulation versus remote control, remote control nodes)	

CHAPTER 2

Desired Functionality and Gap Analysis

After you have documented your existing messaging environment, the next step is to decide what functionality you want and what user functionality gaps must be filled. This chapter walks you through the process of defining requirements and shows how to conduct a gap analysis. Chapter 3, "Setting up a Test Environment," shows you how to put this information to use in testing and designing your Microsoft Exchange 5.5 messaging system.

Define Required Functionality

Now it's time to develop a detailed list of what functions will be implemented in the Exchange Server messaging system. This list may not be the full list identified in a gap analysis, but rather the minimal amount of functionality required to start deployment. Using versions allows the project team to implement functionality in phases to keep the scope and delivery schedule manageable.

Separate the functions into groups:

- User functions
- Administrative functions
- Operation functions
- Coexistence functions or dependencies
- Infrastructure dependencies

Use a formula of *perceived value* versus *costs to implement and support* to develop the functionality list. Use this sequence:

1. Start with a list of functional requirements and function points generated during the gap analysis.
2. Examine each requirement in terms of costs and potential risks.
3. Identify acceptable requirements and add them to the project plan.
4. Move additional requirements to the next version of the messaging system.

Specify Performance Criteria

Specify performance criteria for system operations. Common criteria include:

- Availability of the Exchange servers
- Message delivery time
- Messages per hour

Specify Operational Constraints

In conjunction with the performance criteria, certain constraints should be defined regarding data that will be traveling through the network. If these are not defined, it is difficult to design the system accurately. Items that are normally constrained include:

- Message size
- Server disk space
- Number of recipients per message

Features and Implementation Impacts

At the end of Chapter 3, "Setting up a Test Environment," you can find a list of new features in Exchange 5.5, highlighting their potential benefit, identifying implementation issues, and pointing out action items that must be completed before the feature can be implemented. Use this matrix to plan what features your organization would like to deploy.

Conduct a Gap Analysis

A gap analysis compares the current network and messaging environment with the desired end state to determine what must be done to close any gaps. Four primary areas must be identified:

- Improvements that must be made to infrastructure components to support the end-state Exchange Server.
- Systems that must be implemented to support the coexistence of the end-state Exchange Server.
- Areas where new functionality is strongly desired by users, administrators, or operations.
- Functionality points that users will no longer have or that will significantly change.

Assessing Infrastructure Readiness

Documenting infrastructure readiness relies on network infrastructure information gathered during the information-gathering phase. Compare the state of the current messaging environment to the information in the end-state Exchange Server network dependencies document. The table below lists key assessment areas:

Activity	Finding
Assess connectivity requirements	
Assess protocol requirements	
Assess address management requirements	
Assess name resolution requirements	
Assess network operating system (OS) requirements	
Assess remote access requirements	
Assess Windows NT Server domain model requirements	
Assessing operations readiness	
Assess availability requirements	
Assess security requirements	
Assess fault monitoring requirements	
Assess capacity management requirements	
Assess 7x24 support requirements	
Assessing technical support readiness	
Assess capacity requirements	
Assess escalation requirements	
Assessing migration infrastructure readiness	
Assess directory synchronization requirements	
Assess calendar and scheduling requirements	
Assess distribution lists requirements	
Assessing software distribution readiness	
Assess capacity requirements	
Assess escalation requirements	

Coexistence Infrastructure

This phase identifies what is required to ensure that Microsoft Exchange Server coexists with the existing messaging environment. Each area covered below has been investigated during the information-gathering phase. Add areas requiring special attention to the project plan.

Message Flow

Stable message flow between Exchange Server and the current messaging system is, of course, a primary requirement. Exchange Server provides connectors to cc:Mail and Microsoft Mail for desktop personal computers and Macintoshes. If another system is used, connections often can be made with either X.400 or SMTP. In addition, third parties also provide gateways. Another option is to use the gateways developed for Microsoft Mail and have messages passed through.

Deciding on a technology to use for the connection can have an impact on the logical design of the site topology system.

Distribution Lists

Distribution lists (mail lists) are another functional area where a coexistence strategy must be developed. Most customers find it difficult to keep distribution lists synchronized across systems. A more efficient route is to have the list in one system or the other, based on where most list members are.

Electronic Forms

If any of the existing systems use electronic forms, a strategy must be developed to use forms between systems. Because forms don't generally share content standards, coexistence between messaging systems is difficult. Nevertheless, requirements should be identified.

Note   With Microsoft Exchange Server 5.5, compatibility with Microsoft Outlook forms and active server pages (ASPs) is much easier.

Calendar and Scheduling

The coexistence of electronic calendars and scheduling systems is likewise difficult because of a lack of standards. Exchange Server supports the transmission of Microsoft Schedule+ requests between Exchange Server and other systems. Third-party developers have created systems that integrate with other environments.

This problem can be mitigated by migrating entire workgroups at the same time. Because users generally schedule meetings with others in their immediate workgroup, converting all of them at once eliminates most coexistence requirements.

Directory Synchronization

Directory synchronization with existing systems is critical and the end-state goal should be to have an automated directory synchronization process between the environments. Exchange Server provides for directory synchronization between cc:Mail and Microsoft Mail. Other systems can be integrated using directory synchronization file formats or directory application programming interfaces (APIs). Many planners decide to develop customized synchronization processes or install commercial synchronization processes developed by third-parties.

Mail Applications

You may have to modify any application that uses the existing messaging infrastructure as a transport or as access point so that it works with the new environment, such as an application that receives requests for information through e-mail.

Coexistence and Migration Risk Assessment

Use this table:

Item	Description	Current status	Risk
Data migration	How existing messages will be migrated to Exchange		
Message flow	How messages will flow between systems during coexistence		
Scheduling	How calendars will be accessible during migration, and how requests and notifications will flow		
Electronic forms	How electronic forms will be migrated between systems		
Mail enabled applications (MEAs)	How existing MEAs will interact with the new system		
Directory synchronization	How directory entries will be kept up to date during the migration process		

(continued)

Item	Description	Current status	Risk
Directory naming standards	Standards for critical entries such as alias and directory name		
Distribution lists	How distribution lists will be preserved during migration		

Determine User Functionality Gaps

Compare user functionality available in existing systems with functionality provided by either Outlook or Exchange Client, and document any features that will not be available during migration or that will disappear altogether. Develop mitigation strategies for areas where the lack of functionality will affect operations. It should be noted that Exchange Server provides significant functionality for users, administrators, and operations personnel, and that additional functionality can be added with very little additional cost.

Build the Master Project Plan

After system functions have been identified and the gap analysis completed, construct an overall project plan that provides detailed information on timelines and overall implementation costs. Build the master project plan by:

- **Identifying the plan owner**—The program manager, who must be able to influence resource decision and effectively track the work progress, is the plan owner.

- **Defining the plan scope (time, money, and people)**—Use the gap analysis to build the master project plan.

- **Building the plan**—Include estimated work effort, task assignment, and predecessor, if appropriate.

- **Updating the plan**—Keep the plan up to date by reviewing the plan with project team members on a weekly or biweekly basis.

CHAPTER 3

Setting Up a Test Environment

This chapter discusses how to set up a lab to test a Microsoft Exchange Server deployment. One section uses an upgrade to Microsoft Exchange 5.5 as an example to show how to assess product features and develop a test plan. Testing upgrades and new releases is a continual process that should be included in every project timeline. Maintaining a fully operational test lab gives you the ability to evaluate upgrades and new releases so you can implement them in a timely fashion.

Why Test?

Although designers spend months developing a Microsoft Exchange architecture and deployment plan, the most careful planning cannot anticipate everything that can happen when deployment starts. The best way to validate Exchange architecture is to build a test lab and prototype the design.

Many project managers think their deadlines and budgets don't allow for testing. Testing does indeed have a cost, but so does *not* testing. The only way to assess how Exchange will perform in a production environment is to install it and monitor it, and a test lab is the most practical venue for doing this. Architects can observe a design in operation and fine-tune it without affecting end users. The operations staff can get the feel of the new technology. Business unit users can be brought in to do client and application integration testing.

All of this requires investing some time and some money, but thorough testing ensures that when the time comes to deploy Exchange the architecture has been fine-tuned, the operations staff can support it, and the business units have tested their standard desktop and application configurations. This can eliminate the unpleasant surprises often encountered during deployment, save time and money by reducing or eliminating snags that hamper productivity, and reveal support issues before they incur expense or delay during deployment. The money you spend setting up the lab does not have to stay in the lab: after testing is done you can roll the lab equipment into the production environment. The best strategy is to set up the lab before deployment with several fully configured servers. When it is time to deploy, move some of the servers into production, but keep a base lab configuration in place so that you can test upgrades and service packs without having to rebuild the lab.

Planning Your Test Lab

Planning your test lab is as important as planning your production environment. The two environments should be completely separate, but should operate the same. The lab's primary objective is to validate the Windows NT and Exchange architectures against a working prototype with all the components of the production environment. The lab also allows the various groups responsible for introducing the new technology to test their implementation plans against the production environment. Use the lab to analyze:

- Compatibility between the Windows NT Server domain design and Exchange site design.
- Interoperability between Windows NT and the existing networking environment.
- Interoperability between Exchange and existing mail systems.
- Client workstation configurations.
- Changes in network traffic volumes or patterns that result from introducing Windows NT and Exchange.
- Administration, support, and maintenance procedures.

Install and maintain the lab as if it were a production environment. It is an investment and to pay off it must be usable and dependable. Treating the lab as a production environment also allows the operations staff to test administration, support, maintenance, and troubleshooting procedures. It should always be ready for testing new products, new releases, or product updates and service packs.

Appoint a lab manager or coordinator to oversee installation and testing activity. After the lab is properly configured, implement a change control process to help avoid conflicts between groups using the lab. Basically, this process makes sure that groups using the lab get the lab manager's approval before making any changes to lab hardware or software. This prevents one group from making changes that skew other groups' testing.

A change control process ensures that all testing groups are informed of and agree to any changes to lab hardware or software. Groups with conflicting testing requirements must reserve testing time with the lab manager. The lab manager should post hardware and software status and testing schedules so testers are aware of the lab activity. The lab manager must also have procedures in place to restore the lab to its original state. A change control process keeps the lab environment stable and in a known state. The goal of testing is to obtain approval or "certification " for a product to be deployed in production. If the lab environment mirrors production, then systems and applications can be certified with confidence that the lab test results represent what to expect in production

Production Environment for the Company

The following discussion refers to a fictitious 20,000-user enterprise called the Company. It assumes that Windows NT Server domain and Exchange architectures have been designed and formulated and that necessary Exchange deployment planning has been completed. The discussion centers on how to design and create a test lab that can validate these things.

Windows NT Server Domain Overview

The Company has 20,000 users divided into six business units. The home office, with 5,000 users, is a hub location on the Company's WAN. There are 520 sales offices connected through frame relay with variable speeds—generally, the larger the office the faster the speed. Over half the locations have fewer than 10 users. The production Windows NT Server domain plan is a multi-master account domain, one for each of the six business units and one administration domain containing privileged accounts for the Company's corporate IS administrators and operations staff. Exchange is in its own resource domain. There is a one-way trust from the Exchange resource domain to each account domain, and all domains trust the corporate IS domain. The account domains do not trust each other. Users from the business units share no resources other than Exchange.

Exchange Organization and Site Design

The Company decided to maintain adequate bandwidth to centralize most Exchange servers in a "server farm" at the corporate home office (the Corporate Site). Corporate Site servers contain user mailboxes for staff at this location and at the smaller sales offices. A few large divisional sales offices (1,000 to 2,000 users) require their own servers, but they are connected with lines having speeds of at least 512KB/sec and therefore are in the Corporate Site. Five subsidiaries, each with its own IS staff, administer their own networks and support their own users. The subsidiaries have separate Windows NT Server domains, have installed Exchange servers in their own sites, and connect to the server farm through X.400 connectors over permanent leased line connections with the Internet Mail Server as a backup connection.

The Company uses SoftSwitch to interconnect MS Mail (PC) users (14,000), Professional Office System (PROFS) users (2,500), Macintosh mail users (3,000), and UNIX mail users (500). SoftSwitch is also used for SMTP mail and X.400 mail to a public X.400 service provider. SMTP services are to be migrated to Exchange immediately; X.400 services will be migrated later. SoftSwitch Central is the Mail Directory. The Company has other directories that it uses for telephone numbers and applications.

The long-range migration plan is to bring all of the Company's directory services to Exchange. The plan calls for dedicated messaging servers that contain only user mailboxes (1,000 per server) and dedicated connector servers that handle mail traffic external to Exchange: two for the Internet Mail Service (inbound and outbound), one with X.400 Connectors to the subsidiary sites, two for Microsoft Mail Connectors to connect Exchange to MS Mail (PC). Exchange will use the MS Mail (PC) SNAPI gateways for connectivity to SoftSwitch. Multiple public folder servers will be installed but only one is called for in the initial deployment.

Lab Setup for Networking Environment

The production environment described above is fairly complex. To validate the design, the test lab must include the following components:

- **Windows NT Server domain**—Exchange relies on Windows NT for authentication and access, so the Company must test a prototype with a multi-master domain configuration containing a representative number of the proposed accounts and resource domains with the appropriate trust relationships. In this case, the domains for a valid test environment are the administrator domain, at least two business unit account domains, and a separate Exchange resource domain. This configuration makes it possible to test network and Exchange administration, the Exchange server-to-server access, and the authentication of the business unit user accounts and groups against the Exchange servers.

- **Administration**—Windows NT and Exchange administrator accounts should be created to reflect the production roles, which are fully defined in the architecture plan (including service accounts, global groups, and local groups) and used to administer the lab environment. This allows thorough testing of access rights for administrators, operators, and service accounts.

- **Domain controllers**—There should be one PDC and one BDC each for the administrator domain and the Exchange resource domain. The business unit account domains can be represented by a single PDC, unless end-user application testing is planned. Application testing requires a separate test plan; business units can use the lab to test integration of Exchange with their application. But this discussion explains only how to use the lab to validate Windows NT and Exchange architectures.

- **Backups**—As soon as the initial lab is set up, back up all servers so that you can, if necessary, return to the original state without time-consuming re-installs. The operations groups involved in testing should make sure that the hardware, software, and schedules for backups match the planned production environment. Backup operators can use the lab to test backup and restore procedures and to determine whether full, incremental, or differential backups will be used.

- **Dynamic host configuration protocol/Windows Internet Naming Service (DHCP/WINS)**—Servers and workstations should obtain IP addresses just as they will in production. Servers usually have static IP addresses. To eliminate the need for separate DHCP/WINS servers, test workstations can have an address range reserved for them on the production servers. This assumes that TCP/IP addressing and DHCP/WINS have already been implemented. If TCP/IP has not yet been implemented, add it as a component of the test lab and develop a test plan.

- **Interoperability**—The proposed production design uses Novell servers for files and print services. Several UNIX applications send data through SMTP to internal users and business clients outside the Company. The lab must include Novell and UNIX servers for coexistence and interoperability testing.

- **Protocol support**—The lab servers and client workstations must have all the protocols installed that will be used in production.

- **LAN/WAN connectivity**—Routers that can simulate WAN links and different line speeds should be available in the lab for conducting connectivity testing between Company locations and subsidiaries.

Lab Setup for Exchange Site Design

Sites

One Corporate Site and two subsidiary sites should be installed in the lab. It is important to simulate the site-to-site traffic connecting through the Corporate Site.

Exchange Servers

The production Exchange servers are dedicated to Exchange and configured to hold 1,000 users each. The lab uses two messaging servers for user mailboxes and only two connector servers for the Internet Mail Service, the Microsoft Mail Connector, and the X.400 connectors to the subsidiary sites. One connector has the Microsoft Mail Connector and the IMS (inbound) installed, and the other has the X.400 and IMS (outbound). When a particular connector type is to be tested, the other connectors can be stopped. This reduces the number of connector servers needed. All servers are configured to production specifications for initial testing: two messaging servers and two connector servers. These will be used for benchmarks and throughput testing.

To conserve costs, the disk and memory have been scaled back on the remaining Exchange servers and each will have only one processor. Most lab testing does not require full-scale server configurations because the focus is on Exchange Server *configurations* rather than *stress* testing the hardware. The TechNet CD and the Exchange Web site (http://www.microsoft.com/exchange) have a lot of documentation on users-per-server Exchange benchmarks developed by Microsoft. Computer manufacturers likewise supply information through their local account representatives or on their Web sites. There is no need to repeat this type of benchmark testing on Exchange servers that will be dedicated either to messaging or connectors. The section on server sizing has tables of production hardware configurations that show the details and the differences between the server types.

Naming Conventions and Test IDs

The production design naming conventions for computers, Windows NT Server domains, Exchange, and user names will be used in the lab with the word *Test* appended to the name. This allows operations staff and business unit users to "preview" any required naming changes that will affect them, such as Internet mail addresses, but makes it easy for network and telecommunications personnel to tell the difference between test and production machines. It also distinguishes test and/or pilot users from production users.

The lab manager should set up a block of generic test accounts with the correct permissions so short-term users (such as business units testing applications) can easily schedule a test, use a generic ID, and not incur the administrative overhead of creating and deleting test accounts. A user can come into the lab, sit at workstation *PCTest-01*, and log on using Windows NT account *ExUser1Test* and password *Pass1234*. The workstation profiles should all be set so *ExUser1Test* logs on to the appropriate Windows NT Server domain and the correct NDS context for NetWare servers for file and print services. The mail and fax control panel settings should be set to connect *ExUser1Test* to an Exchange mailbox for *ExTestUser1*.

Only full-time testers need personal test accounts and profiles. Precede their actual name with *ExTest* to identify them as testers and to make it easy to derive a list of all test IDs by sorting the global address lists of all mail systems. Example: User name is "Maureen Tracy Venti," the production display name is "Venti, Maureen Tracy," and the test ID is "ExTest Venti, Maureen Tracy."

Internal Connectivity

The Company currently uses SoftSwitch for internal mail system interconnectivity. As is often the case, no test version of SoftSwitch is available and the lab must be connected to the production SoftSwitch environment for testing mail system interoperability and directory synchronization. Test plans must be carefully written to ensure that the production system is not adversely affected by testing. The lab manager must make sure all testers take this into account when they execute their test plans. Some testing may need to be done after hours.

External Connectivity

The company currently uses SoftSwitch for external mail connectivity through SMTP mail and X.400. SMTP services will be migrated to Exchange immediately upon production implementation. Testing SMTP is relatively straightforward because Exchange can be configured to interoperate with UNIX sendmail hosts. The lab's two connector servers each have an instance of the IMS installed—one inbound, one outbound. The lab is configured to forward outbound mail to a production sendmail host, and DNS entries and MX records have been made to route inbound SMTP mail to the lab IMS. See the Exchange Server documentation for configuration details. There is no need to create an extra "break" in the firewall. Only secured production servers have access outside the firewall. The X.400 services are more difficult to test because only one X.400 MTA connection to an ADMD is valid at any one time. Test connections can be set up, but this takes time and can be costly. In our example, the Company plans to migrate external X.400 connectivity to Exchange in the future. To change from the Company's existing X.400 MTA connection to the Exchange X.400 MTA will require testing with the Company's X.400 provider. This testing will be scheduled for some future time, well in advance of production implementation. For the current Exchange deployment, external X.400 mail will be routed through SoftSwitch through the MS Mail (PC) SNAPI gateways. The SMTP domain in the lab will use the qualifier *test* to distinguish it from production, as in *user@Test.Company.com*.

Mail Systems Interoperability

The Company used as an example in this chapter has five mail systems: Exchange, MS Mail (PC) users (14,000), PROFS users (2,500), Macintosh mail users (3,000), and UNIX users (500). Each type must be installed in the lab—or the lab must access test versions of each. Exchange should be used to send mail messages of various sizes to all mail systems that are part of the production design. Basic messaging is usually trouble free; problems are more likely with CC (carbon copy) and BCC (blind carbon copy), distribution lists (especially those containing a mix of native Exchange users and users on different mail systems), attachments, read receipts, delivery receipts, and SMTP and X.400 mail. Some issues may not be resolvable because of the limitations of older gateways or mail systems. In most cases, mail administrators will already know about these problems, but they should document them and their workarounds so that users can be informed and their expectations adjusted

Directory Synchronization

Directory synchronization is crucial in any enterprise messaging system. As groups of users migrate, there must be a procedure for removing them from their legacy mail system's directory and creating their new Exchange account so their new mail address is propagated to all the other mail systems in a timely manner. The Company has told its business units that all mail directories will be updated overnight. The group of users who will migrate that day get a new Exchange ID in the morning; that afternoon their old mail account is deleted, and then directory updates are run to send changes to all mail systems. The testers will test the procedures for migrating users and synchronizing directories of different mail systems over a period of several days in the lab to ensure that the schedule allows enough time to process that day's updates from every mail system. The commitment to overnight directory synchronization may require scheduling multiple cycles per night for some systems. The mail directories will be checked daily for consistency. During migration, Exchange user names are sent to all legacy systems directories. If the same names display differently in some directories, the testers will analyze the difference and recommend changes to the name mapping rules if necessary.

Client Workstations

The lab must also contain every type of workstation platform for which support will be required. Configure workstations to the company standard first, then add the Exchange client or Outlook client software. Settings for Exchange user profiles, the Exchange services, and client options must be reviewed and tested so that the best choices are made for the user community. The goal of testing is to develop for each workstation platform a recommended Exchange client configuration that is optimized for the users. Each client workstation in the lab should have all production protocols installed, so that they can access other servers in addition to the Exchange servers, as they would in production. Each workstation can be assigned its own user test ID so any user can come into the lab, use the workstation, and have the correct access to test servers and applications for interoperability. See *Naming Conventions* above.

Testing with Subsidiaries

Subsidiaries are encouraged to follow the Company standards for server setup and configurations, naming conventions, and hardware and software versions. Subsidiaries must go through a trial connection to the lab before they are allowed to connect to the production Exchange system. This checks that the subsidiary is following standards and has the appropriate level of training and support to maintain an Exchange site. In addition, naming conventions must be agreed upon and closely followed to avoid conflicts in user names. Exchange notifies administrators of name conflicts within a site, but does not prevent users in different sites from using the same display name. Testing gives you a chance to assess this condition, and to develop and test procedures for avoiding or dealing with it. See the *Naming Conventions Matrix* for more sample naming standards. Exchange is one system: configuration information from one site will replicate to all others when directory replication takes place. Administrators must work closely together to ensure no unnecessary connectors or redundant mail routes are configured inadvertently.

Exchange Server Production Configurations

For the initial lab testing, build all servers to production specifications to make sure that any capacity issues or hardware-related issues are uncovered. The server types and specifications described below are based on the Company's commitment to dedicate servers to a specialized role in the Exchange environment.

Centralized Messaging Servers and Public Folder Servers

Messaging servers located in the server farm have the naming convention CORP–MSG-nn, where *CORP* is the location, *MSG* is messaging and *nn* is a sequential number beginning at 01. Public folder servers have the same configuration. For the example configuration under discussion, assume that nine messaging servers (CORP-MSG-01 through –09) and one public folder server (CORP-PF-01) are already installed. These are located centrally at the Corporate Site and have the software and hardware configuration below (Compaq is used only as an example):

- Message servers will be dedicated to containing user mailboxes
- The majority of the Company's users (75%) are light messaging users.
- No connectors will be installed on a messaging server
- Messaging servers must support 1000 users

Large messaging server (1,000 users)	Compaq ProLiant 5000
PROCESSOR: P166 Pentium Pro	2-Processor L2 512K cache
RAM	256MB
Windows NT, EXE, and PAGEFILE	2x2.1GB (RAID 1)
EXCHANGE LOGS	2x2.1GB (RAID 1)
MAILDATA and DIRECTORY	5x4.3GB (RAID 5)

Connector and Distribution List Expansion Servers

The connector servers located in the server farm have the naming convention CORP–ccc-nn, where *ccc* is the connector type, *MMC* is Microsoft Mail Connector, *IMS* is Internet Mail Server; SITE is the site connector, and *nn* is a sequential number beginning at 01. The connector servers are centralized at the Corporate Site and have this software and hardware configuration:

- Connector servers will have no users.
- Connector servers will be dedicated to one connector type.
- The connector types are:

  Microsoft Mail Connector (PC) to connect to SoftSwitch named CORP-MMC-01 and -02

  Internet Mail Service named CORP-IMS-01 and -02.

  X.400 Connector for connecting subsidiaries naming convention Corp-Site-01

Distribution list expansion server naming convention CORP-DL-01

Connector server	Compaq ProLiant 2500
PROCESSOR: P200 Pentium Pro	2 processor L2 256K cache
RAM	160MB
Windows NT, EXE, PAGEFILE, and EXCHANGE LOGS	2x2.1GB (RAID 1)
MAILDATA and DIRECTORY	3x4.3GB (RAID 5)

Affiliate/Subsidiary Message Servers

Message servers are scaled to suit the number of users at the location. Affiliates need dedicated connector servers if they support many users and anticipate high mail traffic volumes. The server naming convention indicates a server's affiliate and/or location. There are three messaging server sizes: large (the same as for centralized messaging servers—shown above), medium, and small (shown below).

Medium messaging server: (351 to 700 users)	Compaq ProLiant 2500
PROCESSOR: P166 Pentium Pro	2 Processor L2 512K cache
RAM	192 MB
Windows NT, EXE, and PAGEFILE	2x2GB (RAID 1)
EXCHANGE LOGS	2x2GB (RAID 1)
MAILDATA and DIRECTORY	5x4.3GB (RAID 5)

Small messaging server: (up to 350 users)	Compaq ProLiant 2500
PROCESSOR: P200 Pentium Pro	2 processor L2 256K cache
RAM	128MB
Windows NT, EXE, PAGEFILE, and EXCHANGE LOGS	2x4.3GB (RAID 1)
MAILDATA and DIRECTORY	3x4.3GB (RAID 5)

Affiliates must assess how much intrasite traffic their users will generate and how it compares to projected intersite traffic (to the Corporate Site). This ratio can be used to determine whether a dedicated connector server is required or if the connector can run on the same server that contains user mailboxes. As a general rule, it is not good practice to run connectors on servers that support over 500 users. If a connector is run on a server that contains user mailboxes, add at least 64 MB of RAM to the small and medium configurations shown here.

Sizing Servers for the Lab

As mentioned previously, all servers are to be built to production specification for the initial, preproduction testing. The Company used in this discussion has two messaging servers and two connector servers built to production specifications. Small messaging servers are used for subsidiary site testing. Separate servers are needed so that additional sites can be created. The domain controller servers can be built using guidelines from the *Windows NT Server Resource Kit: Networking Guide, Tools and Checklist for Domain Planning: Hardware Requirements.* This information is also in TechNet (CD and online). After the architecture testing is complete, you can move all the servers with full processor, RAM, and disk space configurations into production.

If possible, it is a good idea to maintain the test lab beyond the initial implementation for use in testing upgrades and service packs. To contain costs, replace the full-scale testing servers with the same models that have only a single processor, less RAM, and less disk space. Order replacement servers in advance so there is minimal lab downtime after you swap fully configured servers out into production. The lab manager must work with the testing groups to decide how cutbacks can be made *and* how a valid test environment can be maintained. As a general rule, at least one messaging server built to production specifications should remain in the lab. Even better would be two: one large messaging server and one connector.

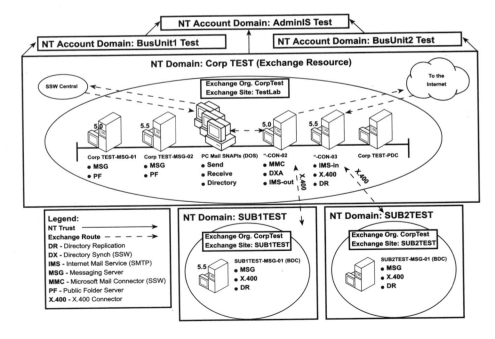

The Company's lab shown above represents all of the architecture's key components. It is helpful to create a lab diagram such as this and post it in the lab so that all testing groups can see the lab plan. The setup also provides administrators and business unit users with a prototype for the Windows NT Server domain plan and the Exchange site design. The connectivity to SoftSwitch and to the Internet ensures that mail interoperability for both internal and external mail can be tested in "real life" scenarios. From this point forward, the Company would plan to test for two to three months before going into production. This much time would be required to test all the areas discussed in the various test plans developed by the Windows NT and Exchange teams.

The next section discusses how to create a test plan and how to leverage the test lab environment to evaluate new releases and service packs while still making progress on a production deployment.

Creating Test Plans: Developing a Strategy on What To Test

Testing can be a moving target. In the software industry, service releases and upgrades are facts of life. As stated in the earlier section, good testing practice for an Exchange deployment requires a stable lab environment with known hardware and software configurations that do not change for the duration of the testing. It is important to target what version of Windows NT Server and Exchange you plan to deploy, and to test that combination from start to finish, even if a new version of Windows NT or Exchange is released before you finish testing. The best method is to "freeze" the test server and client configurations so that after a certain point, unless there is a major problem, no changes can be introduced to the Windows NT/Exchange environment. This ensures that all planned testing is completed and the hardware and software can be certified for production. It also means that quite often you will find yourself deploying a version of Exchange or Windows NT that is no longer the latest release.

This section describes that situation and shows how the Company dealt with it. Here's what happened: while testing was moving along, the Company learned that a new release of Exchange version 5.5, was on the horizon, but they needed to have Exchange in production prior to the 5.5 release. They tested and deployed 5.0, with the understanding that as soon as 5.5 was released, some resources would go back to the test lab and work up a plan to install 5.5. The Company estimated that by the time 5.5 shipped, they would only be 30% deployed. They had to make a decision to simply continue the 5.0 deployment or to try to find a way to introduce 5.5 servers into the deployment. This strategy sounds risky, but the alternative would be to continue deploying 5.0 and then go back and upgrade 25 to 30 Exchange servers—a less risky but extremely laborious strategy. Luckily, the Company came up with a strategy that would enable them to switch from 5.0 to 5.5 as soon as possible. The next section describes this strategy.

Testing While Deploying

The Company had completed the testing for Exchange 5.0 and had completed 30% of the Exchange production deployment. The first group of servers deployed smoothly, and the procedures and documentation had been fine-tuned so that the deployment could be turned over to a third-party solution provider. Deployment was moving along at 1,000 users per month, with the Company's network operations staff managing the day-to-day activities.

Now that the deployment responsibility had been turned over to network operations, the messaging team architects had the time to evaluate Exchange 5.5. The Company's decision to maintain the test lab made it possible to test a new release in parallel with the production deployment. With each new release or service pack, an enterprise must weigh the cost (in diverted resources) of testing the new release against the cost of sticking with the current version and depriving users and administrators of new features and functionality. In the hypothetical case of the Company, the messaging team knew that Exchange versions were interoperable, so 4.0, 5.0, and 5.5 servers could coexist in one environment, given the appropriate service pack levels. Then, too, the more 5.0 servers the Company deployed, the more servers they would have to convert to Exchange 5.5 later.

So the Company's messaging team decided to stop deploying 5.0 servers and start deploying 5.5 servers as soon as possible. That was good news, because Exchange 5.5 has many new features. The bad news was that it has so many of them that it would take months to test them thoroughly enough to obtain the certification and sign-off required before a 5.5 server could be deployed in production.

The following test plan is an example of how the work of testing a new release can be broken down into manageable pieces so that testers can make rapid progress and obtain certification to begin deploying Exchange 5.5 in production.

Exchange 5.5 Test Phases

How To Divide the Work

The most effective deployment method for a new release is to analyze the product and develop a test plan that schedules rapid deployment of some features as short-term deliverables and creates long-term plans for introducing more complex functionality. In other words, assess the features, deploy the easiest or indispensable first, study the more complex or optional, and schedule them for deployment later. Maintaining a post-production test lab makes this phased approach possible.

The Features List in Matrix 1 shows an effective method for assessing features—the important first step, in that you must analyze and evaluate components, functionality, features, benefits, and drawbacks. Only then can you make intelligent planning decisions. The easiest and most effective way to organize this information as you gather it is in a matrix that lets you compare items at a high level. Matrix 1 shows all the new features in Exchange 5.5, highlights feature implementation issues, and lists feature benefits. The last column sets a priority based on a trade-off between the benefits and the ease of implementation. The Action Item is what must be done before the feature can be implemented. Features that will be easy to implement and will have immediate benefit are rated Priority 1. Because the servers will be updated first, client-based features are rated Priority 2. Features that require coordination and longer term planning among IS and business units cannot be implemented for several months, and are rated Priority 3.

Based on this analysis, the messaging team decided to create three test phases. The Phase 1 goal was interoperability for Exchange 5.5. Phase 2 was Exchange Server 5.0 migration and client upgrades; its goal was to go back and upgrade existing Exchange clients and servers. Phase 3 was Exchange and Outlook development, security, and integration of Internet features; its goal was to allow enough time for planning and coordinating the appropriate use of these features.

Matrix 2 shows the results of the analysis of the features listed in Matrix 1. The messaging team decided which features had to be tested to certify Exchange 5.5 for interoperability and to introduce key new features. These items became the focus of the test plan for Phase 1. You can see how the number of features in Matrix 2 is greatly reduced from the complete list in Matrix 1. This process was repeated for Phases 2 and 3, with a similar list generated for each. The matrices became the high-level test plans from which detailed test plans were developed. They also served as a basis for reporting testing status to management.

The three test phases created by the Company's messaging team are described below. This approach can be used for any Exchange upgrade.

Phase 1: Exchange Server Version Interoperability

Not all Exchange 5.0 servers could be upgraded to 5.5 at once. It would take hours to migrate a server with 1,000 users, and in this hypothetical case new users were still being converted to 5.0 from legacy mail systems. The most effective path was to stop deploying 5.0 servers and start deploying 5.5 servers in production as soon as possible. To do this, it was first necessary to determine which features would promote interoperability between Exchange 5.0 and 5.5 and concentrate initial testing on them. When it was determined that there were no coexistence issues with adding Exchange 5.5 servers to the Exchange 5.0 environment, Exchange 5.5 could be certified for production.

Sample Areas for Server Interoperability Testing

- Install an Exchange 5.5 messaging server in the test lab.
- Upgrade lab Administrator Windows NT Workstations to the Exchange 5.5 Administrator program and perform routine administrative tasks against Exchange 5.0 and 5.5 servers—add users, create distribution lists, etc.
- Perform import/export using the Exchange 5.5 Administrator program against the Exchange 5.0 servers.
- Install Exchange 5.5 connectors in the lab with Exchange 5.0 servers.
- Configure folder replication across server versions.
- Configure Exchange Server monitors and link monitors to run across versions.
- Verify all server services are functioning correctly.
- Test the current standard client installations of Outlook 8.02 against Exchange Server 5.5—use the original test matrix developed for production implementation.

Phase 2: Exchange 5.0 Server Upgrades and Outlook Client Upgrade Strategy

Next, focus on developing a solid plan for upgrading existing Exchange production servers to 5.5 and Outlook 8.0x clients to Outlook 98. Exchange servers must be upgraded before clients, but if different groups are testing servers and clients, server migration and client upgrade testing can go on in parallel. The primary goal of this phase is to determine the best way to upgrade the Exchange servers. This phase also includes features that were considered important, but could not be planned and tested in the Phase 1 timeframe.

Upgrade Options

See the Microsoft Exchange Server documentation *Getting Started* manual for full details on upgrade procedures. You can upgrade to Exchange 5.5 from Exchange 4.0 or 5.0. The upgrade Setup program (always back up Exchange server before running Setup) estimates how long the upgrade will take. Basically, it takes longer to upgrade from Exchange 4.0 servers than from 5.0 servers, and Exchange 5.0 servers with many users or large information store databases can take longer than a day. If the estimated time is too long, you can quit Setup. The three upgrade options (fault-tolerant, standard, and move users) are described below.

Fault-tolerant upgrade (not available for 4.0-to-5.5 upgrades)—Backs up each Exchange database to a different, temporary location before upgrading. After all databases are successfully upgraded, the backup databases are removed and replaced by the upgraded databases. This requires available free disk space of at least twice the size of the information store on the Exchange server and it cannot be mapped to a network drive. **Advantage:** If Setup fails, you can reboot and run Setup again. The risk of database restoration is decreased, and recovery from problems is easier because the original database still exists (although you should create a full backup before starting the upgrade). **Disadvantage:** The Exchange server is offline during the upgrade.

Standard upgrade—Upgrades the databases in the same location, so be sure to create a full backup before beginning this upgrade. Use this option when servers do not have double the disk space to perform a fault-tolerant upgrade. **Advantage:** Less free disk space required. **Disadvantage:** If Setup fails during this operation, you must restore the databases before you return to your previous installation or run Setup again. The Exchange Server must be taken offline during the upgrade.

Move users—Sets up a new Exchange 5.5 server, then moves users from Exchange 4.0 or 5.0 servers. **Advantage:** No downtime for users and migration can proceed at a fixed pace, such as 150 user per night. When users are moved, you can reclaim the server for a new Exchange 5.5 installation. **Disadvantage:** Requires more administrator time, more time to move users, and at least one additional server.

For a given situation, one option may be more effective than the alternatives. In the hypothetical Company case, trying to upgrade in an ongoing deployment environment, the messaging team reasoning went like this: move some users to the first production 5.5 server for a production pilot. This may be the quickest way to accommodate business units that need Exchange 5.5 server features. Exchange 5.0 servers that have been installed recently will have smaller databases and will have enough disk space to run the fault-tolerant upgrade. Exchange 5.0 servers that have been installed for a longer period of time will have larger databases and might not have the double disk space needed to perform the fault-tolerant upgrade.

Sample Areas for Server Migration Testing

- Use LoadSim to add users and mail to the lab messaging server. LoadSim is a testing tool that will add users to a server based on a configurable profile. For example, you can add 1,000 light users with 30 mail items each and 7 personal folders. This will put mail into the Exchange private and public information stores. You can find more information on LoadSim from TechNet and from the Microsoft Exchange Web site at **http://www.microsoft.com/exchange**. Note that LoadSim versions must match the Exchange Server version.

- Back up the servers so they can be restored and upgraded as many times as needed. Run upgrade time trials to see how long it takes to upgrade a connector server and a messaging server fault-tolerant upgrade.

- Restore the servers and repeat the process using the standard upgrade.

- Use these times to estimate how long it will take to upgrade a production server.

- Move some users to develop an estimate of how long it takes. Compare times with standard and fault-tolerant upgrades.

Phase 3: Set Future Priorities

Delay adopting features that are merely nice-to-have or that require intensive planning and coordination to implement. Matrix 1 assesses Exchange 5.5 features and their impact on the Company. If outstanding issues are not yet fully understood and you are unsure how a feature will benefit you, sideline the feature until you have time to learn more about it. The last column (Priority and Action Items) is based on feature assessment. The features below represent those that the fictional company rated lower priority because the primary focus of their project was migration of mail users from legacy mail systems to Exchange. It could be that for other Exchange organizations, POP3 and Web access are priorities so they can provide cross-platform support, or that HTML forms and digital signatures are a priority for developing a strategic application. Each company needs to decide priorities for itself.

Sample Features for Phase 3 Testing

- Outlook 98 HTML forms and Internet/intranet integration

- Client alternatives: Web access and POP3

- Mail-enabled applications and public folders

- Encryption, digital signatures, and certificates

- Exchange server side scripting agents

- Exchange directory with lightweight directory access protocol (LDAP) interface as a replacement for all directories

Closing Remarks

The lab setup and testing strategy discussed here can be used with any version of Exchange. The examples are specific, but the process is generally the same. To understand and plan for the deployment of a complex product loaded with new features, you must break it down into testing phases with specific objectives that can be attained within a month or two. This enables you to move quickly through testing cycles, so you can take advantage of new features sooner. An efficient process can also make it feasible to update your system by switching to a newer version "in midstream" because it allows you to test interoperability and introduce new versions methodically.

The fictional Company used for purposes of illustration in this chapter estimated they would be only 30% deployed when a newer version was available. This presented them with a choice: continue deploying Exchange 5.0 and then upgrade all servers, or test Exchange 5.5 as they continued the 5.0 deployment so they could certify the newer version as soon as possible. With efficient testing and evaluation, they were ready to install the first 5.5 server by the time the Exchange 5.0 deployment was 50% completed. This allowed them to take advantage of new features faster and reduced the number of servers they had to convert. Keeping the test lab operational, rather than disassembling it after initial testing, allowed them to perform this complex series of actions easily—at least effectively and with minimal stress.

It costs money to set up a test lab, but this is compensated for when testing reduces conversion time, potential problems, and disruption to the production environment. As the Company was deploying Exchange 5.0, the existence of a complete test lab made it possible to evaluate and test client upgrades quickly, bringing new clients into production as soon as possible. It also enabled the Company to test server migration procedures thoroughly, so that 5.5 server deployment could begin almost immediatelyand server upgrades could be phased over a few months. By the time the original Exchange 5.0 deployment schedule was completed, the entire environment was updated, with all servers on Exchange 5.5 and all clients on Outlook 98.

Luckily, most deployment and upgrade situations are not this complex, but in any situation the benefits of a complete test lab and carefully laid out test procedures are significant.

Matrix 1: Microsoft Exchange Server 5.5 New Features

Matrix 1 lists the new features in Exchange 5.5, highlights their potential benefit to the Company, identifies implementation issues, and points out action items that must be completed before the feature can be implemented. The priority in the last column is based on a trade-off between the benefits and implementation effort:

1. Easy to implement; immediate benefit.
2. Effort or short-term planning required for implementation. For instance, client-based features are rated 2 because the servers must be updated first.
3. Requires coordination and longer term planning among IS and business units; cannot be implemented for several months.

Messaging Foundation: Scalability

Feature	Description	Impact on the Company	Priority—action
Unlimited message store	Size limits on the information store have been increased; storage is limited only by the host hardware.	**Issues:** The Company Exchange server disk size is 20 GB RAID 5 (5X4.2) and 1,000 users per server with a 15-MB mailbox limit. To increase the store, The Company would have to change the RAID 5 set from 4.2- to 9-GB drives. **Benefits:** Users could have larger mailboxes.	2—Review current policies on user mailbox size and server size to determine if a change is needed.
Backup performance improvements	Very large data stores require improved backup performance. The Exchange backup API has been improved to output up to 25 GB per hour.	**Issues:** The Company now does full backups every night. **Benefits:** Faster backups; quicker completion.	1—This would immediately benefit the Company and should be implemented.

Messaging Foundation: Reliability

Feature	Description	Impact on the Company	Priority—action
Microsoft Cluster Server support	Exchange supports Cluster Server technology, providing single-node fail-over support in the event of software or hardware failure. This feature requires Windows NT Server, Enterprise Edition.	**Issues:** Clustering would require the Company to acquire new additional hardware (duplicate drives on Exchange servers) for fail-over. Existing servers cannot be converted to a cluster configuration; they must be re-installed on the new hardware and with Windows NT Server 4.0, Enterprise Edition. **Benefits:** No server outages.	2—Should be considered, but not for immediate implementation.

Messaging Foundation: Security

Feature	Description	Impact on the Company	Priority—action
Enhanced security management	Exchange includes a number of enhancements for managing e-mail security: Key Management (KM) server setup integrated with Exchange server setup; bulk enrollment of users and distribution of certificates; and multiple password validation for administrators.	**Issues:** Responsibility for administration and management: ID administration, messaging team or security? What is the Company's overall strategy for this technology? **Benefit:** Encryption and digital signatures for Outlook users' messages.	3—Develop a Company-wide strategy for using digital signatures and encryption with key IS groups and business units.
S/MIME **(requires an S/MIME-aware client such as Outlook Express or Netscape Communicator)**	Exchange Server allows S/MIME-aware clients to send encrypted mail to one another. The ability to send and receive S/MIME-encrypted or digitally signed mail depends on an S/MIME-aware client.	**Issue:** Current clients do not support this. Outlook Express does today and Outlook 98 will. **Benefit:** Encryption and digital signatures with mail clients outside the Company.	3—Develop a Company-wide strategy for using digital signatures and encryption with key IS groups and business units.
X.509 v3 **(requires an intranet certificate authority such as the Certificate Server in Internet Information Server 4.0 or an Internet certificate authority such as VeriSign)**	Exchange will accept and understand X.509 certificates issued by an intranet certificate authority such as the Certificate Server in Internet Information Server 4.0 or an Internet certificate authority such as VeriSign	**Issue:** What is the Company's overall strategy for this technology? The Company must select a certificate authority as a standard for applications and users. **Benefit:** Secure mail with outside clients and customers.	3-The Company customer applications could take advantage of this. Review with SSGs3. Develop a Company-wide strategy for using secure mail with key IS groups and business units.

Messaging Foundation: Offline User Support

Feature	Description	Impact on the Company	Priority—action
"Change-only" offline Address Book	The offline Address Book downloads only changed items, not a new copy of the entire address book. Downloads are faster and require less bandwidth for remote users.	**Issues:** None. **Benefits:** Faster offline Address Book download for laptop users.	**1**—This would immediately benefit the Company and should be implemented.

Messaging Foundation: Multiple Organization Hosting

Feature	Description	Impact on the Company	Priority—action
Virtual organization support through Address Book Views	Administrators are able to create virtual organizations in Exchange by creating multiple Address Book views within the global address list (GAL) and preventing users from viewing any container other than their own. This allows multiple organizations to be hosted securely on a single server.	**Issues:** None. **Benefits:** Affiliates' GAL entries could be isolated and hidden from each other and from Company users. This could also be used for clients who communicate with a subset of the Company's employees.	**2**—Determine which affiliates do not have their own IS support and will not have an Exchange server. Identify eligible clients companies.

Connectivity: Internet Support

Feature	Description	Impact on the Company	Priority—action
Internet Message Access Protocol (IMAP) 4	IMAP allows users to maintain copies of e-mail messages and discussion items on the server as well as the local message store. Exchange supports the IMAP4 protocol, making it possible for IMAP clients to send/receive mail and participate in discussions.	**Issues:** Training and support. **Benefits:** May be a way for Macintosh and UNIX clients to access Exchange. This would help speed migration to Exchange-based mail. Business units may want to use this feature with LDAP for customer applications or marketing. See below.	3—The Company's development council must work with business units to implement standards.
LDAP v3	Exchange supports LDAP v3, which enables LDAP clients with appropriate permissions to manipulate directory objects. LDAP v3 also supports referrals and directory synchronization with other LDAP servers.	**Issues:** Developer training and support. **Benefits:** May be a way for Macintosh and UNIX clients to access Exchange Address Book. This would help speed migration to Exchange-based mail. Business units may want to use this feature with IMAP4 for customer or ID management applications. See above.	3—The Company's development council must work with business units to implement standards.
Enhanced Internet security	Exchange supports a number of enhanced Internet security features including Secure Sockets Layer (SSL) encryption of SMTP connections between hosts and SASL for authenticating SMTP login. It also prevents spoofing using authenticated login and allows an administrator to accept or reject inbound SMTP connections based upon the type of security being used.	**Issues:** The Company must decide what kind of security is necessary for internal applications and for external customer applications.	3—The Company's development council must work with business units to implement standards.

(continued)

Connectivity: Internet Support *(continued)*

Feature	Description	Impact on the Company	Priority—action
Additional Internet support	Exchange includes support for a number of Internet technologies, including MHTML, which encapsulates HTML content in MIME messages allowing Exchange to store HTML messages, and ETRN (both client-side and server-side support), which allows Exchange to request messages for a selected Internet domain that have been queued on an SMTP server.	**Issues:** This feature is supported today in Outlook Express, but will not be supported in Outlook until Outlook 98. Backward compatibility as Outlook clients upgrade is a potential problem. If this feature is used, workgroups must upgrade together. **Benefits:** HTML messages provide a rich client user experience and can help developers of Outlook forms applications.	2—Determine timeline for client migrations.

Connectivity: LAN and Host-based Systems

Feature	Description	Impact on the Company	Priority—action
Lotus Notes connector	The Notes Connector enables Notes sites to seamlessly exchange e-mail and synchronize directories with Exchange servers.	The Company has made a decision to use only SMTP and X.400 connectors for external connectivity.	N/A
OfficeVision/VM (PROFS) connector	The OfficeVision/VM connector enables e-mail exchange between OfficeVision/VM systems and Exchange.	Same as above.	N/A
SNADS connector	The SNADS connector enables e-mail exchange between SNADS systems such as IBM OfficeVision/MVS or Fisher TAO and Exchange.	Same as above.	N/A

Connectivity: Client Family

Feature	Description	Impact on the Company	Priority—action
Outlook for Windows 3.x and Macintosh	Exchange includes versions of Outlook for Windows 3.x and Macintosh operating systems. These versions of Outlook include the Outlook user interface and interoperability with the 32-bit Outlook calendaring environment.	**Issues:** Requires a Power Macintosh. **Benefits:** Allows Macintosh users to migrate to Exchange-based mail. Macintosh servers could be retired.	**2**—Determine timeline for client migrations.
Updated forms support	HTML forms, created using Visual InterDev or another Web development tool, can be called directly from any Outlook client and launched directly in the default browser.	Same as above re: HTML messages.	**2**—Determine timeline for client migrations.
Outlook Web access enhancements	Outlook Web access now includes calendar objects, allowing users to manage their individual calendar and participate in group scheduling.	**Issues:** Requires a browser that supports frames and Java Script. **Benefits:** Macintosh and UNIX users could migrate to Exchange now. Macintosh and UNIX mail servers could be retired.	**2**—Determine timeline for client migrations.

Tools and Collaboration: Collaboration

Feature	Description	Impact on the Company	Priority—action
Microsoft Exchange scripting agent	Exchange includes server-side scripting for creating event-driven agents, which can be used to create automated collaborative applications and enable simple workflow.	**Issues:** Assess impact on server performance. **Benefits:** More powerful, built-in rules capability for Exchange public folders.	**3**—The Company's development council must work with business units to implement standards.
Microsoft Exchange Chat Service	Exchange Chat Service enables real-time collaboration using any standard Internet Relay Chat (IRC) or IRCX client.	**Issues:** Introduces new concepts for collaboration. **Benefits:** Useful for remote offices and subsidiaries where personnel have joint projects.	**3**-Evaluate this feature to assess how it should be used. Policies for use and user education required.

(continued)

Tools and Collaboration: Collaboration   *(continued)*

Feature	Description	Impact on the Company	Priority—action
Internet Locator Server support	Exchange Internet Locator Server allows users to do ILS lookups using the familiar Exchange directory.	Used with Chat and NetMeeting.	**3**-Evaluate this feature to assess how it should be used. Policies for use and user education required.
Microsoft NetMeeting	Microsoft NetMeeting is integrated into the Outlook client, allowing users to initiate net meetings directly from Outlook.	**Issues:** Introduces new concepts for collaboration. **Benefits:** Useful for remote offices and subsidiaries where personnel have joint projects.	**3**-Evaluate this feature to assess how it should be used. Policies for use and user education required.

Tools and Collaboration: Development Tools

Feature	Description	Impact on the Company	Priority—action
Collaboration Data Objects (CDO) enhancements	CDO (formerly Active Messaging) is the object library used for Exchange ASP applications.	**Issues:** Training and support. **Benefits:** By including objects for e-mail, discussions, calendaring, and directory access Web site developers can create Active Server Pages that make it easy for users to access this information using a Web browser.	**3**—The Company's development council must work with business units to implement standards.
Authoring tools	Design Time Controls, included in Visual InterDev, serve as templates that make it easy for Web site developers to create Active Server Pages. Wizards, available on the Web, allow Web site developers to create Active Server Pages without writing script or HTML using Microsoft FrontPage.	**Issues:** Training and support. **Benefits:** Improved tools could reduce development cycles.	**3**—The Company's development council must work with business units to implement standards.

Feature	Description	Impact on the Company	Priority—action
Visual InterDev	Exchange includes a single user copy of Visual InterDev for creating HTML forms and Exchange ASP applications.	**Issues:** Training and support. **Benefits:** Synergy between Exchange and Web-based functionality enables application developers to leverage the features of each environment.	**3**—The Company's development council must work with business units to implement standards.
Active Directory Services Interface (ADSI)	Microsoft Exchange supports ADSI, which customers can use in conjunction with LDAP to synchronize the Exchange directory with foreign LDAP directories. Customers can also use ADSI to begin writing Exchange applications that will integrate with and take advantage of the Active Directory in Windows NT Server 5.0.	**Issues:** Developer training and support. **Benefits:** This will be the directory API for Windows NT 5.0.	**3**—The Company's development council must work with business units to implement standards.

Management

Feature	Description	Impact on the Company	Priority—action
Deleted item recovery	Deleted items or folders are "soft deleted" and maintained on the server for a specified period of time. During this time, deleted items can be recovered by the end user, freeing up the administrator to do other tasks.	**Issues:** Requires Outlook 8.03. **Benefits:** Administrators and users can recover deleted items without a full server restore. With Outlook 8.03, users can recover their own deleted items.	**2**—Determine timeline for client migrations.
Simple network management protocol (SNMP) support	The MADMAN MIB (RFC 1566) is supported for use with SNMP management consoles.	**Issues:** The Company has no central management console at this time. **Benefits:** Exchange alerts can be integrated with a central management console.	**3**—Network and mail operations groups must agree on a centralized server management console.
Address space scoping	Connectors can be selectively restricted for specific use on an organizational, site, or server basis.	**Issues:** None. **Benefits:** Useful for Company subsidiary Exchange site.	**1**—Exchange administrators will implement this feature.

Matrix 2: Exchange 5.5 New Features To Be Tested in Phase 1

Matrix 2 shows the high-level test plan that results from the feature analysis in Table 1. The Company decided to focus on testing interoperability and a few key features. This greatly reduced the time required for testing and enabled the Company's mail operations team to obtain approval to begin deploying Exchange 5.5 servers in their Exchange 5.0 environment.

Messaging Foundation: Scalability

Feature (tester)	Description	Test plan objective	Results	Complete
Backup performance improvements (Tester 1)	Very large data stores require improved backup performance. In Exchange the backup API has been improved to 25 GB/hour.	Backup has changed and must be tested. Run the same backup tests that were run for 5.0. Document any changes to the backup procedure. Note whether increased performance can improve backup schedule.		

Interoperability: Exchange 5.5 Servers and Exchange 5.0 Servers

Feature (tester)	Description	Test plan objective	Results	Complete
Administrative tasks (Tester 1)	Use the 5.5 Administrator program to administer both 5.0 and 5.5 servers. We will include ID management tasks.	Perform day-to-day administrative functions on both 5.5 and 5.0 servers: Public folder setup Administrator views of server resources Server and link monitors Other configuration changes?		
Outlook 8.02 client (Tester 2)	Test the current Outlook 8.02 Client with Exchange 5.5.	Test to ensure that the 8.02 client can operate against the 5.5 server.		

Feature (tester)	Description	Test plan objective	Results	Complete
Messaging server interoperability **(Tester 3)**	Install 5.5 messaging server to test 5.5 and 5.0 interoperability of clients and server-server communications.	Test that 5.5 and 5.0 server services: • Mail delivery and routing • Directory replication • Public folder replication • Monitors		
Connector server interoperability **(Tester 3)**	Install a mix of 5.5 and 5.0 connectors with 5.0 messaging servers.	NTAU and directory synchronization. Internet Mail Service. Site (to LNW). Upgrade MMC and directory synchronization to 5.5.		

These are the **critical** test items for production implementation

Management: Management

Feature	Description	Test Plan Objective	Results	Complete
Deleted item recovery **(Tester 1)**	Deleted items or folders are "soft deleted" and maintained on the server for a specified period. During this time deleted items can be recovered by the end user, freeing up the administrator to do other tasks.	**Issues:** Requires Outlook 8.03 on the client. Test Exchange administrator and server side functionality for mailboxes and public folders recovery.		
SNMP support **(Tester 3)**	The MADMAN MIB (RFC 1566) is supported for use with SNMP management consoles.	Evaluate possibilities for interfacing Exchange monitoring with network and/or operations monitoring.		
Address space scoping **(Tester 1)**	Connectors can be selectively restricted for specific use on an organizational, site, or server basis.	Test configuration for corporate and subsidiary sites.		

Management: Multiple Organization Hosting

Feature	Description	Test Plan Objective	Results	Complete
Virtual organization support through Address Book Views (Tester 1)	Administrators are able to create virtual organizations in Exchange by creating multiple address containers within the global address list and preventing users from viewing any container other than their own. This allows multiple organizations to be hosted securely on a single server.	Create test customer group as a virtual organization. Verify that test customers are visible only to authorized test users. Verify that access rights are limited to authorized test users. Determine that mail can be sent and received and that the same functionality can be delivered.		

These test items are "nice to have" items on the Exchange Administrator's wish list. They do not have to be completely tested for production implementation because if they are not used, they cannot adversely effect the production system. Testing can be pushed into Phase 3.

Naming Conventions

The Company has already established a unique SoftSwitch name, referred to as the distribution element name (DEN) formed by combining the first seven characters of the last name and the first initial of the first name. This will be used in the new environment where a unique name is required. It was chosen because the users are familiar with it, it is short yet recognizable, and there are procedures in place to ensure unique DENs.

Name	Default and restrictions	Guideline	Company standard	Affiliate requirement
Organization	No default; 64 characters, cannot be changed.	Corporate identity; should be unique, part of every directory object (mailboxes, public folders, etc.); can correspond with X.400 PRMD or SMTP domain.	The Company's name	Same
Site	No default; 64 characters, cannot be changed.	Geographic, physical location, business function.	Corporate	Geographic or Organization name Example: Brazil or Subsidiary Name
Exchange Server	Default is Windows NT Server computer name; 15 characters, cannot be changed, must be unique.	Choose names that are meaningful for users and support personnel (location and function of server, etc.).	Corp-MSG-01 Exchange Messaging Server #1 located in Portsmouth	Affil-loc-MSG-01 Example: Brazil-MSG-01
Display	No default; 256 characters, can be changed.	Name as it will appear in the global address list: Last, First. Be consistent.	Last, First (example: Smithsonian, Pat)	Last, First (affiliate name). This identifies affiliates from corporate employees and prevents duplication of display names in the global address book. Example: Smithsonian, Pat (SubName)
Alias (mailbox)	Default is Windows NT account; 64 characters, can be changed.	Easy to identify.	first.last (example: pat.smithsonian)	Same
First	No default; 16 characters, can be changed.	User's first name.	Pat	Same

(continued)

Name	Default and restrictions	Guideline	Company standard	Affiliate requirement
Initial	No default; 1 character, can be changed.	User's initial; the middle initial is not effective as a tiebreaker because often it is not widely known. A qualifier in parentheses that shows a user's job function is more helpful in distinguishing users on the global address list.	Not used; the middle initial may be used as a tiebreaker for the alias and SMTP name.	Same
Last	No default; 40 characters, can be changed.	User's last name.	Smithsonian	Same
Directory	Default is first alias; 64 characters, cannot be changed; Internal Exchange directory name, **not seen by users**.	Setup maps directory elements such as organization and site according to naming conventions, e.g., o=lmig, ou=homeoffice, cn=recipients, and cn=smtihsop. The directory name is the common name element in the X.500 distinguished name.	SoftSwitch DEN, see below. The directory name is the user's unique identifier, but is internal to Exchange and does not appear to users in the system.	SoftSwitch DEN if they have the same one; otherwise, a unique alias will be created.
SMTP	Default is alias, but can be changed and is configurable. Users can have multiples for inbound mail; but only one is designated as outbound ("From"). No spaces allowed.	Used for Internet mail; should be simple and easily recognizable. First name, followed by last name and separated by a period for readability is recommended.	pat.smithsonian @TheCompany.c om	Some affiliates may require their own unique Internet identity. Evaluate this case by case.
X.400	No default; configurable within X.400 standards, can be changed.	Used for X.400 public network; should be simple and easily recognizable.	A=ATT, P=the Company, g=pat, s=smithsonian	Same as above

Name	Default and restrictions	Guideline	Company standard	Affiliate requirement
SNADS	Distribution Group Name (DGN) x Distribution Element Name (DEN). 8x8.	Used for SoftSwitch, the DEN will be the first 7 characters of the last name followed by the first initial, for a total of 8 characters. Tiebreakers are determined case by case.	Smithsop	DEN
Microsoft Mail	Network /PostOffice /Mailbox. 10x10x10.	Exchange site name becomes the postoffice name. The DEN will be the mailbox name because Exchange will communicate to SoftSwitch using MS Mail SNAPI gateways.	CORP/smithop	AffiliateSiteName /DEN
Exchange Windows NT Server domain	No default; 15 characters.	Easy to identify; geographic or business function	*EXCHANGE* will be the Exchange Windows NT resource domain	Location or affiliate name domain
Windows NT account domains	No default; 15 characters.	Windows NT user account should be short and easy to identify. SoftSwitch DEN will be used to ensure pass-through authentication, compatibility across network directory services, and access to legacy applications.	There will be one master account domain for each business unit. SoftSwitch DEN will be the standard for Windows NT user accounts. The Company will use the HR database as a feed.	Location or affiliate DEN
Company	No default; n characters, can be changed.		The Company	Affiliate name
Office	No default; n characters, can be changed.		Office name	Office name
Department	No default; n characters, can be changed.		Department name	Department name
Phone	No default; n characters, can be changed.		Business phone	Business phone

CHAPTER 4

Site Topology and Server Placement

This begins the discussion on the development phase of deploying Microsoft Exchange, designing the comprehensive messaging system or the Exchange backbone. It covers site topology and server placement. The chapter starts off by considering the logical design, which involves planning the physical network structure and creating the backbone.

Creating the Logical Design

During the development phase of deploying Exchange, the project team creates the **logical design**, the comprehensive design of the entire Exchange Server messaging system. The logical design details the objectives of each network component, configuration and relationship to other components, and design assumptions.

In creating the logical design, your development team relies on the **service offering**, the specification that defines the complete functionality of the Exchange Server messaging system. The team also needs benchmark data collected during the planning phase: current state of the existing network infrastructure and messaging system.

Network Infrastructure Planning

Because many organizations deploy Exchange as the first enterprise-wide client/server application, the development team must plan the network infrastructure to meet capacity and routing requirements. Existing enterprise wide area networks (WANs) that usually handle specific business applications must now support the installation of Exchange on every desktop. The Exchange Server rollout prepares the enterprise network for other client/server applications.

Exchange Server relies on Microsoft Windows NT Server for services such as authentication of administrative access and user access to postoffices. The development team must consider where Exchange servers reside in the Windows NT Server domain model. The team must also plan the number and placement of Dynamic Host Configuration Protocol (DHCP) and Windows Internet Naming Service (WINS) servers, remote access, and naming standards to add and identify sites, servers, gateways, connectors, users, and so forth.

Microsoft Exchange Backbone

In the development phase, your team builds the Exchange backbone, the physical network topology that consists of all the components that provide the routing and connectivity services between the Exchange sites. The components include Exchange site topology, directory replication, server placement, server sizing, external connectivity, naming standards, public folders, forms management, security encryption key management, administrative model, and web, IMAP, POP3, and LDAP connectivity. The development team can build the backbone components in parallel.

Logical Design Checklist

This list helps the development team document steps and components during the build phase.

Activity	Issue or indicator
Defining the infrastructure	
Microsoft Windows NT Server domain model	
Protocol management	
Host name resolution	
Machine naming standards	
Physical network	
Remote access	
Logon ID standards	
Identifying Exchange-related design features	
Site planning	
Server placement	
Server sizing	
Connection topology	

Activity	Issue or indicator
External connectivity	
Naming standards	
Disaster recovery	
Public folder hierarchy	
Public folder replication	
Network news transfer protocol (NNTP) and Internet News Service	
Administrative model	
Alternate-client access	
Forms management	
Clustering	
Security	
Identifying coexistence and migration issues	
Data migration	
Message flow	
Calendar and group scheduling	
Electronic forms	
Mail-enabled applications	
Directory synchronization	
Directory naming standards	
Distribution lists	
Outlook	
IMAP	
POP3	
Web Access	
Planning the deployment process	
Deployment method	
Server deployment	
Client deployment	
Administrator training	
User training	
Service level agreements (SLAs)	

(continued)

Activity	Issue or indicator
Site surveys	
Designing server installation and configuration features	
Software installation	
Hardware installation	
Software configuration	
Hardware configuration	
Designing connector (gateway) installation and configuration	
Connector installation	
Connector configuration	
Designing operations and systems management features	
Failure monitoring	
Performance trending and capacity management	
Remote configuration	
Operations group	
Cost recovery and billing	
Designing the technical support features	
Installation group	
User help desk	
Incident tracking processes	
Incident escalation	

Microsoft Exchange Site Topology

An Exchange messaging network includes a number of servers that administrators logically configure into one or multiple Exchange sites. The network manages a site as a single entity, which reduces messaging server workloads. To achieve the appearance of a single system, servers within an Exchange site communicate frequently. The Exchange server site topology consists of the number of sites and their boundaries, and the routing of messages between the sites. (You should also see "Naming Conventions" at the end of Chapter 3, "Setting up a Test Environment," for guidelines on naming servers and other components.)

Prerequisite Information Gathering

Before planning the details of the Exchange network, your team must determine the site boundaries and messaging hierarchy. Information needed:

- Messaging flows within the organization, using the corporate organizational chart as a starting point.

- Layout of the physical network that hosts the Exchange network, and number of users at each network end point.

- Windows NT Server domain topology.

- Whether the organization has an administrative management domain (ADMD) structure in place that specifies the lines of administration authority and boundaries.

Design Criteria

Considerations in designing the site topology:

- **Administrative costs**—The site topology must minimize administration costs wherever possible.

- **End-to-end messaging performance**—The messaging network should deliver messages end-to-end in less than 20 minutes 90 percent of the time.

- **Client-to-server response time**—The client-to-server response time for actions such as sending messages and reading messages should fall under one second 90 percent of the time. For users accessing across a slow link, a slightly slower response time is acceptable as long as it is consistent.

- **Reliability**—The network must not lose messages during transfer and must generate notices for messages that cannot be successfully delivered.

- **Supportability**—If there are problems, the network must alert the operations group so it can take corrective action.

- **Flexibility**—The network must be able to grow with future organizational and physical networking changes.

Recommendations

The base services of the Exchange server meet most of the requirements in the above section. However, the development team must implement specific steps to meet all of the design criteria:

- **Configure fewer large sites versus many smaller ones**. Base Exchange sites on physical network topology and use as many servers as practical. Large sites provide many advantages, from simplified configuration to ease of maintenance and backup. Sites can span links as slow as 56 Kbps if link usage is kept at or below 50 percent.

- **Include directory replication, message transfer, and possibly server monitoring processes among server communication within a site**. Servers within a site use direct (peer-to-peer) communication and synchronous remote procedure calls (RPCs). The network optimizes these communications when it has minimal latency.

- **Configure sites in a hierarchy to match mail flow and physical network topology**. A mesh topology design does not lend itself well to large messaging systems for a number of reasons:

  1. *A hierarchical topology matches electronic mail flow to organizational structure.* As a general rule, 80 percent of electronic mail remains within a sender's workgroup and the remaining 20 percent goes to the next higher organizational unit.

  2. *The physical network that hosts the messaging system follows a hierarchical model with hubs.* Organizations mirror that topology to avoid inefficient routing.

  3. *A mesh topology costs more to monitor from an operational perspective.* However, operations can easily set up a monitoring system for a hierarchical topology.

  4. *A hierarchical topology allows more flexibility for changes in the organization or physical network.* Administrators can easily move a leaf node (Exchange server) to a different part of the hierarchy if that is required by changes in traffic flows or the physical network.

- **Establish a single route between sites**. Exchange server supports alternate message routing based on criteria such as an administratively controlled cost. Although setting up alternate routes can seem very appealing, administrators should do so only for special circumstances where the underlying communication infrastructure is very unreliable, such as in remote, developing countries.

  Instead, establish a single route between Exchange sites and develop processes to allow administrators to implement alternate routes quickly if necessary. This approach ensures that messages take a consistent route, which benefits operations and technical support and facilitates network capacity planning.

- **Define the security architecture to allow a central operations group to control routing between the sites**. This allows the highly skilled staff to establish alternative routes, track messages, and troubleshoot without requiring them to be near each Exchange server.

- **Do not have Exchange sites span Windows NT Server domains**. Although Exchange sites and Windows NT Server domains operate relatively independently of each other, some dependencies affect Exchange sites. For example, all of the servers within an Exchange site use the same service account, which should not span across Windows NT Server domains.

- **Use RPC-based site connector**. Exchange ships with three site connectors: the RPC, the Internet Mail Service (that acts as a site connector), and the X.400. Each has different characteristics and is designed for different implementations:

  - The **Site Connector** installs easily and is simple to maintain. It transmits messages in their native compressed Exchange format at lower overhead than for the other connectors. Administrators can configure the RPC site connector to send messages to a particular bridgehead server, a selection of servers, or any server in the site. If a server goes offline, the RPC automatically redirects messages to an active server in a hub. It can route all outbound messages through a specific site messaging bridgehead.

  - The **Internet Mail Service**, as a site connector, works for small to medium organizations that communicate using the Internet or with internal UNIX-based users. The Internet Mail Service can provide redundancy in communication paths similar to the RPC site connector, but requires a significant Domain Name Service (DNS) configuration and DNS reliability.

    Administrative tools such as message tracking and single-seat administration do not work with Internet Mail Service.

  - The **X.400 site connector** works best with very slow and unreliable communication lines between two sites. The X.400 connector can schedule connections for batch transmission of messages and perform checkpoint restart. The X.400 connector also operates well connecting sites across public networks.

- **Keep Exchange messages in native format**. Transporting Exchange messages through another messaging system requires additional processing of the message contents, which can affect the contents, and it consumes system resources. It also prevents using the message-tracking tool to trace a message from sender to receiver through all hops.

- **Limit the size of messages flowing through the system**. To ensure standard end-to-end performance, limit the size of the messages through the system. Many organizations set the limit at 2 MB.

- **Minimize the number of gateways to foreign systems**. Gateways traditionally require more support than any other component of the messaging system and frequently become bottlenecks to message flow. Therefore, reduce the number of gateways and locate them near the operations organization.

- **Implement Exchange directory replication**. To ensure that messages take the most efficient route and that messages stay compressed during transit, all sites should participate in directory replication.

Server Placement

Because server hardware represents the major component of an enterprise's messaging system cost, the team should carefully decide how many servers are required. Is a server required in an area with a few users or would it be more economical to put one at a regional location and upgrade the WAN connection if necessary? With previous LAN-based e-mail systems, poor messaging performance prevented accessing servers across a WAN connection. The Exchange client/server architecture allows connection over a WAN link, providing sufficient performance and the ability to centralize servers. This section outlines design factors and some general guidelines to assist the Exchange development team in the decision-making process.

The Exchange directory stores all relevant information regarding Exchange users and those who can be reached through Exchange. The directory also stores configuration information from all of the other backbone components. To make the information accessible to users and Exchange components, Exchange Server must replicate the directory store to other servers in the organization. Directory replication closely matches the messaging topology, but has some unique characteristics that your team must consider to minimize replication latency and reduce network usage. The information presented here assumes a basic understanding of how directory replication works.

Directory replication, not to be confused with directory synchronization, is a complex topic. Refer to the *Microsoft Exchange Server 5.5 Resource Guide* for a detailed overview of Exchange Server directory replication infrastructure and methods.

Design Factors

Server placement takes into account:

- **Performance**—Users must typically have a response time that is less than one second for each action that they perform on the client. The closer users sit to the server, the better their experience.
- **Cost**—The design team should minimize network implementation cost by minimizing the number of servers.
- **Reliability**—An organization should place servers near local support resources.
- **Ownership and responsibility**—Regardless of the technical and cost considerations, organizational structure or policies frequently determine where to place a server.

Performance

The Exchange client communicates with the server through synchronous RPCs. The server holds the client until the transaction has been posted successfully to the Exchange Server in a transaction log. This process ensures message transmission, but every active Exchange user requires 2 kilobytes of bandwidth, which can affect server response time. The following factors can influence Exchange clients across a WAN link:

- **Line type**—Digital links can handle traffic better than analog lines of similar speed. Organizations should use a dedicated line rather than an on-demand one, to increase reliability.

- **Line speed**—The guaranteed speed of a digital link affects its overall capacity.

- **Line usage**—This equals the percentage of time that data transmission uses available bandwidth.

- **Client configuration**—A personal message store can serve to redirect many calls for messages to the local workstation instead of the server.

- **Number of simultaneous users**—This depends on how many users can simultaneously use a given link's capacity.

Costs

These costs are associated with mail servers:

- **Capital equipment costs**—Fewer centralized servers reduce capital cost.

- **Ongoing maintenance costs**—Fewer servers reduce the costs of server hardware maintenance.

- **Software upgrade costs**—In addition to software updates, the upgrade process incurs a cost with each server, even when accomplished remotely.

- **Operations cost**—As electronic mail systems play an increasingly critical role in the enterprise, administrators must monitor them carefully, usually by placing software on each machine to gather data and send it to a central console. More servers in an environment increase cost.

Design Guidelines

After reviewing the factors above, your team should follow these general guidelines:

- **Centralize postoffice servers**. Mailbox servers support user mailboxes. To reduce overall costs, centralize these servers as much as possible while still keeping performance within acceptable thresholds.

- **Consider client bandwidth requirements.** Microsoft Outlook demands the most network bandwidth because it requires an online store to provide functionality such as group scheduling. Next is Exchange Client with server-based storage, followed by Exchange Client with personal storage files (PST). The post office protocol version 3 (POP3) and Internet Message Access Protocol version 4 (IMAP4) clients provide the least functionality, but generate the least amount of network traffic.

- **Place backbone servers in controlled environments.** Organizations usually locate backbone servers in data centers with environmental controls, uninterrupted power supplies, and a 24-hour staff. Locating these critical resources in controlled environments both isolates the machines from external forces and shortens the time necessary to recover from a failure.

- **Weigh the decision to place a remote server.** Instead of adding a remote server, consider increasing the bandwidth of the link.

- **Use validation tools.** Administrators should validate actual performance with testing tools such as Load Simulator and MailStorm, but be careful not to overload a production WAN link with these tools.

CHAPTER 5

Planning Exchange Architecture in a Bandwidth-Sensitive Environment

The biggest challenges in planning an Exchange deployment are deciding server placement and providing the network capacity required to support the various types of clients Exchange can host. This is challenging because it involves two sets of variables: client types *and* their performance with Exchange Server. Rather than focusing just on messaging capability, ignoring the core services that must be delivered to the client desktops to provide messaging, a system architect should consider why Exchange clients behave as they do. This requires understanding the services that provide messaging and their bandwidth requirements.

The second half of this chapter provides a detailed look at how Exchange consumes bandwidth under different configurations and analyzes the traffic between clients and Exchange Server. The discussion is based on the results of three tests: one measuring traffic between an Exchange Client and Server, one measuring traffic between an Internet client and an Exchange Server, and (for comparative purposes) one measuring traffic generated by Microsoft Internet Explorer 3.02 mail client.

You can use the statistics and information in this chapter to better understand network bandwidth loading, including how to set up segments and assign users. It provides a logical framework for evaluating data and understanding the implications of server and service placement inside a distributed organization.

Choosing the Client

Deciding the type and combination of clients simplifies calculations and makes the remaining steps in the planning process much easier. To choose, you must first approximate the bandwidth that clients require, then use these figures to estimate the client's performance against Exchange Server. If you are migrating an existing messaging system to Exchange, you can simply profile a random sample of clients that are accessing a server over a particular WAN link. If you are planning a new deployment, you can extrapolate a client profile from the basic user definitions: very light, light, medium, or heavy.

Definition of Users

The following definitions for very light, light, medium, and heavy users are from the white paper "Exchange Performance: Concurrent Users Per Server," available on the TechNet sample CD-ROM.

Parameter	Very light	Light	Medium	Heavy
Hours in a day	12	8	8	8
Originate new mail (not reply or forward)	2x	2x	4x	6x
Text-only message				
Text-only message				
1K text (ups1k.msg)	100	90	60	50
2K text (ups2k.msg)			16	10
4K text (ups4k.msg)			4	5
1K text message with attachment				
1K text message with attachment				
10K attachment (ups10kat.msg)		10	5	10
Microsoft Excel attachment (upsXLatt.msg)			4	5
Word attachment (upsWDatt.msg)			2	5
Embedded bitmap (upsBMobj.msg)			2	5
Embedded Excel object Object (upsXLobj.msg)			2	10
Recipients per new/forward message	3	3	3	3
Add a distribution list to addressees	Never	30%	30%	30%
Read new mail	12x	12x	12x	12x
Send reply	5%	5%	7%	15%
Send reply all	3%	3%	5%	7%
Send forward	5%	5%	7%	7%
Delete (move to DI)	40%	40%	40%	40%
Move messages	Never	20%	20%	20%

(continued)

Parameter	Very light	Light	Medium	Heavy
Load attachments on read mail	N/A	25%	25%	25%
Maximum inbox size (in messages)	20	20	125	250
Other old mail processing	5x	5x	15x	20x
Schedule+ changes	1x	1x	5x	10x
Empty deleted items folder	1x	1x	1x	1x
Messages sent per day (computed average)	3.6	4.7	14.2	30.7
Messages received per day (computed average)	9.6	22.9	66.3	118.9

It is relatively easy to use a client profile to calculate its overall bandwidth use for a given interaction, and then decide the most efficient configuration for Exchange Servers and core network services. But before proceeding you should consider supporting services required by the client.

Core Services for Messaging

Messaging requires two underlying services—authentication and name resolution—each of which can require considerable bandwidth. It is important to find the best place to locate servers providing these services.

In areas of the architecture with large client populations, it is obvious that you should put authentication and name resolution services for satellite offices on machines other than the Exchange Server. If, for instance, a BDC server and a WINS server are already deployed at the remote location to support other applications, you should leverage the remote location's resources before building a separate messaging architecture. In areas of the architecture with small client populations, however, you must also place authentication and name resolution servers carefully. Bad placement can create a significant and persistent strain on the often already-burdened line to the remote location.

Authentication

During the Exchange client logon action, a Windows NT access token is obtained from the local PDC or BDC that is used for the duration of the Exchange connection. Several servers are involved in passing authentication information as well as the initial view of the inbox. The table below summarizes the various amounts of data transferred by Outlook, Exchange 32, Exchange 16, Outlook Web Access, and POP3 clients. The symbol between (->) indicates the direction of the action.

Initial logon distribution (bytes)	Client-> PDC	Client-> DNS	Client-> Exch	Client-> Bcast	DNS-> Client
Outlook 8.01		790	11574.5	158.75	1010
Exchange 32		790	10084	135.75	1010
Exchange 16		217.25	20439.5	436.5	321.25

Initial logon distribution (bytes)	Exch-> PDC	Exch-> Client	Exch-> Bcast	PDC-> Client	PDC-> Exch	PDC-> Bcast
Outlook 8.01	24643	11160.5	45		23376.5	
Exchange 32	24737	8709			23462.25	
Exchange 16	44960	14783.75	196.5		30413	479.25

Initial logon distribution (bytes)	Client-> DNS	Client-> Exch	DNS-> Client	Exch-> PDC	Exch-> Client	PDC-> Exch
POP3/LDAP	79	815	125	0	1104	0
POP3/LDAP—secure password authentication (SPA)	79	1238.75	140	602	1362	660.5

Because data is not transferred in full frames during this process, frame summaries are included below.

Initial logon distribution (frames)	Client-> PDC	Client-> DNS	Client-> Exch	Client-> Bcast	DNS-> Client	Exch-> PDC
Outlook 8.01		10	86.75	1.75	11	127.25
Exchange 32		7.5	60.25	1	8.25	96.25
Exchange 16		2.75	148.75	3	3.75	209.25

Initial logon distribution (frames)	Exch-> Client	Exch-> Bcast	PDC-> Client	PDC-> Exch	PDC-> Bcast
Outlook 8.01	64.25	0.75		125.75	
Exchange 32	44.5			95	
Exchange 16	151.25	1.75		168	3

Initial logon distribution (frames)	Client-> DNS	Client-> Exch	DNS-> Client	Exch-> PDC	Exch-> Client	PDC-> Exch
POP3/LDAP	1	13	1.5	0	14	0
POP3/LDAP (SPA)	1	16	1.5	3	17	2.25

Here is the traffic generated between Outlook or Exchange clients and the various servers (DNS, PDC, and Exchange) during an initial logon action.

1. Client obtains the address of the DNS/WINS Server (ARP).
2. Client queries DNS server for the directory server's address.
3. Client requests that the directory server return the mailbox server for the client's mailbox or the initial inbox view if the client's mailbox is on the same server.
4. Directory server looks up SID for user attempting to log on and obtains access token for the user from the domain controller on the client's behalf.
5. Directory server returns the mailbox server for the client's mailbox.
6. Client queries DNS for address of the mailbox server.
7. Client initiates connection to the mailbox server.
8. Mailbox server looks up SID for user attempting to log on and obtains an access token for the user from the domain controller on the client's behalf.
9. Mailbox server returns access token and initial inbox view to user.

Note: If the user's mailbox is on the same box queried by the directory server as the client, then steps 5, 6, 7, and 8 are skipped.

This information can help the system architect determine if the BDC and name resolution services should be located on the local subnet. Here is an example. Consider a remote network with 150 Outlook 8.01 users. The first step is to profile the remote link. Inventory the remote location's services (BDCs or local name servers) and isolate line use factors outside the scope of this planning (file and print services, application-specific services such as system management software (SMS) or systems network architecture (SNA) server, voice channels, bandwidth devoted to specialized applications). Now, if the remote subnet contains an Exchange Server and name resolution services but no BDCs, the architecture looks like this:

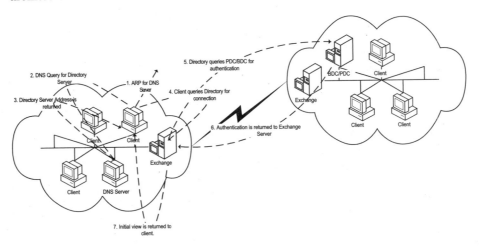

MAPI Logon

A MAPI logon is unique in terms of server usage. It is the only process (except for public folder operations) that generates traffic between the client and non-Exchange servers. It must be completed before any actions can be committed against the Exchange server, and it is incurred only once a day.

Initial MAPI logon for 150 clients in the example above generates about 48 K of traffic per client from the Exchange Server to the authentication server (PDC or BDC). If half the clients log on at the same time, 3.43 MB of authentication traffic is incurred once a day provided users do not disconnect until they go home at the end of the day. All of this traffic is reflected over the WAN link connecting the remote site and the central site, and the architect can assume that much of this traffic will be transmitted in a short amount of time because about half the users will tend to enter the office and log on to Exchange at about the same time every day. Even so, logon actions will be distributed within this concentration because not everyone will arrive at exactly the same time and some logon actions will complete before others are issued. Result: peak usage for initial logon actions on the link will be about 2.34 MB.

Other clients such as POP3 or Microsoft Outlook Web Access (OWA) are often considered lightweight, and some messaging systems designers try to save bandwidth by deploying them at remote locations instead of Exchange clients. The problem is that these OWA clients disconnect after 15 minutes of inactivity (default on IIS, which can be changed), and POP3 clients disconnect immediately after they have completed a download, send, or address resolution activity. Remote clients have to check for new mail on their server several times per day because OWA and POP3 have no provisions for new item notification. Additionally, each check will incur logon overhead if the session has timed out. If 50% of the clients overlap on their mail check requests, the total logon traffic generated for each mail check period, every eight hours, is 19.97 MB per day, about five times the burden with Exchange clients.

Initial logon distribution (bytes)	Client-> DNS	Client-> IIS	IIS-> Client	IIS-> Exch	IIS-> DNS
Outlook Web Access	79	30639	34657.25	11938.75	553

Initial logon distribution (bytes)	DNS-> Client	DNS-> IIS	Exch-> IIS	Exch-> PDC	PDC-> Exch
Outlook Web Access	110	680	19899	17931	16974.25

Initial logon distribution (frames)	Client-> DNS	Client-> IIS	IIS-> Client	IIS-> Exch	IIS-> DNS
Outlook Web Access	79	30639	34657.25	11938.75	553

Initial logon distribution (frames)	DNS-> Client	DNS-> IIS	Exch-> IIS	Exch-> PDC	PDC-> Exch
Outlook Web Access	110	680	19899	17931	16974.25

If the BDC is on the local subnet, different traffic is generated over the WAN link. In this scenario, traffic generated by WINS or DNS replication, BDC replication, Exchange message transfer, and Exchange directory replication supplants the client traffic that was generated in the previous example. In remote office sites that have large to very large client populations, this traffic can actually be much more controllable as it is generated on a schedule. Additionally, because the schedules for many of these replication and synchronization activities are independent and configurable by an administrator, the traffic will often be much more easily approximated than Exchange client activities on the same network.

More scenarios for the placement of servers are listed below in the Scenarios for Server Placement section below.

Name Resolution

Name resolution in Windows networks is accomplished by either DNS or WINS. The second half of this chapter, Bandwidth Test Results, uses DNS as name resolution to capture the actions clients conduct against an Exchange server. Understanding the impact of this recurring traffic is imperative to the design of a smooth-running Exchange architecture.

When using DNS to access an Exchange server from an Outlook or Exchange client, DNS queries are committed only during an initial logon to the Exchange Server and when establishing a connection to a public folder server. After these connections are established, there are no more DNS queries until the MAPI session is terminated. In the case of the Outlook client, the total DNS traffic is 790 bytes in 10 frames (10 DNS queries) sent, and 1,010 bytes in 11 frames (11 DNS responses) received during the initial logon.

DNS/WINS name resolution traffic for connectionless clients such as OWA and POP3 becomes much more significant, with totals varying based on how often the client polls the server for new messages. If a POP3 client polls an average of 6 times per day, each client generates 79 bytes in 1 frame (1 DNS query) sent, and 125 to 140 bytes in 1 to 2 frames (1 or 2 DNS responses) received: a daily total of 474 bytes in 6 frames sent, and 750 to 840 bytes in 6 to 12 frames received. If the client uses SPA for authentication, it generates even more traffic acquiring the name of the PDC in addition to resolving the name of the Exchange server.

The OWA case is similar. If the client polls the OWA server for new messages 6 times per day, each client generates 79 bytes in 1 frame (1 DNS query) sent and 110 bytes in 1 frame (1 DNS response) received. If the IIS server is left at the default connection timeout (900 seconds), the client will generate this DNS traffic each time it connects to the Exchange server. DNS queries are not generated from OWA clients when connecting to public folder servers, only for the initial connection to the Exchange server.

Directory Accesses

Directory accesses in Outlook, Exchange, POP3, IMAP4, and OWA clients are performed each time a client completes initial connection, sends a new message, or manually resolves an address. During initial connection, the directory server is queried for the location of the client's mailbox, and this serves as a referral mechanism if the client's mailbox is not on the server initially connected to. This is documented as an IMAP4 extension currently in RFC (RFC2193).

Depending on the client profile, directory access is committed frequently to resolve addresses for new mail items, less frequently for operations such as querying the directory for recipient information (such as organizational hierarchy, phone number, or physical address information), and least frequently for initial logon activity (except for POP3 and OWA clients). Directory resolution of recipient addresses can be costly on the WAN link, although POP3 traffic for this activity is confined to the client and the Exchange server. In addition to address resolution traffic, the OWA client also creates traffic between the IIS server hosting the OWA ASPs and the Exchange server.

Exchange 16 (bytes)	Client-> Exch	Exch ->Client
Ambiguous address resolution (4 char)	346	630
Address lookup	748	20116
Exchange 16 (frames)		
Ambiguous address resolution (4 char)	2	6
Address lookup	1	14
Exchange 32 (bytes)	**Client-> Exch**	**Exch ->Client**
Ambiguous address resolution (4 char)	459.33	711.33
Address lookup	1398.67	24942.67
Exchange 32 (frames)		
Ambiguous address resolution (4 char)	3.33	1.67
Address lookup	14.33	18.67

Outlook 8.01 (bytes)		Client-> Exch	Exch ->Client
Ambiguous address resolution (4 char)		607.33	968.67
Address lookup		1332.67	24895.33
Outlook 8.01 (frames)			
Ambiguous address resolution (4 char)		3.33	2.33
Address lookup		13.67	18.33

Outlook Web Access (bytes)	Client- >IIS	IIS- >Client	IIS- >Exch	Exch- >IIS
Address lookup	3522	7696	600	844
Outlook Web Access (frames)				
Address lookup	26	15.67	3	2

Looking up a single address in the Exchange directory from an OWA client generates 3,522 bytes in 26 frames sent and 7,676 bytes in 16 frames received. If people use this method 5 to 8 times a day to acquire directory information (organizational hierarchy, phone number, or physical address information), each client will generate 54.67 to 87.48 KB per day. If there are 100 clients at the remote location, this adds up to 5.34 to 8.54 MB per day.

Message Transfer

Here is what everyone wants to know: message traffic patterns. First a few notes about the characteristics of the traffic generated. For Exchange 16, Exchange 32, and Outlook 8.01 clients, traffic for all messaging operations (all operations tested) was generated between the Exchange server and messaging client only. In other words, no other servers generated or received traffic from these clients for the following operations:

- Send an item xK
- Send an item xK no notification
- Send an item with attachment xK
- Send an item with attachment 1M

- Open an item xK
- Open an item with attachment xK
- Open an item with attachment 1M
- Delete an item xK
- Delete an item with attachment xK
- Delete an item with attachment 1M

Tests marked with xK were conducted for message sizes of 1, 10, and 100 KB, and where applicable 1 MB. This distribution allows for easy extrapolation of messages of intermediary sizes up to 1 MB. For a summary of the results of this test please refer to the second half of this chapter, Bandwidth Test Results.

A few observations form the testing are worth noting because they will have substantial impact on any calculations for messaging throughput and network usage. First, with the Exchange 16, Exchange 32, and Outlook 8.01 clients, message bodies are compressed at the client, then sent and stored as compressed Rich Text Format (RTF). The server does not have to uncompress the messages until they go out a connector other than the site connector. This reduces network overhead for the transmission of message bodies for these clients about 33% for a 10-K message and 41.36% for a 100-K message. Attachments are sent and stored as binary images (not compressed).

The Exchange 16, Exchange 32, and Outlook 8.01 clients use cursors for navigating the message store, and they support messaging data stream encryption. Message type is rendered at the client so that rendering an Outlook form generates much less traffic on the wire than rendering the same form in an OWA client.

Additional notes regarding the operation of POP3 and OWA clients include:

Clients send all data as plain text unless a session level security protocol such as SSL is used. To compose messages with verified addresses, the client must connect to the Exchange server using LDAP—one connection for each message address resolution process. Message notification does not exist as a service; new messages are delivered when the client polls the server. Neither text nor attachments are compressed.

Public Folder Accesses

Exchange 16, Exchange 32, and Outlook 8.01 clients handle public folder connections as additional server connections. Outlook Web Access clients generate initial connection traffic for every connection after 15 minutes of inactivity because the client's session with the IIS server is terminated after 15 minutes of inactivity. Traffic observed from the connection of the clients is as follows:

Exchange 16 (bytes)	Client-> Exch	Exch ->Client
Public folder connection (initial)	1,998	1,354
Public folder connection (subsequent)	0	0
Public folder hierarchy enumeration (initial)	1,296	1,172
Public folder hierarchy enumeration (subsequent)	234	198
Exchange 16 (frames)		
Public folder connection (initial)	8	7
Public folder connection (subsequent)	0	0
Public folder hierarchy enumeration (initial)	7	6
Public folder hierarchy enumeration (subsequent)	1	1

Exchange 32 (bytes)	Client-> Exch	Exch ->Client
Public folder connection (initial)	2,990	2,038
Public folder connection (subsequent)	0	0
Public folder hierarchy enumeration (initial)	1,296	1,172
Public folder hierarchy enumeration (subsequent)	226	198
Exchange 32 (frames)		
Public folder connection (initial)	13	11
Public folder connection (subsequent)	0	0
Public folder hierarchy enumeration (initial)	7	6
Public folder hierarchy enumeration (subsequent)	2	1

Outlook 8.01 (bytes)	Client->Exch	Exch ->Client
Public folder connection (initial)	4,732	3,556
Public folder connection (subsequent)	1,200	1,060
Public folder hierarchy enumeration (initial)	1,306	990
Public folder hierarchy enumeration (subsequent)	258	230
Outlook 8.01 (frames)		
Public folder connection (initial)	17	19
Public folder connection (subsequent)	7	6
Public folder hierarchy enumeration (initial)	6	5
Public folder hierarchy enumeration (subsequent)	2	1

Outlook Web Access (bytes)	Client->IIS	IIS->Client	IIS->Exch	Exch->IIS
Public folder connection and hierarchy enumeration	3,076	8,143.67	1,874	1,878
Outlook Web Access (frames)				
Public folder connection and hierarchy enumeration	21.33	16	10	9

For Exchange 16, Exchange 32, and Outlook 8.01, initial connections per logon session are more costly than subsequent connections from the same logon session; amounts vary by client. Outlook clients generate traffic when connecting subsequently to the public folder server, Exchange clients do not. When a new client session is started, initial connection traffic applies as detailed above.

When items are opened in a public folder, the standard open item traffic is generated only between the client and the public folder server servicing the request. Public folder hierarchy enumeration can occur several times during the course of the day, so Exchange architects should consider placing a public folder hierarchy server at each remote location. It should handle light client activity, so it can be hosted on the local user server.

Outlook-Specific Items and Their Accesses

Outlook items such as calendar, task, contact, and note items are accessed in exactly the same way as message items are. Correlation with the appropriate class ID and display in the proper form is a function of the client. Having made these statements, there were no anomalies associated with the traffic observed for the use of these items. Message items can be substituted for them in network load calculations.

Server Placement Scenarios

Here are scenarios showing the traffic patterns that result from server placement in a remote network configuration.

Scenario 1: Everything But the Kitchen Sink

All required messaging resources and core network support resources are at the remote location: BDC, name server, IIS server, and Exchange server, all of which may be on one machine. The implementation of this scenario would look much as follows:

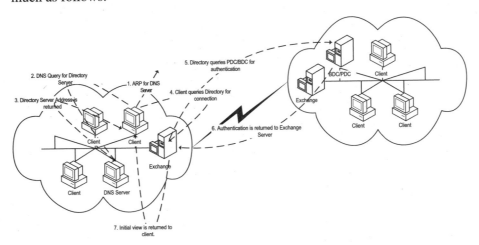

Types of Traffic Generated

This arrangement generates only server-to-server traffic, most likely WINS or DNS replication traffic, BDC SAM replication, Exchange directory replication, and Exchange message transfer. Public folder connection traffic is possible if local replicas aren't available, and there will probably be some public folder replication traffic on the WAN link. This configuration is preferred when remote locations have large client populations or must continue functioning for long periods of time even if a remote WAN link fails.

Advantages

If the link to the remote location is broken, remote clients can still perform all activities except accessing public folder information not in a local replica. With the proper connector, it is even possible to organize schedules so that the remote link can be dial-on-demand or of variable bandwidth. Because support and messaging services are localized, clients can be selected without regard for their bandwidth consumption on the WAN connection.

Disadvantages

Having no onsite administrative personnel at the remote location can drastically raise administrative overhead at that site and require that personnel go to the remote site to manage or troubleshoot. For some client populations, the remote service's use of bandwidth may be much higher than the traffic that could be generated by client activity over the WAN link. This can be the case when organizations deploy server resources to a remote location with few users or users who access e-mail infrequently.

Variations

Many core services are modular and can be relocated without affecting the overall remote client operation, so pull one or more back to the centralized location. OWA services is a good candidate, or you can relocate Exchange messaging services and change the client to POP3.

Scenario 2: One or More Services from a Centralized Location

This is a variation on scenario 1: one or more core services (BDC, Exchange, IIS, DNS/WINS) are moved back to the centralized location.

Types of Traffic Generated

This generates server-to-server and client-to-server traffic. Depending on the number of services relocated to the central location, you might see more client traffic than server-to-server traffic on the wire: WINS or DNS replication traffic, BDC SAM replication, Exchange directory replication, Exchange message transfer, public folder replication traffic, Exchange client traffic (message composition, navigation, public folder navigation, etc.), and OWA client traffic. This configuration is common when remote locations have client populations large enough to require high availability and quick response time on selected services, but not large enough to warrant placing all core network services at the site.

Advantages

Greater administrative control can be exerted on the servers if they are constrained to a single physical location. Depending on the services that are moved to the central location, it might be possible to complete replication more quickly. Suppose an organization has a tremendous amount of turnover resulting in frequent directory changes, but has to synchronize fully every four hours to keep it accurate for critical business needs. If remote locations have varying bandwidth availability and quality, and service level agreements cannot be negotiated to provide acceptable network stability and uptime, you might have to centralize Exchange servers to make this work.

Disadvantages

If core services are centralized, clients might generate excessive traffic on the WAN link. This fact may dictate the choice of client. The choice to centralize some core services may also dictate the SLA for the remote link and the total feature set offered to remote clients.

Variations

The architect should carefully study and select services for centralization, which will affect operations ranging from client functionality to independence from the central site. Centralizing core services increases the probability that remote clients occasionally will generate excessive traffic trying to use some or all of the relocated functions. The architect should study the impact of relocation on other applications deployed at the remote location. Example: a remote location has an SQL server replicated database and Windows NT integrated security. If you centralize the remote BDC to provide for faster SAM replication with the PDC, remote clients will be unable to access remote SQL server data until the link has been reestablished—potentially a costly problem.

Scenario 3: Completely Centralized

All core services—BDC, Exchange, IIS, and DNS/WINS—are moved back to the central site.

Types of Traffic Generated

This generates only client-to-server traffic, most likely, at a minimum: Exchange client traffic (message composition, navigation, public folder navigation, etc.) and, depending on the remote client, OWA client traffic, POP3 message download/send/directory access, and IMAP4 message download/send/directory access/store synchronization. If public folders are used, there is connection traffic, the amount depending on the remote client choice and its frequency of access. This configuration is common at organizations with lightly populated remote locations.

Advantages

Putting all core network services servers in a single environment allows hands-on management and centralization of the support organization. Without WAN links, traffic speeds are high for activities such as replication of distributed data stored in a multimaster capacity (such as the Exchange directory) or data such as the Windows NT SAM. And backups are simplified when all resources are centralized on relatively high-speed networks.

Disadvantages

"Putting all your eggs in one basket" presents problems sooner or later. An architect contemplating this configuration must build in fault tolerance for server configurations and WAN links. One catastrophic failure at the central site can disable the network, so there must be a disaster recovery plan in place. Additionally, because the remote site business needs dictate the service level agreements (SLA) that are established with bandwidth providers, each time new critical applications are added at the site such as e-mail, the SLAs could potentially change. If many mission-critical applications are in use at the remote site, or if their quantity increases rapidly, the high-availability links required to support the environment may be cost prohibitive.

Variations

Change the remote client to one that operates better under the constraints of the link. Change the bandwidth so that clients can carry more features. Possibly even expose public folders as Network News Transfer Protocol (NNTP) newsgroups so that POP3 clients can take advantage of them. Using a POP3 client in this fashion would require the administrator to allow access to the Exchange directory using LDAP (possibly even secured by SSL).

POP3, IMAP4, and OWA: Aren't Internet-Standard Clients the Only Way To Go?

Just because a client complies with an RFC it is not by definition better. An RFC standardizes features so that many vendors can implement them in products, but this process often means that the newest features are not included. If several vendors can't agree on how to implement a function, it is sometimes omitted. And standard is not always best. Consider the POP3 client. It can secure data on the wire only with a session encryption protocol such as SSL, which means the client cannot maintain a server connection and must reauthenticate itself for each message poll or address resolution. Standardized? Yes. Efficient? No.

Internet standard clients have a place in Exchange architectures, but not on every desktop. They provide the greatest benefit when they augment Outlook and Exchange clients. In this configuration, users can simultaneously access an Exchange mailbox from OWA, POP3/IMAP4, and Outlook clients, check calendar and mail contents from a kiosk between meetings, or use one client at home and a richer one at work. Using a kiosk equipped with OWA in this fashion would simplify software management and licensing while still allowing the user to respond to critical items or read stored items.

Internet standard clients provide the greatest benefit when used with richer clients, and Exchange Server is unique in its support of architectures based on multiple client use.

Bandwidth Test Results

The rest of this chapter shows how Microsoft Exchange consumes bandwidth under different configurations. The discussion is based on the results of three tests: one measuring traffic between an Exchange Client and Server, one measuring traffic between an Internet client and an Exchange Server, and (for comparative purposes) one measuring traffic generated by Microsoft Internet Explorer 3.02 mail client. All data is included here, for your reference.

Lab Configuration

Two labs were constructed. The first captured network traffic between a typical client (Microsoft Exchange 32, Microsoft Exchange 16, and Outlook 8.01) and a generically configured server. The second captured traffic on a Microsoft Outlook Web Access (OWA) client using Microsoft Information Internet Server (IIS) and Microsoft Exchange Server. Testers captured traffic resulting from common tasks performed on each client and used it to approximate the overall client impact on a section of a corporation's network.

Note: Approximations of this type cannot predict or reflect random end-user messaging activities or usage patterns. As a rule, however, they are useful and generally accurate methods with which to model communications.

Client Bandwidth Analysis Lab

The lab architecture for the client bandwidth analysis was set up as a five-machine subnet. The machine configurations were as follows:

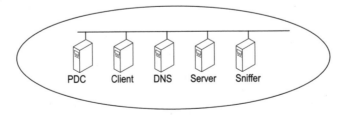

Client Configurations

32-bit client	16-bit client
DEC 200i Personal Workstation	Compaq Prolinea 4/66
Two Intel Pentium Pro 200-MHz processors	16-MB RAM
64-MB RAM	Intel EtherExpress 16 TP network card
Integrated DEC 10/100 TP Ethernet	Windows for Workgroups 3.11 with 32-bit MS-TCP/IP 3.11b
Windows NT Server 4.00.1381 with SP3	Microsoft Exchange 5.0 SP1 16-bit client
Outlook 8.01.3817 or Microsoft Exchange 5.0 32-bit client (depending on test). For the Outlook tests, the client was configured with Outlook 8.01.3817.	Static TCP/IP address
Static TCP/IP address	

Server Configurations

Microsoft Exchange Server	DNS Server
DEC 200i Personal Workstation	DEC 200i Personal Workstation
Two Intel Pentium Pro 200-MHz processors	Two Intel Pentium Pro 200-MHz processors
64-MB RAM	64-MB RAM
Integrated DEC 10/100 TP Ethernet	Integrated DEC 10/100 TP Ethernet
Windows NT Server 4.00.1381 with SP3	Windows NT Server 4.00.1381 with SP3
Microsoft Exchange 5.0 SP1	Static TCP/IP address
Static TCP/IP address	

Other Configurations

Windows NT PDC	Network Monitor
DEC 200i Personal Workstation	DEC 200i Personal Workstation
Two Intel Pentium Pro 200-MHz processors	Two Intel Pentium Pro 200-MHz processors
64-MB RAM	64-MB RAM
Integrated DEC 10/100 TP Ethernet	Integrated DEC 10/100 TP Ethernet
Windows NT Server 4.00.1381 with SP3	Windows NT Server 4.00.1381 with SP3
Static TCP/IP address	SMS 1.2 Network Monitor
	Office 97
	Static TCP/IP address

Configuration Notes

The server in this lab was optimized for:

- More than 500 users on the server
- Multiserver with public and private information stores
- Between 10,000 and 99,999 users in the organization
- Limit memory usage to 48 MB

OWA, POP, and LDAP Bandwidth Analysis Lab

The lab architecture for the client bandwidth analysis was set up as a five-machine subnet with the following machine configurations:

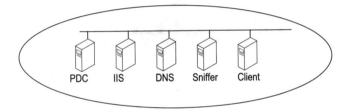

32-bit Client Configuration

- DEC 200i Personal Workstation
- Two Intel Pentium Pro 200-MHz processors
- 64-MB RAM
- Integrated DEC 10/100 TP Ethernet
- Windows NT Server 4.00.1381 with SP3
- Outlook 8.01.3817 or Microsoft Exchange 5.0 32-bit Client (depending on test). For the Outlook tests, the client was configured with Outlook 8.01.3817.
- Static TCP/IP address

Server Configurations

Microsoft Exchange Server	DNS Server	IIS Server
DEC 200i Personal Workstation	DEC 200i Personal Workstation	DEC 266i Personal Workstation
Two Intel Pentium Pro 200-MHz processors	Two Intel Pentium Pro 200-MHz processors	Two Intel Pentium II 266-MHz processors
64-MB RAM	64-MB RAM	64-MB RAM
Integrated DEC 10/100 TP Ethernet	Integrated DEC 10/100 TP Ethernet	Integrated DEC 10/100 TP Ethernet
Windows NT Server 4.00.1381 with SP3	Windows NT Server 4.00.1381 with SP3	Windows NT Server 4.00.1381 with SP3
Microsoft Exchange 5.0 SP1	Static TCP/IP address	IIS 3.0 with ASP
Static TCP/IP address		Microsoft Exchange 5.0 SP1 OWA ASPs
		Static TCP/IP address

Other Server Configurations

Windows NT PDC	Network Monitor
DEC 200i Personal Workstation	DELL 590
Two Intel Pentium Pro 200-MHz processors	1 Intel Pentium 90-MHz processor
64-MB RAM	32-MB RAM
Integrated DEC 10/100 TP Ethernet	Integrated 10 TP Ethernet
Windows NT Server 4.00.1381 with SP3	Windows NT Server 4.00.1381 with SP3
Static TCP/IP address	SMS 1.2 Network Monitor
	Office 97
	VB 5.0 Enterprise
	Static TCP/IP address

Configuration Notes

The Microsoft Exchange Server in this lab was optimized for:

- More than 500 users on the server
- Multiserver with public and private information stores
- Between 10,000 and 99,999 users in the organization
- Memory usage limited to 48 MB

Exchange Client-to-Server Traffic Analysis

A series of tests focused on standard messaging activities, including initial logon, sending and deleting mail with and without attachments, looking up addresses, and scheduling meetings. The tests, described below, focus on three clients:

- Outlook 8.01.3817
- Microsoft Exchange 5.0 32-bit
- Microsoft Exchange 5.0 16-bit

Results for the tests are in the section, Test Results for Each Client, and notes on the tests themselves are in the Extrapolations and Observations section.

"Initial Log on to" and "Exit and Log off from" the Server

This test captures the traffic generated by initial connection and validation of the Exchange Client and Exchange Server to the DNS server and PDC client. Since Exchange uses Windows NT to grant or deny access to mailboxes or other Exchange resources, testing this traffic is an important part of the load calculation. The client was configured to use Windows NT password authentication for the Exchange service defined in the MAPI profile.

Two other tests were conducted to see if the number of messages in a client's inbox affected the amount of traffic generated between the client and server. The first used a just-installed client with only a single sample item in its inbox; the second was run with 100 items in the client's inbox. In both tests the same amount of traffic was generated.

After the initial connection tests were completed, the traffic resulting from a disconnection from the server was tested by selecting *file|exit and log off* the client.

Generic Mail Item Tests

Each client (Outlook 8.01.3817, Microsoft Exchange 5.0 32 bit, and Microsoft Exchange 5.0 16 bit) was tested performing the following actions:

- **Send an item xK**—Send a mail message containing xK of text. Include a simple subject indicating the contents of the message, such as "xK of text." The recipient for the message was the current logged on user.

- **Send an item xK no notification**—Send a mail message containing xK of text. Include a simple subject indicating the contents of the message, such as "xK of text." For this test the recipient of the message was a user other than the currently logged on user.

- **Open an item xK**—Open the item sent above.

- **Delete an item xK**—Delete the item sent above.

- **Send an item with attachment xK**—Send a mail message containing an xK attachment and no other text. Include a simple subject indicating the contents of the message, such as "1-K Attachment (1)."

- **Open an item with attachment xK**—Read the item sent above.

- **Read attachment xK**—Read the attachment after a mail message containing an attachment of x size has been received and opened.

- **Delete an item with attachment xK**—Delete the item sent above.

- **Send an item with attachment 1M**—Send a mail message containing a 1-M attachment and no other text. Include a simple subject line indicating the contents of the message, for example: "1-K Attachment (1)." Enter the correct alias for the user to which you are sending.

- **Open an item with attachment 1M**—Read the item sent above.

- **Read attachment 1M**—Read an attachment of x size with a mail message that has been received and opened. Open the attachment contained in the message, and read that attachment.

- **Delete an item with attachment 1M**—Delete the item sent above.

- **Process read receipt**—Process a 1-k mail message sent with a read receipt. The message was opened on the client (note that this traffic has already been captured in other tests), a sniff was started, and the user double-clicked on the read receipt. The double-click on the read receipt and the closing of the corresponding item was the traffic tested.

- **Create subfolder**—Create a single subfolder in the mailbox.

- **Empty deleted items x - yK item(s)**—Empty the deleted items folder, in which there are x number of yK sized items present in the folder.

Addressing and Address Resolution Tests

Two addressing tests were performed on the three clients. They are:

- **Address lookup**—To capture traffic resulting from users running MAPI query of the addresses in the global address list (GAL), the To: button was clicked when addressing a message and the address book was used to find recipient addresses.
- **Ambiguous address resolution**—To capture the automatic resolution of recipient addresses by Outlook, the first four characters of the user's alias were typed into the To: value box for the mail message being composed.

Public Folder Connection and Hierarchy Enumeration Tests

Because the messaging functionality of each client is similar, these tests were conducted in the same way.

- **Public folders**—When the client double-clicks on the hierarchy of public folders, an initial connection is made to a public folder server. The traffic generated by a query and connection to a public folder server was tested.
- **All public folders**—Browse the hierarchy of public folders within a given organization.

Calendaring/Scheduling, Tasks, and Contact Tests

The Schedule+ client of Exchange and the Outlook calendar operate and perform very differently. Because the Outlook client is the only client that intermittently generates traffic to the server, no comparisons can be made to Schedule+ used by the Exchange 16- and 32-bit clients. As a result, Schedule+ tests measured the traffic generated by synchronization of the .SCD file on the client with a number of task calendar and contact entries.

- **Open calendar**—Initial view of the calendar by double clicking on the calendar item **[For Outlook]**. Initial opening of Schedule+ by clicking on the Schedule+ button in the Exchange Client toolbar **[For Schedule+]**.
- **Add a calendar item**—Create a four-hour meeting in the calendar (from 8 a.m. to 12 p.m. on a specific day) using "Meeting" as the description.
- **Modify a calendar item**—Move the created meeting from 12 p.m. to 4 p.m. on the same day, and rename the meeting to "Another meeting."
- **Delete calendar item**—Delete the item created above.
- **Open tasks**—View tasks by double-clicking on the tasks item **[Outlook Only]**.
- **Add a task item**—Create a task item in the client named "Task" **[Outlook Only]**.

- **Modify a task item**—Rename the task to "Another task" **[Outlook Only]**.
- **Delete task item**—Delete the item created above **[Outlook Only]**.
- **Open contacts**—View the calendar by double clicking on the contacts item **[Outlook Only]**.
- **Add a contact item**—Create a contact with full name, company name, two telephone numbers, business address, and e-mail address, and save **[Outlook Only]**.
- **Modify a contact item**—Rename the contact **[Outlook Only]**.
- **Delete contact item**—Delete the item created above **[Outlook Only]**.

Test and Environment Notes

During the generic mail tests, the bandwidth resulting from sent items reflects the initial notification of mail and the traffic generated by sending the message. Tests of emptying deleted items were conducted in several ways to determine the traffic impact of single instance storage, number of items, and size of item. For a description of single instance storage in Exchange, see the section Single Instance Storage near the end of this chapter.

In all of the tests, the Exchange and Outlook clients pass the same amount of data to the server regardless of the number and size of items in the deleted items folder. This return traffic is proportionately larger because there are more items in the folder. The client uses the return information from the server to populate a progress indicator, which positions the cursor for the next action once an item is read, deleted, etc. For example, when a user deletes one item, the position occupied by the deleted item becomes a cursor that the client can then pass to the server to indicate the next item to be deleted.

Test Results for Each Client

The results listed below are averages for three iterations of each test. The first two tables list results of logon and exit tests. Results of tests for generic mail activities, addressing, public folders, and scheduling tests are compiled into the next three large tables, one for each client tested: Outlook 8.01.3817, Microsoft Exchange 5.0 32-bit, and Microsoft Exchange 5.0 16-bit.

The right-hand table columns list "Bytes" and "Frames," both of which represent total transmission for the action described. For example, the total bytes for sending a 1-K message with an attachment from a server to a client are 2,233; the total frames for the same action equal 9.5. Below the "Bytes" and "Frames" columns are abbreviations for client (Cli) and server (Srv). The symbol between (->) indicates the direction of the action being tested. For example, "Srv->Cli" means that the test measures traffic from the server to the client.

Tests of "Initial Log on" and "Exit and Log off" the Server

Initial logon traffic	Bytes		Frames	
	Srv->Cli	Cli->Srv	Srv->Cli	Cli->Srv
Outlook 8.01 initial logon actions	12500.250	12965.750	77.750	101.500
Outlook 8.01 exit and logoff actions	2382.000	2246.000	21.000	23.000
Microsoft Exchange 32 initial logon actions	10079.000	11039.750	72.750	94.750
Microsoft Exchange 32 exit and logoff actions	2694.000	2877.333	25.000	29.000
Microsoft Exchange 16 initial logon actions	15105.000	21093.250	155.000	154.500
Microsoft Exchange 16 exit and logoff actions	2314.000	2434.000	24.000	25.000

This diagram illustrates the flow of traffic between the various servers (DNS, PDC, and Exchange) and the client during the initial logon process in the test environment.

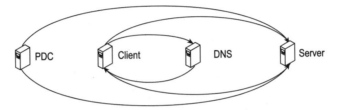

The initial logon sequence for the Outlook and Exchange clients follows this process:

1. Find directory server address (DNS, WINS)
2. Connect to directory (plus authentication)
3. Determine name of mailbox server
4. Find mailbox server address (DNS, WINS)
5. Connect to mailbox (plus authentication)

Results of the protocol distribution for the Outlook 8.01 client against an Exchange Server were averaged from four Outlook initial logon tests. The average number of total frames generated in each of the trials was 434.25. Keep in mind that the client is connecting to the Exchange Server running on a Windows NT Server, to which a user has already logged on to the console.

Outlook 8.01 initial log on protocol distribution	Average frames	Average bytes	% frames of total	% bytes of total
SMB protocol	253.5	17915.25	57.75	23.75
NBT protocol	254.5	1100.5	58	1
MSRPC protocol	247.5	16261	56.5	21.25
R_LSARPC protocol	144	7200	32.75	9

Outlook 8.01 Averaged Results for All Other Tests

Outlook 8.01.3817 test description	Srv->Cli (bytes)	Cli->Srv (bytes)	Srv->Cli (frames)	Cli->Srv (frames)
Send item 1K	2428.000	2286.000	6.500	7.500
Send item 10K	2316.000	6655.333	7.000	9.667
Send item 100K	3218.000	41326.000	20.000	34.000
Open item 1K	2894.000	985.000	3.000	4.000
Open item 10K	7094.000	1088.000	6.000	5.000
Open item 100K	44857.333	3967.333	33.333	25.667
Delete item 1K	660.000	408.000	2.333	4.000
Delete item 10K	518.000	226.000	1.000	2.000
Delete item 100K	430.000	226.000	1.667	2.000
Send item 1K no notification	1536.000	2436.000	6.500	7.000
Send item 10K no notification	1596.000	6686.000	7.000	10.000
Send item 100K no notification	2498.000	41342.000	20.000	34.000
Send item 1K with attachment	2233.000	6869.000	9.500	14.000
Send item 10K with attachment	2290.000	16232.000	17.000	12.000
Send item 100K with attachment	5326.000	113279.500	49.500	85.000
Send item 1M with attachment	46114.000	1452564.000	593.000	1018.000
Open item 1K with attachment	6372.000	1334.000	6.000	6.000
Open item 10K with attachment	6356.000	1334.000	6.000	6.000
Open item 100K with attachment	6404.000	1328.667	6.000	6.000
Open item 1M with attachment	6404.000	1334.000	6.000	6.000
Read attachment 1K	2254.000	858.000	5.000	6.000
Read attachment 10K	12008.000	1248.000	12.000	11.000
Read attachment 100K	109700.000	5060.000	80.333	57.000

(continued)

Outlook 8.01.3817 test description	Srv->Cli (bytes)	Cli->Srv (bytes)	Srv->Cli (frames)	Cli->Srv (frames)
Read 1M with attachment	1120722.000	43428.000	779.000	522.000
Delete item with attachment 1K	534.000	226.000	1.000	2.000
Delete item with attachment 10K	534.000	226.000	1.000	2.000
Delete item with attachment 100K	534.000	226.000	1.000	2.000
Delete item 1M with attachment	516.667	252.667	1.333	2.000
Empty deleted items 1 -1K	642.000	650.000	3.000	5.000
Empty deleted items 1 -1M	856.000	740.000	4.000	5.000
Empty deleted items 10 -1K	1444.000	740.000	5.000	5.000
Empty deleted items 10 -1M	1460.000	740.000	5.000	5.000
Process read receipt (1K item)	7629.000	3599.000	12.500	15.000
Ambiguous address resolution (4 char)	764.000	520.000	2.000	3.000
Address lookup	19518.667	1125.333	14.667	11.333
Create subfolder	1539.333	1062.000	5.000	7.000
Double-click on public folders	1060.000	1200.000	6.000	7.000
Double-click on all public folders	230.000	258.000	1.000	2.000
Open calendar	914.000	958.000	3.000	4.000
Add a calendar item	1229.000	1545.000	4.000	5.000
Modify a calendar item	2144.000	1312.667	3.333	4.667
Delete a calendar item	3196.667	1880.000	6.333	7.667
Open tasks	358.000	354.000	1.000	2.000
Add a task item	1216.000	1640.000	5.000	7.500
Modify a task item	1935.333	1428.333	3.000	5.667
Delete a task item	641.333	397.333	2.000	3.000
Open contacts	406.000	386.000	1.000	2.000
Add a contact item	1023.000	2103.000	4.500	7.000
Modify a contact item	2994.000	1892.000	3.000	4.000
Delete a contact item	774.000	574.000	3.000	5.000

Microsoft Exchange 32 Averaged Results for All Other Tests

Microsoft Exchange(32) 5.5.1458.57 test description	Srv->Cli (bytes)	Cli->Srv (bytes)	Srv->Cli (frames)	Cli->Srv (frames)
Send item 1K	2512.000	2898.000	8.000	11.333
Send item 10K	2614.667	7183.333	9.000	13.000
Send item 100K	3616.000	42108.000	23.000	37.000
Open item 1K	2486.000	664.000	3.000	4.000
Open item 10K	6824.000	784.000	6.000	6.000
Open item 100K	42590.000	2718.667	31.000	22.333
Delete item 1K	350.000	234.000	1.000	2.000
Delete item 10K	342.000	226.000	1.000	2.000
Delete item 100K	464.000	408.000	2.000	4.000
Send item 1K no notification	2150.000	2712.000	7.000	9.000
Send item 10K no notification	2230.000	6928.000	9.000	10.000
Send item 100K no notification	3144.000	41637.000	21.000	34.500
Send item 1K with attachment	2915.333	7221.333	10.667	16.667
Send item 10K with attachment	3014.000	16736.000	13.000	21.000
Send item 100K with attachment	5802.667	113611.333	51.333	88.333
Send item 1M with attachment	37308.667	1117500.000	461.000	789.000
Open item 1K with attachment	5374.000	959.333	5.000	5.000
Open item 10K with attachment	5615.333	1091.333	5.667	6.333
Open item 100K with attachment	5716.333	1151.333	6.000	6.667
Open item 1M with attachment	5294.000	954.000	5.000	5.000
Read attachment 1K	1206.000	242.000	1.000	2.000
Read attachment 10K	11082.000	754.000	9.000	8.000
Read attachment 100K	108530.000	4262.000	75.000	51.000
Read 1M with attachment	1119694.000	42812.000	775.333	518.000
Delete item with attachment 1K	358.000	231.333	1.000	2.000
Delete item with attachment 10K	368.667	226.000	1.000	2.000
Delete item with attachment 100K	480.000	408.000	2.000	4.000
Delete item 1M with attachment	390.000	226.000	1.000	2.000
Empty deleted items 1 -1K	492.000	440.000	2.000	3.000
Empty deleted items 1 -1M	658.000	666.000	3.000	5.000

(continued)

Microsoft Exchange(32) 5.5.1458.57 test description	Srv->Cli (bytes)	Cli->Srv (bytes)	Srv->Cli (frames)	Cli->Srv (frames)
Empty deleted items 10 -1K	990.000	666.000	4.000	5.000
Empty deleted items 10 -1M	792.000	376.000	3.000	3.000
Process read receipt (1K item)	1638.000	846.000	3.000	5.000
Ambiguous address resolution (4 char)	711.333	459.333	1.667	3.333
Address lookup	19566.000	1186.000	15.000	12.000
Create subfolder	326.000	226.000	1.000	2.000
Double-click on public folders	0.000	0.000	0.000	0.000
Double-click on all public folders	198.000	226.000	1.000	2.000
Synchronize Schedule+ 1 - 1K item	1044.000	1180.000	6.000	8.000
Synchronize Schedule+ 10 - 1K item	1044.000	1180.000	6.000	8.000
Synchronize Schedule+ 100 - 1K item	1044.000	1180.000	3.000	4.000

Microsoft Exchange 16 Averaged Results for All Other Tests

Microsoft Exchange(16) 5.5.1458.57 test description	Srv->Cli (bytes)	Cli->Srv (bytes)	Srv->Cli (frames)	Cli->Srv (frames)
Send item 1K	2618.000	2154.000	6.000	8.000
Send item 10K	2274.000	6956.000	8.000	11.000
Send item 100K	3208.000	41920.000	21.000	36.000
Open item 1K	2316.000	490.000	2.000	2.000
Open item 10K	6804.000	692.000	6.000	4.000
Open item 100K	42400.000	2804.000	30.000	22.333
Delete item 1K	380.000	234.000	1.500	2.000
Delete item 10K	342.000	234.000	1.000	2.000
Delete item 100K	342.000	234.000	1.000	2.000
Send item 1K no notification	2210.000	2730.000	8.000	9.667
Send item 10K no notification	2210.000	6956.000	8.000	11.000
Send item 100K no notification	3144.000	41936.000	21.000	36.000
Send item 1K with attachment	2652.000	4222.000	8.000	11.333
Send item 10K with attachment	2832.000	13964.667	11.000	17.667
Send item 100K with attachment	5702.000	111092.667	50.000	84.667
Send item 1M with attachment	36282.000	1117904.000	458.000	784.000

(continued)

Microsoft Exchange(16) 5.5.1458.57 test description	Srv->Cli (bytes)	Cli->Srv (bytes)	Srv->Cli (frames)	Cli->Srv (frames)
Open item 1K with attachment	2828.667	1120.667	3.000	5.000
Open item 10K with attachment	2828.667	938.000	3.000	4.333
Open item 100K with attachment	2886.000	918.000	4.000	4.000
Open item 1M with attachment	2930.000	918.000	3.000	4.000
Read attachment 1K	1206.000	234.000	1.000	2.000
Read attachment 10K	11110.000	654.000	9.000	6.000
Read attachment 100K	110154.000	5274.000	87.000	50.000
Read 1M with attachment	1136960.000	54414.000	904.000	518.000
Delete item with attachment 1K	358.000	234.000	1.000	2.000
Delete item with attachment 10K	358.000	234.000	1.000	2.000
Delete item with attachment 100K	358.000	234.000	1.000	2.000
Delete item 1M with attachment	390.000	234.000	1.000	2.000
Empty deleted items 1 -1K	460.000	392.000	2.000	3.000
Empty deleted items 1 -1M	508.000	516.000	2.000	4.000
Empty deleted items 10 -1K	792.000	392.000	3.000	3.000
Empty deleted items 10 -1M	840.000	516.000	3.000	4.000
Process read receipt (1K item)	1500.000	664.000	2.000	3.000
Ambiguous address resolution (4 char)	630.000	346.000	1.000	2.000
Address lookup	20116.000	748.000	14.000	6.000
Create subfolder	358.000	234.000	1.000	2.000
Double-click on public folders	0.000	0.000	0.000	0.000
Double-click on all public folders	198.000	234.000	1.000	2.000
Synchronize Schedule+ 1 - 1K item	1044.000	1194.000	6.000	8.500
Synchronize Schedule+ 10 - 1K item	1104.000	1164.000	7.000	8.000
Synchronize Schedule+ 100 - 1K item	1044.000	1194.000	6.000	8.500

Extrapolations and Observations

In all of the tests, the clients were connecting directly to the server over a standard 10-Mbps Ethernet. No offline storage was assumed. In addition, traffic generated was primarily between the Exchange Server and the respective client, except for the initial logon action, which resulted in traffic generated between DNS or PDC and the server or client.

Other test-specific comments are below.

Generic Mail Tests

A few anomalies observed during these tests are worth noting:

- Text sent to the server as an attachment was copied directly to the server with no compression. However, when the same text was sent in the body of a message, it was compressed on the client before transmission to the server. Both Outlook and Exchange clients compressed a 10-K message to approximately 6 K and a 100-K message to approximately 41 K. In both the 10-K and 100-K message tests, the compressed message equaled the size of the message in the information store.

- The Outlook 8.01.3817 client and Exchange 5.0.1458 (32-bit) clients used the same Exchange Provider, but used it differently, sometimes causing different traffic patterns.

- On the 16-bit client, tests of the 100-K attached text could not use Notepad and a substitute write was used to open the attachment. Even when the client generated the Notepad error, the data had already been copied over, implying that when a client attempts to open an item with an association, the attachment is fully copied to the client regardless of whether the client succeeds in opening the item.

Public Folder Connections

After the initial connection from the Outlook client to the public folder server, each connection client generated traffic. But no additional traffic was generated on subsequent connections from the Exchange Client to the public folder server after the initial connection generated traffic.

Calendar vs. Schedule+

The Schedule+ client of Exchange and the Outlook calendar operate differently, with different impact on traffic. For example, the Exchange 32- and 16-bit Schedule+ clients did not work from the server in the default installation, which sets up true values on the following attributes:

- Work primarily from local file
- Always synchronize upon exit
- Synchronize every [15] minutes

By contrast, Outlook works primarily from the server by default unless Outlook is configured to not use a PST for message delivery, in which case there is no server-based copy of the calendar details. Running Outlook from the server means that after a MAPI session is established to the server, the client will use that session for calendar and messaging activities. Because two connections are not instantiated, the traffic patterns exhibited by the Outlook client are recurring numbers of small packets for typical actions like creating a calendar item or modifying a calendar item. If the Outlook client is used for scheduling, intermittent traffic is generated at various levels based on the client's interaction with the Exchange Server.

RPC Provider

By default, the Exchange client loads a provider for each possible transport that might be installed on the machine. Default providers are loaded in this order:

- **Ncalrpc**—LRPC-only connection to the server.
- **ncacn_ip_tcp**—IP connection to the server.
- **ncacn_spx**—SPX connection to the server.
- **ncacn_np**—Named Pipes connection to the server.
- **netbios**—NetBIOS.
- **ncacn_vns_spp**—Vines IP connection to the server.

Upon loading, the Exchange Client tries each of the providers (from the registry if it is a 32-bit client or from the .INI file if it is 16-bit). If protocols are loaded that support a specific provider, the load time can be long due to additional traffic and timeouts, so to reduce loading time significantly, match the provider to the protocol.

Load time was improved on the 16-bit Exchange 5.0 Client by using only the TCP/IP parameter with the RPC provider. Starting with the default value for RPC provider, the client generated traffic for more than 5 minutes; starting with the TCP/IP-only RPC provider reduced this to under 1 minute.

Selecting Subfolders

Selecting folders other than the currently selected one causes the client to generate an average of 822 bytes. This amount is determined by the client's current display window size: it appears that the client asks only for the number of items it can display. The amount is also affected by the number of items in the folder: if the client can display all of the folder items in the current window, each folder item sent adds about 80 bytes.

Different Client Modes

Exchange supports different ways of storing, collecting, and managing messages. Some combinations are better suited to an organization's business processes and overall architecture. For example, if a highly dispersed remote office environment uses disconnected clients with remote mail and a set of personal folders on each, new items are delivered directly to the client and stored in a set of personal folders. Opening them creates no traffic, as it would if the item was stored on the server. On the other hand, clients configured to use an offline store continue to generate traffic while connected to the server.

Here are the advantages and disadvantages of personal folders, their location, and overall storage strategies:

Client storage options and storage strategies	Advantages	Disadvantages
Private store	Universal storage method; user can access from multiple clients.	Complicated to restore single mailbox or specific messages (requires separate server).
PST on server	Can archive file through network backup; recoverable.	Slower responsiveness, higher network load; for successful PST backup the user cannot be connected.
PST on local drive	Faster performance and storage flexibility for the user.	Impossible or difficult to automate file backup.
Increase disk capacity of computers running Exchange Server	Enables users to maintain majority of their messages on the Exchange Server. Easier to maintain and back up critical user data. Allows users to create offline storage replicas (OSTs) of server-based folders.	Requires configuring additional hard disks on computers running Exchange Server. Must restore a backup of server's entire private information store to recover a single mailbox.

(continued)

Client storage options and storage strategies	Advantages	Disadvantages
Decrease number of users per server	Enables users to maintain majority of their messages on the server. Easier to maintain and back up critical user data. Allows users to create offline storage replicas (OSTs) of server-based folders.	Requires purchase of additional computers to run Exchange Server. Must restore a backup of server's entire private information store to recover a single mailbox.
Maintain majority of mail messages in personal store (PST) files	No additional hardware expense on computers running Exchange Server. If PST files are stored on a file server and regularly archived, can recover a single user's data without restoring the entire Exchange private information store.	Requires users to maintain all data beyond their 20- to 30-MB storage quota in PST files stored locally or on a network file server. No "single instance storage" means more total disk space used within the organization. No way to create offline storage (OST files) for PST files maintained on a network file server. If PST is password protected and user "forgets" password, no way to recover the file.

Internet Client-to-Server Traffic Analysis

Outlook Web Access (OWA) is often viewed as a lighter client for corporate deployments, but what's overlooked are the costs associated with an OWA-based solution. The OWA client depends on the server for such basic functions as rendering views and forms. From both a user-interaction and a cost-of-deployment standpoint, this server dependence can be restrictive, particularly when network resources are limited.

This section analyzes traffic generated between an OWA client and the Microsoft Internet Information Server (IIS), and between the IIS server and the Exchange Server. Using the load associated with a single OWA client and an IIS server (separate from Exchange Server), it is possible to approximate the overall load associated with a client on available bandwidth. This is an *approximation*—client actions against the server can vary or implementation issues can skew the numbers—but the tests provide a starting point for relatively generic implementations.

Outlook Web Access

For these tests, the IIS 3.0 server was installed as a separate machine with the Outlook Web Access Active Server Pages (version 1458.58 shipped in Service Pack 1 for Microsoft Exchange 5.0) configured to point to the Exchange Server. Only basic (clear text) authentication was permitted in the tests, and Internet Explorer 3.02a was used as the browser.

Initial Logon

Outlook Web Access test description	Srv-> Cli (bytes)	Cli-> Srv (bytes)	Srv-> Cli (frames)	Cli-> Srv (frames)
Initial logon action	34767.250	30718.000	34767.250	30718.000
Outlook Web Access test description	**Srv-> IIS (bytes)**	**IIS-> Srv (bytes)**	**Srv-> IIS (frames)**	**IIS-> Srv (frames)**
Initial logon action	12491.750	20579.000	12491.750	20579.000

Generic Mail Item Tests

Due to the differences between the OWA client and the Outlook and Exchange clients, some tests were modified. Wherever possible, however, the tests conducted on the OWA client were identical to the tests conducted on the other clients. Here is a summary of the tests:

- **Send an item xK**—Send a mail message containing xK of text in the body. Include a simple subject indicating the contents of the message, for example. "xK of text". The recipient for the message was the current logged on user.

- **Open an item xK**—Open the item sent above.

- **Delete an item xK**—Delete the item sent above. Please note that deleting a mail message in OWA is only possible after opening that mail message. For the purposes of this test the opening traffic was not captured.

- **Process read receipt**—Send a 1-K mail message with a read receipt. The message was opened on the client (note that this traffic has already been captured in other tests), then a sniff was started, and the user double-clicked on the read receipt.

- **Create subfolder**—Create a single subfolder in the mailbox.

Generic Mail Tests

Outlook Web Access test description	Srv->Cli (bytes)	Cli->Srv (bytes)	Srv->Cli (frames)	Cli->Srv (frames)
Send item 1K	30177.333	8296.333	30177.333	8296.333
Send item 10K	28418.000	18431.333	28418.000	18431.333
Send item 100K	28876.333	41295.000	28876.333	41295.000
Open item 1K	15141.000	5868.000	15141.000	5868.000
Open item 10K	29146.000	4256.333	29146.000	4256.333
Open item 100K	169996.333	8558.667	169996.333	8558.667
Delete item 1K	1722.000	1207.000	1722.000	1207.000
Delete item 10K	1722.000	1207.000	1722.000	1207.000
Delete item 100K	1722.000	1207.000	1722.000	1207.000
Process read receipt (1K item)	4325.000	1048.000	4325.000	1048.000
Create subfolder	2776.000	1306.000	2776.000	1306.000
Double-click on public folders	8143.667	3076.000	8143.667	3076.000
Send item 1K	4052.000	2506.000	4052.000	2506.000
Send item 10K	23346.000	2926.000	23346.000	2926.000
Send item 100K	64810.000	4148.667	64810.000	4148.667
Open item 1K	347.333	3396.000	347.333	3396.000
Open item 10K	483.333	8941.333	483.333	8941.333
Open item 100K	2590.000	43481.333	2590.000	43481.333
Delete item 1K	1235.333	4336.667	1235.333	4336.667
Delete item 10K	1422.000	9132.000	1422.000	9132.000
Delete item 100K	1196.000	3598.000	1196.000	3598.000
Process read receipt (1K item)	307.333	3431.333	307.333	3431.333
Create subfolder	450.667	486.667	450.667	486.667
Double-click on public folders	1874.000	1878.000	1874.000	1878.000

Addressing and Address Resolution Tests

The address lookup test was conducted with all three clients. In this test, a four-character search with one possible result is returned.

OWA test description	Srv-> Cli (bytes)	Cli-> Srv (bytes)	Srv-> Cli (frames)	Cli-> Srv (frames)	Srv-> IIS (bytes)	IIS-> Srv (bytes)	Srv-> IIS (frames)	IIS-> Srv (frames)
Address lookup	7676.000	3522.000	7676.000	3522.000	600.000	844.000	600.000	844.000

Extrapolations and Observations

Initially, the IE cache was purged before each test, but when it was found that no significant caching was being performed, the tests were rerun without purging the cache. During the tests, it was confirmed that no client-side message compression was being performed. See the POP3 tests below for more information.

Internet Explorer 3.02 Internet Mail

The following tests were conducted on an Internet Mail client (IE 3.02) with POP3 (postoffice protocol) and LDAP (lightweight directory access protocol) to provide a comparison for the MAPI RPC clients listed above. All of these tests were conducted with the client configured to use secure password authentication (SPA).

Initial Logon and Use of SPA in Logon

IE 3.02 Internet Mail test description	Srv->Cli (bytes)	Cli->Srv (bytes)	Srv->Cli (frames)	Cli->Srv (frames)
Initial logon	1229.000	924.000	15.500	14.500
Initial logon with SPA	1502.000	1377.750	18.500	18.500

Generic Mail Item Tests

These tests, summarized below, use all three clients. A table of results follows.

- **Send an item xK**—Send a mail message containing xK of text. Include a simple subject indicating the contents of the message, for example, "xK of text".

- **Send an item with attachment xK**—Send a mail message containing an xK attachment and no other text in the body. Include a simple subject indicating the contents of the message, for example, "1-K attachment (1)". Enter the correct alias for the user to which you are sending.

- **Send an item with attachment 1M**—Send a mail message with a 1-M attachment and no other text in the body. Include a simple subject indicating the contents of the message, for example, "1-K attachment (1)". Enter the correct alias for the user to whom you are sending.
- **Download 1 item xK**—Connect the POP3 client to a maildrop server to download new messages. This test series involves messages of various sizes.
- **Download 10 items xK**—Use the above test scenarios with multiple messages for each download.

POP3 Generic Mail Tests

Test description	Srv->Cli (bytes)	Cli->Srv (bytes)	Srv->Cli (frames)	Cli->Srv (frames)
Download item 1K	2982.000	1319.000	17.333	17.333
Download item 10K	12514.333	1559.000	23.667	21.333
Download item 100K	108455.333	3999.000	88.333	61.667
Download item 1M (attachment)	1120859.000	30199.667	763.667	499.000
Download 10 items 1K	21928.333	2871.667	41.667	39.667
Download 10 items 10K	126282.667	5868.000	116.333	85.000
Download 10 items 100K	1083900.000	29568.000	748.667	483.667
Download 10 items 1M	11240776.667	292308.000	7530.333	4853.667
Send item 1K	3429.000	4353.000	34.000	37.333
Send item 10K	3505.000	14160.000	39.000	47.667
Send item 100K	6351.000	111204.333	84.667	135.667

Addressing and Address Resolution Tests

A new directory service was added into the Windows address book for the POP3 client to allow the resolution of Exchange recipients against the Exchange GAL. The traffic captured in this test was primarily used as a comparison for the address lookup tests conducted earlier against the Outlook and Exchange clients.

In this address lookup test, a four-character search with one possible result was returned using Internet Mail client set up with an LDAP directory service.

LDAP Directory Access Tests

LDAP test description	Srv->Cli (bytes)	Cli->Srv (bytes)	Srv->Cli (frames)	Cli->Srv (frames)
Address lookup	1476.667	2142.667	14.333	18.000

Extrapolations and Observations

During the tests, it was discovered that sending a message with 1 MB of message text is not possible with an Internet Mail client. The maximum message body size for the POP3 client and the Exchange and Outlook clients is 999 K. For the 1-MB download tests, the 1 MB of message text was sent as an attachment. For the Outlook and Exchange clients, the 1-MB message test was separated from the 1-MB attachment test because client-side text compression took place on message body text before the message was sent. This compression did not happen on the Internet mail client, so the tests have been combined.

The tests indicated that the Internet Mail engine on the Exchange server performs compression for all POP3 mail transfers. Outlook 8.01, Exchange 32, and Exchange 16 clients handle this compression on the client side. For example, a 100-K message is stored on the server as approximately 37.6 K.

All of the POP3 tests were conducted using SPA authentication to approximate minimum security deployed in most large organizations. Address resolution tests for the POP3/LDAP client were conducted differently because of the clients' different operations.

Single Instance Store

The Exchange store uses single instance storage. The following terms are encountered in any discussion of this storage:

- FID—Folder ID.
- MID—Message ID that is unique within a store.
- INID—Instance ID of a message.
- MTS-ID—Globally unique identifier of a message.
- GUID—Globally unique identifier that identifies the store.

If the same copy of the message is stored in different folders, only a single physical instance of the message is maintained and is referred to as the INID. Each copy of a message has its own unique MID. To locate any message, the FID and the MID of the message are needed; FID identifies which folder the message is stored in and MID identifies the message in the folder. When the store sends a message to the MTA, the content-correlator, if not set, is filled with a GUID, FID of the Sent Items folder, and the INID of the message.

File Versions

Following are all of the versions of the Address Book Provider, Database Access Provider, Exchange Configuration Library, and Extensions DLL for the respective clients.

Outlook

Filename	File datestamp		File version	File size
Emsabp32.dll	2/21/97	12:00am	8.01.3817	102,160
Emsmdb32.dll	2/21/97	12:00am	8.01.3817	529,168
Emsui32.dll	2/21/97	12:00am	8.01.3817	126,224
Emsuix32.dll	2/21/97	12:00am	8.01.3817	585,488

Microsoft Exchange 32

Filename	File datestamp		File version	File size
Emsabp32.dll	2/20/97	12:00am	5.0.1457.3	102,160
Emsmdb32.dll	2/20/97	12:00am	5.0.1457.3	529,168
Emsui32.dll	2/20/97	12:00am	5.0.1457.3	126,224
Emsuix32.dll	2/20/97	12:00am	5.0.1457.3	585,488

Microsoft Exchange 16:

Filename	File datestamp		File version	File size
Emsabp32.dll	5/23/97	4:25:10pm	N/A	126,080
Emsmdb32.dll	2/20/97	12:00am	N/A	734,944
Emsui32.dll	2/20/97	12:00am	N/A	142,144
Emsuix32.dll	2/20/97	12:00am	N/A	728,160

Sources of Test Errors

Why are the traffic patterns so erratic when sending attachments?

The Outlook and Exchange clients begin copying attachments to the server as soon as the attachment is placed in the message body window. If this copy is permitted to finish before the send action is initiated, only a few subsequent frames have to be sent to the server once the send button is clicked. However, if send is initiated before the copy is completed, the initial copy is cancelled and a new copy started. Because the user is not aware of the completion of the initial copy, he/she may initiate the send before the copy is completed. The data captures in this chapter were conducted with this in mind as a common action in a real-life setting. An average of the traffic generated from the client with a send initiated immediately after the attachment is placed in the body of the message was used because this is typically how users operate.

In what order is host name resolution for TCP/IP addresses performed?

Listed in order of precedence:

1. HOSTS file
2. DNS server
3. NetBIOS cache
4. WINS server
5. Broadcast
6. LMHOSTS file

Closing Remarks

In a complex Exchange environment it can never be assumed, as it was for these tests, that all servers and clients enjoy consistent high-bandwidth conditions. Therefore, system professionals deploying Exchange must understand the *types* of traffic generated for typical actions between the client and the server.

An understanding of the types of traffic generated in the initial logon process provides some insights. For example, to reduce traffic generated over the WAN link in some architectures, Exchange servers have been placed at the end of a WAN connection on the same subnet as clients. Although there is a substantial reduction in traffic for e-mail and calendar activities, a large amount of traffic is still generated by authentication and address resolution for the client. In some cases, it might make more sense to move these services to the same subnet as the client, make sure there is a BDC for the client authentication domain, and place appropriate address resolution services in the same subnet.

Of course, ramifications are inherent in this configuration as well, and the amount of traffic caused by moving services to the remote subnet would have to be studied before you could be sure it was feasible. One consideration is the traffic generated by WINS replication if the address resolution services used by the client are WINS/DHCP. Likewise, the traffic generated for SAM replication should be considered if a BDC is placed in the remote site. In both cases, a few clients at the remote site will generate a certain level of authentication traffic. However, as the number of clients grows in the remote subnet, the traffic generated for the client's authentication and address resolution will outweigh the traffic generated by moving the services to the local subnet.

More Information

Q149217, Title: XCLN: Microsoft Exchange Message Size Limitations

Q163576, Title: XGEN: Changing the RPC Binding Order

Q136516, Title: XCLN: Improving Windows Client Startup Times

Q167100, Title: XCLN: Out of Memory Errors with Microsoft Exchange 5.0 16-Bit Client

Q155048, Title: XCLN: Troubleshooting Startup of Windows Client

Q161626, Title: XCLN: Troubleshooting IPX/SPX Connections

CHAPTER 6

Messaging Components, Server Communication, and External Connectivity

This chapter further discusses designing the comprehensive messaging system, or the Exchange backbone, including public folders, forms management, Key Management (KM) server, the message transfer agent (MTA), and message flow from Exchange servers to internal and external systems. You must determine how the existing network connects to these systems and how Exchange Server can integrate with them. For detailed discussion on connecting to Lotus Notes, Lotus cc:Mail, MS Mail, SNADS, and AppleTalk/Quarterdeck/Starnine mail systems, see Part 3 of this book, "Coexistence and Migration Scenarios."

Administrative Model

Your development team can plan an administration model that is centralized, de-centralized, or a combination. The decision should be made as early as possible in the planning process because it affects directory security and can affect site boundaries. The built-in administration features of Exchange use Microsoft Windows NT services that administrators can manage remotely.

Design Criteria

Messaging system administrators must:

- Minimize administrative costs.
- Support Exchange servers from a single location.
- Remotely manage Exchange servers.
- Move users between servers within a site and between sites.
- Support both central and distributed administrative models.
- Assign different levels of administrative security.
- Back up user data without disrupting messaging.

Recommendations

Although Exchange meets most of the requirements specified above, the development team can implement specific steps to achieve all of them:

- **Implement a centralized administration service model where possible**— Where possible, offer business units a centralized administration service. This reduces overall administrative costs by centrally locating administrators and support technicians.

- **Plan for cases where distributed administration is required**—Business units sometimes manage isolated domains but still must interact with the rest of the organization. A central administrative unit can develop procedures and policies to ensure enterprise-wide standards. To help do this, the development team should:

  - Configure message transfer agents (MTAs) to pass mail properly to the local hub site. If the network uses site connectors, each site must have the other site's service account password and make use of the override page permissions in conjunction with Windows NT 4.0 and Exchange 5.5.

  - Use standard naming conventions. Exchange uniquely identifies objects, such as sites, servers, gateways, connectors, users, and so forth, with logical names that provide consistency across the enterprise. Create Exchange naming standards in conjunction with any existing standards, and maximize interoperability with existing systems.

  - Make sure the Exchange ORG name matches the official ORG name.

  - Configure directory replication within Exchange.

  - Coordinate migration of other messaging systems to Exchange with the central administration unit to ensure proper directory updates in other directory systems.

- **Implement online backup**—Exchange backs up user and directory data without disrupting the messaging system. Specific procedures regarding online backup and restore are available in Chapter 15 of the *Microsoft Exchange Administrator's Guide*. Administrators can remotely manage tape backup jobs by taking advantage of the built-in AT scheduler available in Windows NT Server.

  Go to http://www.microsoft.com/exchange to find a range of third-party backup tools for Windows NT Server. For a discussion on managing the information store, see the section on The Limits of Unlimited Information Store in Chapter 8.

- **Implement container-based security for sites that span business units**—In some situations, a large Exchange site spans multiple business units. Create separate recipients containers for each business unit to restrict administrative authority within the site.

- **Minimize the number of Exchange sites and servers**. An Exchange site is a single administrative unit similar in concept to a Microsoft Mail or cc:Mail postoffice. Exchange sites, however, can consist of multiple servers and can support many more users than a Microsoft Mail or cc:Mail postoffice. Consolidate users within a business unit to as few servers as possible. This reduces hardware costs and *boosts* performance because most e-mail flows within organizational units.

  Reducing the number of sites increases performance and reduces administration. Within an Exchange site, servers use peer-to-peer network communication. Between sites, bridgehead or target servers manage communication, which can add extra hops between the source and destination. The operations group can more easily manage fewer sites because each site requires an open connection. Site planning must consider geographic location and bandwidth.

- **Use personal storage file (PST) for moving users between sites**—The Exchange Administrator program moves a user's mailbox within a site by selecting the desired mailbox and destination server. In this case, the Administrator program can move all the associated user data to the new server. To move a mailbox between sites, the administrator must back up mailbox data to a PST file, delete the original mailbox, then add the file to the destination server.

- **Set limit on mailbox storage**—To ease the administration of server disk space, limit mailbox storage and have the system notify users who reach their limit. Once notified, users can receive mail, but cannot send any until they free up storage space by archiving or deleting messages. You can also limit users on an Exchange 5.5 server to no longer receive mail over a certain threshold.

- **Create separate containers for distribution lists and public folders**—If the development team creates containers for public folders and distribution lists within a site, clients can browse these using the global address book and by searching from the "**To**" field in an e-mail message. The Exchange Administrator program supports simple management of distribution lists and public folders. Use the information store site configuration object to specify a public folder container.

Note Containers can negatively affect system performance by restricting the ability to move objects from one container to another.

- **Use a single transport protocol**—Central operations needs network connectivity to provide single-seat administration. If the messaging system uses a single transport protocol across all servers, operations can connect to and manage any Exchange server in the organization as long as the account privileges have been set correctly.

To complete a logical design that meets the organization's administration needs, the development team must have the following information:

- The enterprise operations structure and administration processes.

- A detailed service-level agreement outlining what services the administrative unit can provide to business units.

- A list of business units and service-level agreements in a distributed administration model.

- The enterprise Windows NT Server domain architecture and administrative model, which the Exchange administration model will closely follow.

Public Folders

With Exchange Server, you can create public folders, storage areas on public information stores (Exchsrvr\Mdbdata\PUB.EDB) that allow users to conveniently share information with others. Users can build collaboration and business applications, such as discussion groups, tracking applications, document libraries, want ads, news services, and so forth, with public folders. They provide efficient database containers accessed by multiple users, storing custom forms for contributing and reviewing information (access control lists), rules for finding, viewing, and organizing items within the folder, and various types of information, from simple messages to complex multimedia clips. Users can design and create public folders from the Microsoft Outlook client.

You can replicate public folders across Exchange servers and sites in your organization using the Exchange Administrator program. Public folder servers contain a replica of the folder hierarchy and automatically ensure that these replicas stay synchronized with the original and with each other. Clients view public folder information independently of where it resides, within a single folder hierarchy, and users never need to know the home public folder server location. Users "pull down" information they need without searching for it.

A centrally located organization connected with a high-bandwidth network can provide access to public folders without creating replicas and synchronizing them, routing users to the original folder. Even if your organization contains multiple sites, you can avoid public folder hierarchy replication as long as user access and response times meet your performance guidelines. This section highlights a few public folder concepts and outlines Microsoft Consulting Services best practices developed through planning public folder strategies for customers.

As an Exchange administrator, you can refer to the *Microsoft Exchange Server 5.5 Resource Guide*, (Chapter 6, "Public Folders"), to familiarize yourself with the fundamentals of public folder architecture, administration, and hierarchy and content replication. The *Microsoft BackOffice Resource Kit, Second Edition* also includes useful tools to modify folder properties, set permissions, configure replication, track public folder usage for capacity planning and successful load balancing, and so forth:

- Public Folders Administration Tool
- Public Folders Information Tool
- Public Folder Reporting Utility
- Public Folders Tree Info Tool
- Public Folder Verification Tool

Managing Top-level Public Folder Creation

Typically, users can see every top-level (root) folder whether or not they have permission to view its contents. The Exchange Administrator program allows you to specify users who can create top-level folders in the public folder hierarchy, controlling permissions and managing public folder growth. Unmanaged folder creation can obscure folder organization and increase the difficulty of finding information. Limiting the number of top-level folders also reduces user frustration of having too many public folders with restricted access. (See *Microsoft Exchange Server 5.5 Resource Guide* for instructions on setting folder permissions.)

An **Employee Compensation Guidelines** public folder with limited access would undoubtedly get a lot of traffic if employees could see it at the root-level, generating many access-denied error messages. The owner of these guidelines should create the folder at a lower level in the tree, "hiding" it under a larger grouping of folders with restricted information. You can also hide this folder in the public folder tree using the **Visible Attribute** in public folder permissions, first introduced in Microsoft Exchange Server 5.0. This attribute allows a public folder owner to hide the folder from any person the owner excludes from the visible list.

Public folder owners can also create views, add forms, and assign permissions, allowing other users to read and create items. Owners can apply permissions to edit or delete their work, and edit or delete all items on a default, per-user, or per-distribution list basis. (See the *Microsoft Exchange Server 5.5 Resource Guide*.)

You can also create hidden distribution lists that map to top-level folder and key subfolders, to easily change ownership roles as employees move through different positions within the organization. Generally, you should restrict the right to *create* new top-level folders to other Exchange Server administrators.

Replication and Site Affinity

When a user adds or changes an item in a public folder, Exchange Server copies that change to every replica of the folder throughout the organization, between two or more servers in the same site and between servers in different sites. Exchange servers with public information stores periodically send out change notification messages. Servers receiving the change notification message then replicate changes to the local server. You can configure notification frequency (default every 15 minutes) and the maximum message size (default 300 KB), by adjusting the public information store object in the Exchange Administrator program.

Public folder replication provides users with a copy of the information in the home Exchange site. Changes made to the replica copy to all other replicas of the public folder, creating a distributed database. Because users work with public folder replicas, two users may simultaneously modify the same form in separate replicas, creating a content version conflicts. Exchange Server handles replica conflicts by assigning revision numbers to all items in a public folder, identifying conflicts, and sending a conflict notification to the user with the appropriate permission to resolve.

Exchange Server also *backfills* public folders replicas quickly, populating new replicas with content and updating replicas on servers that you take down for maintenance or you must restore from tape backup. Subfolders inherit the replication characteristics of parent folders (default). Thus, subfolders will replicate to all servers receiving top-level folder replicas. You can modify subfolder replication using the Administrator program.

Prevent Excessive Replication Traffic

Do not replicate public folders with content that users constantly update by various sources. Replicate folders that *do not* change often, such as those containing standard documents, forms, and corporate policies. Users can access these folders more quickly if replicated to multiple servers.

Your organization's public folder hierarchy and replication strategy will affect the number of clients accessing specific folders over a given timeframe: the busier a public folder server, the slower the access and response times. Increased client access to public folders will slow performance much more than server-to-server public folder communication. Develop your replication strategy within and between sites based on your organization's Exchange site topology, anticipated frequency of changes and client access to public folders, and the overall physical network topology.

Use Subsites to Decrease WAN Traffic

Locations (or subsites) are logical groupings of Exchange servers that can help reduce wide area network (WAN) traffic in organizations with few Exchange sites. Subsites provide Outlook clients a list of local servers within a large site and direct them to a local public folder server rather than searching for a folder replica.

Locate Public Folders by Site Affinity

In practice, implementing site affinity is the opposite of replicating public folders. With site affinity, Exchange servers connect users to the original instance of the selected folder, not to a local, replicated copy, using remote procedure calls (RPC) via connected sites. Site affinity provides these advantages:

- You maintain only one copy of the public folder.
- Users can immediately see all changes.
- You avoid replication traffic for high-usage folders.

However, a high-usage folder accessed over a WAN can place a strain on network resources. A site affinity configuration also requires trust relationships across account domains to grant folder access.

Should you use replication or site affinities? You can connect public folder information that only local users modify with site affinity, assuming minimal interest from remote users. You can also configure stable folders with corporate policy materials for site affinity. However, you should replicate folders with few updates *and* frequent access by many users across multiple sites, minimizing network traffic. Study high-usage folders that involve many updates, such as threaded discussion lists, to determine the best configuration. Start with site affinity and monitor the response times. If all is satisfactory, continue with that approach. If users experience poor response times, strategically locate replicas, but keep these to a minimum to reduce replication traffic. Increase the number of replicas only when performance demands.

Combine site affinity and folder replication to provide your organization with the Exchange Server configuration to meet user needs and network capabilities. And you should continue monitoring the messaging system, providing data to correct problems, optimize public folder usage, and make decisions about future needs.

Choosing a Public Folder Hierarchy Design

You design the public folder hierarchy based on your organization's objectives. Typically, organizations choose for one of three approaches:

- **Participant folders**—A static folder hierarchy in which common users do not have the right to create subfolders in the hierarchy. Users can participate in discussions and read and post items to folders, but cannot create their own collaboration solution. This design requires more public folder administration, but provides controlled growth of the public folder hierarchy.

- **Semi-structured folders**—A combination of participant folders and locations for user creation. Your organization can choose a temporary location for folder creation, placing limits on them so that the Exchange server can automatically manage cleanup.

- **Open folders**—An open approach where users can create subfolders without restrictions. Few organizations choose this option because it allows an unmanageable folder hierarchy.

For many organizations, the semi-structured approach represents the best design choice. By creating folders open for user postings and others for corporate collaboration, the flexible hierarchy design accommodates the collaboration needs of most corporations.

Here are some public folder design best practices:

- **Naming public folders**—Regardless of which hierarchy design you choose, public folder names provide the primary method of locating useful information within the hierarchy. Avoid naming folders by organizational divisions and locations because these change, making the naming structure obsolete. Name folders by their function as these persist over time. If a folder provides help, name it "Help."

- **Quick navigation**—A flat hierarchy allows users to quickly navigate folders for information. Keep the hierarchy three to four folders deep so users can exchange a folder location name at the water cooler and remember it on the way back to their desks.

- **Views**—Create multiple views within folders, maximizing folder usage. For example, if the training group wants to post training offerings at multiple locations in a single folder, you could define fields for each location instead of adding subfolders. As trainers add new classes, they specify locations. Filters can automatically sort items as users change views.

Public Folder "Re-homing"

Exchange Server replicates public folders between sites using a directory replication connector that depends on an established site connector. After implementing a directory replication connector, you should not disable or disconnect it because deleting it removes data about the other site (B) from the current one (A). All objects in Site B, including users, resources, and distribution lists, will no longer exist in Site A. The public folder hierarchy will still exist, but you will lose data on public folder owners whose accounts reside in Site B.

If you remove the directory replication and site connectors, *and* intend on re-establishing the connection, *do not* run a DS/IS consistency check. It will reset ownership of any orphaned public folders, assigning "new homes"—re-homing them—in Site A. Public folder operation will seem okay until you reconnect the sites and they resynchronize. The same folder in both sites will have different owners, and folders deleted from Site A, whose original owners reside in Site B, will now disappear from all sites as Exchange backfills the replicas. It is difficult to predict accurately the outcome, especially with a complex hierarchy of folders and subfolders that has grown over time.

How can you avoid this situation? For starters, Microsoft Exchange 5.5 allows administrators to lock a public folder's home site so that it cannot be re-homed (default). Do not delete directory replication connectors unless you never intend to reconnect the sites—disassembling an Exchange organization is very complicated. If you *must* break replication and you *intend* to reestablish it later, remember *not* to perform a DS/IS consistency check while the sites are disconnected. Exchange 5.5 will provide you with dialogue boxes and warnings to remind you.

Forms Management

Microsoft Exchange 5.5 supports workgroup applications through several varieties of electronic forms. An organization's development group can design forms using the Exchange Forms Designer (EFD) development tool that comes with Exchange. Outlook 97 and Outlook 98 can also easily create forms. With Exchange Server 5.5, web clients can view web forms using the active server pages (ASP) technology. The web forms contain script that accesses Exchange through active messaging to generate forms in HTML.

Users or the organization's IT group can install forms in Exchange folders for client access. Exchange also replicates forms throughout the system. An organization can use forms for a variety of purposes including the help desk requests, workflow and expense reporting, discussion groups, human resources information, product ordering, and so forth.

Requirements

- From the user perspective, loading forms must not be greater than the time loading Exchange client.
- Offline users should have access to electronic forms.
- Forms should distribute easily and upgrade automatically.
- Electronic forms must be easy to support.

Exchange Server base services meet most of the requirements in the above section, but the IT development team can implement steps to ensure that design criteria are met. Recommendations for implementing Exchange electronic forms are described below.

Configuration Recommendations

- **Secure the organization forms library**—Control who can create items in the organization forms library. By default, forms saved to an organization forms library are available to all users to read and compose messages.
- **Tune forms cache on client computers**—Exchange clients experience optimal performance when reading recently used forms from the local cache. If an organization uses many forms, administrators should increase the default forms cache on clients.
- **Replicate public folders in a hub structure**—Because the organization forms library is a public folder that stores forms, administrators should configure the public folder affinity between sites to point to hub machines. This minimizes the number of sites searched if a folder does not exist on the local site.
- **Create an organizational forms library for each language**—Foreign language clients attempt to locate forms in the forms library that match the language being used on the client (default). Therefore, localize the forms these clients need and save them into all existing foreign language libraries.
- **Create an Exchange application library**—The library should provide developers with examples of forms and a design architecture reference.

Process Recommendations

- **Use available form design tools**—These include the EFD, a graphical design environment that allows users and development groups to create custom electronic forms, a Form Design Wizard that uses templates, and ready-made form templates. Outlook 97 and Outlook 98 include their own forms environment, but forms created in Outlook are not compatible with Exchange clients.

- **Develop procedures for business units to develop their own applications**—Business units can then develop and post forms to their local public folders.

- **Follow existing user interface (UI) design guidelines**—This provides a consistent look and feel for graphical user interface (GUI) applications.

- **Use naming standards**—Define categories and subcategories within the organization forms library. Also standardize names of e-form applications.

- **Use organization forms library for global forms**—Save forms in one of three libraries: organization forms, public folders, and personal folders. The organizational forms library allows the network to distribute forms globally. Public folders make forms available to users. Personal folders store forms for individuals.

- **Use Microsoft Visual Basic 4.0 to extend forms when required**—Source code for forms applications is in standard Visual Basic syntax. EFD 1.0 uses the Visual Basic 4.0 engine to build a GUI interface. Visual Basic 4.0 can enhance forms applications with features such as Open Database Connectivity (ODBC), field calculation, spell check capabilities, and usage tracking. When creating forms with Outlook 97 or Outlook 98, you can use VBScript to add logic that will perform other functions.

- **Backup source code of forms**—To change a form application, developers must access the source code. Backup copies can help if source is lost or damaged somehow.

For more information, see "Microsoft Exchange Forms Designer Fundamentals" and "Extending Microsoft Exchange Forms" on the TechNet sample CD-ROM.

Security Encryption Key Management

Exchange supports digital signing and encryption of messages with a combination of public and private keys. To facilitate the creation and management of these keys, Exchange Server provides the Key Management (KM) component, an option that the development team can install on an organization's KM server.

The KM server performs a variety of important tasks, including generating public and private encryption keys. It also acts as your certificate authority (CA) by creating public signing and encryption X.509 certificates. After the KM server has generated keys and certificates and user security files have been created, the server doesn't need to be running for users to send and receive encrypted and signed messages. The KM server also maintains a secure copy of every user's private encryption key in an encrypted database in case an administrator needs to retrieve a key after it's been issued.

The KM server maintains and distributes a certificate revocation list (CRL). The CRL enables administrators to revoke user certificates if they have been compromised and are no longer secure. It is stored in the directory on every server. Exchange Clients store a replica of the CRL to check certificates during offline work.

As part of the backbone design and server installation process, the development team decides the logical placement of the KM server in the network. For an extended discussion on deploying the KM server and security issues, read Chapter 7, "Exchange 5.5 Advanced Security and Its Implementation."

Configuring and Tuning the MTA

Since it first shipped with Microsoft Exchange 4.0, the Message Transfer Agent (MTA) has been improved to provide greater scalability, better performance and more reliability in constrained network conditions. You can easily use the Exchange Performance Wizard to configure and tune the MTA service on bridgehead servers that handle large volumes of message traffic. As the workhorse in Exchange, the MTA receives messages from other servers, mail connectors, or users in other mail systems and manages the complex task of routing messages to their intended destinations. Because every Exchange server installs and uses the MTA for message flow, establish your MTA configuration and tuning standards early in the deployment project. (For more information on how the MTA operates, read Chapter 5, "Addressing and Routing," in the *Microsoft Exchange Server 5.5 Resource Guide*.)

This section discusses how to configure and tune the MTA in your Exchange deployment. The majority of fine-tuning required by the Exchange Server 5.5 MTA involves X.400 connectors operating over slow links. A brief scenario later in this section provides suggestions for this situation.

Configuring MTAs and Transport Stacks

Because the Exchange system uses Message Transfer Agents for intra-site mail delivery and external communications with other mail systems, you could potentially have many MTAs to configure. Each MTA has property pages to control:

- How an Exchange Server site MTA functions.
- Messaging parameters for an individual MTA.
- How other MTA instances operate on a server.

You can access **MTA Site Configuration Properties** through the MTA site configuration object in the site configuration container of the Exchange Administrator program. The general page allows you to enable message tracking for the site, recording every transferred message into the daily logs. To have complete message tracking, you must also configure the information store and other connectors. This illustration shows the **General** properties page for the MTA site configuration object.

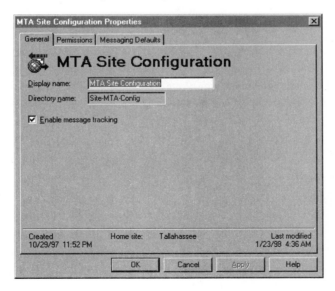

The **Messaging Defaults** page controls the parameters for messaging time-outs within the site. These values directly affect the messaging defaults when you setup a new X.400 connector within the site. The scenario provided later discusses what these values are and how to tune them for your environment. The next illustration shows the **Messaging Defaults** properties page for MTA site configuration.

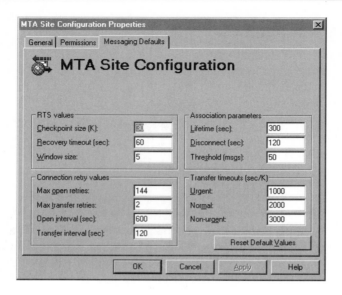

The server Message Transfer Agent Properties pages (**General**, **Queues**, and **Diagnostics Logging**) control how the MTA on a specific server operates. The **General** page allows the administrator to set the local MTA name and password, the maximum message size, conversion of X.400 to Exchange message format, and distribution list expansion behavior. Although you can override the local MTA and password with the X.400 connector properties, establish the local MTA name and a password for each connector you configure separately. You can also use the **Recalculate Routing** button here to manually recalculate the routing tables on the local server.

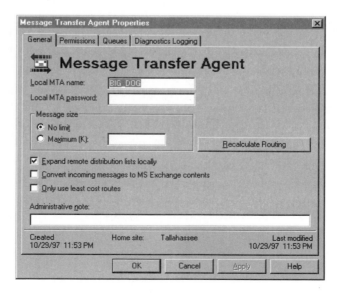

X.400 Standards and Connectivity

Based on the 1988 X.400 MTA specification X.413, the Microsoft Exchange Connector for X.400 integrates tightly with the Exchange MTA and is supported on the following OSI transports:

- TP0/X.25
- TP4/(CLNP)
- TP0/RFC 1006 to TCP/IP

The X.400 connector also supports many textual message body part standards, such as International IA5, T.61 (Teletex), ISO 6937, and ISO 8857-1, ensuring that mail addressed from foreign language messaging systems will have the majority of characters transferred in a displayable format. The X.400 connector also supports file attachments using the following binary body parts:

- BP9—For embedding and forwarding messages based on the X.400 standard.
- BP14 (1984 specification)—Simple transport of binary attachments.
- BP15 (1988 specification)—X.400 standard for sending attachments.
- File Transfer Body Part (1992 specification)—For file name, size, properties, and other information.

Exchange converts other X.400 body parts not listed above to messaging application programming interface (MAPI) binary attachments.

The X.400 connector can connect two Exchange Server sites, allowing administrators a higher level of control over the behavior of the MTA than with other connectors, scheduling message transfer activity, managing message size, and assigning cost routing. X.400 connectivity provides the best solution for organizations with slow or unreliable links, or limited bandwidth, and handles directory replication between sites.

To create an X.400 connector, you must first create an MTA transport stack in the Exchange Administrator program by clicking **File**, **New Other**, **MTA Transport Stack**, and then selecting the appropriate type. You can create MTA transport stacks on X.25, TP4 and TCP/IP, but normally you will use TCP/IP. You can also optionally configure the OSI TSP information for legacy system connections, but this is unnecessary for native Exchange connections.

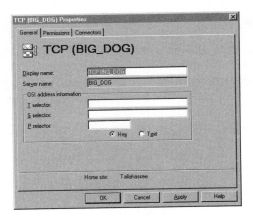

After you configure the appropriate MTA transport stack, create an X.400 connector by clicking **File**, **New Other**, **X.400 Connector** in the Administrator program. The dialogue will prompt you for the MTA transport stack to use before starting the **General** properties page, which displays the connector's directory name, the remote MTA name and password, and options for word-wrap and remote client MAPI support.

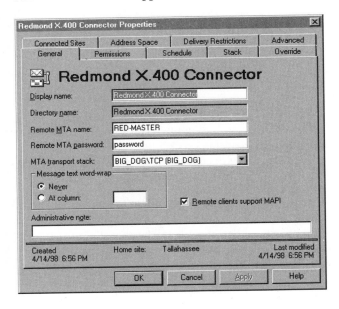

Use the **Schedule** properties page to specify times the X.400 connector can make connections to a remote MTA and allow a remote-MTA initiated transfer, provided that you've configured both MTAs for the **Two-way-alternate** option found on the **Advanced** properties page. The **Stack** properties page is similar to the MTA transport stack **General** properties page, except that you must specify the address of the remote MTA, which varies depending on the MTA transport stack. Typically, the remote MTA address is the TCP/IP address of the remote server running the MTA.

If you deploy hundreds of Microsoft Exchange sites throughout your network, the task of configuring all those MTA transports and X.400 connectors can be quite daunting. Fortunately, you can create an unattended server installation routine, covered in Chapter 16,"Deploying Outlook Clients and Exchange Servers," configuring the transports and X.400 connectors on as many Exchange servers as you need.

Tuning Bridgehead Servers and X.400 Override Values

You can separate Exchange MTA tuning into two parts: tuning a bridgehead server MTA and tuning a X.400 connector for slow or unreliable links. You optimize a bridgehead server MTA by configuring registry parameters with the Performance Wizard. Running the wizard with the "**-v**" option allows you to review and edit registry values that control MTA resources and scalability properties. At the beginning of the wizard, select **Connector/Directory import** and **Multi-server** for tuning a bridgehead server. Remember that overriding default values by increasing them will require more memory or processor resources.

Tuning X.400 override values allows you to make adjustments for slow link or limited bandwidth networks, providing the most control over connection behavior and how MTA associations operate over the link. These values affect the overall patience and reliability of X.400 connections to remote sites.

For example, company XYZ uses modem dial-up lines and X.400 connectors, linking their central Exchange site with 30 other remote locations. Remote sites connect to the central site using standard dial-up lines and Microsoft Routing and Remote Access, establishing a PPTP connection over the Internet. The average connection speed is 28.8 Kbps even though the company has installed 56-K modems on servers because not all locations can support 56-K connections. All X.400 connectors at the 30 various locations and the central office connect and transfer mail every 15 minutes. The following changes to X.400 override values will optimize MTA performance.

RTS Values

- **Checkpoint size (KB)**—Amount of data transmitted before the MTA must acknowledge an inserted checkpoint. Configure this value to be smaller than the bandwidth (28.8-KB average), between 20-27 KB, or even smaller on unreliable links.

- **Window size**—Number of checkpoints that can go unacknowledged before the MTA suspends message transfer. Increase this to 10-15 checkpoints maximum, assuming the link will support only Exchange traffic. Use this equation: (window size) x (checkpoint number) = received memory size allocation. The memory size allocation should be less than 300 KB.

- **Recovery timeout (sec)**—Length of time to cache unacknowledged checkpoint data. An MTA continues to transfer messages with unacknowledged checkpoints for a set period before it timeouts. It then restarts the transfer from the beginning, deleting all acknowledged checkpoints when the message is completely sent. Configure the timeout between 180 to 240 seconds maximum, less than the total estimated connection time scheduled (15 minutes).

Association Parameters

When one MTA communicates with another, it can manage multiple associations. In this example, there should only be one association from the central bridgehead server to a remote site bridgehead server.

- **Lifetime (seconds)**—Length of time an MTA should hold open an association after sending a message through (default 300 seconds). Configure this long enough to catch immediate replies or non-delivery reports (NDRs) but less than 5 minutes maximum, probably closer to 1½ to 2 minutes.

- **Disconnect (seconds)**—Amount of time to wait before terminating a connection after closing an association, ½ to 1 minute. Add this to the lifetime value to determine how long the connection will stay open after message transfer completes.

- **Threshold (messages)**—Number of messages in the queue before the MTA opens another association. Should be greater than the expected total per scheduled connection interval, around 100. The maximum threshold should be 250.

Connection Retry Values

- **Maximum open retries**—Maximum number of times the connector attempts to open a connection before a message returns an NDR (default 144). Configure this between 100 and 120 attempts because the connection is slower and will take longer to transfer replies.

- **Maximum transfer retries**—Number of retries in sending a message during an open connection before the message returns an NDR. Set this number between 5 and 15 (default 2).

- **Open interval (seconds)**—Amount of time to wait before attempting to re-open a connection that previously ended in error (default 600 seconds). Set this value greater than the time it takes to re-establish a dial-up connection, but never less than 60 seconds.

- **Transfer interval (seconds)**—Time to wait before resending a message across an open connection after a previous attempt failed (default 120). Configure this between 60 and 90 seconds.

Transfer Timeouts (seconds/K)

How long the MTA should wait before sending an NDR message for failed message transfer:

- **Urgent messages**—Should be less than the total time connected (15 minutes in this example, default 1,000 seconds/K). Increase this value if urgent messages return NDRs too frequently.

- **Normal messages**—Default 2,000/K is appropriate for most conditions, but can be higher if you get excessive NDRs from timeouts.

- **Non-urgent messages**—For low-priority messages, default is 3,000/K, which you should not change.

Web Connectivity

With Microsoft Exchange Server 5.5, users can access their e-mail and calendar along with public folders using a web browser. Because an Internet browser is a thin client (the server hosts most of the application functionality), the server processes much of the messaging functionality. The decision to offer e-mail, calendar, and public folder access through a web browser affects server sizing and placement decisions that your team should keep in perspective when deciding these issues.

POP3 Connectivity

Microsoft Exchange Server 5.5 also allows Post Office Protocol version 3 (POP3) clients to access Exchange servers. POP3 clients access messages through the POP3 protocol, but send messages through Simple Mail Transport Protocol (SMTP). Your development team must decide whether to direct POP3 inbound messages to the same server as outbound messages or to a centralized server.

TechNet includes other resources on POP3 administration with Exchange 5.5: "Module 5: Post Office Protocol 3 (POP3) Service" of the *Microsoft Exchange Server 5.5 Upgrade* training on TechNet.

IMAP4 Connectivity

Exchange Server 5.5 allows Internet Message Access Protocol version 4 (IMAP4) clients to access Microsoft Exchange Servers. Similar to POP3 clients, IMAP4 clients access messages through the IMAP4 protocol, and send messages through SMTP. As with POP3, your team needs to decide whether to direct IMAP4 inbound messages to the same server as outbound messages or to a centralized server.

Lightweight Directory Access Protocol Connectivity

Exchange Server supports Lightweight Directory Access Protocol (LDAP), which allows users of other directory applications to browse and search information from the Exchange Server directory. With Exchange Server 5.5, clients can also write to the Exchange directory using LDAP. LDAP clients access the Exchange directory over TCP/IP. LDAP also allows organizations to publish their directory, or portions of it, to outside users. Administrators choose which directory attributes, such as e-mail address, phone number, manager, and so forth, to publish to nonauthenticated users. Installing Exchange Server enables LDAP support (default), allowing LDAP clients to search the directory immediately following server setup.

Because Exchange administrators can configure LDAP to permit anonymous (nonauthenticated) access to certain types of data, you should consider the additional load on the server and review security policies.

TechNet includes other resources on LDAP administration with Microsoft Exchange 5.5: "Module 6: Lightweight Directory Access Protocol (LDAP)" of the *Microsoft Exchange Server 5.5 Upgrade* training on TechNet.

C H A P T E R   7

Exchange 5.5 Advanced Security and Its Implementation

Exchange 4.0 was the first version that allowed users to secure messages (using digital encryption) and seal/sign them (using digital signature). Security standards and technology continue to evolve rapidly as needs are intensified by rapidly growing networks, of which the Internet is only an example. And the topic of network security itself is complex, comprising many concepts, techniques, and methods. Not surprisingly, users sometimes need more information than is provided in standard documentation, more explanation of what various security components are supposed to do and how. This section explains how common cryptography processes secure messages and how Exchange and Outlook implement them.

Encryption Basics

Symmetric (Secret) Key vs. Public Key Cryptography

There are two common types of cryptography: symmetric key and public key. They differ in how they execute and how they manage keys

Symmetric key encryption uses the same key to encrypt and decrypt all transmissions, usually with an algorithm such as RC2, RC4, CAST, DES, or Triple-DES. (These and other terms are defined at the end of this chapter.) Both parties in the communication must have the encryption key, and it must be transferred between them. This is best done over separate media so that if either the key or the text is somehow intercepted it is useless. For example, you can put the key on a floppy and snail-mail it to a business associate, then send encrypted data over the Internet.

Public key encryption was introduced to eliminate the need to transfer the key between users. It generates a key pair for each user: a public key for encryption (only) and a private key for decryption (only). In X.500-compliant directories, public keys are published as user attributes; users' X.509 certificates contain their public key as well as the information needed to verify it.

The public/private key model eliminates the need to transfer the key between users, so intercepted communications are not decipherable to outsiders. A sender need only obtain a recipient's public key from a trusted source (an external organization selected to verify the identity of other organizations) and then send encrypted data. Only the owner of the public key used for encryption can decrypt it.

Cryptographic Hashing

Hashing secures message and private key data by using them as elements in a mathematical function that creates a digital fingerprint or "checksum" of the package. The algorithm then is used on the receiving end to decrypt. Hash algorithms include MD-4, MD-5, and SHA-1.

Certificates/Certificate Authorities and Authentication

What Is the Difference Between a Public Key and an X.509 Certificate?

Public keys and X.509 certificates are not interchangeable, and do not perform the same function. A public key is used to encrypt a transmission. An X.509 certificate contains and supplies verification for a user's public key. When an X.509 certificate is signed by a trusted authority, a user can verify the integrity of another user's public key as well as what applications the key was granted for and is valid for.

X.509 Certificates

By 1993, the International Telecommunications Union had defined X.509 standards for creating certificates that can be used to authenticate secret/public key techniques in X.500 directories by binding a user identity (username/password combination) to a public key. Certificates do not dictate which cryptographic algorithm is used in the user's public key; they merely associate the public key and the user's identity in a verifiable way. X.509 also specifies the format of certificate revocation lists (CRLs) that administrators can use to revoke pre-existing trusts. For example, company A terminates a partnership with company B. The Company A administrator can add Company B to a CRL, which prevents its certificates from continuing to be trusted within Company A.

What Is the Difference Between X.509v1 and X.509v3 Certificates?

Version 1 X.509 certificates include fields for version, serial number, signature algorithm ID, issuer name, validity period, user name, public key information for the user, and signatures on each of these fields. Version 3 certificates add support for issuer-unique identifier, subject unique identifier, and extensions such as subject and issuer attributes, certification policy information, and key usage restrictions. Either of these versions can be used to digitally sign items (verify sender identity and that the contents of the item have not changed) or encrypt them.

Network Privacy vs. Message Content Encryption

When transferring messages, you can use network security or message item security. These techniques are very different. Network level secures a transmission path for multiple "clear" items. It is established along with the network connection and re-established each time a new network connection is made. Message level secures a specific item for routing over a clear or encrypted transmission pipe.

Exchange supports two network security mechanisms: NTRPC and SSL. Message content encryption and signing techniques are performed on each item with public and private key information obtained from the Exchange directory or stored in the user's private security file, on their machine or a floppy.

Network Security Options

Windows NT RPC Security

Windows NT 4 uses RSA RC4 stream encryption to provide both secure network and PPTP VPN connections. You can use this connection for encrypted SMTP mail, which is by definition sent as plain text between Windows NT servers hosting Exchange Servers. If you configure Exchange 5.0 and 5.5 SMTP connections to use NTRPC, you can establish 128-bit secure connections between servers in North America and 40-bit connections elsewhere. RPC encryption automatically negotiates the encryption level based on the lowest level of encryption used in the connection. The SMTP connection can be authenticated by Windows NT challenge/response authentication when using this option. If you require a secure client-server connection, you can enable NTRPC on Exchange and Outlook 32-bit clients.

Secure Socket Layer (SSL) Encryption

Similar to NTRPC, SSL also uses RSA RC4 stream encryption to secure client-server and server-server connections, providing (for all client-server platforms) 128-bit encryption within North America and 40-bit encryption elsewhere. It provides a secure network connection for SMTP mail between servers. Authentication is provided through X.509v3 certificates or by using SASL in Exchange 5.5 later. SSL can also secure client-server connections for LDAP, POP3, HTTP, NNTP, and IMAP4.

Authentication Mechanisms for Secure Exchange Connections

Several mechanisms can authenticate Exchange server-server and client-server communications:

Mechanism:	Used for:	Description:
Basic authentication	Server-to-server or client-to-server	Plain text ID and password sent over wire
SASL/AUTH	Server-to-server	Plain text ID and password sent over wire
Windows NT challenge/response authentication	Server-to-server or client-to-server	The user's password is never sent on the wire. The username, password, and machine name are verified based on a "shared secret" between the server and the client.
Secure Socket Layer (SSL) server authentication	Server-to-server	Client trusts server's certificate primarily to establish channel encryption
SSL client authentication	Server-to-server or client-to-server	Server trusts client's certificate (used in Web shopping, membership transactions, etc.)

Message Content Encryption and Signing

Digital signatures and digital sealing are based on encryption technologies. However, Exchange uses different pairs for each task in its implementation of these technologies. See the section below on Key Generation (Enrollment) for more details on the keys Exchange uses to perform these actions, as well as detail on how they are generated and populated in the Exchange directory.

Message Body Encryption

This security option provides for a completely opaque message body (and signature). It generates a one-time symmetric key and encrypts it in the recipient's public key, so that only that key owner can decrypt it, then sends the message. On the recipient end, the private key is used to decrypt the symmetric key, which is then used to decrypt the message. This process is transparent to the user. It is performed with no interaction between client and additional network services except for a directory query to obtain the recipient's public key.

Digital Signatures

When a digital signature is added to a message, the message contents are used to compute a hash value that identifies the sender and serves as a "digital fingerprint" that verifies the message has not been altered in transit. A message digest algorithm, the message contents, and the sender's private key are used to generate the hash value. The recipient decrypts the original hash value with the sender public key, which is readily obtainable from a trusted directory, such as the Exchange directory, or it can be sent with the signed message. The message is decrypted, then a new hash value is computed from the received text and compared to original hash value. If they match, the contents and the sender's identity are verified.

Securing Items in Exchange

Exchange uses several components to secure items:

- **Exchange Administrator**—Manages the advanced security operations for an organization, including issuance and revocation of certificates, recovery of certificates, and setting of site encryption algorithm preferences.

- **Archive database**—Stores keys/certificates.

- **Directory**—Stores certificates/preferences for client encryption and signing. For example, clients state in the directory the maximum strength security they support. Others clients use this information to secure messages in ways the other clients are able to decrypt.

- **Client (Outlook)**—The client interface to advanced security. It reads, from the directory, other users' certificates, performs all cryptography on mail messages, and protects private keys in a secure store.

Exchange Administrator (KM Server) Functions

The Exchange Administrator program allows you to control Key Management server functions through objects—a CA object at the site configuration level, and additional property tabs on recipients in the organization. The CA object shows up this way in the Exchange Administrator:

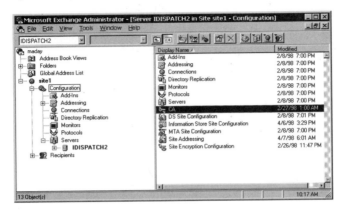

The recipient security tab (which appears when the recipient's properties are displayed) allows you to enroll, revoke, and recover the recipient's keys.

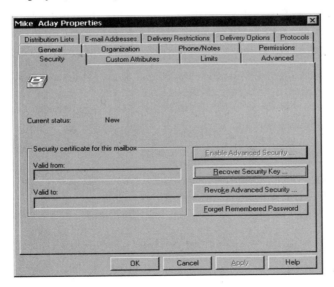

Exchange 5.5 enhanced security with multiple password policies (missile-silo), automated token distribution using e-mail, and bulk enrollment by recipient container.

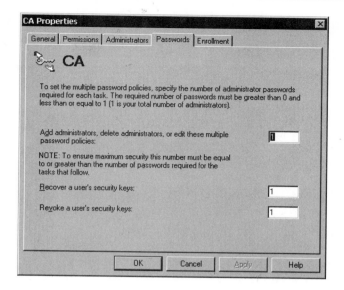

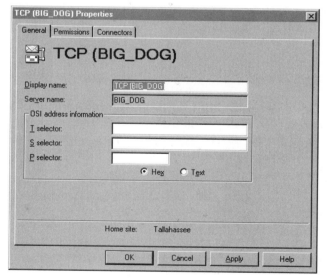

Key Generation (Enrollment)

The administrator can enable advanced security per user or per recipient container, sending enrolled users a message (usually through e-mail) containing a token that they use to generate the signing key pair.

When enrolling users in advanced security, the administrator must choose a certificate type: Exchange Server version 4.0 through 5.5 support X.509v1 certificates, and Exchange 5.5 Service Pack 1 (SP1) extends support for X.509v3 certificates. Both X.509v1 and X.509v3 certificates can be issued to ensure backward compatibility. If SP1 is installed, the administrator can elect to change the preferred certificate type and is then required to provide the name of the certificate server for the organization. Because Exchange 5.5 SP1 supports S/MIME clients, the administrator must also choose preferred secure message format—either Exchange 4.0/5.0 format (X.509v1 certificates) or S/MIME format (X.509v3 certificates).

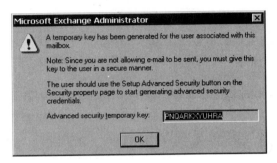

The token is used with a temporary password and the permanent password to generate a 1,024-bit key pair, which is then encrypted with the permanent password that the client supplied and sent to the system attendant service. It sends the new key pair to the Key Management server, which sends it to the Cryptography Service Provider (CSP), which generates the encrypting key pair, archives the private data encryption key, and returns the data encryption key pair to the KM server. The KM server gets a public key certificate for the new pair from the Certificate Server (CS) then archives it.

Next, the KM server requests a signing key certificate from the CS, receives it, then stores it in the archive database. The KM server sends the signing public key certificate, the encryption public key certificate, the encrypted private data encryption key, and the CA's signing certificate to the system attendant, which assembles these into a single message to the client.

The client creates a USER.EPF file (where USER is the alias that the user is currently logged on under, this file contains the user's certificates and private keys, encrypted with the user's permanent KM server password), then publishes the two certificates (for public signing and encrypting keys) in the Exchange directory. If the client accepts other certificates, they are added to the user's . EPF file. The entire enrollment process is detailed below.

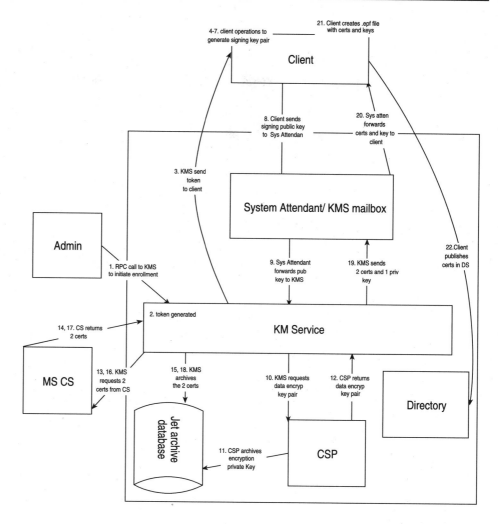

Key Renewal

A certificate system must allow administrators to revoke or expire user certificates because users leave the organization, working relationships with units or other organizations change, etc. All certificates generated by Exchange Server must be renewed every year (default). Administrators can renew them forcibly at any time. The renewal process has five steps.

1. Client sends a certificate renewal request to the system attendant (SA), which forwards it to KM server. (Requests are sent to the SA automatically during enrollment in advanced security; the client does not have to address them.)

2. KM server creates a new data encryption key pair, gets a certificate for the newly generated public key from the certificate server, and returns the new key pair to the client using the system attendant.

3. Client creates a new signing key pair, then sends the new signing public key to KM server using the system attendant. KM server gets a certificate for the new signing public key from certificate server and returns it to client using the system attendant.

4. Client adds the new signing and encrypting certificates and keys to its .EPF file, and KM server adds the new security information to the key recovery database.

5. The client publishes the new certificates in the Exchange directory.

Key Recovery

When users lose keys or forget passwords, they need KM server for key recovery. KM server can recover an encryption key pair so that previously encrypted items can be accessed. Signing keys are treated differently—no one ever needs to forge an identity on a mail item, and only users with valid private keys can send signed items. When the client generates a new key pair, the new public key is placed in the directory in place of the previous one.

Note that in the Exchange 5.5 SP1, Certificate Server becomes the Certificate Authority (CA) for KM server, which allows KM server to provide key-recovery for Certificate Server. This requires that each Exchange KM server must point to a Certificate Server (CS). Multiple KM servers within an organization can point to the same CS, but if it is not on same machine you must install the CS client on the KM server.

There are a couple of things to watch out for. First, CS hierarchies will not be supported until Windows NT 5, so there can be no subordinate trust relationships between CSs. Second, once a KM server points to a CS, it cannot point to a new one without invalidating the root of trust and causing all mail encrypted with certificates issued from this root to be inaccessible.

Don't confuse moving a KM server with moving clients from one KM server to another. If you move an entire KM server to a new machine, no clients are detached from their archived keys. To move a KM server, execute these steps:

1. Stop the system attendant on the machine running KM server.

2. Backup the Jet key archive database.

3. Restart the system attendant.

4. Run Exchange Setup to remove the KM server component.

5. Run Exchange Setup on the new machine and install the KM server component.

6. Copy the old Jet database over the newly created empty database.

Key Revocation

To revoke keys, administrators mark certificates for individual users or entire organizations as no longer usable. This is made relatively easy by the Certificate Revocation List (CRL), which is stored in the Exchange directory. It lists all revoked certificates, and is signed by the KM server (the CA for the organization). Every time a client logs on to check mail the CTL is checked to verify signatures on received mail.

Archive Database Details

Version 4.0/5.0 of Exchange Key Management server allows for recovery of users' archived data encryption keys. Version 5.0 and earlier of KM server store keys in encrypted text files (one file for each user) on the KM server. With the 5.5 release of Exchange, a new KM server utility transfers the keys to an archive database by going through the user key files serially and transferring them to the new database format.

A user can have multiple entries in the new database, each entry representing a layer of certificate history. If old certificates are not maintained, users cannot decrypt old encrypted mail. Each record in the database contains up to four certificates, and related state information and certificate data (serial number, expiration date, etc.). Stored certificates include two data encryption certificates (an X.509v1 certificate generated by KM server and an X.509v3 certificate generated by MS Certificate Server) and two signing certificates (one for each v1 and v3).

If administrators turn off Exchange 4.0/5.0 backward compatibility, newly generated records will not contain either of the X.509v1 certificates. The signing certificate and the encryption certificate differ only in that the encryption private key is encrypted and archived, and the signing private key is generated once and never leaves the client's computer.

Finally, the archive database contains a two-field record for each KM server administrator—security ID (SID) and password. When an administrator's privileges are revoked, the corresponding SID and password are deleted from the database.

The Exchange Directory

Public information is stored in and retrieved from the Exchange directory. The directory also contains KM server information clients need to use advanced security:

- X.509v1 and v3 public signing and data encryption certificates for each enrolled user. Publication of these certificates allows clients to look each other up in the directory (rather than exchange keys manually).

- Exchange 5.5 SP1 allows you to store cross certificates of other certifying authorities in the directory. Publication of these certificates allows clients to authenticate and trust the root certificate of external organizations and other Certifying Authorities (CAs) within their organization. For instance, if Microsoft and Company A both use the same CA, the establishment of a trust between Microsoft and Company A would be facilitated because initial identity negotiation would not be necessary: both organizations are automatically valid.

- Certificate Revocation Lists (CRLs) for both the home organization and cross-certified organizations. CRLs must be public in the directory so clients can determine if a message should be trusted.

Client Functions

Enrolled clients can send/receive signed mail, receive encrypted mail, send encrypted mail to enrolled recipients, and have KM server administrators recover their private key history. Clients generating secured and signed messages perform all cryptographic operations with local private, public, and public keys derived from the Exchange directory. After enrollment has concluded for generating secure or signed messages, no traffic is generated between client and Key Management server.

If you send a message to several users, the symmetric key for message encryption or item signing is generated at the lowest level common to the recipients (value queried from the directory). Symmetric keys are generated to send a message and used only once. If someone derives a symmetric key by attacking a message, it is good only for that message.

The newly released Outlook98 provides a fully interoperable S/MIME client, uses standard X509v3 certificates, and supports the Exchange 4.0/5.0 format for backward compatibility. Outlook Express cannot address a KM server, so it obtains X.509v3 certificates from another CA and therefore does not support Exchange 4.0/5.0 format secured messages. Each time a client connects, Exchange reads the CRL from the directory to verify signatures.

Exchange KM Server Implementation Details

Exchange 5.5 has a Cryptography Service Provider (CSP) that isolates all KM server cryptography functions into one dynamic link library (DLL). This isolation allows the addition of new encryption algorithms as they are developed, without having to wait for an Exchange KM server revision.

Exchange versions through 5.5 allow only one KM server per organization. Multiple-site architectures must configure individual sites to point to one KM server. Exchange 5.5 SP1 KM server supports Certificate Trusts Lists (CTLs), which allow cross-certification between organizations and up to one KM servers per Exchange site. CTLs contain certificates from other trusted CAs (even those outside the Exchange architecture), are signed by the root CA for the Exchange organization, and are stored in the Exchange directory. CTLs allows inter- and intra-organization webs-of-trust which clients can use to validate certificates attached associated with received items. Should the need arise, administrators can easily revoke trust for CTL certificates.

MS Certificate Servers also become Certifying Authorities (CA) for Exchange 5.5 SP1 KM servers, and the ability to have multiple KM servers per organization does have caveats. One issue is preservation of user histories (old encryption keys). If a site is modified to point at a new KM server, user key histories are lost. To minimize such loss, you should create new KM servers only when you create new sites. Upgrade considerations are outlined in the next section.

Upgrading Pre-SP1 KM Server Implementations

Networking KM servers is complex and risky, so configure them with care. Here are some example topologies:

1. **Single upgraded KM server per organization**—4.0/5.0 customers upgrade and do not install additional servers. No changes in topology. All sites still point to this single KM server. One MS CS is set up and the single KM server points to it. No risk.

2. **Single upgraded KM server plus installation of additional servers**—After the upgrade, a KM server is added for the site named Special-site. All Special-site users now point to (and must be enrolled in Advanced Security for) a new KM server. Since archive databases are unique to each KM server, Special-site users can no longer recover keys from their old KM server and may not be able to recover mail encrypted that used the old keys. In addition, the KM server administrators may choose to set up either one MS CS for all KM servers to point to, or up to one MS CS for each KM server. KM servers pointing to different CSs will need to cross certify each other.

3. **Clean installation of multiple KM servers (no upgrade)**—If multiple KM servers are set up cleanly (no upgrade), users cannot lose the ability to recover their key history: no databases have been established so there is no history to lose. As above, KM servers pointing to different CSs must cross-certify each other.

Administrators who move users to a new KM server should encourage them to protect their mail. Have them use a bulk decryption tool (such as Sectool, in the BackOffice Resource Kit) to decrypt all their mail, move to the new KM server, then re-encrypt with the new recoverable key.

Deploying Exchange Security

When deploying Advanced Security for an organization, first determine the organization topology. Locate the KM server in a secure but accessible spot. Location becomes more important when you deploy SP1 with multiple CSs and KM servers. A smart placement plan for CSs and KM servers can simplify backup and recovery of KM databases and the key issuance policies.

Next deploy the Exchange servers. If you intend to support S/MIME clients, you must deploy at least one SP1 server. Note that since SP1 uses Certificate Server to generate public and private keys and certificates, there must be CSs already deployed in the architecture. When deployment is complete, you can decide the client functionality. If you want to deploy S/MIME clients, you should deploy Outlook 98. If you want to sign and secure items within the organization and are not concerned about compliance with S/MIME standards, you can deploy any of the Outlook or Exchange clients.

Exchange 5.5 SP1 provides a new server-side feature that gives non-S/MIME clients two options for handling S/MIME signatures: Preserve and Toss. "Preserve S/MIME signature" stores the entire signed message in an attachment to the message. Messages go through a conversion process when they are received into the Exchange store: if even one bit is changed during this process the signature would be invalid, even though the message may not have changed. Using the preserve option and encapsulating the original mail message as an attachment preserves the signature on the item. "Toss S/MIME signature" removes the signature associated with the message. Using this method, S/MIME clients lose ability to verify signatures on messages, but all clients get readable text.

Establishing a Trust Hierarchy

When the supporting architecture is in place, you can set up a trust network with external organizations.

First step, decide which external organizations or CAs your organization should trust, then obtain their X509v3 root certificates. Conduct this crucial transfer out-of-band. With the CAs in hand, you can populate the CTL property page, which directories access to verify certificates. Note that this process is performed on each KM server, not each CS.

Once the trust is established, you should regularly import CRLs for trusted external CAs (and send yours to them) to guarantee that revocations are reflected in the CRL. When other organizations establish trust with yours, they will request your root certificate and CRL. You can obtain them by exporting them to a file from your CS. As before, transmit these out of band.

Scenarios for Exchange Server Security

Exchange Server offers several options for secure transmission, digital signature, and digital encryption. There are three types of connections available:

- Options that secure transmissions by securing the underlying transmission medium (network privacy)
- Options that secure item transmission or verification of the sender's identity by securing or signing the item being transmitted (message content encryption and signing)
- Options that support session level and item level security

All of these are possible through the implementation of the previously discussed network and message security options, and are listed as a practical implementation framework.

Secure Transmission

Exchange version 5.5 supports authentication of SMTP delivery between servers in three ways: a combination of SASL and AUTH, a combination of SASL/AUTH over SSL, or via Windows NT Challenge/Response and NTRPC.

SASL/AUTH with SSL Encrypted Connection (No Item Encryption/Signing)

SASL provides a simple base level of authentication and optionally allows two communicating hosts to negotiate a security protocol. Exchange 5.5 supports SASL as an authentication mechanism between SMTP mail transfer hosts, and AUTH (an SMTP extension command) which similarly allows for the authentication of the connection between two mail hosts. When combined with SSL, these authentication and session security techniques provide an encrypted and authenticated connection between the transfer hosts for the "clear" SMTP transfer.

Windows NT Challenge/Response and NTRPC Connection (No Item Encryption/Signing)

NT Challenge/Response is an encrypted authentication protocol used between Windows NT servers. If NTRPC encryption is turned on (default between servers) the communication stream between the Windows NT servers is encrypted with 128-bit strength RC-4. This means that the SMTP mail transfer is encrypted, even though the underlying SMTP transfer format is clear text. The items are secure while being transferred over the Internet and only "clear" after they have been received by the authenticated destination server.

Digitally Signed or Sealed Items

X.509v1 Key Exchange (Item Encryption and Signing)

Exchange versions 4.0, 5.0, and 5.5 support the issuance of X.509v1 certificates to recipients in the Exchange organization. Using a supplied form with Exchange, the certificate exchange form, users in one organization can send their certificates to users in another Exchange organization. After certificates are swapped, the users can send and verify messages that are digitally encrypted, digitally signed, or both.

X.509v3 Key Exchange (Item Encryption and Signing)

Exchange 5.5 SP1 supports the issuance of X.509v3 certificates to recipients in the Exchange organization. Using a form supplied with Exchange, users in one organization can send their certificate to users in another Exchange organization. After the certificates are swapped, the users can send and verify messages that are digitally encrypted, digitally signed or both.

Session and Item Encryption

SASL/AUTH with SSL Encrypted Connection (X.509v1 Item Encryption and Signing)

NTLM Encrypted Connection (X.509v1 Item Encryption and Signing)

Combinations of other techniques, these options provide the highest available security: secure transmission, individually secured or signed items, and non-repudiation and verification of "opaque" content. These options are most efficient in small client populations.

SASL/AUTH with SSL Encrypted Connection (X.509v3 Item Encryption and Signing)

Windows NT Challenge/Response and NTRPC Connection (X.509v3 Item Encryption and Signing)

These options require the presence of at least one Exchange 5.5 SP1 Server to generate X.509v3-compliant certificates and to establish cross-certification between organizations.

Definitions

Here's a quick list of security terms. Go to http://www.rsa.com for a basic security and algorithm information.

CAST A variable key length encryption algorithm developed by Carlisle Adams and Stafford Tavares of Northern Telecom Research. This algorithm supports keys 40 to 128 bits long.

Clear item An unencrypted item; readable without decryption.

Data Encryption Standard (DES/Triple DES) An IBM symmetric encryption block cipher which uses a fixed 56-bit key. It was defined and endorsed by the U.S. government in 1977 as an official standard. Regarded as the most widely used cryptosystem in the world. A process of encrypting plain text three times with DES and three different potential series of actions. DES-EEE3 (three DES encryptions with three different keys), DES-EDE3 (three DES operations in the sequence *encrypt-decrypt-encrypt* with three different keys), or DES-EEE2 and DES-EDE2 (same as the previous formats except that the first and third operations use the same key).

MD (Message Digest Algorithm, MD4, MD5) Developed by Rivest, this takes a message of arbitrary length and produces a 128-bit message digest. The algorithm is optimized for 32-bit machines. Description and source code for MD4 and MD5 can be found as Internet RFCs 1319 – 1321.

Opaque item An encrypted item; cannot be read without being deciphered.

RC2 A variable key-size block cipher designed by Rivest for RSA Data Security, designed as a faster, "drop-in" replacement for DES. Variable key size enables it to be made more or less secure than DES. The algorithm is confidential and proprietary to RSA Data Security.

RC4 A variable key-size stream cipher with byte-oriented operations designed by Rivest for RSA Data Security.

SASL Simple Authentication and Security Layer. Defined in RFC2222.

Secure Hash Algorithm version 1 Published in 1994 as a federal information-processing standard (FIPS PUB 180). Similar to the MD4 family of hash functions, this takes a message of less than 2^{64} bits and produces a 160-bit message digest. It is slightly slower than MD5 but is more secure against brute-force collision and inversion attacks.

X.509 A standard released by the International Telecommunications Union that specifies the formatting of a mechanism to verify public keys issued to security principals in an organization.

More Information

- Q177492, Title: XADM: Key Management Server Fails to Reissue Key
- Q148432, Title: XADM: Location of the Key Management Server Software
- Q177309, Title: XADM: Setup Cannot Initialize the Key Management Database
- Q177734, Title: XADM: KM Server Features Not Supported in Exchange 5.5 release
- Q176737, Title: XADM: Key Management Server Fails to Start and Logs Event 5060
- Q174743, Title: XADM: Cannot Install 4.0/5/0 KMS After Installing 5.5 Server
- Q156713, Title: XADM: KM Server Stops Intermittently on Alpha Servers
- Q154531, Title: XADM: Moving the KM Server to Another Server in the Site
- Q153394, Title: XADM: Error When Selecting Security Tab for Mailbox
- Q152849, Title: XADM: How to Recover from a Lost Key Management Server
- Q151689, Title: XADM: Error Starting Key Management Server
- Q149333, Title: XADM: The Basics of Advanced Security
- Q152498, Title: XADM: Unable to Enable Advanced Security on User Account
- Q169519, Title: XADM: Exchange 5.5 Remove All Option Removes Database Files
- Q146464, Title: XCLN: Err Msg: Unable to Obtain a Valid…Revocation List
- Q152686, Title: XCLN: How Expired Encryption Key Pairs Work
- Q154089, Title: XCLN: Cannot Send Sealed Message when Offline
- Q147421, Title: XFOR: How Exchange Encryption is Disabled on French Servers
- Q176681, Title: XGEN: Description of Microsoft Exchange Server 5.5
- Q146463, Title: XGEN: KMS Cannot Write Certificate Revocation List
- Q143380, Title: XGEN: Exchange Server Services and Their Dependencies
- Q170908 INFO: Key Management Server Functions not Exposed to Developers

CHAPTER 8

Advanced Backbone Design and Optimization

This chapter describes in depth how to construct an Exchange Server backbone: design, connector choice, directory replication process, background traffic, and general performance tuning. It is written for administrators and systems integrators who are already familiar with Exchange Server. The information is based on version 5.5, although many of the principles apply to earlier versions. You may also find it useful when troubleshooting directory replication problems. It concludes with a discussion of how the Exchange 5.5 "unlimited" information store affects tuning and capacity planning.

Caution This discussion explains changes to the Exchange raw directory and Windows NT Registry. Before you apply *any* changes to a live system, test them first in a lab environment. Document carefully any changes you make in a live environment.

You can also refer to the *Microsoft Exchange Server 5.5 Resource Guide,* Chapter 15, for a detailed overview of Exchange Server directory replication infrastructure and methods and the Exchange directory structure, covering which Exchange directory schema objects determine when, where, and how data will be replicated.

First Steps

Building Blocks

Exchange Server is unique in how it integrates with the underlying environment and how it forms a collective of knowledge between the servers. Although Exchange can be deployed out of the box in simple environments, designers of larger environments may need to tune components to achieve maximum performance and efficiency. Getting the right design in place is crucial to the operation and support of the Exchange infrastructure. You can always make changes afterwards, but things are far easier when deployed correctly from the day one.

Issues You Will Come Across

Basic design questions:

- Should I have multiple sites or a single one?
- How do I know if my network will accommodate Exchange?
- Which connector should I use between sites?
- Which messaging topology should I use, mesh or hub-and-spoke?
- Should the directory replication topology match the messaging topology?
- What if I want to change it all afterwards?
- How can I know if the system is performing at its best?
- Can I control the number of system messages generated?

This section makes general recommendations and offers ideas on how to decide upon your design. It is based on field experience in different environments working with clients who wanted different functionality and performance. When you have worked through the process, don't worry if your result differs from the recommendations presented in this chapter: the solutions you derive will reflect the size and intent of your enterprise.

Technical Design

Single Exchange Site Environments

Although you might think that only small Exchange installations deploy a single site, many sizeable companies enjoy the simplicity of having a single Exchange site that spans, sometimes, the world. So the first question to confront is: should you deploy one or more Exchange sites? It can be a relatively easy question to answer, for although a single-site configuration has some prerequisites such as authentication for the Site Services Account and administration policy, in most cases it simply is a matter of how much network bandwidth is available.

Network Bandwidth for a Site

Site boundaries are perhaps the toughest topic for Exchange designers. The rule of thumb is that, to place Exchange servers in the same site, you must have an average of 64 KB/seconds of available bandwidth. The problem with this is the same as with any rule of thumb; it doesn't cover all circumstances. Can you put 50 Exchange servers at each end of a 64-KB link? If the available bandwidth falls below 64 KB will Exchange "break"?

Another problem is rooted in human nature. Ask the people in charge of the network if there is an average of 64-KB available bandwidth and, normally, they will ask you to specify how much traffic Exchange will produce and at what times of the day. It is a perfectly reasonable question, and a lot safer than trying to derive an answer to yours, but it doesn't get you any closer to a decision.

To cut this knot, consider these Exchange site technicalities:

- Both the directory service and message transfer agent (MTA) components talk directly with each other within a site.

- Any Exchange server can communicate directly with any other Exchange server in the site.

- RPC produces errors if it can't get a response (directory service or MTA) within 30 seconds of making a request.

- Changes to the Exchange directory are replicated every 5 minutes (default).

- User generated messages are sent immediately and cannot be scheduled.

- The knowledge consistency checker runs (every 3 hours, hard-coded) on each server, causing intrasite traffic (more on this later).

- Backup replication occurs every 6 hours, also causing intrasite traffic (more on this later).

Obviously, it is difficult to assess exactly how much intrasite traffic Exchange generates. This chapter can help you assess the situation generally. The first clue is, in general, don't be afraid of creating large sites—they can make system administration much easier. More decision-making help is in the sections that follow.

Domain Structures

Before you install the first Exchange server, you should have a clear strategy for whether you will install your Exchange servers in one of your existing Windows NT Server domains, or if you will create a new resource domain. This decision for many companies depends upon whether the existing domain structure is "tidy" or whether it has grown organically over the years and is not simply and cleanly organized. In companies with a multitude of account domains, many Exchange designers tend to create a separate resource domain for the Exchange servers.

Separate Resource Domain

If you decide to build a separate Windows NT Server domain, deploy separate non-Exchange servers to act as the domain controllers (one PDC and at least two BDCs, for resilience). These are solely used for Exchange Server startup and process authentication. For best performance, deploy all Exchange servers as member servers. The resource domain should have a trust to each domain that holds user accounts (for mailbox mapping). This topology works well for companies that have user accounts in different domains but cannot implement trusts between them for security or political reasons.

Existing Accounts Domain

If you decide to use an existing account domain, install all dedicated connector servers as member servers. Now the question is whether to install mailbox and public folder servers as member servers or as BDCs. The latter choice can improve client performance, but there are other factors to consider. When an Exchange client logs on to the mailbox, its account credentials must be validated against the domain controller with the accounts database—even if the user is already logged on to the Windows NT domain. If all Exchange servers are built as member servers, clients logging on have to wait while the Exchange server checks credentials. This wait is reduced if the Exchange servers are built as BDCs, but BDCs must participate with the PDC in domain replication and sometimes general client authentication, so too many BDCs in a domain can degrade Windows NT and network performance. If you configure Exchange servers as BDCs, allow for extra processing and memory overhead when you create specifications for the hardware.

Hub-and-Spoke vs. Mesh

If you decide on a multiple-site environment, you must choose between hub-and-spoke or mesh architectures. This is based mainly on the projected ultimate size of the system: if there will be more than 20 Exchange sites, use the more scalable hub-and-spoke. Mesh designs allow full use of Exchange's rerouting capabilities, but when sites proliferate the routing tables grow exponentially until route calculation time and pressure on the MTA become unacceptable.

The best performing Exchange installations are generally hub-and-spoke. The hub site is usually a small collection of Exchange servers dedicated to message routing and directory replication. Spoke sites are located at regional offices and linked to the hub using a standard Exchange connector (site, X400 or IMS) with a piggy-backed directory replication connector. All hub servers should run Exchange Server 5.5, even if the spoke sites run previous versions. It has an enhanced message transfer agent capable of coping with much greater loads than previous versions.

Centralized Hub Sites

If all hub servers are in one location with high bandwidth and high availability links, it is called a *centralized hub*. This design works best when the network has a clearly defined central point and regional offices have direct network connections to it. This design increases site connector options because any server in the hub can act as the local messaging bridgehead.

Distributed Hub Sites

If you want to provide a local hub access point for satellite offices, deploy the hub servers over a wide-area, medium bandwidth network. This design works best for companies with numerous separated large offices but no clear network center. This design can work well and can be more efficient than a centralized hub (by reducing directory replication traffic), but it does limit site connector options. If the design allows any Exchange server in the hub to connect to the spoke, the network may flood or RPC may timeout.

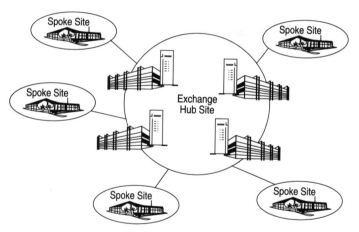

Number of Spoke Sites

Always try to limit the number of Exchange sites in the organization to simplify administration and reduce directory replication traffic. If a design requires more than 30 Exchange sites, these elements must be carefully tuned:

- Schedule on the directory replication connector.
- Address Book views replication schedule (defaults to every 6 hours).
- Public folder hierarchy replication.
- Public information store status messages.

Expanded explanations of replication and public folder traffic are presented later in this chapter.

If a design requires a very large number of sites (over 200), make sure the correct tuning parameters are in place, and deploy hotfix software if any Exchange 4.0 or 5.0 servers are running within the system. Contact Microsoft Premier Support Services to obtain hotfix software for installations with greater than 212 Exchange sites.

Choice of Messaging Connector

When you have defined site boundaries, you must decide which connector to use to link the sites. Your main choices are:

- Site connector (using RPC)
- X.400 connector
- Internet Mail Service
- Dynamic RAS Connector

Some instances indicate a type of connector rather obviously. For example, if a company already pays for a public X.400 connection to a provider, the X.400 connector is an obvious choice for the Exchange network. Other instances require some decision-making. For example, if the enterprise has available only a couple of modems and standard telephone lines, you can approach connectivity in three ways:

- Use the Dynamic RAS Connector for point-to-point transfer.
- Use a dial-up connection to the Internet and use the Internet Mail Service.
- Deploy Windows NT routing technology that provides dial-on-demand connectivity, then deploy the X.400 connector.

Perhaps your greatest dilemma is when there is either a WAN using leased lines or dial-on-demand Integrated Services Digital Network (ISDN). In principle you could use either the site, X.400, or Internet Mail Service to link the sites together.

Use the site connector whenever possible; it is the fastest and provides the most resilience. To use it, a network must support synchronous RPC and Windows NT authentication. Although you can deploy a site connector in a Windows NT model where there are no domain relationships, you may have to implement one temporarily to carry the authentication while you set up the site connector. This involves setting up a two-way trust, assigning Exchange permissions for the local site services account in the adjacent site. After the connector is in place, you can remove the trust relationship.

The rule of thumb says that you should use the site connector when bandwidth is good, the X.400 connector when bandwidth is limited, and the Internet Mail Service when you link sites over the Internet. Fair enough, but what is *good* bandwidth? Many people are too timid when it comes to estimating available bandwidth, so they use the "safest" connector (X.400). This does use less bandwidth than other connectors, but it introduces resilience and security issues. To help you compare connectors, the tables below show how much data is seen on the network when transmitting a message between two sites using each of the available connectors.

Table 1. A simple plain text message. Traffic includes binding and authentication of the MTAs.

Connector	Traffic sent (bytes)	Traffic received (bytes)	Total frames	Comments
Site (RPC)	7,484	3,889	60	Secure connection, whole session encrypted
X.400	4,087	751	19	Message header and body part names in plain text
Internet Mail Service	6,962	1,376	30	Uses NTLM authentication and encryption

Table 2. A simple plain text message. MTAs already bound.

Connector	Traffic sent (bytes)	Traffic received (bytes)	Total frames	Comments
Site (RPC)	4,744	1,434	24	Secure connection, whole session encrypted
X.400	3,653	319	13	Message header and body part names in plain text
Internet Mail Service	6,962	1,376	30	Used NTLM authentication and encryption

Table 3. A message with a 304-KB attachment. MTAs already bound.

Connector	Traffic sent (bytes)	Traffic received (bytes)	Total frames	Comments
Site (RPC)	342,302	19,629	471	Secure connection, whole session encrypted
X.400	332,366	12,279	454	Message header and body part names in plain text
IMS	453,164	13,258	523	Used NTLM authentication and encryption

As you can see from the tables, the X.400 connector is most efficient on the network. However, it does not provide the level of security that the other connectors offer. You will also notice that there is not too much overhead on the Site Connector as the size of the message increases. Designers in general, still favor the Site Connector for its resilience capabilities.

Directory Replication Connectors

The simplest arrangement is to layer the directory replication topology directly onto the messaging topology. If you decide to deploy "shortcut" messaging connectors, document them carefully and use them sparingly: if you deploy many of them in a large multiple-site Exchange system, the Gateway Address Resolution Table (GWART) can get extremely large, which puts significant overhead on route calculation, which can retard message routing and delivery.

In a pure hub-and-spoke environment, stagger directory replication times between the hub and the spokes so that the whole environment is updated in one cycle.

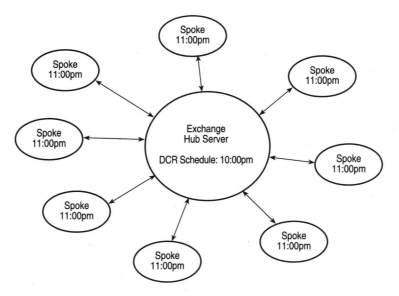

This figure shows each hub-to-spoke directory replication connector set to request updates at 10:00 p.m. and each spoke-to-hub DRC set to request updates at 11:00 p.m. This one-hour gap ensures that the hub site has complete knowledge before the spokes start requesting updates. This is significant: reverse the request times and it would take two days to replicate new objects to the entire organization (assuming the replication occurred only once per day).

Setting Limits on the Backbone

To keep the messaging system fast and efficient, you must set a maximum message size. There are lots of opinions on this, of course, but 5 MB is a common maximum. When you choose a limit, there are various ways to impose it. If you have complete control of the Exchange environment you can set the *Outgoing Message Size Limit* on individual mailboxes, which allows certain users or agents to send larger messages if required. Although this limit can't be set at the information store level, you can automate the setting using ADSI. A different approach is to set the maximum message size limit directly on the MTA, thus limiting every user automatically.

Exchange system traffic is allowed to exceed the message size limit. For example, you cannot use it to restrict large messages in a replicated public folder. To enforce a restriction in this case you would have to use a rule to affect a specific public folder.

Tuning a Messaging Bridgehead Server

Large Exchange installations usually deploy dedicated message switching servers in the hub site for performance reasons. In these scenarios the MTA process must take precedence over all other tasks in the server, Exchange and non-Exchange. To fully tune a connector server, you have to "break" the normal Exchange rules of hardware design and configuration.

CPU, Memory, and Network Interface Cards

Dedicated Exchange MTA servers are normally processor-bound: you will get far more performance out of a dual-processor Pentium II 333 Mhz than you will from a quad-processor Pentium Pro 200 MHz. Current architectural limitations prevent Pentium II–based servers from supporting more than two processors. For mailbox/public folder servers, a Pentium Pro–based server offers higher performance because of the more tightly coupled L2 cache memory.

Dedicated messaging servers often need only 128 MB of memory because their information stores are small compared to those of mailbox and public folder servers.

If your hardware vendor supports multiple-failover network interface cards, it is a good idea to install them. This will ensure that the server stays running even in the event of a network failure.

Disk Configuration

Connector and mailbox/public folder servers differ in hard disk arrangement. Both types should use a quality Redundant Array of Inexpensive Disks (RAID) controller that supports hardware level RAID5 and RAID1. For mailbox and public folder servers, place the information store databases and transaction logs on separate disks; for connector servers, place both components on the same disk because the MTA does not pass messages through the store. To boost performance, spread the *exchsrvr\mtadata* directory over as many spindles as possible. The reason for this is that when the MTA is receiving a message, it is written to the hard disk as a DAT file in the *mtadata* directory and, after the routing decision has been made, the data is passed directly to the MTA of another Exchange server, thus bypassing the information store.

There are a few exceptions to the above rules: connectors based on the Exchange Development Kit use virtual queues (MTS-IN and MTS-OUT) which *are* held in the information store, so for servers with these connectors (Internet Mail Service, cc:Mail connector, Notes connector, and most third-party connector products), it is a good idea to place the logs and the information store on separate disks for performance and resilience. It should also be noted that the directory service acts as a client to the information store, and so it passes incoming directory replication requests through the information store.

The write-back memory cache on a quality RAID controller can also be enabled to improve performance. Quality controllers have heavy parity ratio and a battery backup. If it allows you to set the read/write cache ratio, such as the Compaq SMART Array controller, configure it as 25% read and 75% write for maximum performance.

Performance Optimizer

After installation is complete, you can boost performance by running the Exchange Performance Optimizer and selecting the correct options for your server. If you don't run it, performance may be sluggish and the server may generate error messages in the application event log. For a pure Exchange messaging bridgehead server, deselect the **Private** and **Public Store Server** check boxes, and select **MultiServer**. This increases the number of available Kernel threads and RTS threads in the MTA from 1 to 3.

Manual Registry Tuning

Depending on the total number of connectors supported by the hub servers, you may want to change some MTA registry settings. Exchange Server 4.0 and 5.0 required specific registry adjustments if more than 10 Site Connectors were configured on a single server. This was because of the number of control blocks and threads set aside for MTA-to-MTA communications. The Exchange 5.5 MTA is much more dynamic and you will find that many of the MTA registry keys are now redundant, although the Performance Optimizer will still change them. For example, the LAN-MTA parameters are now dynamically adjusted and allocated as needed, but the Performance Optimizer will still adjust the parameters when the **Connector/Directory Import** option is selected.

Some of the MTA registry values do not work as expected. For example, Performance Optimizer always sets the value for *Dispatcher threads* to 2, although the MTA when it starts allocates 6: 2 for the Router, 2 for Fanout, and 2 for Results. Therefore, the *Dispatcher threads* value that is visible in the Registry should not be taken as the absolute number of threads allocated to this component. This value indicates how many threads each subcomponent can allocate.

You almost never have to alter MTA registry parameters in Exchange Server 5.5. The only common case is if you have more than 20 X.400 connectors on a bridgehead server, in which case you must adjust the *TCP/IP control blocks* to equal the total number of X.400 connectors.

MTA registry parameters can be found under HKEY_LOCAL_MACHINE /System/CurrentControlSet/Services/MSExchangeMTA/Parameters.

Urgent Associations

The Exchange 5.5 MTA is the first version to assure that important messages are not held up behind lower priority ones. It creates an urgent association dynamically for a priority message as soon as it arrives in the queue.

Tuning a Directory Replication Bridgehead Server

The executable for the directory service is called DSAMAIN.EXE, and it is fully multithreaded and multitasking. Upon startup of the directory service, the program allocates threads to handle client requests and directory replication from other Exchange servers. The Registry parameter **Max Threads (EXDS+NSP+DRA)** controls exactly how many threads can be allocated for the directory service process. The Exchange Performance Optimizer always sets this value to 50 no matter which options are selected. These threads are shared between the different directory service tasks:

- **EXDS**—Process that handles LDAP and DAPI requests.

- **NSP**—Name Service Provider handles directory requests from MAPI clients.

- **DRA**—Directory Replication Agent handles server-to-server replication tasks.

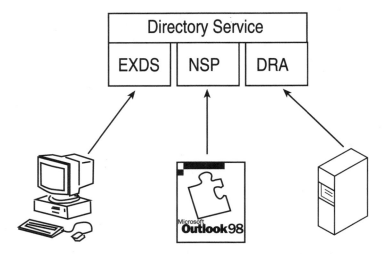

All of these subcomponents compete for threads from the directory service. If the Exchange server contains a large number of mailboxes (more than 1,500) and is slow responding to client requests, increase this registry value by 30 to ease the bottleneck. Use Windows NT Performance Monitor to see how many threads are in use by the directory service (Object "Process," Counter "Threads in use," Instance "DSAMAIN").

Although DRA threads are allocated out of the master pool, you can adjust the number reserved for this subcomponent. If an Exchange server can't keep up with replication requests or if you have a dedicated Exchange server for directory replication (directory bridgehead), you can increase the *Replicator maximum concurrent read threads* registry parameter, doubling, for instance, the 10 set aside by Performance Optimizer. Remember: threads come out of the master pool, so you may need to increase the *Max Threads (EXDS+NSP+DRA)* registry parameter as well.

DS registry parameters can be found under HKEY_LOCAL_MACHINE /System/CurrentControlSet/Services/MSExchangeDS/Parameters.

Changing Directory Replication Connectors

The network infrastructure in an enterprise often changes, so it may sometimes be necessary to adjust Exchange to make best use of underlying networks. The most common requirement is to change directory replication connectors.

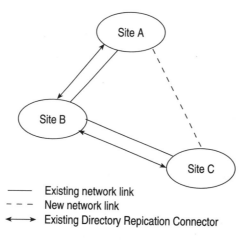

—— Existing network link
- - - New network link
←——→ Existing Directory Repication Connector

Unfortunately, Exchange will not allow the configuration of triangulated directory replication connectors and so the directory replication link must be torn down between sites before another can be established.

Rebuilding directory replication connector links is tricky. For instance, objects in the public folder hierarchy will have been replicated between the sites already. As long as you don't initiate any form of DS/IS consistency adjustment when the directory replication connector has been torn down, you should have no problems with any public folder replication or affinity when replication is formed again. Even public folder permissions are retained during a teardown.

Distribution lists present the biggest challenge. As soon as you tear down a DRC, distribution lists lose any recipients that are no longer present in Address Book. You can avoid this by exporting distribution list (DL) membership out of the organization, simply by specifying the GAL as the export point. If the DLs belong to different sites, you must import the membership into each site individually.

Directory Replication Architecture

The Replication Model

Unlike a Windows NT Server domain, which maintains one central copy of the directory, in an Exchange site all Exchange servers are considered as masters and can modify any object within the site, regardless of where it was created. Between sites, all Exchange servers receive a read-only replica of all objects. The only exception to this rule is the Address Book Views naming context, which is read/write between Exchange sites.

When a modification is made to the Exchange directory, a change notification is sent to all servers in the site, informing them that an update has taken place. It is then up to those servers to pull the updated entries from the notifying server. Change notification timings are controlled by Registry parameters.

Change notifications are not uses between sites. Instead, at a specified time, a bridgehead server sends request messages to an adjacent bridgehead server, which processes the requests and sends back the necessary response.

Background Traffic

There is no doubt that Exchange is a robust messaging product; however, for the product to notice inconsistencies, a level of background traffic (mostly directory replication and status information) will be seen between Exchange servers intra- and intersite. Although Exchange can automatically detect and correct problems, enterprise-style installations may want to throttle this automatic facility if network resources and bandwidth are limited.

Invocation-Ids

Every directory service has a unique identifier called an **Invocation-Id** associated with it. To see the ID for a given Exchange server, run the Exchange Administrator program in raw mode (ADMIN-RAW), then drill down in the navigation bar and select the local server name. The right hand panel shows the **Directory Service** object. If you get the raw properties of, say, the directory service and select the "Invocation-Id" attribute, you'll see a 32-digit hex string that is the unique signature for the local directory service. It looks like this:

```
00F4355CE15AD111900800A02470DBE1
```

DSA-Signatures

Whenever an object is modified, the Invocation-Id of the local directory service is stamped against that object. The information is exposed through the DSA-Signature raw attribute on the directory object. These signatures provide the basic building blocks for intra- and intersite replication. When a directory replication request is made to an Exchange server, the local DSA returns only objects stamped with its signature.

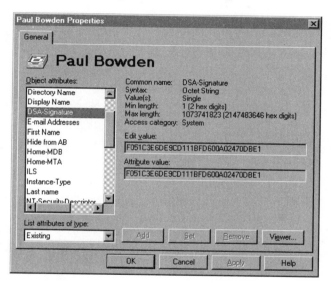

There are only two instances when an Exchange Server can inform other servers of directory data that it doesn't "own." The first is when a directory replication bridgehead server passes along information it has learned from connected sites. The second is a little more complex. Imagine three servers in the site: A, B and C. If C is down, A and B replicate modifications to each other freely. If A is taken offline and C is then restarted, server B informs C of its own changes *plus* modifications that were made on server A. This scenario occurs only when Exchange services are started up, not if there is a break in communications such as a network fault.

Update Sequence Numbers

Whenever a change is made to the Exchange directory, the local directory service stamps the next available Update Sequence Number (USN) on that object. Starting at 1 and going up to 2,147,483,647, USNs are crucial to directory replication. Even so, USNs are not synchronized between servers in a site—each Exchange server maintains its own count, although the counts should be fairly close because directories should contain about the same number of objects.

Local directory services stamp one of their own USNs against all objects, regardless of whether they were created locally or replicated from another Exchange server.

To see the current USN of a given server, you must make a modification to the existing directory. The easiest way see the last USN is to modify a field on a current object like a mailbox, then look at its USN-Changed attribute.

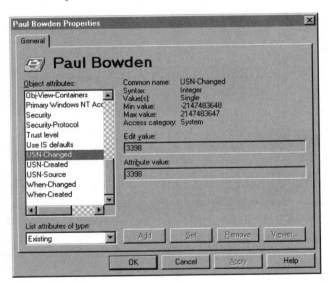

USN Fields

In raw mode, each directory object has a set of fields relating to USNs:

- **USN-Changed**—The USN applied by the local directory service the last time this object was modified.

- **USN-Created**—The USN assigned by the local directory service when this object was originally created in the local directory.

- **USN-Source**—The USN assigned by the directory where the object was first created or last modified. This either relates to the USN assigned on absolute time of creation if local, or the latest USN assigned on this object if replicated from another server.

Object-Versions

When a new object is created, it is stamped with version "1." Whenever it is changed, the directory service making the modification increments the version number. Replicated out to other directory services (untouched), version numbers are the directory service's primary tool for finding replication conflicts. If the directory service finds an object with the same version number but different DSA-Signatures, it knows the object has been changed independently on two different servers. The directory service resolves the conflict by saving the version with the latest time signature (When-Changed raw attribute).

Naming Contexts

An Exchange 5.5 directory has five naming contexts (Exchange 4.0 has four). Modifications always take place within a naming context. When a change takes place, a change notification is sent out for that context. For example, if you change two objects in different contexts on the same server, two push notifications are sent out to the other servers in the site. You can see the context names in the Event Log if diagnostic logging for directory replication is turned up:

Table 4. Naming context identifiers in the Event Log

Naming context	Referred to as
Organization	/o=*orgname*
Site	/o=*orgname*/ou=*sitename*
Schema	/o=*orgname*/ou=*sitename*/cn=Microsoft DMD
Configuration	/o=*orgname*/ou=*sitename*/cn=Configuration
Address Book Views	/o=*orgname*/ou=_ABViews_

For example, a modification to a mailbox in the recipients container occurs in the site naming context. A modification made to an X.400 connector occurs in the configuration naming context.

Note The Windows NT Event Viewer is a great troubleshooting tool that Exchange Server uses with directory replication diagnostic logging. See Directory Replication Logging Events later in this chapter.

Local Modifications

When you use the Exchange Administrator program, you must log on to an individual Exchange server. When you select an object in the site naming context, the data is always retrieved from the logged-on server. When changes are made to the configuration naming context, the data may be retrieved locally (for example, from the X.400 connector) or pulled from the source server (for example, from the MS Mail (PC) connector).

When you create new objects or make modifications to existing entries, that data is written locally, even if the object's "home" is another server. This applies even when creating mailboxes on a server in the site that you are not logged on to. In this scenario, the mailbox is created only after replication has occurred.

REPS-TO and REPS-FROM

Each directory service retains a list of all other servers in the site with which it performs replication. These lists can be seen in raw mode on each naming context. The REPS-TO list is not too interesting, but the REPS-FROM list shows all of the other servers in the site that replicate to this one. More important, especially for troubleshooting, it shows the last USN received from that server. When looking at the REPS-FROM list for a particular context, keep in mind that the number reflects the last change made within that context, not the last change made on that server. Make it a habit to refresh (F5) the Exchange Administrator program before looking at USN numbers.

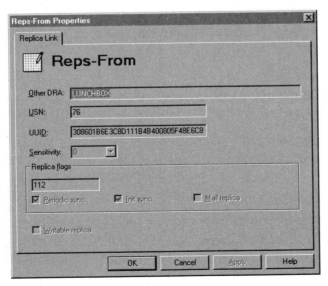

Directory Service "Channels"

Because directory services in the same site must authenticate to each other directly, a low-overhead communication channel is established between them and stays open for about 15 minutes. Data can flow freely over the channel without re-authentication between the servers. Directory service authentication generates roughly 8 KB of traffic.

Intrasite Directory Service Binding

When directory services communicate with each other, they do so through RPC. Because RPC itself relies on an underlying network protocol such as TCP/IP, IPX/SPX and NetBEUI, a Registry parameter controls the prioritized transport list for binding. This is found under:

HKEY_LOCAL_MACHINE\Software\Microsoft\Exchange\ExchangeProvider

Value: RPC_SVR_BINDING_ORDER

Default: ncacn_ip_tcp,ncacn_spx,ncacn_vines_spp

To help Exchange reduce the binding latency, place the correct transport protocol at the start of the list and remove the others. If a remote Exchange server is temporarily down or there is a short-term network problem, the local Exchange server may waste CPU cycles and time (increasing latency) trying the other network protocols.

Objects Received from Remote Sites

It is always useful to see the last object replicated from a particular server or site. Just as you can look at the REPS-FROM list for contexts within your own site, you can also look at REPS-FROM information relating to other sites by calling up the Raw Properties on naming contexts in the read-only portion of your directory. This information should tell you about the last USN received from the remote bridgehead.

Object Replication

When an object such as a mailbox is modified, the entire object must be re-replicated. The directory service does not support field-level replication. This is a consideration if you are populating all of the fields for directory entries or if you perform bulk directory updates.

Manual Refreshing

When modifications are made to the local directory, they are normally seen immediately. If, however, changes are made through replication, you may need to refresh the window (F5) before you notice the change.

Tombstones

When an object is deactivated and marked for deletion from the Exchange directory, it becomes a tombstone entry. Because this is considered to be a change on the local directory, it is replicated to all other servers. Before being deleted, tombstone objects are kept for 30 days (the default) to leave enough time for the deleted object to be replicated throughout the organization. After 30 days, each Exchange server will expunge tombstoned entries, which does not involve additional replication.

Replication Traffic

Amount of Replication Traffic Generated

Let's return to the question: how much traffic does Exchange generate on the network? This is an important element in planning. Some Exchange designers try to minimize traffic by populating the fewest fields possible in the directory (display name, alias, and primary Windows NT account); others use the directory to its maximum potential. As a rough guideline, a mailbox created (or modified) with the minimum fields populated produces about 3.5 KB of traffic to all other servers in the site, and a fully populated one produces about 5.8 KB. These are rough figures and you can't multiply them when calculating directory replication traffic for multiple directory entries because data is bundled together.

Because servers within a site are presumed to have good bandwidth to each other, intrasite data is not compressed. Intersite, the local bridgehead servers can compress replication information before submitting messages.

Traffic Seen When Joining a Site

All Exchange servers in the organization must receive a complete copy of the Exchange directory. It is important to understand how this fact affects the network transmission rates, especially in cases such as adding a server to a large organization when it is at the end of a slow link.

In some companies, the overhead of replicating the directory to a new server over a slow link is too great. For scenarios such as these, other options are available such as building the new Exchange server on a high-speed network and then physically moving the server to its destination.

Intrasite Backup Replication Cycle

Regular backup traffic must be taken into account. Regardless of the amount of change, every server in a site initiates a full backup replication to every other server every 6 hours by default. This does not burden the network as much as you might think. Exchange Servers pass only delta information and because all servers are kept close to up to date, this traffic can be fairly small in small sites. In large sites it may be significant, and you may want to change the bit mask to extend the interval between backup replication cycles.

A backup replication initiates this sequence of events between a local server and every other server in the site:

1. Local DSA requests an update for the **Organization** naming context and waits for a response.

2. Remote DSA processes the request and sends any changes.

3. Local DSA requests an update for the **Site** naming context and waits for a response.

4. Remote DSA processes the request and sends any changes.

5. Local DSA requests an update for the **Schema** naming context and waits for a response.

6. Remote DSA processes the request and sends any changes.

7. Local DSA requests an update for the **Configuration** naming context and waits for a response.

8. Remote DSA processes the request and sends any changes.

9. Local DSA requests an update for the **Address Book Views** naming context and waits for a response.

10. Remote DSA processes the request and sends any changes.

Backup replication requests go to each Exchange server in the site. The local server updates its knowledge grouped per naming context, not by server. For example, if there are three servers in the site, the local server asks for the Organization naming context from server B, waits to complete, then asks for the Organization naming context from server C. After these have been received, it then moves on to the Site naming context. If one of the servers is down for maintenance, the next task is attempted without further delay. DSAs have a fixed timeout of 35 minutes. If an adjacent server cannot be contacted within this time, an error 13 is raised in the Event Log.

Assuming that each naming context is already up to date, allow for about 20 KB of replication traffic for each server, each way. This can be significant in large sites. An Exchange site with 50 servers would see 47.8 Mb of total traffic (#Servers-1) 20 (#Servers) staggered over 6 hours. To see if this is acceptable, you must analyze the speed and topology of the network links dividing the Exchange servers.

You can adjust the backup replication schedule by changing the raw *Period-Rep-Sync-Times* attribute (each naming context has one of these) in the directory. The field contains 168 hex digits, each digit controlling a one-hour timeframe, which means you can shift the cycle over a seven-day period. On some servers you may notice that the string is populated with 1s, which indicate the first 15-minute period of the hour; on others you may see 8s, which equate to the third 15-minute period. Click on the *Editor* button to see/set the time schedule for replication.

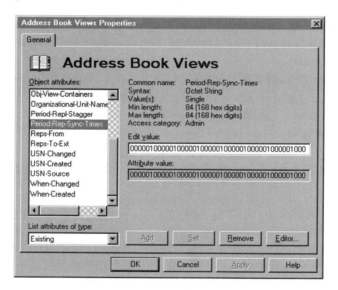

Intersite Backup Replication Cycle

There is no intersite backup replication cycle, but every six hours a single request message passes between bridgeheads asking for updates to the Address Book Views context. The number of ABViews request messages from each site depends on the total number of sites in the organization (# of sites − 1). This action can be controlled via the *Period-Rep-Sync-Times* attribute for the Address Book Views naming context.

The Knowledge Consistency Checker

At each three-hour interval the Exchange Knowledge Consistency Checker (KCC) executes to verify that server knowledge is consistent throughout the site. The KCC runs on each Exchange server and verifies that all servers have knowledge about each other. The KCC checks the number of servers in the site that it knows about against the number of servers in the site that its partner has listed. If it finds that the local server does not have the same knowledge as the partner server, it establishes replication links to the new server. Partner servers are defined as the result of a *stricmp* calculation against the list of servers in the site. In general terms, the local KCC moves from one server to the next in numeric or alphabetic order. In a large complex site, you can directly influence the KCC connections and latency by correctly naming your servers. The same amount of data is generated no matter how you name your servers, but you can use your knowledge of the underlying network to optimize the connections.

Failure to consider the underlying network when planning Exchange server names can increase overhead on your WAN and pressure on Exchange.

Consider this example of a poorly designed site. For simplification, the Exchange servers are literally called A, B, C, etc. Black lines represent the network structure, and green boxes represent Exchange servers.

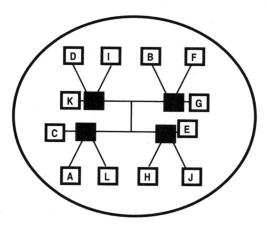

This structure will cause knowledge links to be established over multiple network hops and over the WAN. Using different server names could alleviate much of this unnecessary traffic, with corresponding improvement to network performance.

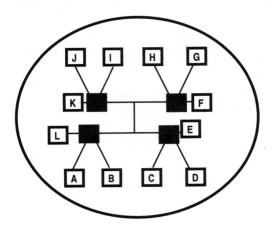

The "last" server in the site establishes its knowledge link with the "first." When another Exchange server joins or leaves the site, full knowledge of that change should be propagated within a few hours. In this context, "last" and "first" do not refer to when the servers were installed, but to their alphabetic position in the configuration context.

When all servers are up and running, this ring is consistent. If a server goes down for some reason, its upstream partner continues calling it. If there is no response in 30 seconds, the upstream server gives up and binds to the inactive server's downstream partner.

The KCC also has a role to play for intersite knowledge. During initial replication, the KCC can create placeholders for other sites. These can be seen in the local Administrator program as an "empty" site name and configuration container. Once these objects exist, the directory service populates them with the information contained in the directory replication response messages received from adjacent bridgehead servers.

Intrasite Replication Packets

The table below outlines the packets sent and received on the network during intrasite replication. Packets lengths can vary with different naming conventions; the values used here are offered as a general guide.

Table 5. Intrasite replication traffic.

Packet description	Length
Context change notification	214 bytes
Notification acknowledgment	118 bytes
Context pull request	246 bytes
Response to pull request	Multiples of max frame size
Context received acknowledgment	60 bytes

Replication Events

Each part of the directory replication process raises an event as it executes. If diagnostic logging is turned up, this information can be seen within the application event log. In the following table the DRA is the *Directory Replication Agent.*

Table 6. Replication event IDs generated by the directory service.

Event ID	Description
1068	Local DRA told to pull updates from the remote server
1070	Local DRA has been asked to supply changes to a remote server
1071	Local DRA has calculated the number of objects to be replicated
1199	Local DRA has compressed the replication message
1058	Local DRA has successfully received an update for the context
1099	Local DRA has received a request message from another site
1101	Local DRA submitted a response messages to another site

DRA Option Values

Whenever requesting directory replication, a DRA specifies the options criteria for the request. These can be seen in the application event log when diagnostic logging for replication is turned up.

Table 7. Option values seen against events in the application event log.

Option value	Description
3	Normal intrasite replication
4000	Manually invoked request updates
4041	Normal replication for bridgehead servers, or downstream servers requesting updates for remote site naming contexts from the local bridgehead in the site
4051	"Backup" replication cycle
C000	Manually invoked request all objects

Intersite Replication Messages

The mechanics of intersite directory replication differ from those of intrasite replication. Activation is controlled through the schedule tab on the directory replication connector on each bridgehead server. Be careful when setting the activation schedule. It is easy to select a one-hour time block, which would generate four update request messages per context within that hour, and therefore four complete replication cycles. You should instead choose a single 15-minute block in the schedule tab for each desired replication cycle. When the schedule becomes active, the directory service on the local bridgehead composes a number of messages and addresses them to the directory service on the remote bridgehead.

Table 8. Intersite replication request messages.

Msg	Contents	Size (bytes)
1	Request Configuration naming context	144
2	Request Site naming context	120

The total number of request messages composed depends upon the number of sites gained through this connector. If the directory replication topology is hub-and-spoke (20 satellites), each satellite bridgehead composes 40 messages on each directory replication schedule (2 x 19 other satellites and 2 requests for the hub site). All directory update requests are sent to the adjacent bridgehead in the hub site. The hub site responds to these requests on behalf of the other satellite sites. This means that if the hub site does not have full knowledge of a particular satellite site, it cannot pass on any more information than what it has to the requesting satellite.

If there has been no change to the requested context, a response message is sent saying so. If there have been changes, the objects are gathered, compressed (if necessary), and then sent in a single mail message per context (up to the "packet size" defined in the Registry). A response message is sent for each request.

If there are problems with the underlying message transport, you will see many directory replication requests in the MTA queues. The bridgehead must *always* respond to requests, so once message routing resumes you will see many responses in the queues. So if replication appears not to be working, don't request a full directory update between sites—the requests will just pile up, and when message routing resumes the responses will pile up. Failure to receive responses usually means a problem in the underlying message transport, not with replication. Most new Exchange Administrators are not used to the pause between setting up a new directory replication connector and the population of the stubs. They therefore assume that directory replication is not working and try to manually request updates, which just makes the MTA queue up with more directory replication messages.

Manually Asking for Updates from a Remote Site

If you believe that your local Exchange site is out of synchronization or you want immediate delivery of recent changes from another site, you can hit the *Request Now* button for a remote site on the directory replication connector. There are two update options: updates since the last communication, and re-request of all objects. A "re-request all objects" effectively produces a directory replication update message where the starting USN is "1."

Update requests are always sent for the three naming contexts in the table below. Message lengths vary with different naming conventions, and the numbers below are provided as a general guide. The DRA does not have to request or process the contexts in any specific order.

Table 9. Intersite replication request messages sent on demand.

Context	Request length (bytes)
Request Site naming context	120
Request Configuration naming context	144
Request Address Book Views naming context	120

For the Address Book Views request only, the local bridgehead server requests updates within the site before sending the request message.

After the remote bridgehead has received the requests, it works out the number of objects that it needs to return and then submits the response messages. If there have been no updates within each context, the response messages are small. Message lengths vary with different naming conventions, and the numbers below are provided as a general guide.

Table 10. Intersite replication response message sizes (Exchange level, not network level).

Context	Response length (bytes)
Site naming context	1,400
Configuration naming context	1,320
Address Book Views naming context	1,176

If there have been updates to the context, the information is bundled up and sent in the response message. The amount of replication traffic caused by modified objects depends on the number of fields populated, so it is not accurately predictable for planning purposes. Allow anywhere between 2 and 5 KB for each replicated object. If necessary, the response message will be compressed.

When the local bridgehead receives updates from another site, it propagates that information (even if the responses indicate no changes) to servers within the local site through normal intrasite replication.

Compression

Exchange servers in the same site normally have good bandwidth, so they do not compress objects that they pass to each other for replication. Between sites, where bandwidth is not always plentiful, bridgehead servers compress replication traffic over 50 KB. Under this amount it is more efficient to send the information as-is rather than use CPU cycles to compress it. The target bridgehead decompresses information, before entering it into the local directory. The compression ratio is roughly 5:1.

Intersite Replication on Startup

Some companies prefer to perform offline backups of their Exchange servers. While this method is fast and complete, taking down a directory bridgehead and restarting it (either a shutdown or NET START) causes a full intersite replication. Five minutes after the directory service makes contact with the MTA process (on the same Exchange server), directory replication request messages are sent to adjacent bridgeheads.

You can stop these directory update messages from being sent using a new Registry parameter implemented in Exchange 4.0 SP5, Exchange 5.0 SP2, and Exchange 5.5 SP1.

Directory Replication Registry Parameter Tuning

The Registry parameters that control how the directory service process works are found under:

HKEY_LOCAL_MACHINE/System/CurrentControlSet/Services /MSExchangeDS/Parameters

Value: Replicator Notify Pause After Modification (seconds)

Data type REG_DWORD

Default 300

Description This sets the period that must elapse on the local directory service before it sends notification packets for modifications made in the local directory. These notifications are sent to all of the other servers within the site.

Advice If you have a large Exchange site spread over a WAN, you may want to increase this value on the servers where you make directory modifications so that directory changes are batched up for more than 300 seconds. Increasing this value increases the time it takes to replicate directory information throughout the site. Generally, a value of 30 minutes (1,800 seconds) is acceptable to most companies.

Value: Replicator Notify Pause Between DSA's (seconds)

Default 30

Description This sets the wait time interval between notifying servers in the site that a change has taken place. The wait ensures that the modified directory service is not overloaded with update requests all at once.

Advice If you have a large Exchange site spread over a WAN, you may want to increase notification time between the servers to 120 seconds, which is acceptable in most situations.

Value: Intrasite Packet Size

Data type REG_DWORD

Default 100

Description This sets the maximum number of updated objects that the local directory service will send in a RPC response when responding to a directory replication update request. If the local directory service has more than this number of objects, it informs the remote directory service (using direct RPC) to request more objects. This acts as a checkpoint and ensures the communication link is still valid.

Advice Leave this value alone unless you have a specific requirement.

Value: Intersite Packet Size

Data type REG_DWORD

Default 512

Description For a directory service acting as a bridgehead server, this sets the maximum number of directory update objects it will send in one message when responding to a directory replication update request message. If the local directory service has more than this number of objects, it tells the remote directory service (using a message) to request more objects.

Advice Leave this value alone unless you have a specific requirement.

Value: Replicator Inter site Synchronization at Startup

Data type REG_DWORD

Default 1 (not present)

Description The default means that a full intersite replication occurs when a directory replication bridgehead is restarted. Change this to zero and there is no automatic replication.

Advice Change this only if you frequently restart directory bridgehead servers.

Public Folder Replication and Status Messages

Public Folder Hierarchy Replication

When public folders are created, modified, or deleted, update information must be sent to all other public information stores within the organization. The information store service is responsible for this action. By default, a thread runs every 15 minutes to check for changes in the public folder hierarchy. If it finds none, it exits without generating data. If it finds changes on the local server, it creates an update message(s) and submits it to the MTA. Default limits for a single message are 20 new/changed folders and/or 500 deleted folders. The message is sent to all public stores in the organization, propagating changes as if in a mesh relationship. The update message size depends on the number of changes made in the hierarchy.

Table 11. Hierarchy replication message sizes.

Number of changes	Size of message (KB)
1	2
2	3
3	3
4	4

To reduce the frequency of hierarchy change replication, go to the Exchange Administrator program, and under *Server* in the public information store object raise the value of the *Replicate always interval (minutes)* parameter. The next time the thread executes it will re-read this value and adjust its execution time. You do not need to stop any services for this change to take effect.

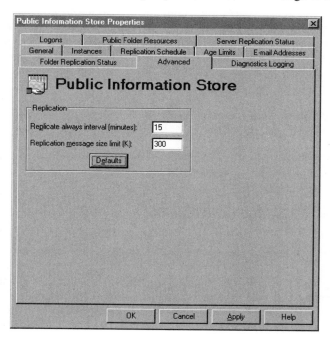

Public Folder Hierarchy Status Messages

Even when public folders are not used for housing information, the existence of a public information store on an Exchange server (default) creates traffic throughout the enterprise. By default, an store thread runs every 12 hours (at 12:15 a.m. and 12:15 p.m. GMT) to determine if a public folder hierarchy status message has been sent out in the last 24 hours. If one has not been sent, one is composed and sent; if one has been sent, no action is taken. The message contains the status of the public folder hierarchy folder, and its size depends on the number of folders in the hierarchy. Note that the thread runs on GMT and is completely independent of the Windows NT locale, time zone, and daylight savings settings.

This mechanism can be troublesome for large environments. First of all, the public folder hierarchy status message is addressed to all other servers that have a public information store. These stores do not see site boundaries, so the message is sent to every public store in the organization. Removing unused public information stores from servers can reduce this traffic. A second problem is the send time of the status message. Depending upon when the information store service is started, it dictates when the status message is sent out, just after midnight or just after midday. The calculation for working out when the status message will be generated is:

Information store startup time + 24 hours + time to next thread execution (every 12 hours)

For example, if the information store is started at 3:00 a.m., Monday morning, the status message will be generated at 12:15 p.m., Tuesday afternoon.

General Public Folder Status Messages

If public folder replication is configured between two or more Exchange servers, the information is truly synchronized between the two systems. If replication messages are somehow lost, the public folder components can recover by identifying inconsistencies and back-filling information. This is a good arrangement, but it generates background status messages.

For efficiency reasons status messages for each replicated public folder are sent as a single message wherever possible. To reduce the number of status messages flowing through the Exchange network you should:

- Replicate public folders only when you need to.
- Try to establish a common *replication topology.*

Replication topology refers to the number and identity (names) of servers that have an instance of a given public folder. Say you have 200 folders replicated between servers A, B, and C in the same Exchange site. Although each folder must transmit its status, this topology requires only six status messages: A sends one to B and one to C, B sends one to A and one to C, and C sends one to A and one to B. Because all 200 folders are replicated to the same servers, the status information can be bundled into one message.

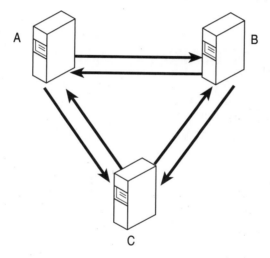

If you create another 50 public folders and replicate them between A, B, and C, you will still have only six status messages, although they will be slightly larger. If you now add another 10 public folders and replicate them only between A and B, *eight* status messages will be generated. Because these 10 folders are not replicated to C, status information cannot be bundled, so separate messages are generated: one from A to B and one from B to A.

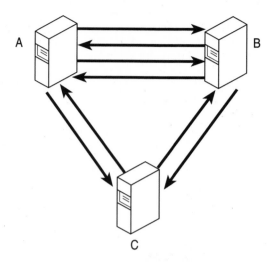

Public Store Registry Parameter Tuning

These parameters control the transmission of status messages by the information store service. By default, none of these parameters exists, and so manual creation is required under the section:

HKEY_LOCAL_MACHINE/System/CurrentControlSet/Services/MSExchangeIS /ParametersPublic

Store Status

Value: Replication Send Status Timeout

Data Type DWORD

Default 84,600 seconds (24 hours)

Description This is the minimum amount of time to wait before sending a public folder status message to the rest of the organization.

Advice If there are more than 50 sites in the organization with slow links involved, you may want to adjust this parameter on each public store server. Increasing this value lowers the total amount of system traffic generated, although it increases the time required to resolve inconsistencies in the public folder hierarchy.

Value: Replication Send Status Alignment

Data Type DWORD

Default 42,300 *seconds (12 hours)*

Description Minimum period to wait before the public folder status store thread runs.

Advice Leave this parameter alone.

Value: Replication Send Status Alignment Skew

Data Type DWORD

Default 0 *seconds*

Description This sets an amount of time after 12:15 a.m./p.m. GMT to run the public folder status store thread.

Advice If the network has to move many system messages during the day, find out when most of the messages are being generated and adjust this parameter to delay generation until quiet times of the day. Some companies adjust this parameter so that all system messages are generated at 6:15 a.m. or 6:15 p.m. local.

Store Startup

When the information store process is started, two status messages are sent to all of the other public stores within the organization to ensure public folder consistency. In environments where Exchange servers are restarted regularly (after nightly offline backups, for instance), this can deluge the hubs with mail. A new Registry parameter allows you to prevent status messages on startup. It is recognized only by Exchange 4.0 SP5, Exchange 5.0 SP2, and Exchange 5.5 SP1 or the relative hotfix.

Value: Disable Replication Messages at Startup

Data Type DWORD

Default 0

Description Prevents the information store from sending status messages for public and system folders on startup.

Advice Adjust this parameter only if public store servers are regularly restarted.

Note Offline backups cause extra administrative burden and do not ensure the integrity of the data within the information store. Use online backups wherever possible.

Intrasite Directory Replication Example

Here is an example that shows the intrasite replication process as it is initiated after creation of a new mailbox on Server 1, one of three Exchange servers in the base configuration:

Server	Current USN
Server 1	1053
Server 2	1060
Server 3	1049

1. The Administrator creates the mailbox directly on Server 1. The new object is stamped with 1054 on all three USN fields. Server 1's DSA-signature is written on the object and version 1 is assigned.

2. Exactly five minutes after the change is made, a change notification is sent first to Server 2. If these two directory services have not communicated in the last 15 minutes, they authenticate to each other. Once authenticated, the push consists of a single 214-byte packet containing the updated naming context. An internal timer now counts down from 30.

3. In response to the push, Server 2 sends to Server 1 an acknowledgment consisting of a single 118-byte packet.

4. Almost immediately, Server 2 requests to synchronize its copy of the naming context with Server 1. It informs Server 1 that it wants to obtain all new objects starting with 1054 and options 3 (normal replication). With "replication" diagnostic logging turned up, this is signified by event 1068 in Server 2's application event log. The request consists of a single 246-byte frame.

5. When Server 1 receives the pull request, it finds all the objects that are stamped with USN 1054 or higher and with its own DSA-signature. This process is signified with event 1070 in Server 1's application event log.

6. After Server 1 completes this process, the DSA reports the number of objects found that match the criteria (event 1071) and starts to transmit the information. This will be seen on the network as multiple packets of the maximum frame length for that topology (1,514 bytes for Ethernet, 4,202 bytes for Token Ring).

7. After Server 2 receives all of the information, the DSA sends back a single frame of 60 bytes as an acknowledgment and then reports event 1058 to signify that the replication completed successfully. The new mailbox object is assigned the following USN values in Server 2's directory:

   USN-Changed: 1061

   USN-Created: 1061

   USN-Source: 1054

8. Even though Server 2's current USN has incremented because of the new object, the DSA knows that it shouldn't replicate this information onward because the object does not have its DSA-signature.

9. Server 2 updates its REPS-FROM list on the site naming context for Server 1. This reflects USN 1054.

10. After the timer in step 2 has expired, Server 1 performs this same process for Server 3, although without the timer because there are no other servers in the site to replicate to. After completion, Server 3 assigns the following USN values to the new mailbox object:

USN-Changed: 1050

USN-Created: 1050

USN-Source: 1054

Tuning Scenario

Based on an actual large Exchange deployment, the example shows the number of system messages generated and how design and deployment mistakes can cause problems.

Configuration Details

Network topology Data center with 128-KB/second lines (shared) to each office

Number of Exchange sites 140 (139 single server sites)

Messaging topology Pure hub-and-spoke using X.400 connectors

Directory replication topology Pure hub-and-spoke

Number of Exchange servers 141 (all Exchange 5.0)

Problems

- MTAs in the hub site crashing three times a day.
- MTACHECK would generally run okay, but sometimes an MTAWIPE had to be performed.
- Thousands of system messages (directory service and public store) were in the queues.

Resolution of MTA Stability

The primary issue was MTA instability. There were only two servers in the hub site, each with 70 X.400 connectors and 70 directory replication connectors. Although this is theoretically possible, it cannot be accomplished without manually tuning the 5.0 MTA. Unfortunately, because the MTA kept crashing, more messages would back up in the queues and the sheer number of messages would crash the MTA again, etc.

Changing MTA Registry parameters (doubling the number of threads for the kernel, dispatcher and TCP/IP) relieved contention on the MTA and reduced crash frequency to every other day.

Although the MTA in Exchange Server 5.5 would have resolved many of these problems, the full release code wasn't ready at the time and so the only way to relieve the pressure was to double the number of hub servers to four. This action stabilized the hubs, although there were still a huge number of messages in the queues.

Working Out Where the System Messages Came From

The next task was to determine why the messages were being generated. A full directory replication cycle was being performed once a day, early in the morning. The hub-and-spoke DRC schedules were staggered appropriately by three hours, but a one-hour time block had been set, not 15 minutes.

Hub Directory Replication

When the hub DRC schedule became active at 1:00 a.m., the hub servers would send two directory update request messages to each spoke site. Because a one-hour time block had been set, six additional directory update request messages would be sent to each spoke.

- Total number of request messages generated: 1,112
- Total number of response messages generated: 1,112

Spoke Directory Replication

When each of the spoke DRC schedules became active at 4:00 a.m., each spoke server would send two directory update request messages (addressed to one of the hub servers) for each site obtained through the directory replication connector. Because a one-hour time block was set, six additional directory update request messages would be sent for each site.

- Total number of request messages generated: 154,568
- Total number of response messages generated: 154,568

Hub-to-Spoke Address Book Views Replication

As Address Book Views are not replicated as per the DRC schedule, every six hours the hub would send each spoke a single update request message.

- Total number of request messages generated in 24 hours: 556
- Total number of response messages generated in 24 hours: 556

Spoke-to-Hub Address Book Views Replication

Every six hours each spoke server would send an updated request message for each site gained through the connector. These messages would be processed by one of the hub servers.

- Total number of request messages generated in 24 hours: 77,284
- Total number of response messages generated in 24 hours: 77,284

Public Folder Hierarchy Status Messages

Every 24 hours, each server with a public information store sends out the status of the public folder hierarchy. There must be at least one public information store per site, which means there had to be at least 140 public stores in this organization. In fact there were 141 as both original bridgehead servers also had public stores. Although each of the spoke servers sent only one status message to the hub, this message would get fanned out at the hub because each message was addressed to all public stores in the organization.

- Total number of status messages generated in 24 hours: 19,881

Overall Analysis

This adds up to nearly half a million system messages every 24 hours. Obviously, this is unacceptable and serious tuning was begun. Some obvious errors had been made when installing the directory replication connectors, and these were fairly easy to solve. Most of the other tuning had to be accomplished with Registry settings and raw mode of the Exchange directory.

To determine how to go about tuning the system, the consultants asked the system owners three fundamental questions about basic Exchange use:

- How often do you want a full directory replication to occur?
- Do you actively use Address Book Views?
- Do you actively use public folders?

The system owners wanted one full directory replication a day. They did not use Address Book Views or public folders, but wanted to leave the functionality enabled in case they decided to use them.

Active Tuning

Having defined what the company wanted and secured agreement for a general plan of attack, the consultants began tuning.

Directory Replication

The one-hour time block was changed to 15 minutes on each directory replication connector. Activation times were left as they were. Here is how this affected traffic:

Hub to spoke:

- Total number of request messages generated: 278
- Total number of response messages generated: 278

Spoke to hub:

- Total number of request messages generated: 38,642
- Total number of response messages generated: 38,642

Address Book Views Replication

Because the functionality was left enabled, there had to be some sort of replication in place, so the *Period-Rep-Sync-Times* attribute on the hub servers was set to Saturday 10:00 a.m. and on the spoke servers to Saturday 10:00 p.m. Here is how this affected traffic:

Hub to spoke:

- Total number of request messages generated in 7 days: 139
- Total number of response messages generated in 7 days: 139

Spoke to hub:

- Total number of request messages generated in 7 days: 19,321
- Total number of response messages generated in 7 days: 19,321

Public Folder Hierarchy Status Messages

Public folder functionality was also kept, but to reduce traffic redundant public information stores were deleted. As it was, the only one that could be deleted was at the hub, and this reduced traffic levels insignificantly. Next, the daily automatic status message was changed to weekly, with a Registry key. Unlike Address Book Views, the status message cannot be explicitly scheduled for a certain time and day: instead it is sent every *xx* hours. The client company generally took servers down for maintenance only on weekends, so a seven-day schedule fit nicely. For more protection, the consultants implemented a six-hour time skew so that status would be sent at 6:15 a.m. and 6:15 p.m.—that is, always outside normal working hours. Here is how this affected traffic:

Total number of status messages generated every 7 days: 19,600

The Result

Tuning reduced total system traffic from the original half million to 136,360. The hub servers were eventually upgraded to Exchange Server 5.5 to provide higher throughput on the connections. Although the figures still seem a little high, you must remember that this is a week's total system traffic for all servers. Because Exchange sites can span 128 KB/second links, the company is redesigning the system to consolidate sites.

Future versions of Windows NT and Exchange Server will make it possible to reduce system traffic even more.

Directory Replication Diagnostic Logging Events

This section discusses directory replication diagnostic logging events and their significance. For continuity with the *Microsoft Exchange Server 5.5 Resource Guide*, the scenario used below follows the guide's example organization (Ferguson and Bardell). The Windows NT Event Viewer provides a great troubleshooting tool that Exchange Server uses with directory replication diagnostic logging, allowing you to track the status and flow of directory replication.

To enable directory replication diagnostic logging, open **Properties** under **Org**, **Site**, **Configuration**, **Servers**, **<*Server*>**, **Directory Service**. Select the **Diagnostic Logging** tab and set the logging level for replication to "Maximum."

Basic Events

When working with replication across Exchange sites (intersite replication), look for eight basic events (chronological order):

Generated by the requesting server:

- **Event ID 1068**—Directory requests the directory replication agent (DRA) to get changes from a remote naming context.
- **Event ID 1100**—Details requested changes and from which server.
- **Event ID 1058**—Indicates receipt of a successful request transaction.

Generated by a remote directory service:

- **Event ID 1099**—Shows receipt of the request message.
- **Event ID 1070**—Remote directory asks local DRA to package up requested changes.
- **Event ID 1071**—Remote DRA acknowledges that it has packaged the changes.
- **Event ID 1101**—Sends response.

Logged onto the requesting server:

- **Event ID 1099**—Requestor server acknowledges receipt of remote DRA's replication message.

A Closer Look

In this scenario, server Boston01 requests changes from naming context /o=Ferguson&Bardell/ou=NAmerica-W (server SanFrancisco01). Both are directory replication bridgehead servers, Boston01 as the requestor server and SanFrancisco01 as the remote directory service. Event ID **1068** signals Boston01's initial request for changes, detailing the naming context that must send changes and from which directory. In the description box of the **Event Detail** dialogue, "options 4041" specifies that this naming context is synchronized periodically by name (not Invocation-ID) with asynchronous (Async) replication. (You can find definitions of these options in "Options and Flags in Diagnostic Logging Details.") Here's what the **Event Detail** description says:

```
Internal event: The directory replication agent (DRA) was asked to
synchronize replica of /o=Ferguson&Bardell/ou=Namerica-W from directory
ID EX:/o=Ferguson&Bardell/ou=NAmerica-
W/cn=Configuration/cn=Servers/cn=SanFrancisco01/cn=Microsoft DSA with
options 4041.
```

When the message is sent (Event ID **1100**), the event description shows that server Boston01 generated this event, requesting changes to the configuration naming context from SanFrancisco01:

```
During intersite replication, the directory replication agent (DRA)
successfully submitted a message with a length of 136 while requesting
updates in naming context /o=Ferguson&Bardell/ou=Namerica-
E/cn=Configuration from the directory at
EX:/o=Ferguson&Bardell/ou=NAmerica-
W/cn=Configuration/cn=Servers/cn=SanFrancisco01/cn=Microsoft DSA.
```

Event **1058** states that the requestor server successfully packaged and sent the request for a replication update:

```
Internal event: The directory replication agent (DRA) call completed
successfully.
```

The remote DRA (SanFrancisco01) generates the next four events. The remote DRA first generates Event **1099**, saying that it received the replication request message. Match the length in this event description with the one in 1100 to confirm delivery:

```
During intersite replication, the directory replication agent (DRA)
received a message with length of 136 from the directory at
EX:/o=Ferguson&Bardell/ou=NAmerica-
E/cn=Configuration/cn=Servers/cn=Boston01/cn=Microsoft DSA.
```

Event ID **1070** shows remote server SanFrancisco01 asking the DRA to package changes for the requestor server Boston01. You can see the naming context requested and (for the first time) what update sequence number (USN—unique numbers that every directory keeps to track database changes) value passes. In this scenario, the requestor server asks for changes greater than USN 1237:

```
Internal event: Directory d6149c3a935fd11aaee00c04fb68e14 asked the
directory replication agent (DRA) to get changes from naming context
/o=Ferguson&Bardell/ou=NAmerica-W starting at update sequence number
(USN) 1237 with flags a80 and sensitivity 100.
```

Event ID **1071** logs the DRA packaging changes, including the number of changes and the latest USN being sent:

```
Internal event: The directory replication agent (DRA) got changes
returning 4 objects and entries up to update sequence number (USN) 1442.
```

The remote directory server then generates Event **1101**, indicating it submitted the message, and specifying the updated naming context and the requestor server receiving the changes. The event description also details the message length that you can verify against the requestor server:

```
During intersite replication, the directory replication agent (DRA)
successfully submitted a message with a length of 5592 while updating
the replica of naming context /o=Ferguson&Bardell/ou=NAmerica-W on the
directory at EX:/o=Ferguson&Bardell/ou=NAmerica-
E/cn=Configuration/cn=Servers/cn=Boston01/cn=Microsoft DSA.
```

The final intersite directory replication event (**1099**) logs on the requestor server Boston01, describing the receipt of changes from remote DRA SanFrancisco01. The message length should match the length in 1101, confirming that this is the same replication message:

```
During intersite replication, the directory replication agent (DRA)
received a message with a length of 5592 from the directory at
EX:/o=Ferguson&Bardell/ou=NAmerica-
W/cn=Configuration/cn=Servers/cn=SanFrancisco01/cn=Microsoft DSA.
```

Replication within a site (intrasite replication) generates similar events with the exception that the local "notification" server has changes to replicate *and notifies* other directories in the site. The remote DRA server receives notification, and then requests changes. Look for four basic events in intrasite replication (chronological order):

Generated by the remote DRA:

- **Event ID 1068**—States that it has been notified to get changes from the local "notification" server.

Generated on the local "notification" server:

- **Event ID 1070**—Remote DRA asks server for changes.
- **Event ID 1071**—Indicates that changes were sent back to the remote DRA.

Generated on the remote DRA:

- **Event ID 1058**—Shows the replication call was successful.

In the scenario, Boston01 has changes at the /o=Ferguson&Bardell /ou=NAmerica-E site container that it needs to replicate to other servers in the site. NewYork01 is the only other server in the site. Boston01 is local "notification" server and NewYork01 the remote DRA.

Event **1068** notifies server NewYork01 that server Boston01 has changes that NewYork01 must request. "Options 3" in the event description refers to "Async replication, set by notify caller," indicating intrasite replication. (See the Options and Flags in Diagnostic Logging Details section below.)

```
Internal event: The directory replication agent (DRA) was asked to
synchronize replica of /o=Ferguson&Bardell/ou=NAmerica-E from directory
ID ee6cf383865bd1118cfb00c04fb169ac Boston01 with options 3.
```

On the local notification server DRA (Boston01), Event **1070**'s description shows remote DRA NewYork01 asking for changes from the notification server's site naming context. The **Event Detail** also shows which USN the DRA marks as the starting point.

```
Internal event: Directory 52d4c132f161d111b1b900c04fb169f3 NewYork01
asked the directory replication agent (DRA) to get changes from naming
context /o=Ferguson&Bardell/ou=NAmerica-E starting at update sequence
number (USN) 2535 with flags 71 and sensitivity 100.
```

The next event (**1071**) generated on notification server Boston01 states that it successfully packaged the changes that remote DRA NewYork01 requested, including the number of changes sent and the latest replicated USN. Because intrasite replication is based on Remote Procedure Call (RPC), this information instantly replicates between the two directories.

```
Internal event: The directory replication agent (DRA) got changes
returning 3 objects and entries up to update sequence number (USN) 2544.
```

The final event (**1058**) logs on to remote DRA NewYork01, indicating that NewYork01 successfully completed the replication process as requested by requestor serverBoston01.

```
Internal event: The directory replication agent (DRA) call completed
successfully.
```

Remember that there are cases during intrasite replication when the first event (1068) does not have "options 3," for example, when the bridgehead server replicates objects from other sites. Because the bridgehead server must also provide notification messages for other servers within its site, it will use a different option, in most cases "4041." You may also see "options 4051" when intrasite naming contexts replicate by schedule.

Options and Flags in Diagnostic Logging Details

When viewing the Event ID 1068, you can identify the options passed by extrapolating the hex values of specific attributes:

4041 = Sync by Name, Sync Replica periodically, Async Replication

```
0x4000   // Sync by name, not UUID
0x0040   // Sync replica periodically
0x0001   // Asynchronous replication
```

4051 = Sync by Name, Sync Replica periodically, Writeable Replica, Async Replication

```
0x4000  // Sync by name, not UUID
0x0040  // Sync replica periodically
0x0010  // Writeable replica
0x0001  // Asynchronous replication
```

General Attributes

```
0x0001  //Asynchronous replication
0x2000000   // Only wait 10 minutes on sync call
```

Install Option

```
0x0010  // Not first DSA in site
```

Replica Option Flags

```
0x0010  // Writeable replica
0x0020  // Sync replica at startup
0x0040  // Sync replica periodically
0x0080  // Mail replica
0x0100  // Complete replica asyncly
0x1000  // Change source of replica
```

Replica Deletion Flags

```
0x0100  // Ignore error if replica source DSA unavailable
0x1000  // Don't try and contact other DRA
0x2000  // Delete subref (nw replicas only)
0x4000  // Allow deletion even if NC has Reps-To
0x8000  // Replica has no Reps-From
```

Synchronization Flags

```
0x0002  // Set by notify caller
0x0004  // Set when this is a retry sync
0x0008  // Sync replica from all sources
0x4000  // Sync by name, not UUID
0x8000  // Sync from scratch
0x40000 // Daemon queued sync
0x100000// Always q, never discard
0x400000// Sync abandoned due to lack of progress
0x800000// Performing initial sync now
0x1000000   // Sync attempt was preempted
0x200000// Not synced since boot or replica add
0x0200  // Sync getting objects modified by any DSA; Also passed to
        replica_add and get NC changes
```

Flags To Update Refs When Replicas Added or Deleted

```
0x0004 // When NC replicated
0x0008 // When replica NC deleted
```

GetNcChanges Flags

```
0x0400 // Return replica dest mods
0x0800 // Include ancestors
```

Backsync Required

```
0x10000 // Backsync needed
```

The Limits of Unlimited Information Store

Microsoft Exchange Server 5.5 removes the hardware limitation of 16 GB per database that existed in Exchange 4.0 and 5.0, improving the scalability of the information store. The store service has been streamlined, effectively scaling across four processors, and making use of as much RAM as you can add. The improved storage engine removes the need for maintenance-related server downtime, and the backup API works with the fastest backup hardware available in the PC server market. But have we really come to a point where we can scale Exchange servers indefinitely? How does the unlimited information store— "storage limited only by hardware"—impact capacity planning? This section discusses issues that govern an information store database and makes recommendations for setting limits.

"Hard" Limits

All servers have a maximum hardware configuration. This affects the information store size in two ways:

- **Physical partition size**—There is a maximum physical data partition size that can be configured for the information store database.

   (Of course, hardware vendors continue leapfrog each other in an effort to push the boundaries of what PC server technology can achieve.)

- **Maximum configuration**—Servers have a maximum configuration in terms of number and types of processors, amount of RAM, and so forth. There are also limits in what can be configured to run under Windows NT, such as 2 GB (3 GB with Windows NT/E) maximum memory available to applications, which affect the number of users you can put on one server.

   We will discuss later why you will also want to limit the amount of space you allow each user, resulting in a maximum size for the store at any one time.

"Soft" (Operational) Limits

With Exchange 5.5's "unlimited" information store, network administrators initially look to maximize servers by adding as many users per server as possible. However, several hardware-dependent operational issues can outweigh plans to reach a target information store size. The administrator must:

- **Set acceptable risk levels for servers going down**—Downed servers leave temporarily stranded users. Effectively managing this risk can cost money, and so the administrator must balance server configuration with the number of users and risk of lost user performance during an unfortunate outage.

- **Estimate impact of online backup on system performance**—Although the online backup of Exchange should not affect user access, approximate the maximum operational window of time and bandwidth to allow a full system backup.

- **Calculate database restore performance**—Keeping in mind that the restore operation is only one step in recovering a server, estimate the maximum acceptable time to restore a database.

A New Planning Framework

This section provides a framework to plan large-server stores in a consistent manner that systems administrators can readily support. It does not address detailed performance tuning or capacity planning issues. See the second book in this series, *Managing and Maintaining Microsoft Exchange 5.5*, for an in-depth discussion on that topic. For Exchange administrators, capacity planning is even more critical for very large servers than for the "medium-sized" servers typically deployed in the past. Here's why:

- **The cost of inadequate planning for 2,000 users is simply greater than the cost of inadequate planning for 500 users.** For example, a RAID5 partition to hold the information store databases on a "medium" server can consist of seven 4-GB drives, with a nominal throughput of 500 I/O operations per second. You could scale this up for 2,000 users by going to a RAID5 partition consisting of seven 18-GB disks. This array still only has a throughput of 500 I/O operations per second. This disk subsystem can have a greater overall affect on performance in the 2,000-user server, increasing the risk of creating a bottleneck during peak loads.

- **Many existing Exchange 4.0 and 5.0 servers are "over-specified."** Organizations restricted the number of users per server, conservatively estimating against the 16-GB limit on store size. For example, if you allow each user 50 MB of server storage, you can support 320 users per server with 16 GB. Experience allows them to safely predict that a dual Pentium Pro server with 256-MB RAM and "sensible" disk configuration—dedicated transaction log disk, database partition striped across four to five disks—can readily handle this load. And given the competitive pricing of servers with this specification, an IS manager can make "safe" purchasing decisions with relatively little research.

These factors that allowed us to make "safe" server specifications have disappeared, leaving us with the challenge of specifying hardware to support large user numbers with large stores. Some guidelines exist in the form of performance white papers published by Compaq, Digital, and Hewlett Packard. Given the relatively narrow parameters of even the best performance tests, carefully weigh these results.

A "Safe" Specification for 2,000 Users

For the IS professional looking for a "safe" specification approach, here is an outline for a 2,000-user mailbox server, based on MCS experience with an Exchange 5.5 "early adopter" enterprise.

Component	Specification	Comments
Processors	Four Pentium Pro 200, 512-KB level II cache.	Processors with 1-GB level II cache offer increased performance at a higher cost (roughly three times the same processor with 512 KB), but a 512-KB cache is quite adequate for 2,000 users.
Main memory	512 MB.	With improved buffer management, Exchange 5.5 uses all 512 MB. Because there is minimal swapping in and out of the memory, you need not add more memory.
Disk configuration	Dedicated system disk, dedicated transaction log disk, RAID5 partition for databases consisting of at least 10 disks.	With a 2,000-user load, a dedicated spindle for transaction logs is essential. The RAID5 database partition must have enough disks to spread the load and achieve required throughput.
Array controllers	Caching array controllers with ECC (Error Checking and Correction) protection and battery backup.	2,000-user performance will not be achieved without write caching enabled on array controllers. Because corruption of data loss in the cache can lead to a corrupt store, ensure adequate protection of data in transit.
Network	Fast Ethernet or FDDI.	Client/server traffic for 2,000 users will (at least during peak loads) swamp an ordinary Ethernet segment; a fast network is important.
Backup hardware	Single DLT7000 or array of four DLT7000s.	Install the fastest available hardware. (Backup and restore performance are discussed in more detail below.)

This configuration is for a dedicated mailbox server. Additional services that you can install on an Exchange server (Event Service, Outlook Web Access, Internet Mail Service, various connectors, and so forth) add a significant and unpredictable load. Because this is a "safe" server configuration, do not install additional services on this dedicated mailbox server.

Capacity Planning and Management

Controlling Information Store Size

Effective Exchange network support is about keeping control. This is particularly important when it comes to managing the information store database size on large servers. Nothing will compromise your ability to maintain an efficient and reliable messaging service faster than a runaway store. In planning Exchange 5.5 server deployment specify the following:

- Maximum store size for the hardware platform.
- Per-user storage quota to manage the store size within this maximum.
- Monitoring system to track the growth in store size.
- Contingencies for dealing with stores that reach the maximum size.

Because Exchange allows for a great deal of flexibility regarding the actual storage values and monitoring triggers that your organization can adopt, create a clear information store policy and follow it. Failure to manage store sizes increases the risk of one of several severe conditions:

- Database can no longer be backed up to the installed backup device, potentially leading to extended running without a current backup.
- Backup takes much longer to restore than originally planned and allowed for, affecting messaging service.
- Database runs out of disk space, bringing the Exchange server to a stop.

Maximum Store Size

An Exchange planning team will go through several rounds of capacity planning. After you have an idea of how much space your organization will need and how much disk space to purchase, you'll have come to the point of drafting a detailed policy for maintaining the server store size. The specific issue now is determining exactly how much of the available physical disk to allocate for the information store.

To effectively manage a partition's space, you'll first want a clear organization of everything residing on that partition. With Exchange servers, dedicate one large partition to the databases. Because transaction logs write to a dedicated spindle (in our "safe" hardware configuration), the database partition should contain only database files. Make sure MTA database files and other work files go somewhere else, such as the system disk.

There are two approaches to limiting store size:

- **Manage "in good faith"**—Set a safety margin for used space that allows time to respond. (70% full is a good general guideline.)
- **Take maximum risk avoidance**—Set a maximum store size to 50% of available disk space if you are concerned about the risk that you may one day need to perform an offline defragmentation of the store database.

Exchange 5.5 eliminates the need to schedule an offline defrag (eseutil /d). However, if your server ever requires this operation you will need enough free space to hold the new defragged database. This space doesn't have to be in the same partition (or on the same server), but in operational terms it is much simpler if it is.

Per User Quotas

Setting user storage quotas eases the burden of managing an information store within a maximum size limit. Although not an exact science, size quotas allow you to estimate the maximum size your store can grow to, and prevent "runaway" users from pushing it beyond the limits you set. You can derive an approximate store size from average mailbox size and single instance ratio, a rough ratio of the storage users will consume, and the store's physical size. For an average e-mail item shared by two mailboxes, the single instance ratio is 2:1. In reality other factors affect the store size, such as number of indexes, level of fragmentation, and so forth, but in practical terms, estimates turn out to be remarkably accurate, based on this calculation:

```
((number of users) x (user quota) x (% of quota used)) /
(single instance ratio)
```

Number of users	User quota (MB)	% of quota used	Single instance ratio	Store size (GB)
2,000	50	75	1.5	50
2,000	50	75	2	38
3,000	50	90	1.5	90
3,000	50	90	2	68
4,000	50	75	1.5	100
4,000	50	75	2	75

It is obviously difficult to estimate single-instance ratio without existing data. In practice, ratios between 1.25:1 and 2:1 seem most common. We would expect better ratios (in the 2:1 range) with larger stores because with more users on a server the likelihood that messages and attachments remain shared is higher.

Tracking Store Size

To manage the information store you will need to:

- Track the historical growth of stores, important for calculating future needs.
- Implement an alert system that triggers events when the information store approaches set limits.

(You can use Windows NT Performance Monitor or other system management software to trigger an alert when disk free space falls below a threshold.)

Because the information store does not report comprehensive or detailed information, some interpretation is required when looking at space consumption. First, track the free physical space on disk. Although this is a rough number, you want to manage Exchange server's store size. Track the physical size of each database. On a day-to-day basis, file size does not represent an accurate counter because the Exchange database file size updates only when services stop.

Keep an eye on the amount of space consumed by the Deleted Item cache. On a mature store, with the retention set to a week or less, the amount of space used should remain relatively small. Windows NT PerfMon provides counters to monitor this, but keep in mind that these counters give only an indication, not a precise measurement of storage consumed.

Finally, you may need to determine the amount of free space within the database file. The file size itself represents a "high water mark." Generally many items will have been deleted and the space they occupied reclaimed by the store service. Although a file occupies 79% of disk space, there may be a lot of free space internally, with little risk of an increase to 80% or beyond. Exchange 5.5 SP1 adds a new "space dumper" switch to ESEUTIL (/ms) that reads out an estimate of how much space an offline defrag would reclaim.

The issue of offline defrag is discussed below under The Defrag Issue.

Dealing with "Oversize" Stores

When the information store approaches the set limit, we can respond with one of several options:

- **Delete old mail from mailboxes.** Users will not appreciate this severe measure, although some organizations may have this kind of housekeeping already in place.

- **Add more disk space to the database partition.** This option carries its own risks:

  - Deviation from a standard server configuration that simplifies maintenance or disaster recovery can potentially increase overall support costs.

  - Increasing the maximum information store size to a new value requires re-evaluation of backup capacity, restore window, and so forth.

- **Move some users to another server.** By tracking space usage on all servers, you will generally know where you can move a group of mailboxes. The number of situations that require commissioning a new server should be few. This option maintains system stability. There are no abrupt changes to server configuration, operating model, or administrative policy. For these reasons, MCS generally recommends this option.

Note Within an Exchange site the Move User operation attempts to preserve single-instance storage, but watch for situations where single instancing breaks for individual messages.

The Defrag Issue

Exchange 4.0 and 5.0 performed a daily housekeeping routine that consisted of limited tuning of the host of indexes maintained by the store and very little in the way of reclaiming free space within the information store database. For this reason, many administrators instituted a regular offline defrag (EDBUTIL /d) as part of their maintenance schedule to reclaim space and optimize indexes. Offline defrag takes a long time, and Microsoft advises against doing this regularly on a very large store. The Exchange product development team improved the online defrag processing performed during daily maintenance. With Exchange 5.5, administrators do not need to perform an offline defrag for general maintenance reasons.

You would need to perform an offline defrag only if you needed to shrink the physical size of the database file, for example, after a major fragmentation event such as moving a large number of mailboxes (for example, 100 mailboxes or more) off a server, or removing a large number of newsgroups. You can generally avoid these scenarios by managing the information store within set limits. Nevertheless, set up a contingency plan to perform an offline defrag. As indicated in Maximum Store Size, there are two approaches, depending on how you assess the risk: reserve 50% of physical disk on every Exchange server or set aside capacity within the network that can be used as the target for defrag processing.

Resilience and Disaster Planning

There is no getting round this fundamental fact: bigger servers with more users concentrate the risk of server outage on fewer components. An organization's implementation of large Exchange 5.5 servers must address this issue. Exchange administrators can configure most high-quality, off-the-shelf servers with a range of options providing resilience from uninterrupted power supplies, to RAID protection for disks, duplexing of disk controllers, redundant NICs, and so forth. You may be able to build an Exchange server so that the only single point of failure is the motherboard.

Exchange 5.5, Enterprise Edition supports clustering (Microsoft Cluster Server— MSCS), which provides failover against components like the motherboard. Clustering support works, and it works well. Managed failover (which implies a clean shutdown of one node) is exceptionally fast (as fast as stopping and starting Exchange services on the same node, but without the delay normally due to the operator). Failover because of an error condition can be just as fast (if services can be shut down cleanly on the failing node) or can be a little slower if it involves a replay of transaction logs.

Before choosing to implement clustering you should thoroughly evaluate the possibilities offered by your chosen hardware vendor:

- **Some component failures may not actually be prevented.** A cluster may offer protection for only a few more components than a stand-alone server with a full set of resilient options, and those components have a low risk of failure. For example, the component you want to protect such as a disk array controller may still be a shared single point of failure in a cluster.

- **Components delivering high levels of performance for several thousand users may not work in clusters.** Because of the way MSCS was developed (disk subsystems driven by dual-initiator SCSI controllers) many high-end disk array controllers, as well as other advanced devices, may not be supported.

Clusters do have an advantage over stand-alone systems in their ability to minimize planned downtime by failing over to the standby node to carry out maintenance work on the primary node.

Deploying large Exchange 5.5 servers also includes developing a disaster and recovery plan. The next book in this series, *Managing and Maintaining Microsoft Exchange 5.5,* covers details on this. For those (hopefully few) recovery situations that require restoring an information store from tape (or other media), make sure you know how long the restore operation will take and that the procedure has been tested.

Backup and Restore Performance

Although some vendors offer specialized hardware backup solutions, this section discusses a traditional backup technique using mainstream controllers and devices. Unless your organization has specific reasons or requirements, there seems little cause to abandon the many benefits of staying with commodity hardware. If you do need a specialized solution, such as disk mirroring, for very large servers, consider these potential issues:

- Some solutions involve, even if only briefly, stopping Exchange services to take an offline copy of the information store database. This requires managing regular interruptions to the service.

- Offline backup copies only disk sectors. The Exchange online backup involves reading all database pages through an API and examining the checksum on each page for corruption not picked up by other methods. Regardless of the backup and recovery design implemented, perform online backups regularly.

Standard solutions can offer impressive performance, but before throwing a lot of effort into investigating specialized hardware solutions consider:

- Performance enhancing options of "standard" solutions such as support for tape RAID.

- Focusing on restore scenarios because restore performance is more important than backup performance.

The "fast" backup device on today's high-end servers is the DLT 35/70. Achieving good backup speeds depends on balancing the throughput of the reading device with the throughput of the writing device. The DLT 35/70 can read several standard 7,200-rpm disks in parallel while writing to a single DLT 35/70 disk at full speed. And this is fortunate given that a disk partition spreads over several disks, supporting a large information store database.

If a disk partition spreads over more than (for example) seven disks, you can achieve even faster backup speeds by writing to several DLT drives in parallel. This requires backup software with this capability, such as RAIT options for tape devices—the ability to combine several tape drives into a single logical partition similar to a disk RAID partition. MCS has worked with organizations that have achieved 30-GB/hour backup rates from seven disks to a single DLT 35/70 (using ARCserve) and 40-GB/hour backup rates from 13 disks to an array of four DLT 35/70s configured as a RAID5 set (also using ARCserve).

Unfortunately, restore rates are not as impressive as backup rates. Most disk array controllers are not optimized for bulk restore, and writing RAID5 parity data to disks reduces restore speeds. The same configurations that achieved 30- and 40-GB/hour backup speeds can only manage restore speeds of 16 and 20 GB/hour, respectively. You can expect better performance without the RAID5 overhead, but this discussion has focused on RAID5 subsystems as they are almost universally implemented for Exchange database partitions. Test and document restore rates for your servers, planning for the total time to restore the Exchange databases and how large to grow the stores.

C H A P T E R   9

Exchange Inter-Organization Directory Synchronization Planning

As organizations merge, reorganize, and expand, their messaging systems must be restructured. Depending on how many sites, business units, and servers are involved, a Microsoft Exchange Server might have to be added, removed from one unit, incorporated in another, and so on. Many organizations have found it difficult to change their messaging topology without forcing the administrator to re-create the Exchange server in a new location. This process can result in lost messages.

This chapter describes two tools for implementing inter-organizational directory synchronization for Exchange and provides guidelines for selecting the right tool and planning the synchronization. These are:

- **InterOrg Synchronization Tool**, developed by Microsoft Consulting Services (MCS) in Atlanta and now available in the *Microsoft BackOffice Resource Kit, Second Edition.*
- **LinkAge Directory Exchange (LDE)**, developed by LinkAge Software, Inc. (which was acquired by Microsoft in June of 1997), and available through MCS.

Note Inter-organizational directory synchronization is a complex process and should be undertaken only by certified Exchange specialists. In addition, both tools discussed in this document are provided separately and with limited or no support.

Selecting a Synchronization Method

InterOrg and LDE each have unique advantages that make them more effective in certain situations. This section describes the pros and cons of each tool and provides criteria for selecting tools.

InterOrg Synchronization Tool

The InterOrg Synchronization Tool uses a central Jet database to store all directory updates received from each organization (typically via one bridgehead server from each organization). Each bridgehead server sends its updates to the master. After those are processed, the master sends back the latest update of the master directory. This solution uses SMTP as the transport mechanism between bridgehead servers. This solution requires Microsoft Exchange Server version 5.0 with SP1 or later and Microsoft Windows NT 4.0 with SP3.

One bridgehead server is identified as the *master* and all other *requestor* bridgehead servers must be registered with the master to be validated for sending and receiving directory updates. To send and receive the directory messages (because the tool uses a message-based transport), each bridgehead server must be configured with a master and a requestor mailbox.

The master server has two primary functions. It must have sufficient disk space to host the Microsoft Access-compatible Jet database to send/receive updates, and it must keep a list to validate the identity of the different requestors involved. (Details on size limitations are below.) This server must also be a requestor or its own Exchange directory will not receive the Inter-Organizational directory updates.

Note The InterOrg Synchronization Tool is part of the *BackOffice Resource Kit* and not supported by Microsoft's Premier Support Services (PSS) at this time.

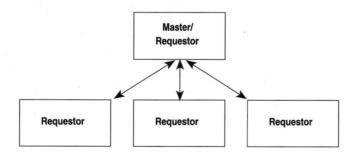

Pros

- It uses SMTP as the transport mechanism for directory update messages, so any asynchronous connection can be used between organizations including dial-up.
- Simple to implement.

- Requires simple routine administration.
- Supports both full reloads and updates only of the inter-organizational directory.
- Included as part of the *BackOffice Resource Kit*.
- Can export from/import to specified recipient containers.
- Can use Exchange trust levels to determine which recipients are exported from a specified container.
- An administrator can append additional information to the user's display name to make it easier to identify the various users from multiple companies.

Cons

- Routine maintenance of the master and requestor mailboxes is required (archiving, deleting, etc.).
- It will exchange only a predefined set of attributes; special or custom attributes are not supported.
- Synchronizing several large organizations could exceed the Jet database's maximum size of 1 gigabyte. However, the InterOrg Synchronization Tool was written to use ODBC drivers and therefore can be configured to use SQL Server and bypass the 1-gigabyte limitation.
- Updates are scheduled only once a day, so multiple organizations will be out of synchronization for up to 24 hours until the next scheduled update.
- It has minimal tracking abilities to determine the success or failure of an update.
- Microsoft does not provide direct support for it.

LinkAge Directory Exchange (LDE)

LDE is an inter-system directory synchronization solution from LinkAge Software that requires Exchange Server. Current supported versions of Exchange are 4.0, 5.0, and 5.5. It is comprised of three main components:

- A directory exchange manager (DXM)
- Various directory exchange agents (DXAs)
- A GUI administrator interface (LinkAge Administrator)

In addition, a transport mechanism (connector) is often required to communicate with foreign mail systems and other organizations running Exchange.

At this time, LDE is not an official product and is only available to trained MCS consultants and designated partners. The length of time needed by consultants to implement LDE varies between 5 to 20 days depending on the complexity of the environment. If after reading this document LDE seems like the appropriate solution, you can engage the services of your local MCS practice or contact the Exchange Connectivity Competency Center (EC3).

Note The LDE Tool is not supported by Microsoft's Premier Support Services (PSS).

DXM

The DXM is based on an SQL Server database to house a multimail system directory (a "meta-directory"). The DXM provides the following:

- Data warehousing for all directory entries from each participating mail system.
- Centralized monitoring and management of the DXAs activities.
- Creation of mapping rules between directories.
- Setting of synchronization schedules.

DXA

Each type of mail system requires its own DXA, which reports changes to its own directory and applies updates from the master directory. DXAs are available for Lotus Notes, Microsoft Exchange, and PROFS. Other mail system use a Universal DXA (UDXA), which employs a flat file system imported from or exported to the foreign mail system. In the case of Exchange, the DXA runs on a designated bridgehead server of the Microsoft Exchange server of the organization it will synchronize.

LDE Synchronization

Inter-organizational synchronization is accomplished with LDE by employing a single DXM and an Exchange DXA for each organization. Typically, EC3 recommends a directory synchronization bridgehead server for each organization and one server to host the DXM.

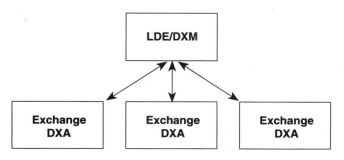

Transport Mechanisms

LDE uses message interchange format (MIF) files to communicate directory updates between the DXM and the DXA. For these MIF files to be sent between the DXA and the directory exchange manager, a transport mechanism is required. The transport mechanism between Exchange organizations can be configured as needed, including these configurations:

- **SMTP**—Update messages are sent using Internet Mail Service Connectors using the SMTP protocol.
- **X.400**—Update messages are sent using X.400 Connectors using the X.400 protocol.
- **LAN/WAN connection (shared file access)** —Requires rerouting of messaging queues for LDE.

Queue Routing

In addition to a transport mechanism, the routing of the messaging queues is very important. The LDE solution takes advantage of the SNADS connector's properties to bundle the MIFs for transport across an SMTP or X.400 connection.

Pros

- It can synchronize several directory types even if they are of the same type, such as multiple Exchange organizations, and can synchronize only selected attributes between organizations, including custom attributes defined at either organization.
- The association between directory types can be customized.
- Scheduling of updates is configurable.
- Delivery and receipt of updates can be scheduled as separate events.
- Update tracking is simplified using logged activities.
- The only routine maintenance is the archiving of logs if desired.
- It includes multiple transport choices (such as LAN, SMTP, and X.400).

Cons

- It is more difficult to install/configure.
- It has higher resource requirements because of the prerequisite of Microsoft SQL Server.
- Because of the robust nature of mapping rules, more thought must be given to how the different directories will map to each other.

Synchronization Tool Recommendations

The following table lists scenarios and recommended tools.

If ...	Select ...	Because ...
Organizations are small and SMTP is available between them	InterOrg	Simple to install and can handle the job well.
Budget is an issue and SMTP is available between organizations	InterOrg	Will not take many service hours to implement.
No LDE trained consultant is available and SMTP is available between organizations	InterOrg	Premier will not support LDE if a trained installer did not install it.
Total number of seats involved is less than 5,000 and SMTP is available between organizations	InterOrg	LDE is provided by EC3 to limited customers.
Full PSS support is required for solution	LDE	InterOrg is not supported.
Nonstandard attributes or custom attributes must be propagated	LDE	InterOrg only supports a subset of the attributes in Exchange.
Synchronization must be up to date every day or more frequently	LDE	InterOrg will lag roughly 24 hours.
At least one organization cannot install an Exchange version newer than 4.0	LDE	InterOrg is not supported on Exchange Server 4.0.
SMTP traffic between organizations is not possible, but there is LAN shared file access or X.400 Connector can be used	LDE	InterOrg requires SMTP as the transport since because it only propagates SMTP addresses as the TA (Target-Address attribute) for custom recipients.
There are groups of users who should not be propagated and are not within a particular container	LDE	Supports filtering of addresses.
Additional address proxies are required (for example: Notes)	LDE	InterOrg does not propagate addresses other than SMTP.

Planning/Data Collection

A thorough understanding of the requirements and the environment is necessary to synchronize two or more Exchange servers successfully. The following tables will assist you to collect the necessary information.

Network Connectivity

Questions	Expected answers	Significance
What LAN wiring topologies are used within each organization?	Token Ring, Ethernet	Needed to plan NIC for bridgehead server in each organization.
What are the current and/or planned LAN/WAN connections between the organizations?	X.25, Frame Relay, ISDN, packet switching, ATM, fiber optics, dial-up	Required to determine which routing mechanisms can be used.
Which network protocols are used in each organization?	TCP/IP, NetBEUI, IPX/SPX, DLC	Required to determine which routing mechanisms can be used.
Is there currently SMTP traffic being sent in each organization between Exchange and the Internet?	Yes, no	Required to determine which routing mechanisms can be used. Needed to choose a solution.
If SMTP traffic, what solutions are being used for DNS and firewalls, and where are they located?	DNS: hosts file, Microsoft DNS, proxy server, third party Firewall: third-party name Location: Local, hosted at ISP	Required to plan changes needed for added components and servers.
What are the domain names in each organization, and in which ones will the bridgehead servers reside?	Windows NT Server domain names	Required to plan Machine Names for bridgehead servers.
Is there currently or is there planned LAN shared file access between organizations?	Yes, no	Required to determine routing mechanisms that can be used for LDE.
If yes to LAN shared file access, are any domain trust relationships established and what is their nature?	Yes, no None, one- or two-way trust	Required for service account authentication and to determine which trusts need to be set up.
If yes to LAN shared file access, can an Exchange bridgehead server for each organization be put on a shared LAN segment?	Yes, no	Required to determine routing mechanisms that can be used for LDE.
What version of Windows NT is in place and which service packs?	Windows NT 3.1 (not supported by either product), Windows NT 3.51 (SP1-SP5), Windows NT 4.0 (SP1-SP3)	The InterOrg Synchronization Tool requires Windows NT 4.0 SP3, while LDE will function on Windows NT 3.51 SP5.
What is the preferred transport mechanism if LAN shared file access cannot be used?	SMTP or X.400	Required to determine routing mechanisms that can be used for LDE or the InterOrg Synchronization Tool. The InterOrg Synchronization Tool supports only SMTP addressing.

Business Units Involved

Questions	Expected Answers	Significance
What is the nature of the relationship between the business units?	Amalgamation, acquisition, joint venture, etc.	Amalgamations and acquisitions may typically require a full directory synchronization; a joint venture may typically require only that select groups be synchronized.
Where are the business units (that are being synchronized) located?	Cities, states, countries	Required to plan implementation and budget.
What is the accessibility of these locations?	High security; no business hours access to production	May assist in determining timelines and implementation planning.
Are there multinational locations, or languages other than English required?	Yes, no If yes, which languages?	May want to add test cases to reflect different time zone and language issues. May require update scheduling planning for different time zones.
Is there complete buy-in from the groups representing each organization?	N/A	Often one or more of the organizations may not be co-operating wholeheartedly, which is best to know up front.

Exchange Architectures Within Each Business Unit

Questions	Expected answers	Significance
What is the number of sites and servers?	N/A	Required for capacity planning and bridgehead server location planning.
How is Exchange administration currently handled within each organization?	Centralized, distributed	Required to determine who will be responsible for the implemented solution at each.
What versions of Exchange are currently being used?	4.0, 5.0, 5.5, and applicable service packs	Needed for compatibility issues (InterOrg not tested on 4.0).
What client versions are being used?	Exchange (DOS, 16 bit, 32 bit) Outlook (97, 98, Express)	Required to be able to set expectations of information that can be shared between organizations.
What routing issues are there between sites currently?	Internet Mail Service in use, for example	Required for setup planning of either solution. If there is an Internet Mail Service, will the same one be used or will another one be setup? Care must be taken that no unintended traffic is sent to a new Internet Mail Service.

Questions	Expected answers	Significance
Currently, what is the structure of the recipients container in each organization?	Single, multiple, nested	Required to determine the repositories for the custom recipients being added.
How are the various GALs organized and is this one company with multiple Exchange organizations or multiple companies with multiple organizations?	Type and format of user information entered, for example: Display name generation <Last Name, First Name Initial> for John R Smith Example: Smith, John R	A single company with multiple organizations may prefer to standardize on how the user information is entered for consistency. If this is not possible or multiple organizations are involved, manipulate the user information between directories so the data conforms to each organization's requirements, such as the mapping rules capability of LDE.
How many directory entries must be synchronized from each organization?	N/A	Required for capacity and replication planning as well as determining hardware requirements of bridgehead servers.

Foreign Mail Systems

Questions	Expected answers	Significance
Is there currently connectivity to other foreign mail environments throughout any of the business units?	N/A	Consider if any of these foreign environments can be targeted for a migration to Exchange and plan accordingly.
Are any connectors being used, and if so, which ones and at which sites/servers?	cc:Mail, Notes, SNADS, PROFS, MS Mail (PC), third party	Will their associated mail environments be participating in the synchronization?
What addressing proxies are currently being used in each organization?	Microsoft Exchange, MS Mail (PC), cc:Mail, Notes, X.400, SMTP, SNADS, PROFS, etc.	Do these need to be propagated and used?
What will be the interoperability requirements between the foreign mail environments and the inter-organizational environment?	For example, does the Notes community in one organization that talks to Exchange need to be able to talk to the "foreign" organization?	This will require some planning around the propagation of target addresses and how they are resolved.
What is the current network connectivity for the foreign mail system?	SMTP, natural connectors (such as Connector for cc:Mail), third-party solutions	If foreign mail systems are involved, can the current solutions be used or will they require upgrading/replacement?
Are there any plans to replace any of the foreign mail system?	N/A	LDE was designed to handle multiple mail environments and may assist in these other directories as well.

Inter-Organizational Requirements

Questions	Expected answers	Significance
Which business units need to synchronize with whom?	N/A	Required for planning and determining project scope.
Do business units cooperate well?	N/A	Required for approving recommendations for bridgehead server deployment and recipient container organization.
What are the centralized versus distributed management requirements?	Business units responsible for administering the solution in each organization	Required to develop contacts and to plan training of all necessary people.
What is the desired synchronization schedule?	Daily, weekly, etc.	Required to plan solution and to choose between LDE and InterOrg Synchronization Tool.

Technical and Business Contact List

Questions	Expected answers	Significance
Is there a list of all the technical, business, and project manager contacts?	Network administrator, mail administrator, Microsoft Exchange administrators, etc.	Required to organize the team and plan the synchronization.

The Basics of the InterOrg Synchronization Tool

This section provides a synopsis of the steps to analyze InterOrg and its performance.

Basic Installation Information

The first step is to setup two mailboxes (a master and a requestor) on all bridgehead servers involved in the directory synchronization. This process communicates via SMTP, so Internet Mail Service Connectors must be installed in each organization to allow SMTP traffic to flow between servers. Be sure to confirm that SMTP messages can flow between the organizations.

The next step is to run the installation program, which will install the initial InterOrg add-in and allow you to configure the Exchange server as either a master/requestor or simply a requestor. Configuring the InterOrg add-in will create additional add-ins, one for a master and one for a requestor, in the form of property pages that are used to configure both these components and directory synchronization. The master property page principally consists of a validation list of participating requestors. Most of the directory synchronization configuration occurs on the requestor property pages.

The requestor agent can export multiple containers, and it's necessary to specify each of the containers individually. For example, a container must be selected from each site in an Exchange organization with multiple sites. The next step is to select the type of contents within each container that will be exported, including mailboxes, distribution lists, and custom recipients.

Important Issues

The following InterOrg components and issues require special attention.

Master/Requestor Mailboxes

Both the requestor and master mailboxes send and receive the directory synchronization messages and require regular maintenance. Export information is copied to the *sent* container and import information is removed from the Inbox to the *deleted* container. Periodically, archive and delete these messages because they can become quite numerous, particularly after a full reload.

USN

An Update Sequence Number (USN) is assigned to each entry received by the master, which processes updates that have an USN greater than the stored one. By default, only deltas to the directories are sent and processed. If a full reload is needed for a particular organization, you must reset that requestor's USN number manually in the property page of the requestor. The options available are to reset the *export USN* to send a full reload or to reset the *import USN* to receive a full reload.

Jet Database

InterOrg relies on the ODBC Jet drivers and is subject to any limitations of an Access database. Other databases used by InterOrg are located in the directory synchronization folder on the master server, which stores the multi-organizational global address list (GAL) in .MDB format. The InterOrg Synchronization Tool can be reconfigured to use SQL Server instead to remove the 1-gigabyte limitation.

Update Scheduling

Updates occur every 24 hours so an initial requestor will be out of synchronization for 24 hours when the master receives or sends back any updates.

SMTP Messaging Structure

InterOrg's reliance on SMTP for the exchange of directory synchronization messages makes it an excellent solution for organizations that do not have a dedicated WAN link or much bandwidth. It also can be implemented using dial-up links, with the caveat that slow links may prohibit large messages or full reloads to GALs.

Configurable Parameters

- Recipient containers to export
- Which objects to export from the selected recipients containers
- Reset the import USN (request a full reload)
- Reset the export USN (send a full reload)
- The size of directory synchronization messages to send
- Recipients container to import into
- Which domains to import (you can hide some organizations from a particular location)
- Which time you want to synchronize at (set locally at each requestor server)
- Which days of the week you want to synchronize at
- Requesting Immediate synchronization

Benchmarks

A GAL of 35,000 entries was tested with full reloads and updates on two test organizations without problems. Internet Mail Service and the necessary mailboxes were set up in both machines. The two organizations were:

- *Orange* acted as the master/requestor on a Pentium 166 MMX with 80-MB RAM and a 2-GB disk
- *Apple* was a requestor on a Pentium Pro 200 with 64-MB RAM and two 2-GB disks

The tests started with both machines having an initial load of 10 addresses on each to establish basic directory synchronization. The full load was with the 35,000-entry directory with the following fields: last name, alias name, display name, and e-mail addresses. The update load used the same directory to test 100 deletions, 10 additions, and 11 deltas.

The tests did not check SMTP transfer times because this depends on the network connection and bandwidth or the time for *Apple* to import the 35,000-entry .CSV file. The results are summarized below.

Load type	Event description	Duration (minutes)
Full	*Apple* requestor activated and message sent to *Orange* master.	29:48
Full	*Orange* master receives and processes inbound message from *Apple* requestor.	21:32
Full	*Orange* requestor activated and request sent to *Orange* master; response received from *Orange* master and processed.	35:12
Full	Total time for full reload. not including SMTP travel time.	86:12
Update	*Apple* requestor activated and message sent to *Orange* master.	00:23
Update	*Orange* master receives and processes inbound message from *Apple* requestor.	04:21
	Orange requestor activated and request sent to *Orange* master, response received from *Orange* master and processed.	01:07
Update	Time for Update – Not including SMTP travel time.	05:51

Frequently Asked Questions

Question   Can the schedule be adjusted to make directory synchronization happen every couple of hours?

Answer   No. There is only one schedule time. You can select which days of the week you would like to directory synchronization on, but there is only one field for time that will apply to all selected days.

Question   Does it send deltas or full reloads?

Answer   Both. The Update Sequence Number (USN) assigned to every change provides the information needed for the default delta updates. Resetting the USN (in the property pages) makes full reloads possible.

Question   Is there any way to capture the data as it is sent from one server to another?

Answer   Yes. The Jet database stores update messages, which are sent to and from master and requestor mailboxes. All outbound mail is copied to the sent mail on the sending side, and all incoming mail ends up in the deleted container. Regular maintenance of InterOrg entails emptying these containers, which is especially important after a full reload of a large GAL.

Question   What are the best uses of InterOrg?

Answer   InterOrg uses SMTP (Internet Mail Service) to send messages from one organization to another, making network connectivity more or less irrelevant. In addition, InterOrg is easier to install.

The Basics of LDE

Two services installed by LDE (LinkAge Controller service and LinkAge Directory Exchange service) can coexist on one bridgehead server. Both the Microsoft Exchange Connectivity Controller service and the connector-specific service are added when Microsoft Connectors (Notes, SNADS, or PROFS) are installed.

Note When using Exchange 5.5, the LinkAge Controller service interferes with the Connectivity Controller. Because the LinkAge Directory Exchange service depends on the LinkAge Controller service, registry changes must be made to allow the LinkAge Directory Exchange service to remove the need for the LinkAge Controller service. For more information, please contact MCS.

To illustrate how LDE works, the following scenario outlines three organizations that must be synchronized. All machines mentioned below should be running:

- Windows NT Server 4.0 with Service Pack 3 and networking configured with DNS or hosts file

- Microsoft Exchange 5.5 (the LDE box can be an earlier version) with either Internet Mail Service or X.400 configured, unless in a LAN/WAN shared-file-capable network

- SQL Server 6.5 with Service Pack 3 on DXM box only

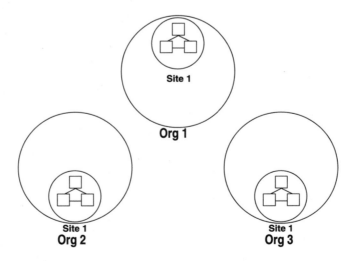

Directory Exchange Manager Server (DXM)

The first step is to create a Directory Exchange Manager Server (DXM) for these organizations. The DXM is comprised of one Exchange 5.5 Server running the LDE DXM and providing the necessary queue routing and inter-organizational connectivity (either SMTP via an Internet Mail Service or X.400 via an X.400 Connector). It can be installed in one of the existing organizations or in its own organization, depending on where the administrative group is located.

If you install DXM in an existing organization, it is a wise practice to place it in its own site to avoid routing conflicts with other Internet Mail Service or X.400 implementations. By putting DXM in its own site, you also can control replication of inter-organizational directory information to the local organization using the Directory Replicator Connector, provided the Site Connector is not used.

Either way, you will have one of the following configurations:

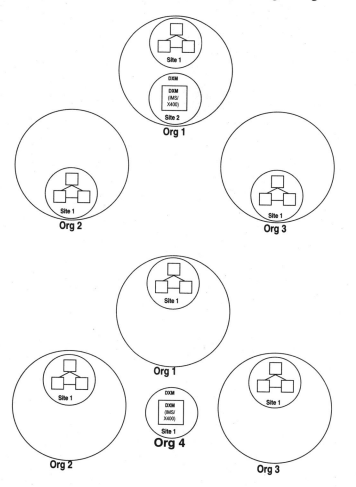

Directory Synchronization Bridgehead Server (DXA)

After the DXM Server is in place, each organization participating in the synchronization will require a Directory Synchronization Bridgehead (DXA) server (DXA). The DXA server requires Microsoft Exchange 5.5 for routing and the LDE Directory Exchange Agent (DXA). The DXA server is considered to be remote to the DXM unless you choose to install the DXM into an existing organization, in which case you don't need to install a separate DXA server. In this scenario, the DXM will have a DXA running on it that will not require the remote configuration because it will use LAN/WAN shared file access to exchange messages with the Exchange directory.

Depending on the placement of the DXM server, the entire topology will reflect one of the following architectures:

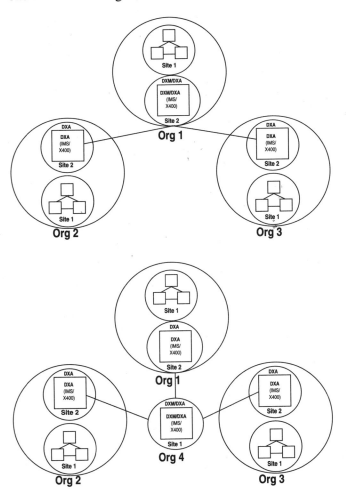

Understanding Routing and the Queues

This section provides an overview of routing by describing how MIF (message interchange format) files are processed.

DXM Server to DXA Server

The MIF passes through several queues before reaching its destination. First, it goes to the LSI2GML queue and undergoes the LSI2GML transformation. After that, the MIF gets placed into DIA2MEX.in queue. From there, the SNADS Connector detects the MIF and reads the message into Exchange, where the connector will do an address resolution and detect the SMTP address for the DXA.

The MIF then travels through the SMTP to the remote Internet Mail Service, where address resolution occurs again and Exchange detects the SNADS address for the DXA. After in the SNADS Connector, the ROUTE.TBL routes any messages for ORG.DXAMEX to the GML2LSI.in queue where it undergoes the GML2LSI transformation. After processing, the GML2LSI process places the MIF into the DXAMEX.in, where it is detected by the DXA.

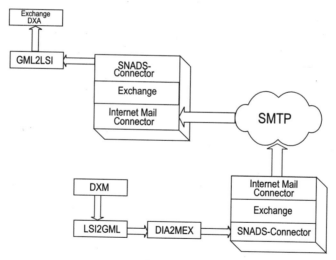

DXA Server to DXM Server

On the return trip to the DXM, the MIF follows a slightly different path. First, the MIF is deposited into the LSI2GML.in queue and undergoes LSI2GML transformation. From there, LSI2GML places the MIF into the DIA2MEX.in queue for the SNADS Connector to pick up and handle address resolution. After detecting the SMTP address for the DXM, the connector sends the message to the local Exchange box using SMTP, where address resolution occurs again. The message is routed back to the SNADS Connector and routed on to GML2LSI, where it undergoes the GML2LSI transformation. Finally, it is placed into the DXM.in queue, where the DXM detects it.

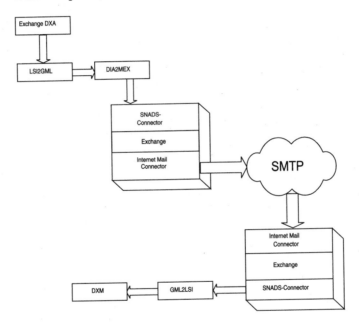

C H A P T E R   1 0

Lotus Notes

This chapter helps you install and operate the Microsoft Exchange Connector for Lotus Notes (Connector for Notes). It begins with an overview of the connector, including information on hardware and software prerequisites. It describes how Exchange and the Lotus Notes environments interact, provides information on the connector's internal queues and processes, and walks through installation and configuration (for connectivity), then discusses advanced configuration topics such as directory synchronization, mapping rules, and filter rules. It concludes with several labs on troubleshooting scenarios and common problems.

To get the most from it, you should thoroughly understand Exchange and its internal message flow and have access to the Exchange 5.5 CD-ROM documentation. A basic understanding of Notes helps, but is not required.

Microsoft Exchange Connector for Lotus Notes

Overview

The Exchange Connector for Lotus Notes provides message delivery and directory synchronization between Microsoft Exchange and Lotus Notes. It provides:

- Rich text format messaging between Notes and Exchange Server users with minimal loss of fidelity.
- File object transfer (video, graphics, word processing documents, and spreadsheets) between the two systems, with file name, icon, and launch capability preserved.
- Support for OLE attachments.
- Support for Lotus Notes Document Links (doclinks).
- Directory synchronization between Notes and Exchange Server.

- The Microsoft Exchange Connectivity Administrator, with which you can monitor processes and view connector activity logs.

- The Notes Configuration Utility, which automatically sets permissions, creates database files required by the connector, and updates several Notes settings.

- Conversion of mail objects such as attachments and Notes doclinks.

In a standard configuration, the connector runs as a service on a single Exchange Server computer. It uses a Notes client on the Exchange Server computer to establish a network connection to a single Lotus Notes/Domino server. The Exchange Server computer on which the connector is installed and the Notes server computer with which the connector communicates are called *bridgehead servers*. The connector can also connect downstream Exchange Server sites with Notes domains.

You can administer the connector from the server running the connector or from a remote Windows NT Server or Windows NT Workstation computer. You can administer the connector locally or remotely using the Exchange Server Administrator program or the Exchange Connectivity Administrator. For example, you can install the Connectivity Administrator program on a computer other than the one the connector is installed on to monitor connector processes or log connector status information.

Both the Exchange Server Administrator program and the Exchange Connectivity Administrator can be installed on a Windows NT Server or Windows NT Workstation computer.

Hardware Requirements

The connector requires the same hardware as Exchange Server. For specifics, see *Microsoft Exchange Server Getting Started*.

Note You can use Digital Alpha computers to run Exchange and to send and receive messages through the connector, but this version of the connector runs on Intel only.

It is recommended that you run the connector on a computer separate from the Exchange Server computer that supports production end-user mailboxes. To do this, you need at least a Pentium computer with a 1-GB hard drive and 32-MB RAM. If you run it on the same computer, you need a minimum of 64-MB RAM and 1 GB (for the connector software and data files) plus the space required for Exchange Server requirement (including space for mailboxes and other message transfer agents).

Software Requirements

The connector requires the same software as Exchange Server 5.5 (see *Microsoft Exchange Server Getting Started* for details) plus:

- Lotus Notes Client for Windows NT, release 4.52
- A network connection to a Lotus Notes version 3.*x*, 4.*x*, or Lotus Notes/Domino Server version 4.5*x*

For information on establishing a LAN-based, client/server connection for Lotus Notes and a list of network connections, see the *Lotus Notes Release 4 Network Connection Guide*.

Note Do not run Lotus Notes clients or other OLE-enabled application software on the same computer as the connector while the connector is running: it interferes with the connector's OLE processing.

The Connectivity Administrator can run on the same Windows NT Server as the connector, or on any LAN-connected Windows NT Server or Windows NT Workstation.

User Account Permission Requirements

The Windows NT user account requires specific permissions to install, administer, and run the connector:

- To install, upgrade, and remove the connector, you must be a Windows NT administrator and an Exchange Server service account administrator on the server running the connector.
- To administer the connector, the Windows NT user account requires Read and Write access to the CONNECT$ share created during Exchange Server Setup.
- To start and stop the connector service, you must be a Windows NT administrator on the server running the connector.
- To view and control the connector processes running on either a local or remote Windows NT Server, the Windows NT user account that the Connectivity Administrator runs under must have permission to start and stop services on the server running the connector.

Connection of Downstream Sites with Lotus Notes Domains

You can place several Exchange Server computers at the same site as (or downstream from) the server running the connector. A Lotus Notes network can have many Lotus Notes/Domino servers within the same domain as, or downstream from, the bridgehead server.

For the connector to route Lotus Notes messages to users at downstream Exchange Server sites, you must install the Lotus Notes E-mail Address Generator on a Exchange Server computer at each downstream site. To enable the connector to route Exchange Server messages to Notes domains that are not directly connected to the server running the connector, you must identify those domains using the Exchange Server Administrator program.

Connector Performance

Performance planning for Exchange Server is a trade-off between serving local users and processing traffic through connectors. One approach is to establish one Exchange Server computer for all connectors and another one (or more) for hosting mailboxes. Or you can run connectors on dedicated computers connected over the LAN to a hub Exchange Server computer, which can also support mailboxes. Don't install the connector on the Exchange Server computer that supports end-user mailboxes.

Directory Synchronization with Multiple Lotus Notes/Domino Servers

You must periodically synchronize the Exchange Server and Notes directories to ensure messages are delivered successfully in each environment. If your Notes domain contains several servers, you can simplify the directory synchronization process.

When you configure the Lotus Notes/Domino bridgehead server, use NAMES.NSF (the Lotus Notes Name and Address Book) as the Target Name and Address Book. This ensures that Exchange Server addresses are replicated automatically to other Notes/Domino servers in the domain. Using NAMES.NSF as the Source Name and Address Book ensures that Notes addresses are replicated automatically to the Exchange Server directory. If you use another name for the Target Name and Address Book, you must create (or include) the Target Name and Address Book in the Master Address Book for the Lotus Notes domain or set up cascading Address Books. For more information, see the Lotus Notes documentation.

The Connector for Notes Messaging Architecture

The Role of Exchange

Exchange Server facilitates the connector's connectivity and functionality. Connector service requests are passed to the information store, which uses Exchange services such as the Message Transfer Agent (MTA) for distribution list expansion and resolution.

How the Connector Works with Lotus Notes

The connector also requires access to a Notes release 4 client. The connector interfaces with the Notes server as a Notes client and requires the services of certain Notes-client DLLs, as well as a NOTES.INI and ID file for Notes API calls. Unlike Exchange, Notes uses a single interface for both client and server administration. The Notes server administration is provided by an administrator ID created when the Notes server is installed. In a typical implementation of the connector, the Notes server and the connector reside on separate workstations. This requires that the Notes client interface be installed on the workstation hosting the connector.

Location of Notes Server

For production environments, it is **highly** recommended that the Notes server be on a separate server from the Exchange connector. For the self-study exercises in this chapter, however, you can configure the Notes server on the same machine as the connector. If you are running the Notes server, you should add the following line to the NOTES.INI file.

```
serverkeyfilename = server.id
```

If the Notes server and the connector are on the same machine, shut down the server before you install the connector. Setup Wizard's response time becomes **extremely** slow if the Notes server is running.

How the Connector Uses Notes Databases

In the Notes/data directory, every Notes server has a mailbox database (MAIL.BOX) with outbound, undelivered mail for local recipients. If a server cannot deliver the mail, Notes attempts to send a Delivery Failure Report to the sender indicating why the mail message could not be delivered. Messages from Exchange to Notes users are also placed into MAIL.BOX, and Notes Server delivers them.

For the connector to pass messages between Notes and Exchange, two additional databases must be created: **EXCHANGE.BOX** and **EXCHANGE.BAD**. Notes transforms mail destined for Exchange (or to other recipients served by Exchange) into Exchange format and stores it in EXCHANGE.BOX, until the connector can forward it. The connector places messages it cannot transform in EXCHANGE.BAD, its secondary mail file.

When you create these databases, use the EXCHANGE.BOX and EXCHANGE.BAD default names unless they conflict with other file names on the Notes server. If you use other names, you will have to supply them when you run the Configuration Utility or change them in the connector property pages under the routing tab.

Notes Permissions Required by the Connector

The connector requires *at least* **Depositor** (which is the default) access to MAIL.BOX. Depositor is usually sufficient because the connector only needs to deposit mail into MAIL.BOX.

The connector also requires *Manager* with *delete* permission access to EXCHANGE.BOX. This allows Notes messages sent with Notes OLE links to traverse the connector, and allows the connector to perform maintenance (deletions, etc.) on its queues.

When a Notes document link (doclink) is included in a message to an Exchange user, it can either be converted to a rich text (*.RTF) attachment sent as an OLE object, or for Lotus Notes Domino servers sent as an HTTP link. If a doclink is sent as an RTF attachment, the connector user ID must have at least **Reader** access to the document (and hence, the database) associated with the doclink. To grant the appropriate access to the connector, you can either add the user ID created for the connector to an appropriate Group in the Public Name and Address Book or update the ACL of each database directly.

If doclinks are converted to OLE objects, recipients must have a Notes client installed on their workstation to view the document and must have access to the database (or a replica) in which the document is stored.

Queues and Processes

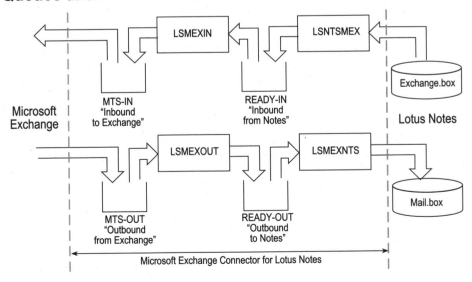

The Exchange-Notes Connector interacts with Exchange for message handling using the following MAPI queues and processes. These queues are created by the connector's Setup program and are maintained by Exchange.

For processing of inbound (to Exchange) messages:

- **MTS-IN** is an inbound queue, serviced by the **LSMEXIN** process. **MTS-IN** is the actual queue name in Exchange; however the queue will be shown in the Exchange queue viewer with the following friendly name "**Inbound to Exchange.**" This queue maintains information in Exchange native TNEF.

- The **READY-IN, "Inbound from Notes"** queue is serviced by the LSNTSMEX process. It queries the EXCHANGE.BOX database in which Notes stores foreign mail.

Notice in the diagram that the **LSNTSMEX** process queries EXCHANGE.BOX and transforms any mail into the **READY-IN** queue in Exchange format. The **LSMEXIN** process queries this queue and takes any mail into the **MTS-IN** queue, which is then ported into Exchange for processing.

For processing of outbound (from Exchange) messages:

- The **MTS-OUT, "Outbound from Exchange"** queue receives messages destined for Notes. The **LSMEXOUT** process queries this queue and translates any messages from TNEF and transports them into the **READY-OUT, "Outbound to Notes"** queue.

- The **LSMEXNTS** process is triggered by mail arriving in the **READY-OUT** queue. Messages within are transported into MAIL.BOX, the Notes Mail Router mailbox.

The **LSNTSMEX** and **LSMEXNTS** processes perform message transformation between Notes and Exchange and Exchange to Notes, respectively. **LSNTSMEX** resolves doclinks and polls EXCHANGE.BOX for Notes-to-Exchange messages.

LSMEXNTS is triggered by messages arriving in the **READY-OUT** queue. No polling is done. These messages are transported to MAIL.BOX for processing by Notes.

The **LSMEXIN** and **LSMEXOUT** processes are responsible for address translation, message tracking, statistics gathering.

Table 1. Message transformation between Notes and Exchange

Objects	From Notes to Exchange	From Exchange to Notes
Regular attachments	Icon positioned as in originating message: no change.	Icon positioned as in originating message: no change.
Notes Documents Links (Doclinks)	You can configure three options:	RTF attachments are preserved across connector.
	Converted to a rich text format regular attachment with the icon positioned as it was in the originating message. The rich text format attachment is preserved.	OLE Notes links are translated back to Notes Doclinks. (The Notes client is needed to open the Notes OLE links.)
	Sent as an OLE Lotus Notes link. The recipient user ID used must have Reader access to the document associated with the doclink and must have access to a Lotus Notes 4.52 client.	
	Sent as a Web hyperlink. This causes links to Lotus Notes documents, views, and databases to be converted to an icon representing a Uniform Resource Locator (URL) in the Exchange Server message. This is valid only for Notes/Domino servers. The recipient user must have appropriate access rights.	
Exchange message attachment	N/A	Converted to an *.RTF regular attachment with the icon positioned as it was in the originating message. Embedded messages (multilayered messages) and attachments within embedded messages are not supported.
Exchange message links	N/A	Converted to OLE object with the icon positioned as it was in the originating message.
OLE	Converted to OLE object, with icon, positioned as in originating message.	Converted to OLE object, with icon, positioned as in originating message.

Installation Outline

▶ **To install the Exchange Connector for Lotus Notes**

1. Exchange Connector prerequisites.

2. Build the connector server.

3. Set up the Exchange Connector Notes ID/mailbox, with the appropriate permissions, in the Notes/Domino environment.

4. Set up the Notes client on the Exchange connector server.

5. Install the Connectivity Services.

6. Configure the Lotus Notes/Domino server with the Notes Configuration Utility.

7. Install and configure the Exchange Connector for Lotus Notes.

The next sections of this chapter each explain one part of the installation outline in detail. Dependencies require that the steps be done in this order.

Exchange Connector Prerequisites

- **Lotus Notes server**—The connector supports only Notes Server releases 3.x and 4.x.

- **Lotus Notes client**—A Lotus Notes client version 4.0 or higher must be installed on the Exchange connector server: without it, the connector won't function.

Note For Domino servers, version 4.52a or later of the Notes client is recommended.

- **Exchange Server 5.5, Enterprise Edition**—The connector ships with the Standard and Enterprise Editions of Exchange Server 5.5.

Build the Connector Server

Server recommendations:

- Make the Exchange connector server a dedicated server and host mailboxes on a separate Exchange server.
- Keep the Notes server separate from the Exchange connector server if Notes is hosted on Windows NT.

Configuration recommendations:

- Pentium 200 for a Notes-only connector server.
- Pentium Pro or higher for a multiple-connector server
- 64 MB of RAM or higher for a dedicated server
- Add 32 MB for each additional connector
- Windows NT Server version 4.0 with Service Pack 3 or higher installed

Set Up the Exchange Connector Notes ID/Mailbox

1. Open a Lotus Notes client with administrative permissions.

2. Start the Lotus/Domino Server Administration program by clicking **File > Tools > Server Administration.**

3. On the **Register People** menu, click **People**.

4. On the register person dialog, select **Yes** to confirm a license has been purchased.

5. Enter the administration password and click **OK**. The **Register Person** dialog box appears.

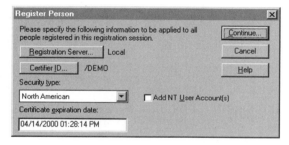

6. Select **North American** or **International** for the **Security type**.

7. Click **Continue.** The **Register person – Basics** dialog box should appear.

8. Type **NOTECON** or another descriptive name for the Notes connector in the **Last Name** field. **Do not** use forward slashes in this name.

9. Set the **minimum password length** to **0** and leave the **password** field **blank**. Removing password protection allows unattended operation of the connector and DXA when accessing its databases on the Notes server. **Note:** Microsoft Product Support only supports a blank password for the connector.

10. Select the license type of **Lotus Notes Desktop** for the connector.

11. Click the **Mail** icon.

> **Note**   Substitute your *Notes Server Name/Organization* combination where you see VEGA/Demo in these screen shots.

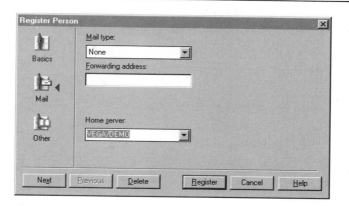

12. In the **Mail type** drop-down menu, select **None**.

13. In the **Home Server** drop-down menu select the Notes server where the connector's databases will be located.

14. Click **Other** to specify additional **Public Address Book** information.

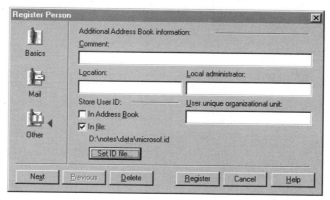

15. Verify the **In Address book** option is not selected because the password is set to blank.

16. Select the **In File** checkbox to generate the user ID.

17. Click **Set ID file** and name the file **NOTECON.ID** or another descriptive name. Make sure that you have a disk in drive A; otherwise, you'll get an error message.

18. Save this file to floppy or a network share for the Exchange connector Notes mail client to use this ID.

19. Click **Register**.

20. On the **File** menu, click **Close**.

21. Open the Public Address Book. On the **View** menu, click **People** and double-click on the **NOTECON** users. Click **Administration** and set the **Foreign Directory Synchronization** field to **No**.

22. **Save** the **Person** document.

23. Highlight the **Address book database.**

24. From the Lotus Notes Administrator, on the **File** menu, click **Database** and then click **Access Control**.

25. From the **Access Control List** window, click **Add**.

26. From the **Add user** window, type **NOTECON** or name of connector mailbox.

27. From the **Access** drop-down list, click **Manager** and select **Delete documents**.

28. In the **Roles** window, select every role.

29. Click **OK**.

30. On the **Start** menu, start the Lotus Domino Server by clicking **Programs** and clicking **Lotus Domino Server**.

Set Up the Notes Client on the Connector Server

You must install the Lotus Notes client on the Exchange connector server. Follow these steps:

1. Insert the floppy containing the NOTESCON.ID file or file name created in the previous section.

2. Run Install.

3. Select **Standard install**.

4. On the **Start** menu, click **Programs, Lotus Applications,** and then **Lotus Notes**.

5. Select **Network LAN connection** and select **Your Notes user ID has been supplied to you in a file**.

6. Click **OK**.

7. Click **OK** to copy file to local directory.

8. Type in the Home server name/org name.

9. Select **Time Zone**.

Install the Connectivity Services

First, Exchange Server 5.5, Enterprise Edition must be installed on the dedicated connector server. Then you can install the Exchange Connectivity Services for Lotus Notes. Follow these steps:

1. Insert the Exchange Server 5.5, Enterprise Edition CD-ROM.
2. Click **Setup Server and Components**.
3. Select the **Connector for Lotus Notes**.
4. Select the Microsoft Exchange Connector for Lotus Notes and Notes E-mail addressing component. Clear any OV/VM options and SNADS options if not used. Click **Next**.
5. Type in the appropriate Exchange service account and password: *domain\exchangesvc*. Click **Next**. It will default to the person you are logged in as, and this more than likely is not the Exchange service account.
6. Click **Yes** and then click **Next**.
7. Leave the Lotus Notes Domain Name as *Exchange*.
8. Exit Setup.

Configure the Lotus Notes/Domino Server

Gathering Configuration Information

The next step in preparing to use the Configuration Utility is to gather:

- Notes bridgehead server name
- Domain name to be used for the Exchange Mail system
- Location of the NOTES.INI file
- User ID which will configure Notes for the connector
- Source and target Name and Address Book
- Notes server registration

The Notes bridgehead server name is the name of the Notes server with which the Notes connector will communicate.

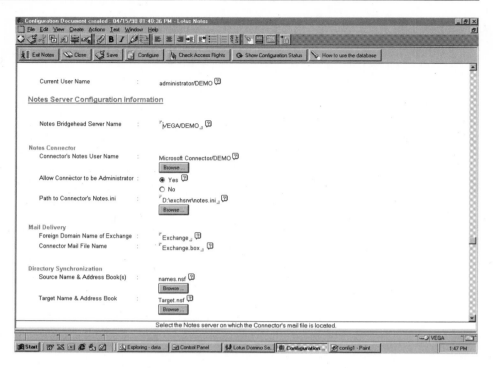

The next piece of information is the domain name (default *Exchange*) that is used to represent Exchange to the Notes users.

Make a copy of the NOTES.INI file and store it in the Exchange server directory. Edit the .INI file. Search for "keyfilename", and replace everything to the right of the equal sign with the path and name of the ID file that you created. Save the file.

Fourth, you need a Notes ID that has the appropriate permission to configure Notes. See the Permissions for the Configuration Utility section below for details on permission levels.

For directory synchronization, you need the source Name and Address book and a target Name and Address book. The source Name and Address book are your current Name and the Address book that contains the Notes users (default NAMES.NSF). It is common practice to create a target Name and Address book rather than using the existing NAMES.NSF to partition the Notes users from the Exchange users. The Configuration Utility will create a target Address book if this is the case. However, you can select an existing Name and Address book.

Finally, you must make sure that the Notes Server Name (if it is not the same as the workstation or server name) is registered in the DNS. If it isn't, you must add it to the local HOSTS file on the Exchange server (if using TCP/IP as the primary communications protocol).

Permissions for the Configuration Utility

When using the Configuration Utility, the ID that is used to configure Notes needs these permissions:

- **Manager access to MAIL.BOX**—If using the SERVER.ID file, you must assign the user manager access as a user and not a server.
- **Manager access to Source Name and Address Book**—The Configuration Utility will create an entry in the Name and Address Book for the connector.
- **The ability to create Databases on the Notes Server**—The Configuration Utility will create several databases for the connector.

What the Configuration Utility Does

The Configuration Utility creates and configures several items for the connector automatically. It:

1. Creates a deposit database for messages traveling from Notes to Exchange. Created from the mail router mailbox template, this by default is called EXCHANGE.BOX. There is no reason to change this name unless it conflicts with another database of the same name. **Note:** If the Notes Server is on a UNIX machine, upper/lowercase matters.

2. Creates a deposit database for storing bad or malformed messages that the connector cannot transfer. It is rarely used, but necessary. Created from the mail router mailbox template, this by default is called EXCHANGE.BAD. There is no reason to change this name unless it conflicts with another database of the same name.

   Note   If the Notes server is on a UNIX machine, upper/lowercase matters.

3. Gives editor rights with delete privileges to the databases created in steps 1 and 2.

4. Creates a foreign domain document in the source Name and Address Book. This foreign domain will represent Exchange. Also the mail router will use this document to move the mail into the deposit database for the connector to process.

5. Assigns the connector's ID file read permissions on the source Name and Address Book, to allow DirSync.

6. Assigns the connector's ID file manager rights to the target Name and Address Book.

7. Makes the connector's ID a part of the administrators group to perform maintenance on the databases created for message transfer.

Use the Notes Configuration Utility to set up the Notes/Domino server connectivity and directory synchronization.

1. From the **Start** menu, click **Programs, Microsoft Exchange Connectivity,** and **Notes Configuration Utility.**

2. Click **Yes** to Cross Certify.

3. On the **File** menu, click **Close.**

4. Click the **New Configuration Document** button.

   Configure the following fields on the Lotus Notes Configuration Utility document:

   Current User Name: NOTECON or other connector name/*<Lotus domain name>*

   Notes Server Configuration Information

   Notes Bridgehead Server Name: *<computer name>/<Lotus domain name>*

   Notes Connector

   Connector's Notes User Name: Click **Browse**, select the <domain name> Address Book and select the NOTECON or equivalent account. The account should be entered as NOTECON/<Lotus domain name>.

   Allow Connector to be Administrator: Select **Yes.**

   Path to Connector's notes.ini files: *<winnt path>*\NOTES.INI

   Mail Delivery

   Foreign Domain Name of Exchange: *Exchange*

   Connector Mail File Name: *EXCHANGE.BOX*

   Directory Synchronization

   Source Name & Address Book(s): Click **Browse** and select **NAMES.NSF** (this is the source address book sent to Exchange from Notes).

   Target Name & Address Book: Click **Browse** and select **Yes** to create a new address book target name. Type **EXCHANGE.NSF** (this is the source address book sent to Notes from Exchange. Be sure to add the .NSF extension). Or you can select an existing Name and Address Book.

5. On the Notes/Domino Server in the Administrators workspace, right-click on the *<Organization name>* Address Book and select **Access Control** and verify that NOTECON/*<organization name>* or the equivalent connector name has Manager permissions with deleted documents and all of the Roles are selected. Next, under the **Advanced** button, specify an Administration Server as *<bridgehead notes server>/<organization name>*.

6. Click the **Configure** button.

7. Click the **Save** button.

8. Click the **Close** button.

9. Restart the Notes server (more specifically, its router) Until you restart it, mail you send to the Exchange Domain from Notes is not delivered, and a non-delivery report (NDR) is returned saying no route was found to the foreign domain.

You can manually create the databases and set their permissions. See the Notes connector documentation (on the Exchange 5.5 CD-ROM under \DOCS\WORD_DOCS\CONNECTIVITY\NOTES) for the procedure.

Install and Configure the Connector

Before you install the connector:

You must add *<drive letter:>*\NOTES to the Windows NT search path for the connector services to start.

▶ **To change the path**

1. In **Control Panel,** click **System** and then click **Environment.**
2. Select the Path variable.
3. Add in: *;<drive letter:>*\NOTES to the existing path.
4. Search for multiple **NNOTES.DLL** files on the connector server. Remove any old copies and any residing in the *<winnt>*\system32 directory.
5. Reboot the Windows NT Exchange connector server. To expedite the reboot, stop the Exchange System Attendant service first.

▶ **To Install the Exchange Connector for Lotus Notes**

1. On the **Start** menu, click **Programs, Microsoft Exchange Connectivity,** and **Setup.**
2. Click **Next** on Configure Microsoft Exchange Connector.
3. Click **Next** on Microsoft Exchange Connector for Lotus Notes.
4. Click **OK** and slick **Exit Setup.**
5. Launch the Exchange Server Administration program.
6. Within the Exchange Administration program, select **Site.**
7. Click **Connections.**
8. Click **Connector for Lotus Notes.**
9. Configure the following tabs:

   Import Container—Specify the Recipients container or Lotus Notes specific container to import Lotus Notes Users.

   Export Container—Specify the containers to export to the Lotus Notes environment.

Options—Polling interval default is 15 seconds.

Dirsync Schedule—Check **Enable Directory Synchronization**.

Select the synchronization frequency.

10. Click **Apply** and then **OK**.

11. Stop and restart the Microsoft Exchange Connectivity Controller service.

12. Restart the Microsoft Exchange Connectivity Controller and Microsoft Exchange Lotus Notes Connector service.

13. On the **Start** menu, click **Programs, Exchange Connectivity**, and **Exchange Connectivity Administrator**.

14. At the **Select a server** dialog box, select **local** and click **logon**.

15. Click the **Process manager** button.

16. Verify all six services have started by the green icon next to each service:

   - Transfer to Exchange for Notes
   - Convert Exchange to Notes
   - Transfer from Exchange to Notes
   - Convert Notes to Exchange
   - DX Agent for Lotus Notes
   - DX Agent for Microsoft Exchange

17. In the Exchange Server Administrator, open the **Lotus Notes Connector** object.

18. Click the **Dirsync** tab.

19. Perform **Immediate Full Reload for Exchange to Notes** and **Immediate Full Reload for Notes to Exchange**.

20. Verify mail flows from Exchange to Notes and Notes to Exchange. Verify Notes addresses have propagated to Exchange and Exchange addresses have propagated to Lotus Notes.

Duplicating the NOTES.INI File

▶ **To make a duplicate NOTES.INI file (highly recommended)**

1. Copy the NOTES.INI file from the \winnt directory and put a copy in the \exchsrvr directory.

2. Use Notepad to open the NOTES.INI file in the \exchsrvr directory. Search for KeyfileName. Change this value to the NOTES.ID file created for the connector using the full path.

3. Go to the Advanced Property page of the Notes Connector in the Exchange Administrator. Change the NOTES.INI file here to point to the copy that you made in the \exchsrvr directory. Click **OK**.

4. Restart the Notes Connector service.

Customize the Connector

Configure Downstream Exchange Sites and Downstream Lotus Notes Domains

If you want a connector to route Lotus Notes messages to users at downstream Exchange server sites, you must install the **Lotus Notes E-mail Address Generator** on one Exchange server within each downstream site. When installing **Lotus Notes E-mail Address Generator** on a server in a downstream site, it is best to keep the foreign **domain name** the same as the upstream Exchange connector server foreign domain.

To enable the connector to route Microsoft Exchange server messages to Lotus Notes domains that are not directly connected to the server running the connector, you must identify those domains using the Exchange Administrator program.

▶ **To configure**

1. Identify the downstream Lotus Notes domains.

2. Open the Exchange Administrator Program.

3. On the **File** menu, click **Properties** and be sure that the **Connector for Lotus Notes** object is highlighted.

4. Select the **Routing** tab.

5. In the **Routable domains:** field, type the names of any downstream Lotus Notes domains. Use a comma to separate each domain name.

6. Restart the Microsoft Connector for Lotus Notes Service.

Change the Default Lotus Notes Address Format

Exchange organizational names and sites names may contain characters that are invalid in the Lotus Notes environment. You can modify the default Lotus Notes e-mail address naming rule to overcome this or to change its appearance within the Lotus Notes Address Book.

The default format for Lotus Notes e-mail address for Exchange recipients is:

&d/site/organization@domain name

Where:

- **&d** is the Lotus Notes display name of the user
- **site** is the user's Exchange Server site name
- **organization** is the user's Exchange server organization name
- **domain name** is the Lotus Notes foreign domain name created to represent the Exchange server organization

▶ **To change the address format**

1. Open the Exchange Server Administrator.
2. Open the site where the connector is installed and click **Configuration**.
3. Double-click **Site Addressing.**
4. Click the **Site Addressing** tab.
5. Click **Notes**, and then click **Edit**.
6. Type the new e-mail address format using the symbols in the table below

To substitute	Use this symbol	Notes
User's alias	&M or &m	the mailbox name
User's initials	&I or &I	middle initial
Display name	&D or &d	blanks are discarded.
User's given name	&G or &g	first name
User's surname	&S or &s	last name
& character	&&	& must be escaped with itself

7. Click **OK**. Click **Yes** to update existing Lotus Notes addresses.
8. Stop and restart the Microsoft Exchange Connector for Lotus Notes service.

Site Addressing Rule examples:

Substituting First Letter of the User's Given Name and Surname:

&g1&s/site/organization@domain name

Substituting a User's Display Name:

&d/site/organization@domain name

Doclinks

You can specify how Lotus Notes doclinks appear in messages bound for Exchange Server recipients. A doclink can be converted to an OLE object, and RTF attachment or, if you have a Domino server, a URL shortcut.

▶ **To change the format**

1. Click the **Advanced** tab with the Exchange Connector for Lotus Notes properties.

2. In the **Convert Notes Doclinks to** menu, select an option.

3. Click **OK**.

4. Restart the connector service.

Mapping Rules

Mapping rules allow the Exchange administrator to map attributes from one mail system to attributes in another mail system. For example, Full Name in Notes may be *First Name Last Name* and in Exchange may be *Last Name, First Name*. Mapping rules can allow for different name standards.

For more on configuring mapping tables see Knowledge Base article Q180517, Title: Customizing Dirsync between Exchange and Notes.

Installation Issues

Alias Autonaming Rules If you want to customize alias autonaming rules for the connector, you must set the alias autonaming configuration for the service account you are using for the connector. To do so, log on to Exchange Server using the service account and verify that the autonaming rules are set appropriately.

Starting the Lotus Notes Configuration Utility

When you start the Lotus Notes Configuration Utility, a message appears asking you to cross-certify the organization that created the configuration database. This message appears because the Lotus Notes database file containing the utility was created by an organization unknown to your Lotus Notes installation. Select **Yes** or **No** depending on whether you want this message displayed when you run this utility in the future.

Removing and Reinstalling E-mail Address Generators with Exchange Connectivity Setup

When e-mail address generators are in use by the Exchange Server System Attendant, Connectivity Setup cannot remove the e-mail address generator files. If the e-mail address generator is in use when reinstalling, the new version will not overwrite the existing copy.

To solve this problem, stop the Exchange Server services and restart them. Ensure that no modifications are made to any site addressing information because this causes the e-mail address generators to be reloaded when the server is restarted.

One-off Addressing of Notes Messages to Exchange Server Recipients

For mail to be correctly delivered from Notes to Exchange Server recipients, Notes users must use the fully qualified Notes e-mail address for the Exchange Server recipient as it appears in the Exchange Server directory. The easiest way to ensure that addresses are specified correctly is to enable directory synchronization between the two systems and encourage users to address messages by selecting the intended recipient from the Name and Address Book. If, however, users type addresses manually, the e-mail address field in the Notes message must contain the address in Notes abbreviated canonical form. The address must look similar to this:

FullName/OrganizationalUnit/Organization@NotesDomain

This address must match the full Notes e-mail address of the user within Exchange Server. No spaces can surround the @ sign.

Notes users can add Exchange Server addresses to their personal address books using the supplied address template.

Viewing Updated Notes Name and Address Books After a Directory Synchronization Cycle

When you access a view of a Lotus Notes Address Book for the first time after a directory synchronization cycle, there may be a delay as Notes updates the index used for sorting the view. When the index has been updated, you can open the Address Book more quickly.

Viewing Graphics in Lotus Notes Messages on Non-Windows Platforms

On Windows platforms, graphics in messages sent from Exchange Server to a Lotus Notes recipient appear as they did in the original Exchange Server message. If the recipient's Lotus Notes client program is running on a platform other than Windows (for example, Macintosh), the graphic image appears as an icon in the message in Lotus Notes. Open the icon to see the graphic that the icon represents.

Message Formatting

The following formatting is not supported when sending messages between Exchange Server and Notes:

- Bulleted and numbered lists
- Table formatting in Notes messages
- Collapsible sections in Notes messages

Assigning Names to Foreign Domains in Lotus Notes

When setting up foreign domains in Notes, avoid using Exchange Server reserved address types (such as MS Mail (PC), SMTP, and cc:Mail) as foreign domain names. Using them can prevent the connector from delivering mail from Exchange Server to the foreign domains.

Using URL Support for Notes Doclinks

When you configure the Exchange Connector for Notes, you can choose how Lotus Notes Document Links (Doclinks) should be represented in messages when they are sent to Exchange Server recipients. One option is to have the Doclink represented as a URL that points to a document on the originating Lotus Notes/Domino server.

By default, the TCP/IP port number that the Lotus Notes/Domino server uses for HTTP links to documents is 80. The port number is defined in the HTTP server section of the server document. If the Notes administrator changes this value, you must add information to the connector's initialization file to ensure the connector includes the correct port number when it generates the URL for the Doclink.

▶ **To update the initialization file, follow these steps:**

1. Using Notepad, edit the Exchsrvr\Connect\EXCHCONN.INI file.

2. Add a new section to the file called [LME-NOTES-DOMINOHTTPNAMES]. Place this section immediately before an existing section or add it at the end of the file.

3. For each Lotus Notes/Domino server for which the TCP/IP port number for HTTP links has been redefined, add an entry to the new section as follows:

   keyword=NotesServerName==DominoHTTPName

   where *keyword* is a unique alphanumeric string that identifies this mapping, *NotesServerName* is the name of the Notes server (in Notes canonical or abbreviated form), and *DominoHTTPName* is the HTTP domain and port number the Lotus Notes/Domino server is known by.

For example:

```
[LME-NOTES-DOMINOHTTPNAMES]
mapping1=Server1/NAmericaE==www.FergusonAndBardell.com:8080
mapping2=Server2/NAmericaE==www.FergusonAndBardell.com:8085
```

UNC Name Must Be Used to Configure the Qroot Parameter

If you customize directory synchronization or configure the server so that queues are not on the same server as the connector or so that connectors on different servers share queues, you must change the parameters located in the [QM] section of the EXCHCONN.INI file. These parameters manage the connector and directory synchronization queues. The qroot parameter specifies the path to the root of the queue directory subtree. This parameter is normally qroot=*drive*:\Exchsrvr\Connect\Exchconn\q.

To change the value of qroot, you must use the universal naming convention (UNC) name for the path where the queues are located, instead of a drive letter. Drive letters cannot be used because drive letter mappings are lost when the administrator who started the connector services logs off. An example follows.

```
[QM]
qroot = \\server_name\share_name\connect\exchconn\q
```

Sending Delivery Reports and Read Notifications to Lotus Notes Users as Embedded Objects

Delivery reports and read notifications sent to Lotus Notes users as embedded objects do not appear in the message received by the Lotus Notes user. They can be forwarded to Lotus Notes users, in which case they are delivered as standard text messages.

Connector Does Not Detect Changes to the Source Name and Address Book for Directory Synchronization

When you add or delete a Source Name and Address Book in the Lotus Notes **Address Books** property page, the connector does not detect the change. Lotus Notes users in a newly added Name and Address Book are not imported into the Exchange Server directory, and Lotus Notes users in a deleted Source Name and Address Book are not removed from the Exchange Server directory.

To update the Exchange Server directory after adding or deleting a Source Name and Address Book, request an immediate full reload from Notes to Exchange Server on the **Dirsync Schedule** property page.

Connector Does Not Detect Change to the Import Container for Directory Synchronization; Processes Updates in Old Container

After you change the Import container to the new container name in the Exchange Server Administrator program, you must delete the custom recipients for Lotus Notes users from the old container and from the **Dirsync Schedule** property page. Then run an immediate full reload from Notes to Exchange Server. When directory synchronization is complete, custom recipients for the Lotus Notes users are re-created in the new import container.

Connector Does Not Detect Change to the Export Container for Directory Synchronization

Further result: Exchange Server recipients in a newly added export container are not imported into the Lotus Notes Target Name and Address Book, and Exchange Server recipients in a deleted export container are not removed from the Lotus Notes Target Name and Address Book.

To update the Lotus Notes Target Name and Address Book after adding or deleting an export container, request an immediate full reload from Exchange Server to Notes on the **Dirsync Schedule** property page.

Services Must Be Restarted to Make Changes in the Directory Synchronization Schedule

If you change the scheduled directory synchronization time in the **Dirsync Schedule** property page, you must stop and restart the Exchange Connector for Notes and the Microsoft Exchange Connectivity Controller services for the change to take effect.

Lotus Notes Client DLLs Must Be Available on the System Path

The Connector for Notes requires access to the DLLs that are installed as part of the Lotus Notes client installation process. If the DLLs are not available to the connector, a "DLL Initialization Failed" error occurs.

Verify that the path to these DLLs is added to the Exchange Server computer's system path before starting the Connector for Notes.

Hidden Text in a Lotus Notes Message Is Visible When Sent to an Exchange Server Recipient

When the **Hide paragraph when document is** property is set as **Opened for editing** or **Opened for reading** on messages sent from Lotus Notes to Microsoft Exchange Server, the message arrives with all text visible to the Exchange Server recipient.

Running the Notes Server and the Exchange Connector for Notes on the Same Computer Is Not Supported

Installing and running the Lotus Notes server and the Microsoft Exchange server with the Connector for Notes on the same computer is not supported. For additional information, see the Microsoft Product Support Services Knowledge Base available on the Web at **http://support.microsoft.com/support.**

Lotus Notes Domain Names More Than 30 Characters Are Truncated

When you configure the Lotus Notes foreign domain name used by Exchange Server to generate Lotus Notes e-mail addresses for Exchange Server recipients, verify that the domain name does not exceed 30 characters.

Lotus Notes does not support foreign domain names of more than 30 characters and truncates them during directory synchronization.

Attachment Link or Shortcut Could Not Be Located or Accessed

The Connector for Notes can resolve Windows shortcuts sent to Lotus Notes users. When a Windows shortcut cannot be accessed, the following text is provided in an attachment:

```
Attachment Link or Shortcut could not be located or accessed. Please
contact sender to send this attachment as an embedded object or regular
file attachment:
```

```
\\Servername\Share\Sample.nsf
```

The connector requires read access to the location indicated in the shortcut to resolve it successfully.

Lotus Notes User Names with High Bit and Unicode/Far East LMBCS Characters Are Not Supported

Directory synchronization between a Japanese Lotus Notes Name and Address Book and a Japanese version of Exchange Server, adds only single-byte character set names to the Exchange Server directory. This Notes e-mail address generator does not support Unicode characters greater than 255, and mail cannot be sent to or from Notes users with these characters in their names.

Known Limitations

- When you add non-Lotus Notes users to a Notes Name and Address Book (for example, users with Internet, X.400, or cc:Mail addresses) you must specify a user name and a domain name. Although Notes does not require this information, the connector uses it when propagating directory information to Exchange Server. Specify the domain to which the connector is attached.

- Messages sent to users on foreign systems through the connector can result in delivery or receipt messages being returned to the sender. These messages usually carry a prefix, inserted into the subject of the message, which describes the status of the delivery: Not Read, Read, Delivered, and Not Delivered. If, however, the original message was sent from an MS Mail (PC) user who connects to the foreign system through the Microsoft Mail connector, a prefix is not included on this return message. The body of the return message informs the sender about the status of the original distribution.

Testing Connector Connectivity

Test the configuration to ensure that e-mail can cross the connector.

On the Exchange server:

1. Create a new Windows NT account using a **first name** of *New* and a **last name** of *Guy*. Click **Ignore** or **Cancel** when the Exchange extension window appears.

2. Open the Exchange Administrator.

3. Highlight the **Recipients** container.

4. On the **File** menu, click **New Mailbox**.

5. In the *First Name* field enter **New**, in the *Last Name* field enter **Guy**. A **Display Name** and **Alias** is automatically generated.

6. Click the **Primary Windows NT Account** button.

7. Select **an existing Windows NT account** and click **OK**.

8. Select the **New Guy** account. Click **Add** and then **OK**. The Exchange user properties appear.

9. Click **OK**.

10. Click the **Recipients container,** and double-click on **New Guy** in the right-hand pane.

11. Click the **E-mail Addresses** button, and write down the New Guy's Notes e-mail address. For Notes users to send e-mail messages to New Guy, this address must be placed in the **To** field of the memo.

Now, go to the Notes server and:

12. On the Notes server create a Notes user with a first name of **Golden** and a last name of **Arm**.

13. Create a memo to New Guy on Exchange by entering the address you wrote down previously in the Notes **To** field.

14. Type "**testing**" in the subject box.

15. In the body, type some text and send the message.

16. On the connector workstation, launch the Exchange client. When the Exchange client starts, the **Choose Profile** dialog appears.

17. You can create a profile for New Guy by clicking **New,** but in this case allow the profile to be automatically generated. Enable only the **Exchange server** option and click **Next**.

18. Enter **New Guy** for the *Profile Name* and click **Next**.

19. For the Exchange server, enter the Exchange Server Name; for the Mailbox name, **New Guy**. Click **Next**.

20. Select **No** when asked if you wish to travel with this computer. Click **Next.**

21. For the personal address book, highlight the **mailbox** section of the path and enter **newguy**. Click **Next**.

22. Verify that the only services being used are the **Exchange Server** and the **Personal Address Book**. Click **Finish**.

23. The **Choose Profile** screen returns. Highlight **New Guy**'s profile and click **OK**.

24. The Microsoft Exchange client appears.

Verify that the LinkAge connector services (under Windows NT) are started. The message could take a few minutes to traverse the connector. When it does arrive on Exchange:

25. Open the message.

26. Write down the address of **Golden Arm** (the address in the from field) and reply to the message. You will refer to it in a later exercise.

27. Wait until the message arrives in Notes.

Results: The message sent from Notes to Exchange should have arrived, as should have the reply to the Notes ID, indicating that connectivity has been established.

Connectivity Lab 1: Testing Read and Delivery Receipts

From the Exchange client send a message from **New Guy** to **Golden Arm** on the Notes server. The steps are listed below:

1. Open the Exchange client and click the **New Guy** profile.

2. Click **Compose/New mail message**.

3. On the **To** line type the addresses of *Golden Arm* (this is the address you wrote down previously when you received the message from the Notes user, *Golden Arm*) or click the **To** button, click **New**, click **Notes address** (put this address in the personal address book). Click **OK**. For the **user name** type *Golden Arm*, and for the **domain** enter the Notes Domain Name and click **OK**.

   The compose message screen returns.

4. For subject, type "Testing Of Read And Delivery Receipts".

5. In the body, type some text.

6. From the **File** menu, click **Properties** and select the Read and Delivery receipts.

7. Leave the **Importance** and **Sensitivity** as **Normal**.

8. Send the message.

   Wait until the message arrives in the Notes client.

   As soon as the message arrives in Notes, a delivery receipt should appear in the Exchange inbox. Read this message.

9. On the Notes client read the message sent from Exchange.

10. On the Exchange client, wait a few minutes until a message arrives. This should be the read receipt.

11. Open and read.

Expected Results

When the message arrives in MAIL.BOX, the Notes server attempts to route it to a valid recipient. Once delivered, a delivery receipt for the message should be generated and sent back to the connector, which sends it to Exchange.

When the message is opened in Notes, a read receipt is generated and sent back to Exchange.

Connectivity Lab 2: Test NDR Using a Nonexistent Foreign Recipient

From the Exchange client, send a message from *New Guy* to *Big Paws* on the Notes system.

Format the message as described in **Lab 1**, substituting **Golden Arm** with **Big Paws** where necessary.

Expected Results

You should receive a message stating that the recipient does not exist.

Connectivity Lab 3: Testing Operation of Notes Doclinks

In this exercise, you compose a message in the Notes client with a document link and send it to an Exchange user.

1. On the Notes client workspace, Double-click the icon entitled **Golden Arm on Server2**.
2. Click the **New Memo** button.
3. In the **To** field enter **New Guy/site1/org1@exchange**.
4. In the **Subject** field type "**Test Of Doclinks**".
5. In the body, type some text.
6. Now create a Notes doclink: To send a Doclink, go to another open Notes document. (Open one if necessary.)
7. From the **Edit** menu, select **Copy as link**, then select **Document link**. This creates a doclink on the clipboard for the other document.
8. Return to the memo.
9. Place the cursor in the document and click **Paste** from the **Edit** menu.
10. A small icon will appear in the location the cursor was posted.
11. Send this message.

Wait a few minutes for the message to traverse the connector.

Expected Results

On the Exchange client, open and read the new message. Observe the location of the icon. It should be positioned as in the memo created in Notes.

Launching the icon will open the Notes document in RTF format (viewed in Word).

Connectivity Lab 4: Test OLE Links

There are three ways to handle Notes doclinks inserted into messages that are sent to Exchange users:

- The doclink can be added as an OLE object.
- The content of the document referenced by the doclink can be inserted into the memo in read-only rich text format (RTF).
- For Domino servers, an HTTP shortcut can be created.

For the connector to send Notes doclinks as OLE objects, the property page in the Exchange Administrator must be changed. On the **Advanced** tab are three selections for changing how the connector will handle the doclinks (Convert Notes DocLinks to): OLE Document Link, RTF Attachment, and HTTP shortcut. Select **OLE Document Link.** After the changes have been applied, restart the services.

A Notes client is required on the recipient's computer

Repeat the instructions that appear in Lab 3.

Expected Results

When the message arrives at Exchange, open it, and double-click on the doclink icon. The Notes document referenced by the doclink should appear in a Notes window.

Connectivity Lab 5: Test HTTP Links

You need a Lotus Notes/Domino Server to perform this lab.

Notes doclinks inserted into messages that are sent to Exchange users can be handled in three ways:

- The doclink can be added as an OLE object.
- The content of the document referenced by the doclink can be inserted into the memo in read-only rich text format (RTF).
- For Domino servers, an HTTP shortcut can be created.

For the connector to send Notes doclinks as an HTTP shortcut, you have to change the property page in the Exchange Administrator. On the **Advanced** tab are three selections for changing how the connector will handle the doclinks (Convert Notes DocLinks to): OLE Document Link, RTF Attachment, and HTTP shortcut. Select **HTTP shortcut**. After the changes have been applied, restart the services.

- This lab requires that the recipient's computer have a Web browser.
- Start the HTTP server on the Domino server: from the Notes Server command window enter: "load http".

Repeat the instructions that appear in Lab 3.

Expected Results

When the message arrives at Exchange, open it, and double-click on the http shortcut icon. The Notes document referenced by the doclink should appear in the Web browser window.

Advanced Configuration

Proxy Address Generators

Customizing the Site Addressing

To customize proxy address generators, use generation rules, which can be altered through the Exchange Administrator Site Addressing property page.

The rules for the proxy address generators are:

```
&M or &m:    Alias
&S or &s:    Surname
&G or &g:    Given Name
&I or &iInitials
&D or &dDisplay Name
```

Combinations can be used, for instance: &gx&s uses x characters from the given name and the rest from the surname

Installing for Downstream Exchange Sites

Each downstream Exchange site must have the proxy address generators installed on at least one server before they can receive mail from Notes.

▶ **To install the proxy address generators into a downstream site, run the Phase 1 setup**

1. Run Setup from the Exchange CD-ROM found in a subdirectory under \server\exchconn. The exact path varies depending on whether Exchange Server is Standard or Enterprise Edition.

2. This brings up an information screen. Read it and click **Next.**

3. Select **Microsoft Exchange Connectivity Services**. Click **Next.**

4. Select the **Microsoft Exchange Connector for Lotus Notes** from the available connectors, as well as the **Notes E-mail Addressing Component**. Click **Next.**

5. Setup prompts you to make sure no applications currently running are using the ODBC DLLs. Close any that are. Click **Yes.**

6. The files are copied into exchsrvr on the local drive and a program group called the Microsoft Exchange Connectivity is created.

7. Setup prompts you for a Lotus Notes Domain Name, which is used to generate Notes proxy addresses for the Exchange users and custom recipients. In other words, Notes users send to this domain when they want to send to Exchange users. For example, if you enter **Exchange** (the default) in this field, a Notes user would send to **user@Exchange** (where **user** is the recipient's alias). Enter a Lotus Notes domain name that will identify Exchange. Click **Next.**

Setup is complete.

Directory Synchronization

Configuration

After you establish messaging connectivity, configuring directory synchronization requires:

1. Selecting an import container
2. Selecting a container to export
3. (Optional) selecting a destination address book for each domain

Selecting an Import Container

1. Go to the **Notes connector** property pages.
2. Click the **Import Container** tab.

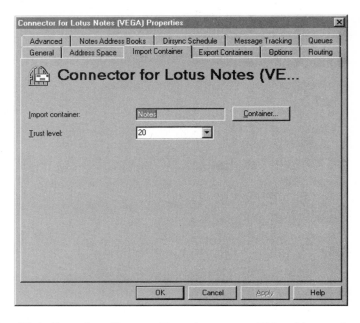

3. Click **Container Button.** From here you will be able to select a container that Notes users will be placed into.

Selecting an Export Container

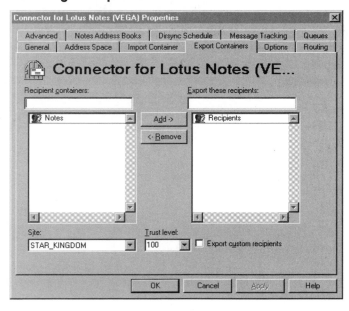

1. Go to the **Export Containers.** Select a **Recipients container** to export to the Notes Directory.

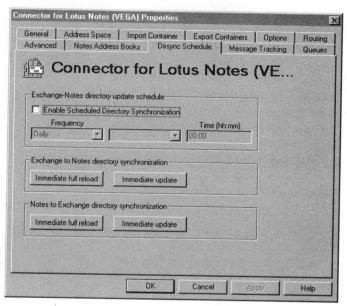

2. Click the **Dirsync Schedule** tab.
3. For the Exchange to Notes Directory Synchronization, click **Immediate Full reload.** This transfers the Exchange directory to the Notes directory.
4. For the Notes to Exchange Directory Synchronization, click the **Immediate Full** reload. This transfers the Notes directory to the Exchange directory. You have completed a directory synchronization cycle. Look in the Exchange Administrator for the new entries.
5. For troubleshooting, use the Connectivity Administrator to find errors.

Selecting a Target Address Book for Each Domain

Within the Notes connector you can assign different target address books for each Notes domain specified within the Exchange directory. For instance, if Site One has its proxy address generators set to the domain of Exchange_Site_1 and Site Two has its proxy address generators set to the domain of Exchange_Site_2, you can assign a target address book to Site One and a target address book for Site Two.

How Directory Sync Works

Directory synchronization between Notes and Exchange uses two file-based queues: **DXANOTES.in** (target of Notes) and **DXAMEX.in** (target of Exchange). These queues are located in the \exchsrvr\connect\exchconn\q directory.

.RDY files are passed between these queues. They contain pointers to the directory information contained in .MIF files. When a directory load is requested (for example, Exchange to Notes) the connector places in the destination queue (in this case DXANOTES.in) an .RDY file that contains a pointer to an .MIF file (which contains the actual directory information). Each .MIF file can hold up to 9,999 entries. For example, 25,000 updates would require three files. The .MIF files are stored in the \exchsrvr\connect\exchconn\q\archive directory. After processing of the .RDY has commenced, the .RDY extension changes to .MPB (MIF Partition Block). These .MPB files are used to organize and track the .MIF files being processed. After processing is done, the .MPB files are removed.

Attributes and Mapping Rules

Overview

The connector maps Exchange and Notes attributes this way:

1. It reads the attributes from the directories, which is controlled through a configuration file called the AMAP.TBL (see next section below).

2. It passes the attributes through a set of mapping rules to transform them into a sensible format for the corresponding directory. For instance, mapping rules change the Notes Full Name format (*Last_Name, First_Name*) into Exchange format (*First_Name Last_Name*).

3. After the mapping rules are complete, the attributes are inserted into the corresponding directory using its AMAP.TBL. For example, the AMAP.TBL file for Exchange is used to read/write the attributes from the Exchange directory.

4. The attributes are passed to the mapping rules (MAPMEX.TBL) and transformed into a Notes format, and then are written into the Notes directory using the AMAP.TBL for Notes.

In the opposite direction, the attributes are read using the Notes AMAP.TBL and passed to the mapping rules (MAPNOTES.TBL), after which the attributes are written into the Exchange directory using the AMAP.TBL for Exchange.

AMAP Tables

First the attributes are taken from and put into the directories using an AMAP.TBL file located in either \dxamex or \dxanotes directory in the Exchconn directory.

The format of the AMAP.TBL depends on the particular directory that is being accessed. The following describes the Exchange AMAP.TBL found in the \dxamex directory:

Friendly name	Length	Exchange common name	Key attribute
ALIAS	64	Mail-nickname	

Where:

- **Friendly Name** is the name used by the connector internally to define a particular attribute.

- **Length** is the length of the particular attribute. If this is larger than the space allocated, the attribute is truncated.

- **Exchange common name** is the common name within Exchange for a particular attribute. These common names can be found using Exchange in raw mode. See the Mapping Rules List at the end of this chapter for more details.

- **Key attribute** marks the attribute as unique within the directory system. If there are more than one in the column, the connector combines the attributes to ensure uniqueness. If the attribute or combination of attributes is not unique, the connector rejects a particular directory update. If not a key attribute, it can be left blank or have a NULL in the column. If there is more than one key attribute indicated (by numbers), the connector change-searches the attributes indicated in priority sequence. For example, User1 has a MailDomain of Exchange and User2 has a MailDomain of Exchange. The key attribute in the AMAP.TBL for Notes is MailDomain 1 and FullName 2. The connector checks the MailDomain for uniqueness first; if it is not unique, the connector combines the highest priority key attribute with the next attribute to create a unique value. If that doesn't work, the connector adds in the next attribute and so on until it creates a unique string.

The format for the Notes AMAP.TBL is:

Friendly name	Length	Notes field name	Key attribute
FIRSTNAME	64	FirstName	NULL
LASTNAME	64	LastName	NULL

Where:

- **Notes field name** is the document field name within a document of a database. See the Mapping Rules List at the end of this chapter on how to find these field names.

- The same fields apply for **friendly name, length,** and **key attribute**.

Adding and Removing Attributes

To remove an attribute from the AMAP.TBL simply add a semicolon to the beginning of the line to comment it out. For example commenting out the LastName in the Notes AMAP.TBL:

```
;LASTNAME 64 LastName NULL
```

> **Caution** Do not delete attributes from the file. This results in non-unique directory entries, which are rejected from the directory.

To add an attribute, you must fill in the columns with the appropriate information. For the Exchange AMAP.TBL it is the friendly name, length, Exchange common name, and the key attribute fields. For the Notes AMAP.TBL it is the friendly name, length, Notes field name, and the key attribute fields. However, several attributes within the AMAP.TBL files are commented out. Simply remove the semicolon to add the attributes.

Attributes added to the AMAP.TBL file are read by the connector but are not active until an appropriate mapping rule is created between the two schemas.

Mapping Rules

Mapping rules transform attributes in one schema to another schema using predefined functions. These mapping rules are stored in two configuration files:

- **MAPMEX.TBL**—Stored in \exchsrvr\connect\exchconn\dxanotes, this maps the attributes from the Exchange schema to the Notes schema (into the Notes directory).
- **MAPNOTES.TBL**—Stored in \exchsrvr\connect\exchconn\dxamex, this maps the Notes schema to the Exchange schema (into the Exchange directory).

The format of the mapping rules is fairly simple.

Destination Attribute = FUNCTION(Source Attribute, ...)

Mapping rule	Description
Destination Attribute	Friendly name of the attribute in the AMAP.TBL
Source Attribute	Friendly name of the attribute in the opposite AMAP.TBL.
FUNCTION	mapping function (optional).

This example is taken from the \dxamex directory from the MAPNOTES.TBL file.

FullName = X500(FullName, "CN")

Mapping rule	Description
FullName	Friendly name from the AMAP.TBL in the \dxamex directory
The second **FullName**	Friendly name from the AMAP.TBL in the \dxanotes directory.
X500 (NFullName,"CN")	A function that locates the common name (CN) from the source of the second FullName

A full list of mapping functions is in the Mapping Rules List at the end of this chapter.

Example

Original files

Exchange AMAP.TBL (located in \exchsrvr\connect\exchconn\dxamex)

```
ACCOUNT 32 Assoc-NT-Account
COMPANY 64 Company
DEPARTMENT 64 Department
FULLNAME 128 Display-Name
FIRSTNAME 64 Given-Name
ALIAS 64 Mail-nickname
OFFICE 64 Physical-Delivery-Office-Name
LASTNAME 64 Surname
NOTESADDR 128 Proxy-Addresses(NOTES:)
USNCreated 12 USN-Created
Initials 5 Initials
Title 32 Title
Phone 20 Telephone-Office1
MobilePhn 20 Telephone-Mobile
Fax 20 Telephone-Fax
```

Notes AMAP.TBL (located in \exchsrvr\connect\exchconn\dxanotes)

```
FULLNAME 220 FullName 1
MAILDOMAIN 31 MailDomain 2
COMPANY 64 CompanyName NULL
DEPARTMENT 64 Department NULL
FIRSTNAME 64 FirstName NULL
LASTNAME 64 LastName NULL
LOCATION 128 Location NULL
SHORTNAME 8 ShortName NULL
UNID 64 $$UNID NULL
DN 256 $$DN NULL
```

```
USNCreated 16 $$USN
Initials 5 MiddleInitial NULL
Title 32 JobTitle NULL
Phone 20 OfficePhoneNumber
MobilePhn 20 CellPhoneNumber
Fax 20 OfficeFAXPhoneNumber
```

MAPNOTES.TBL (located in \exchsrvr\connect\exchconn\dxamex)

```
Alias = ISEQUAL( ShortName, "", SUBSTR( FullName, 1, 64 ), ShortName )
FullName = X500( FullName, "CN" )
TA = "NOTES:" Strip( FullName, ";", "L", "R" ) "@" MailDomain
DN = UNID
FirstName = FirstName
LastName = LastName
Company=Company
Department = Department
Office = Location
Initials = Initials
```

MAPMEX.TBL (located in \exchsrvr\connect\exchconn\dxanotes)

```
FullName = Trim( Strip( NotesAddr, "@", "R" ), "B" )
MailDomain = Trim( Strip( NotesAddr, "@", "L" ), "B" )
ShortName = Alias
LastName = ISEQUAL( LastName, "", FullName, LastName )
FirstName = FirstName
Company = Company
Department = Department
Location = Office
UNID = "00000000-00000000-00000000-00000000"
USN = USNCreated
DN = DN
Initials = Initials
```

Overview

This example adds the attribute for the X.400 addresses to be directory synchronized. When this attribute is in place, the connector synchronizes the X.400 addresses in Notes with the X.400 proxy addresses in Exchange.

Adding an Attribute and Setting a Mapping Rule

1. Add attribute to both AMAP tables. Edit and save each of the two files as follows:

   Exchange AMAP.TBL

   ```
   ACCOUNT 32 Assoc-NT-Account
   COMPANY 64 Company
   DEPARTMENT 64 Department
   FULLNAME 128 Display-Name
   ```

```
FIRSTNAME 64 Given-Name
ALIAS 64 Mail-nickname
OFFICE 64 Physical-Delivery-Office-Name
LASTNAME 64 Surname
NOTESADDR 128 Proxy-Addresses(NOTES:)
USNCreated 12 USN-Created
Initials 5 Initials
Title 32 Title
Phone 20 Telephone-Office1
MobilePhn 20 Telephone-Mobile
Fax 20 Telephone-Fax
```

X400E 256 Proxy-Addresses(X400)

Notes AMAP.TBL

```
FULLNAME 220 FullName 1
MAILDOMAIN 31 MailDomain 2
COMPANY 64 CompanyName NULL
DEPARTMENT 64 Department NULL
FIRSTNAME 64 FirstName NULL
LASTNAME 64 LastName NULL
LOCATION 128 Location NULL
SHORTNAME 8 ShortName NULL
UNID 64 $$UNID NULL
DN 256 $$DN NULL
USNCreated 16 $$USN
Initials 5 MiddleInitial NULL
Title 32 JobTitle NULL
Phone 20 OfficePhoneNumber
MobilePhn 20 CellPhoneNumber
Fax 20 OfficeFAXPhoneNumber
```

X400N 256 x400Address NULL

2. Edit mapping rules for Notes into Exchange.

MAPNOTES.TBL (located in \exchsrvr\connect\exchconn\dxamex)

```
Alias = ISEQUAL( ShortName, "", SUBSTR( FullName, 1, 64 ),
    ShortName )
FullName = X500( FullName, "CN" )
TA = "NOTES:" Strip( FullName, ";", "L", "R" ) "@" MailDomain
DN = UNID
FirstName = FirstName
LastName = LastName
Company=Company
Department = Department
Office = Location
Initials = Initials
```

X400E = X400N

3. Edit Mapping rules for Exchange into Notes

    MAPMEX.TBL (located in \exchsrvr\connect\exchconn\dxanotes)

    ```
    FullName = Trim( Strip( NotesAddr, "@", "R" ), "B" )
    MailDomain = Trim( Strip( NotesAddr, "@", "L" ), "B" )
    ShortName = Alias
    LastName = ISEQUAL( LastName, "", FullName, LastName )
    FirstName = FirstName
    Company = Company
    Department = Department
    Location = Office
    UNID = "00000000-00000000-00000000-00000000"
    USN = USNCreated
    DN = DN
    Initials = Initials
    ```

    X400N = X400E

4. At this point the mapping rules and attributes are added. You must stop and start the connector for the configuration information to be accepted.

Filter Rules

Filtering allows you to prevent certain directory entries from being propagated to the partner directory. If, for example, you don't want the names of suppliers distributed throughout your entire enterprise, you can apply filter rules to control the propagation.

Common attributes are the key to filtering: it is much easier to filter out all members of a particular department, rather than filter out selected users.

Filter rules take this form:

filter_rule_name = <AttributeName>, <OPERATOR>,<value1> | <value2> ...

Any valid directory attribute that can be edited by an administrator can be used in a filter. The attribute name specified must match either the Exchange friendly name (for filtering Exchange entries) or the Notes friendly name (for filtering the Notes entries) found in the AMAP.TBLs.

These operators are supported:

- **EQ**—Propagate if the given attribute is equal to a specified value.
- **NE**—Propagate if the given attribute is not equal to specified value.
- **SW**—Propagate if the given attribute starts with a specified string.
- **DNSW**—Propagate if the given attribute does not start with a specified string.
- **CN**—Propagate if the given attribute contains a specified string.
- **DNCN**—Propagate if the given attribute does note contain a specified string.

If you use multiple values, you must separate EQ, SW, and CN with a vertical bar (l) and NE, DNSW, and DNCN with an ampersand (&).

Example:

filter_site = Site, EQ, Toronto | Ottawa

The connector will only propagate any entry with a site of "Toronto" or "Ottawa".

filter_dept = Department, NE, Supplier & Temps

The Exchange DXA will propagate any entry with a department other than "Suppliers" and "Temps."

The results of multiple filters are logically ANDed together to determine if the entry should be propagated. If mutually exclusive filters are used, no propagation takes place. Define filtering rules carefully.

Filter rules are placed in the [LME-NOTES-DXAMEX] section of EXCHCONN.INI.

ORGINAL [LME-NOTES-DXAMEX]

```
executable = lsdxamex.exe
title = DX Agent for Microsoft Exchange
params = &s -l
; className = EXCHANGE
; MIFVERSION = 2
; InputQ = DXAMEX.IN
OutputQ = DXANOTES.IN
AGENT = MS.DXAMEX
MANAGER = MS.DXANOTES
RECIPIENT = local:DXANOTES.IN
PROPSCHED = dxamexsched
AdminRole = PEER
MIFMap.MS.DXANOTES = DXAMEX\MAPNOTES.TBL
SendGroups = Yes
; CreateAccount = FALSE
; DeleteAccount = FALSE
USNTable = DXAMEX\USN.TBL
AMAP_TABLE = DXAMEX\AMAP.TBL
TABLE = DXAMEX\PCTA.TBL
EXTERNALTABLE = DXAMEX\EXTERNAL.TBL
timeoutlimit = 0
```

For example:

[LME-NOTES-DXAMEX]

```
executable = lsdxamex.exe
title = DX Agent for Microsoft Exchange
```

```
params = &s -1
; className = EXCHANGE
; MIFVERSION = 2
; InputQ = DXAMEX.IN
OutputQ = DXANOTES.IN
AGENT = MS.DXAMEX
MANAGER = MS.DXANOTES
RECIPIENT = local:DXANOTES.IN
PROPSCHED = dxamexsched
AdminRole = PEER
MIFMap.MS.DXANOTES = DXAMEX\MAPNOTES.TBL
SendGroups = Yes
; CreateAccount = FALSE
; DeleteAccount = FALSE
USNTable = DXAMEX\USN.TBL
AMAP_TABLE = DXAMEX\AMAP.TBL
TABLE = DXAMEX\PCTA.TBL
EXTERNALTABLE = DXAMEX\EXTERNAL.TBL
timeoutlimit = 0
```

filter_site = Site,EQ, Toronto | Ottawa

will propagate only the sites that contain **Toronto** or **Ottawa**.

Testing Directory Synchronization

Lab 1: Propagate Full Load—Exchange to Notes

For this lab, the Notes server, the Exchange server, and the Notes connector
should be running.

On the **Dirsync** tab of the Notes Connector property pages, click the **Immediate
full reload** button in the **Exchange to Notes Directory Synchronization** section.
How would you determine the results of the directory synchronization?

Expected Results

The Connectivity Administrator contains all information and logging for the
directory synchronization. The log browser has the logs for the directory
synchronization and will tell you if the synchronization succeeded. The logs
will tell you if any particular transactions have failed (for example, there is a
duplicate entry in the directory). Check the Target Name and Address Book in
Notes for the Exchange addresses.

Lab 2: Propagate Full Load—Notes to Exchange

For this lab, the Notes server, the Exchange server, and the Notes connector should be running.

On the **Diraync** tab of the Notes Connector property pages, click the **Immediate full reload** button in the **Notes to Exchange Directory Synchronization** section. How would you determine the results of the directory synchronization?

Expected Results

The Connectivity Administrator contains all information and logging for the directory synchronization. The log browser has the logs for the directory synchronization and will tell you if the synchronization succeeded. Also the logs will tell you if any particular transactions have failed (for example, there is a duplicate entry in the directory). Check the Exchange Administrator for the Notes addresses.

Lab 3: Propagate Updates Only—Exchange to Notes

For this lab, the Notes server, the Exchange server, and the Notes connector should be running.

Change the first name of an existing Exchange user. On the **Dirsync** tab of the Notes Connector property pages, click the **Immediate updates** button in the **Exchange to Notes Directory Synchronization** section. Check to see if the DirSync sent the change.

Expected Results

Again the Connectivity Administrator contains all information and logging for the directory synchronization. The log browser has the logs for the directory synchronization and will tell you if the synchronization succeeded. Check the Target Name and Address Book in Notes to determine if the update has been sent for the Exchange user. **Note:** You must double-click on the user and examine the first name. Depending on your mapping rules, the user name may not change.

Lab 4: Propagate Updates Only—Notes to Exchange

For this lab, the Notes server, the Exchange server, and the Notes connector should be running.

Change the first name of an existing Notes user. On the **Dirsync** tab of the Notes Connector property pages, click the **Immediate updates** button in the **Exchange to Notes Directory Synchronization** section. Check to see if the DirSync sent the change.

Expected Results

Again the Connectivity Administrator contains all information and logging for the directory synchronization. The log browser has the logs for the directory synchronization and will tell you if the synchronization succeeded. Check the Exchange directory to determine if the update has been sent for the Notes user. **Note:** You must double-click on the user and examine the first name. Depending on your mapping rules, the display name may not change.

Lab 5: Change Mapping Rule—Exchange to Notes

For this lab, the Notes server, the Exchange server, and the Notes connector should be running.

1. Notepad the mapping rules file (MAPMEX.TBL) found in \exchsrvr\connect\exchconn\dxanotes.

   The original mapping rule for LastName and FirstName is:

   LastName = ISEQUAL(LastName, "", FullName, LastName)
   FirstName = FirstName

2. Change it to:

   LastName = ISEQUAL(FirstName, "", FullName, FirstName)
   FirstName = LastName

   Restart the connector for the mapping rules to take affect. On the **Dirsync** tab of the Notes Connector property pages, click the **Immediate full reload** button in the **Notes to Exchange Directory Synchronization** section. Check to see if the DirSync sent the change.

Expected Results

In the Notes Name and Address Book, the FirstName will be swapped with the LastName, and the LastName with the FirstName. For a user "John Smith" in Exchange, the user will end up with the last name of "John" and a first name of "Smith" in Notes, with the changed mapping rules.

Lab 6: Change Mapping Rule—Notes to Exchange

For this lab, the Notes server, the Exchange server, and the Notes connector should be running.

1. Notepad the mapping rules file (MAPNOTES.TBL) found in \exchsrvr\connect\exchconn\dxamex.

   The original mapping rule for FullName is:

   FullName = X500(FullName, "CN")

2. Change it to:

   FullName = LastName ", " FirstName

Restart the connector for the mapping rules to take affect. On the **Dirsync** tab of the Notes Connector property pages, click the **Immediate full reload** button in the **Exchange to Notes Directory Synchronization** section. Check to see if the DirSync sent the change.

Expected Results

In the Exchange Administrator, the display names of the Notes users will be swapped from using the FullName in Notes to using "LastName, FirstName". For a user "John Smith" in Notes, the user will end up with the Exchange Display Name being "Smith, John" with the changed mapping rules.

Lab 7: Adding a New Directory Synchronization Attribute to Exchange and Notes

For this lab, the Notes server, the Exchange server, and the Notes connector should be running.

This lab adds the telephone number attribute to the directory synchronization process.

1. Notepad the AMAP.TBL file found in \exchsrvr\connect\exchconn\dxamex.

2. Add the following line to the end of the active attributes (the ones with out the ";" in front)

    Phone 30 Telephone-Number

    Note   Telephone-Number is the common-name attribute for the phone attribute in Exchange. This can be found by using the Exchange Administrator in RAW mode.

    ---

3. Notepad the AMAP.TBL file found in \exchsrvr\connect\exchconn\dxanotes.

4. Add the following line to the end of the active attributes (the lines that do not begin with a semicolon):

    PHONE 30 OfficePhoneNumber

5. Notepad the mapping rules file (MAPNOTES.TBL) found in \exchsrvr\connect\exchconn\dxamex.

6. Add the following mapping rule:

    Phone = Phone

7. Notepad the mapping rules file (MAPNOTES.TBL) found in \exchsrvr\connect\exchconn\dxanotes.

8. Add the following mapping rule:

    Phone = Phone

Fill the phone attributes for the Exchange users and the Notes users. Restart the connector for the mapping rules to take affect. On the **Dirsync** tab of the Notes Connector property pages, click the **Immediate full reload** button in the **Exchange to Notes Directory Synchronization** section. Check to see if the DirSync sent the change.

Expected Results

The phone attribute should be propagated to both the Exchange directory and to the Notes Names and Address Book.

Lab 8: Adding a Filter Rule to Exchange—Part 1

For this lab, the Notes server, the Exchange server, and the Notes connector should be running.

1. Create two users in the Exchange directory: New Person, Happy Person.
2. Notepad the Exchconn.ini file found in \exchsrvr\connect\exchconn\.
3. Search for: [LME-NOTES-DXAMEX]
4. At the bottom of this section add:

   filter_Person = LASTNAME, EQ, Person

   Restart the connector for the mapping rules to take affect. On the **Dirsync** tab of the Notes Connector property pages, click the **Immediate full reload** button in the **Exchange to Notes Directory Synchronization** section. Check to see if the DirSync sent the change.

Expected Results

The new entries in the Target Name and address book should be only the new people that you created (Exchange1 Person, and Exchange2 Person).

Lab 9: Adding a Filter Rule to Exchange—Part 2

For this lab, the Notes server, the Exchange server, and the Notes connector should be running.

If continuing from Lab 8 skip this step:

- Create two users in the Exchange directory: Exchange1 Person, Exchange2 Person.
1. Notepad the EXCHCONN.INI file found in \exchsrvr\connect\exchconn\.
2. Search for: [LME-NOTES-DXAMEX]

   At the bottom of this section add (if continuing from Lab 8 change the filter rule to):

   filter_Person = LASTNAME, NE, Person

Restart the connector for the mapping rules to take affect. On the **Dirsync** tab of the Notes Connector property pages, click the **Immediate full reload** button in the **Exchange to Notes Directory Synchronization** section. Check to see if the DirSync sent the change.

Expected Results

The new entries in the Target Name and Address Book should be all entries that do not have the last name of Person (that is, Exchange1 Person, and Exchange2 Person are not in the Notes Name and Address Book).

Lab 10: Adding a Filter Rule to Notes

For this lab, the Notes server, the Exchange server, and the Notes connector should be running.

1. Create two users in the Notes directory: Note1 Person, Note2 Person.
2. Notepad the EXCHCONN.INI file found in \exchsrvr\connect\exchconn\.
3. Search for: [LME-NOTES-DXANOTES].
4. At the bottom of this section add:

   filter_NPerson = LASTNAME, NE, Person

   Restart the connector for the mapping rules to take affect. On the **Dirsync** tab of the Notes Connector property pages, click the **Immediate full reload** button in the **Exchange to Notes Directory Synchronization** section. Check to see if the DirSync sent the change.

Expected Results

The new entries in the Exchange directory should be all entries that do not have the last name of Person (that is, Note1 Person and Note2 Person are not in the Exchange Directory).

Troubleshooting

Lab 1: Notes Server Down—Part 1

With the Notes server and the connector running, exit the Notes server. The connector should have two inactive processes. What are they? Familiarize yourself with the error messages

Expected Results

The processes in the Notes connector that are down are: "Convert Notes to Exchange," and "Convert Exchange to Notes." If you ran a DirSync, the "DX Agent for Lotus Notes" would be down as well.

Lab 2: Notes Server Down—Part 2

This lab continues on Troubleshooting Lab 1. If you have not completed Lab 1, do so now.

Send an e-mail from Exchange to Notes. Where is the message queued up? Note the error messages in the Connectivity Administrator.

Expected Results

The message should be queued up in the "Outbound to Notes" queue. You can find this queue in the **Queue** tab of the Notes Connector property pages. In this tab is a drop-down menu for seeing the queues. The "Outbound to Notes" queue is here.

Lab 3: Notes Server Down—Part 3

This lab continues Lab 1. If you have not completed Lab 1, do so now.

- Send an e-mail from Notes to Exchange. Where is the message queued up?

Expected Results

The message should be queued up in the EXCHANGE.BOX database on the Notes server. You can access this queue with the administrator's ID from the Notes Client. By opening this database, you should see the message you sent from Notes to Exchange.

Lab 4: Notes Problem—Part 1

If continuing from Lab 3, restart the Notes server.

1. For this lab, the Notes server, the Exchange server, and the Notes connector should be running.
2. In the Notes server console, type "drop router". Send a message from Exchange to Notes. Where is the message queued up? Note the logs in the Connectivity Administrator.

Expected Results

The message should be queued up in the MAIL.BOX database on the Notes server. You can access this queue with the administrator's ID from the Notes Client. By opening this database, you should see the message you sent from Exchange to Notes. **Note:** The logs in the Connectivity Administrator indicate that everything is normal because the connector has completed its job in delivering the message to the Notes environment. The message router in Notes has not picked up the message and delivered it to the Notes user.

Lab 5: Notes Problem—Part 2

If continuing from Lab 3, restart the Notes server and type "drop router" in the Notes server console.

1. For this lab, the Notes server, the Exchange server, and the Notes connector should be running.
2. Send a message from Notes to Exchange. Where is the messaged queued up? Note the logs in the Connectivity Administrator.

Expected Results

The message should be queued up in the MAIL.BOX database on the Notes server. You can access this queue with the administrator's ID from the Notes client. By opening this database, you should see the message you sent from Notes to Exchange.

Note   The logs in the Connectivity Administrator will indicate that everything is normal and the message that was sent from Notes to Exchange is not in the logs. The mail has been transferred to the MAIL.BOX but has not been transferred from there to EXCHANGE.BOX because the router is down. This would be a Notes problem.

Lab 6: Connector Down

If continuing from Lab 3 or Lab 5, restart the Notes server.

1. For this lab, the Notes server, the Exchange server, and the Notes connector should be running.
2. Stop the services of the Notes Connector. The service is "Microsoft Exchange Connector for Lotus Notes."
3. Send a message from Exchange to Notes. Where is the message queued up?

Expected Results

The message should be queued up in the MTA of the connector's Exchange server. From the Exchange Administrator, highlight the connector's Exchange server. In the window on the right, double-click the Message Transfer Agent. In the MTA window is a **Queue** tab. On its drop-down menu you will see a queue for the connector. The message should be queued here.

Lab 7: Wrong Configuration

1. For this lab, the Notes server, the Exchange server, and the Notes connector should be running.

2. From the property pages of the Notes connector, change Notes server name. This can be done from the **Options** page of the Exchange administrator. Restart the connector.

3. Observe the Connectivity Administrator's logs. Also check the process manager for the Connectivity Administrator.

Expected Results

The processes in the Notes connector that are down are "Convert Notes to Exchange" and "Convert Exchange to Notes." If you ran a DirSync, the "DX Agent for Lotus Notes" would be down as well. Also note in the logs that the connector reports that it could not connect to the Notes server.

Lab 8: Wrong Notes ID

1. For this lab, the Notes server and the Exchange server should be running. The Notes connector should be down. If continuing from Lab 7, correct the configuration.

2. Edit the NOTES.INI file that the connector is using. Search for the word "keyfilename". To the right of the word "keyfilename" is the ID file that the connector is using to access Notes. Change this ID file to another user's (not the administrator's) ID file.

3. Restart the connector. Note the logs. Send messages from Exchange to Notes. Send messages from Notes to Exchange. Try a DirSync in both directions.

Expected Results

If the ID file does not have the same permissions as the connector's ID file, messages from Exchange to Notes will work with no problems. Messages from Notes to Exchange will fail, depending on whether the ID has read access to the EXCHANGE.BOX. DirSync from Notes to Exchange succeeds if the ID has read access to the Name and Address Book, but it fails from Exchange to Notes because the ID does not have write permissions in the Name and Address Book.

Note This is a common problem if a duplicate NOTES.INI file is not made.

Lab 9: Removing Stuck Messages

1. The Notes server, the Exchange server, and the Notes connector should be running properly for this lab. If continuing from Lab 8, use the correct ID file for the connector.

2. From the Connectivity Administrator, open the process manager. Highlight the process "Convert Exchange to Notes." From the **Menu** bar, click **Process manager** and select the **Stop One Process** option. This stops the "Convert Exchange to Notes process." Mail will still flow from Notes to Exchange, but will not flow from Exchange to Notes.

3. Send message from Exchange to Notes, using two different user names.

Expected Results

1. Go to the property pages of the Notes connector. Click the **Queue** tab. The messages in the "Outbound to Notes Queue" are sorted alphabetically by sender, which can make it difficult to find the oldest message.

2. To find the oldest message, use a utility called MDB View found in the Exchange resource kit.

Note The Windows NT ID that you log in with must be the service account for the connector to see the connector profile. When using MDB View, simply use the connector profile to log in. (Outlook or the Exchange client must not be running.) Open the message store for the mailbox of the connector from the MDB tab. From the **MDB** tab, click **Open Root Folder**.

---

3. This brings you to the queues of the connector. For this lab, double-click the READYOUT queue. The top message in the **Messages in Folder** window should be the oldest message. Double-click the oldest message. Here you can see who sent the message.

4. Go back to the property pages of the Notes connector under the **Queues** tab. From here you can remove the message in three ways: export it into a TNEF format (good if you want to send the message to diagnose the problem), delete it with the delete button, or can NDR it (sends a non-delivery receipt) to the sender.

Lab 10: Directory Synchronization Problems—Notes DXA

1. This lab requires the Notes server, the Exchange server, and the Notes connector to be running.

2. Stop the Notes server. Go to the property pages of the Notes Connector. Select the **Dirsync Schedule** tab. Click the **Full Reload** button for the Exchange to Notes DirSync. The Exchange DXA tries to send the Exchange directory to the Notes DXA. The Notes DXA tries to access the Notes server to write the information into the directory. The Notes DXA tries to access the Notes server and fails. Try to clear the DirSync load.

Expected Results

To remove, remove the job file in the \exchsrvr\connect\exchconn\q \DxaNotes.IN directory. To do this, go to the directory. There may be several files here (for this lab, only two). The file that you want to remove is the .MPB or .RDY file. This will remove the directory load from the connector. After the Notes server is restarted, the connector will not try to start a reload.

Note Do not remove the .QCR file. If you do, copy it from the \DxaMEX.IN directory into here.

Lab 11: Directory Synchronization Problems—Exchange DXA

1. This lab requires the Notes server, the Exchange server, and the Notes connector to be running.

2. Stop the DX Agent for Exchange in the Connectivity Administrator. Go to the property pages of the Notes Connector. Click the **Dirsync Schedule** tab. Click the **Full Reload** button for the Notes to Exchange DirSync. The Notes DXA will try to send the Notes directory to the Exchange DXA. The Exchange DXA will not process the directory because it was stopped. Try to clear the DirSync load.

Expected Results

To remove the load, remove the job file in the \exchsrvr\connect\exchconn\q \DXAMEX.IN directory. To do this, go to the directory. There may be several files here (for this lab, only two). The file that you want to remove is the .MPB or .RDY file. This will remove the directory load from the connector. After the DX Agent for Exchange is restarted, the connector will not try to start a reload.

Note Do not remove the .QCR file. If you do, copy it from the \DXANotes.IN directory into here.

Common Troubleshooting Problems

Here are common problems encountered when installing the Notes connector.

The Notes client cannot connect to the Notes server.

If the name of the Notes server is different from the NetBIOS name of the host machine, the Notes server name should be registered in the WINS server. Alternatively, the Notes server name can be registered in the DNS, or the HOSTS file on the local server.

When executing setup, nothing appears to happen or response is very slow.

Ensure that the Windows NT control panel and Notes server are not running on the server where the Connector Setup program is being executed.

When starting the connector a dialog box appears indicating that it cannot find nNotes.DLL.

The Notes connector requires that the Notes 4 client be installed on the same machine. The Notes installation program does not add the location of the Notes client to the system path. You will need to do this manually and reboot your server.

Caution Do not make multiple copies of the nNotes.DLL files. Even if the Notes client is added to the system path, the connector will not work if there are multiple nNotes.DLLs.

When starting my Connectivity Controller I am getting the following error:

```
Warning {Not found} - Could not obtain the value of the <INI PARAMETER>
keyword in the <LME PROCESS> section. Using the default value
'<DEFAULT>'
```

Should I be worried? No. This indicates that at least one parameter has not been found in the EXCHCONN.INI and the default value is used. Often this error occurs when initializing parameters for sections of the software that are not being used. To avoid seeing this error, locate the entry within the EXCHCONN.INI configuration file and comment it out.

When sending a message from Notes to Exchange, I get a message back that indicates that there is no route to the domain in the Notes Server.

Check the Notes foreign domain document to make sure it is pointing to the correct mail routing database and that the connection server's name is fully qualified. After it has been added, restart the mail router on the Notes server by restarting the server.

I can send messages successfully from Exchange to Notes, but messages from Notes never make it to Exchange.

Open EXCHANGE.BOX on the Notes server. If you find messages, check the access control list on the database. The Notes ID that the connector is using must have Read and Delete privileges.

The DX Agent for Notes or the DX Agent for Exchange seems to be processing for a long time for a small number of entries.

There may be a stuck directory exchange message (.RDY file or .MPB file). To remove the message, go to \exchsrvr\connect\exchconn\q\dxanotes.in. If any .MPB or .RDY files are here, remove them. Go to \exchsrvr\connect\exchconn\q \dxamex.in and remove any .MPB or .RDY files you find. If the problem persists, go to \exchsrvr\connect\exchconn\dxanotes. Within this directory, there should be only the AMAP.TBL, the EXTERNAL.TBL, the MAPMEX.TBL, and the PCTA.TBL. Remove the other four files from this directory.

Mapping Rules List

A mapping rule defines how to derive a target field in a target directory class using fields/constants from a source directory class. String functions are provided to formulate these mapping rules. The list below shows all mapping functions and briefly explains them.

Notational Conventions

AND()
Returns the concatenation of two non-null strings or the null string if either of the two strings specified is null.

CFGPARM()
Returns a value from the connector's .INI file.

ISEQUAL()
Returns a configurable value, depending on whether two expressions are equal.

LEFT()
Returns the left n characters of an expression, padded on the right if necessary.

LOWER()
Converts a field to lower-case characters.

NAMEF()
Returns a person's first name or initial from a preformatted string.

NAMEL()
Returns a person's last name or initial from a pre-formatted string.

NAMEM()
> Returns a person's middle name or initial from a pre-formatted string.

POS()
> Determines the position of a particular string within an attribute.

PROPER()
> Converts a name field to proper-name format.

REPLACE()
> Converts a name field to proper-name format.

RIGHT()
> Returns the right n characters of an expression, padded on the left if necessary.

SUBSTR()
> Returns a specified substring of a string, padded with extra characters if necessary.

STRIP()
> Locates the left-most or right-most occurrence of one string in another and removes characters.

TRIM()
> Returns a field with leading and/or trailing blanks removed.

UPPER()
> Converts a field to upper-case characters.

WORD()
> Returns a specified number of words from a string.

X500()
> Extracts an attribute from an X.500-style hierarchical address.

Mapping Functions

Notational conventions	Description
UPPERCASE type	Used for function names
[ ]	Used to indicate optional arguments. If an optional argument is omitted, its default value is assumed.

In the examples, each sample call is followed by the result it produces. Although the examples use only string literals as arguments, remember that each argument can itself be an arbitrarily complex string expression, including nested function calls.

AND() Mapping Function

Syntax:

AND(*exp1,exp2*)

Description:

Returns the concatenation of two non-null strings or the null string if either of the strings involved is null.

Examples:

```
AND("A", "B" ) "AB"
AND ("", "B") ""
AND("A", "") ""
```

CFGPARM() Mapping Function

Syntax: **CFGPARM**(*exp1*[,*exp2*])

Description: CFGPARM returns the value of a parameter in the EXCHCONN.INI file. Exp1 specifies the parameter value to be returned; exp2 specifies the section within the .INI file. If the section is omitted, then the DXA's home section is used. If neither the section nor the parameter is found, the result is an empty string.

Examples:

```
CFGPARM( "executable") "lsdxamex.exe"
CFGPARM( "locale", "dxm") "English"
```

ISEQUAL() Mapping Function

Syntax: **ISEQUAL**(*exp1*, *exp2*, *val1*, *val2*)

Description: ISEQUAL returns the value of *val1* if *exp1* equals *exp2*; otherwise, it returns the value of *val2*. ISEQUAL is not case-sensitive.

Examples:

```
ISEQUAL( "remote", "remote", "R", "L") "R"
ISEQUAL( "remote", "local", "R", "L") "L"
ISEQUAL( "remote", "REMOTE", "R", "L") "R"
```

LEFT() Mapping Function

Syntax: **LEFT** (*field*, *length*, [, *pad*])

Description: LEFT returns the left-most *length* characters of field. If *field* has fewer than *length* characters, the result is padded on the right with the *pad* character.

The default *pad* character is a blank.

Examples:

```
LEFT ( "416-862-7148", "3" ) "416"
LEFT ( "triple", "9" ) "triple "
LEFT ( "triple", "9", "x" ) "triplexxx"
```

LOWER() Mapping Function

Syntax: **LOWER** (*field*)

Description: LOWER returns the value of *field* with any upper-case letters converted to lower-case.

Examples:

```
LOWER ( "LinkAge" ) "linkage"
LOWER ( "Bonnie" ) "bonnie"
```

NAMEF() Mapping Function

Syntax:

NAMEF (*field*, [, *style*])

Description:

If *field* contains a person's name in a specified format, *NAMEF* returns the person's first name or initial. Two styles are supported:

1. The name is in the form *First Middle Last*.
2. The name is in the form *Last, First Middle*.

The default style is 1 if *field* does not contain a comma, 2 if it does.

Initials or strings of initials are treated as first or middle names. If a name has only one part, it is considered both first and last name, regardless of the style.

Examples:

```
NAMEF ( "Sarah Elizabeth Turner" ) "Sarah"
NAMEF ( "S. E. Turner" ) "S."
NAMEF ( "SE Turner" ) "SE"
NAMEF ( "Turner, Sarah E.", "2" ) "Sarah"
NAMEF ( "Madonna", "2" ) "Madonna"
```

NAMEL() Mapping Function

Syntax:

NAMEL (*field*, [, *style*])

Description:

If *field* contains a person's name in a specified format, NAMEF returns the person's last name. Two styles are supported:

1. The name is in the form First Middle Last.
2. The name is in the form Last, First Middle.

The default style is 1 if *field* does not contain a comma, 2 if it does.

Initials or strings of initials are treated as first or middle names. If a name has only one part, it is considered both first and last name, regardless of the style.

Examples:

```
NAMEL ( "Sarah Elizabeth Turner" ) "Turner"
NAMEL ( "S. E. Turner" ) "Turner"
NAMEL ( "Sarah Turner" ) "Turner"
NAMEL ( "Turner, Sarah E.", "2" ) "Turner"
NAMEL ( "Madonna") "Madonna"
```

NAMEM() Mapping Function

Syntax:

NAMEM(*field*, [, *style*])

Description:

If *field* contains a person's name in a specified format, NAMEF returns the person's middle name or initial.

Two styles are supported:

1. The name is in the form *First Middle Last*.
2. The name is in the form *Last, First Middle*.

The default style is 1 if *field* does not contain a comma, 2 if it does.

Initials or strings of initials are treated as first or middle names. If a name has only one part, it is considered both first and last name, regardless of the style. Anything that is not identified as a first or last name is considered a middle name.

Examples:

```
NAMEM ( "Sarah Elizabeth Turner" ) "Elizabeth "
NAMEM ( "S. E. Turner" ) "E. "
NAMEM ( "Turner, Sarah E." ) "E. "
NAMEM ( "Turner, Sarah", "2" ) ""
NAMEM ( "Turner, Sarah E.", "2" ) "E."
NAMEM ( "Turner, Sarah E. M", "2" ) "E. M."
```

POS() Mapping Function

Syntax: POS (*field*, *target*)

Description: POS returns the position of the string *target* within *field*.

If *target* is not in *field*, POS returns zero.

Examples:
```
POS ( "Title: President", "Ti" ) "1"
POS ( "Title: President", ":" ) "6"
POS ( "Title: President", "Manager" ) "0"
```

PROPER() Mapping Function

Syntax: PROPER (*field*)

Description: PROPER returns the value of *field* with lower- and upper-case letters converted to mixed-case, as if *field* were a proper name.

Examples:
```
PROPER ( "linkage" ) "Linkage"
PROPER ( "john") "John"
PROPER ( "o'malley" ) "O'Malley"
```

REPLACE() Mapping Function

Syntax: REPLACE (*field*, *what* [,*with*])

Description: This mapping function enables you to remove specific characters from an ID or replace selected characters with substitute characters. It scans *field* for any characters in the *what* string and replaces them with the corresponding character from the *with* string. If the *with* string is shorter or is not provided (meaning that one of more characters in what have no corresponding characters in with), those characters are elided (removed) from field.

Examples:
```
REPLACE ("James Martin"," ","_") "James_Martin"
REPLACE ("Sales & Marketing Email Group"," ",".")
"Sales.&.Marketing.Email.Group"
REPLACE ("Constantine Raîch'al", " î'", ".i") "Constantine.Raichal"
```

RIGHT() Mapping Function

Syntax: **RIGHT** (*field*, *length* [,*pad*])

Description: RIGHT returns the right-most length characters of *field*. If *field* has fewer than *length* characters, the result is padded on the left with the *pad* character.

The default *pad* character is a blank.

Examples:
```
RIGHT ( "416-862-7148", "7" ) "62-7148"
RIGHT ( "416-862-7148", "8" ) "862-7148"
RIGHT ( "node", "5", "@" ) "@node"
```

STRIP() Mapping Function

Syntax: **STRIP** (*string1*, *string2*, [scan-from-direction] , [strip-toward-direction]),
where   [scan-from-direction]   = "L" | "R"
            [strip-toward-direction] = "L" | "R"

Description: STRIP locates the left-most or right-most occurrence of *string2* in *string1* and removes characters from the right or left, including *string2*.

The value for scan-from-direction determines whether STRIP looks for the left- or right-most occurrence of *string2* in *string1*; the value for strip-toward-direction determines whether characters are removed from the left or right of where *string2* starts.

If the either the scan-from- or the scan-toward-direction parameters are omitted, the value for the missing parameter is assumed to be the same as the one that is specified. If both these parameters are omitted, the default for both is assumed to be "R" (right).

Examples:	STRIP ("Senior Vice President", "Vice", "L") " President" (Note the leading space)
	STRIP ("Senior Vice President", "Vice", "R") "Senior " (Note the trailing space)
	STRIP ("Senior Vice President", " " , "L") "Vice President"
	STRIP ("Senior Vice President", " ", "R") "Senior Vice"
	STRIP ("Senior Vice President", " ", "R", "L") "President"

SUBSTR() Mapping Function

Syntax:	**SUBSTR** (*field*, *start* [*,length* [*, pad*]])
Description:	SUBSTR returns the portion of *field* starting at position *start*, with *length* characters, padded with the *pad* character if necessary.
	The default for *length* is (length of string - start + 1). The default *pad* character is a blank.
Examples:	SUBSTR("Vice-President", "6") "President"
	SUBSTR("Vice-President", "2", "3") "ice"
	SUBSTR("Vice-President", "7", "9", "s") "residents"
	SUBSTR("Vice-President", "11", "4") "dent"

TRIM() Mapping Function

Syntax:	**TRIM** (*field* [*,option*])
Description:	TRIM returns *field* with leading or trailing blanks removed. *Option* specifies whether to remove leading blanks (L) trailing blanks (R), or both (B).
Examples:	TRIM (" Title ", "B") "Title"
	TRIM (" Title ", "L") "Title "
	TRIM (" Title ", "R") " Title"

UPPER() Mapping Function

Syntax:	**UPPER** (*field*)
Description:	UPPER returns the value of *field* with any lower-case letters converted to upper-case.
Examples:	UPPER ("LinkAge") "LINKAGE"
	UPPER ("Bonnie") "BONNIE"

WORD() Mapping Function

Syntax:	**WORD** (*field*, *n* [*, m*])

Description: WORD returns *m* blank-delimited words starting with the *n*th word in *field*.
WORD returns an empty string if *field* contains fewer than *n* words. The default
value for *m* is 1.

Examples:
```
WORD ( "one of a kind", "1" ) "one"
WORD ( "one of a kind", "1", "2" ) "one of"
WORD ( "one of a kind", "3", "2" ) "a kind"
WORD ( "one of a kind", "5" ) ""
WORD ( "Sarah E. Turner", "3" ) "Turner"
```

X500() Mapping Function

Syntax: **X500** (*address*, *field name* [,*index*])

Description: X500 returns the contents of *field name* for the specified address. If the address
has two identical *field name*s, the index value is used to specify the correct one.

The following X.500-type addresses are supported:

- Microsoft Exchange Canonical (for example,
  /o=org/ou=site[/cn=container...])

- Lotus Notes Canonical (for example, cn=name/ou=site..../o=org/c=country)

- Lotus Notes Abbreviated Canonical (for example, name/site/org/country)

Examples: For example, suppose the value of the DN field were that provided in the sample
X500 address below:

```
/o=StarMart/ou=Sales Office/cn=Recipients/cn=Notes_Users
```

The function would provide the following result:

```
X500 ( DN, "ou") "Sales Office"
X500 ( DN, "o") "StarMart"
X500 ( DN, "cn", 2) "Notes_Users"
```

More Information

- Q180517, Title: XFOR: Customizing Dirsync Between Exchange and Notes

- Q174207, Title: XFOR: Notes Proxy Domain Name Over 31 Characters
  Stripped

- Q169393, Title: XFOR: Messages Containing Doclinks Are Getting Stuck in
  Exchange

- Q177597, Title: XFOR: Delivery and Read Reports Do Not Appear in Lotus
  Notes

C H A P T E R   1 1

Lotus cc:Mail

Integrating two different mail systems is a difficult task that requires in-depth knowledge of the messaging environments, the process for connecting the two, and any necessary configuration changes. Even migrating from one system to another requires some level of coexistence so users can communicate with each other during the transition.

This chapter describes how to link Lotus cc:Mail with Microsoft Exchange Server 5.x and how to migrate from cc:Mail to Microsoft Exchange. The focus is on correctly configuring the two mail systems using the Microsoft Exchange Connector for Lotus cc:Mail supplied with Microsoft Exchange Server 5.0 and 5.5. A section about halfway through discusses the Connector for cc:Mail and gives some best practices for implementing it. A corresponding section at the end of the chapter gives best practices for migrating from cc:Mail to Exchange.

To get the most out of this chapter, you should be using Lotus cc:Mail DB6 or DB8 and either Microsoft Exchange Server 5.0 or 5.5. You should thoroughly understand Exchange Server's connectors and architecture, including the message transfer agent (MTA), directory service, and information store. The next few sections provide technical details on cc:Mail and outline the information you must determine for coexistence.

Caution Part of this discussion explains registry changes. Before you apply *any* changes to a live system, test them first in a lab environment. Document carefully any changes you make in a live environment.

Usage Scenarios

You should deploy the Connector for cc:Mail so that it can accommodate different situations. Each of the four usage scenarios outlined below requires a different migration or coexistence strategy:

- An existing Lotus cc:Mail system must coexist with a Microsoft Exchange network. For example, two departments have separate messaging systems but must be able to communicate, or two companies have merged.

- The use of several messaging systems requires a company to establish a message switching service to improve communications.

- A company with a small existing cc:Mail network (fewer than four postoffices) wants to migrate everything to Exchange.

- A company with a medium- to large-size existing cc:Mail network wants to migrate everything to Exchange.

The first two scenarios require installing one or more Connectors for cc:Mail in the Exchange Server network, with data migration to follow at a later stage. Companies in the third scenario may be able to move everyone to Exchange in one step without using any Connectors for cc:Mail. Companies in the fourth category must install one of more Connectors for cc:Mail in the Exchange Server network as they plan for migration. With a large cc:Mail network, it may not be possible to move everyone over to Exchange in a weekend, so temporary connectivity is required.

Analyzing cc:Mail Versions

The Lotus cc:Mail product has evolved over the years with different components for front-end clients, back-end databases, gateways, and monitoring programs. Many companies (yours, perhaps) have added and deleted components to the point where they may not be certain what version or versions they have.

Postoffice Database Versions

The first task is to determine the version number, particularly of the postoffice database, that is already deployed. This database is a set of files held in one directory usually called *\ccdata* and is hosted on server operating systems that support file sharing and record locking. Most cc:Mail postoffices are on Novell NetWare, Windows NT, or IBM OS/2 operating systems. Companies running OS/2 should be aware that many cc:Mail service and maintenance utilities are also available for OS/2; these are identified by the "2" appended to the utility name (for example, ADMIN2 and RECLAIM2).

The version number determine which options to choose to ensure correct connectivity between cc:Mail and Exchange. The table below shows the relationships between database and cc:Mail versions.

Database version	Platform suite	Comments
DB5	cc:Mail 3.x for MS-DOS	Database structure is more than 6 years old and seldom found still in use.
DB6	cc:Mail 4.x for MS-DOS cc:Mail 1.x for Windows cc:Mail 2.x for Windows cc:Mail 6.x for Windows	The most common database structure and version found.
DB7	cc:Mobile 2.x cc:Mobile 6.x	The physical structure of this database is similar to DB6, but only one user can log on because it's primarily for remote use.
DB8	cc:Mail 6.x for Windows cc:Mail 8.x for Windows	Relatively new version using very different file structures from other database versions. cc:Mail 6.x for Windows can communicate with DB6 postoffices as well as DB8.

Determine the Database Version Number

Use cc:Mail's ANALYZE.EXE utility, which checks the integrity of the file structures and identifies corrupt postoffices, to determine the postoffice version. You can also find the version by looking within the \ccdata directory. The following table provides clues:

Database version	Indicators
DB5	No upgrade for 6+ years. ANALYZE.EXE is not in the \ccadmin directory because it wasn't shipped with DB5. A program called *gateway* is being used and was the previous name of the router MTA program before Lotus renamed it.
DB6	The cc:Mail for Windows 2.x or 6.x client is used on the desktop. ANALYZE.EXE reports database version 6. There are files in the \ccdata directory with the following names: MLANDATA CLANDATA NFTERROR.LOG USR*xxxxx*
DB7	cc:Mobile is installed on the machine. Only one USR*xxxxx* file is in the \ccdata directory. Unsuccessful logon attempts to the postoffice using the ADMIN.EXE program.
DB8	cc:Mail for Windows 6.x or 8.x client is used on the desktop. ANALYZE.EXE reports database version 8. There are files in the \ccdata directory with the following names: CCPOMS.*xx* CCPODS.*xx*

Note The Connector for cc:Mail cannot directly communicate with DB5 postoffices.

Overview of the \ccdata Directory

Understanding the file architecture for cc:Mail helps when troubleshooting is required. The major files that make up a postoffice are listed in the following tables for DB6 and DB8.

DB6 Postoffices

File name	Purpose
MLANDATA	Message database. Every message in a user's mailbox or bulletin board will be housed in this single file. cc:Mail uses single-instance storage, which is similar to Exchange Server.
CLANDATA	Postoffice information, directory, and message index. This file has many functions. The first sector (512 bytes) holds the postoffice name and password, the second sector stores the encryption key, and the rest is used for message allocation tables, the main directory list, and the master pointer index to the messages within MLANDATA.
USRxxxxx	Each user has a USR file, which is numbered logically (hex). This file holds information such as the user's name, password, private folder names, and pointers to messages held within MLANDATA.
NFTCHECK	A dummy file that is always 512 bytes. When a cc:Mail client logs on to a postoffice, data is written, read back, and compared to verify that the connection is good.
NFTERROR.LOG	Logs any serious errors, including read and write errors. Generally errors found in this log can be attributed to network problems or postoffice corruption. The Connector for cc:Mail can also log errors here.
CCPODOWN	A dummy file (normally zero bytes) that indicates that a postoffice is shut down. Each cc:Mail component checks this upon logon and backs out if necessary.
TRANSIT.LOG	Used by cc:Mail routers for tracking which queues are being worked upon.

DB8 Postoffices

File name	Purpose
CCPOMS.*xx*	Message store. The equivalent of MLANDATA in DB6. The file extension changes with the postoffice version (when it was last defragmented or RECLAIM-ed).
CCPODS.*xx*	The postoffice name, password, encryption key, and master directory.
CCPOMI.*xx*	The allocation tables and master message pointer index.
U*nnnnnnn.xx*	User names, passwords, private folder names, and pointers to the master list.
CCNFT.LOG	Equivalent of the NFTERROR.LOG in DB6.

Impact on Exchange

Microsoft's Connector for cc:Mail uses a Lotus-compatible format to aid message transfer and directory synchronization. Utilities used by the connector are IMPORT.EXE and EXPORT.EXE, both of which are included on the cc:Mail software CD-ROM. Different versions of IMPORT and EXPORT are available, so be sure to match the correct one with the postoffice database, as indicated in the following table:

IMPORT/EXPORT version	Postoffice database
IMPORT 5.15/Export 5.14	DB6
IMPORT 6.0/Export 6.0	DB8

One of the most common configuration problems occurs when DB6 is configured for IMPORT/EXPORT 6.0. As the table indicates, DB6 should be configured for IMPORT 5.15/Export 5.14.

Note IMPORT/EXPORT 8.0 is not currently supported by the Connector for cc:Mail.

Connector for cc:Mail Architecture

All versions of Exchange Server 5.*x* include the Connector for cc:Mail. Based on the Exchange Development Kit (EDK) connector series, the Connector for cc:Mail automatically executes the EXPORT utility to extract information from the cc:Mail postoffice into plain, structured text. Two-way message communication is possible because the Connector for cc:Mail can also write information into the format that the cc:Mail IMPORT program expects. Synchronization of directories between cc:Mail and Exchange is achieved through extracting and grafting the user directory with the same programs.

Connector for cc:Mail and Microsoft Mail Connector Similarities

The Connector for cc:Mail moves messages from the Exchange information store into the foreign cc:Mail postoffice, in more or less the same way that the Microsoft Mail Connector works with Microsoft Mail postoffices. However, the architecture of the two differs in the following ways:

- **No shadow postoffice**—The Microsoft Mail Connector translates messages from the Exchange information store and places them in a temporary Mail-like routing postoffice. The Connector for cc:Mail translates messages and places them directly into a standard cc:Mail postoffice.

- **No router MTA**—With the Microsoft Mail Connector, After the message is in the shadow postoffice, a configured MTA moves it to the destination Mail postoffice. Because the Connector for cc:Mail does not use a shadow postoffice, an Exchange-based MTA is not necessary.

- **One postoffice connection only**—The Microsoft Mail Connector allows for direct connectivity to many postoffices, whereas the Connector for cc:Mail can only communicate directly with one cc:Mail postoffice. Exchange must funnel messages to one postoffice and onward routing is carried out by cc:Mail router programs.

- **Does not support asynchronous or X.25 connections**—The cc:Mail postoffice must be available on the LAN or WAN so Exchange Server can connect to the share point for the \ccdata directory.

Connector for cc:Mail Directory Structure

All Connector for cc:Mail–related data is held in the ccmcdata directory, a subdirectory of \exchsrvr, which holds the structured text files in transit and some configuration information. The following subdirectories appear under ccmcdata:

Subdirectory of \ccmcdata	Purpose
Bad	Corrupt messages not in the normal, consistent structure.
Export	Messages exported from the cc:Mail postoffice.
Export.bak	Copies of messages exported. Entries will appear here only if the relevant registry flag is set.
Import	Messages to be imported into the cc:Mail postoffice.
Import.bak	Copies of messages imported. Entries will appear here only if the relevant registry flag is set.
Submit	Temporary working directory for message submission *from* Exchange.

Another directory called Dirsync appears after the Connector for cc:Mail has been configured and started.

Connector for cc:Mail Registry Entries

The registry holds the bulk of the Connector for cc:Mail configuration information. Special .INI files built from the registry information every time the connector is started are placed within *ccmcdata*, where they are used to automate the IMPORT and EXPORT processes. The Connector for cc:Mail uses the registry values held under:

HKEY_LOCAL_MACHINE\SYSTEM\CurrentControlSet\Services
\MSExchangeCCMC

n the majority of cases, any entries that must be adjusted are located under the *Parameters* subkey. Alterations to these values are discussed later in the chapter.

Message Routing from Exchange to cc:Mail

The diagram below illustrates how a message is routed from the Exchange Server to a cc:Mail postoffice.

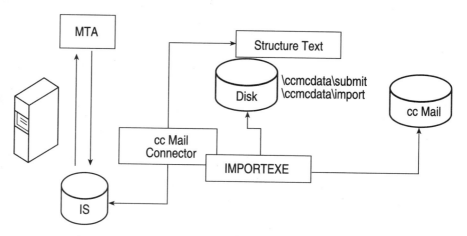

For example, a message sent from an Exchange user to a recipient on cc:Mail is routed as follows:

1. The Exchange user composes a message and addresses it to the cc:Mail recipient either by choosing the name if directory synchronization (dirsync) has been implemented or by entering the cc:Mail address in the To: field of the Exchange message.

   [CCMAIL:Jim Beam at PO1]

2. The Exchange information store receives the message, evaluates the address, identifies that it is not destined for a local recipient, and passes it to the Exchange MTA for routing.

3. The Exchange MTA evaluates the address in the "To:" field. If dirsync has been implemented, the MTA replaces the recipient name with information from the Exchange directory, then uses the gateway address routing table (GWART) to work out which connector can accept this type of message. If the Connector for cc:Mail is local, the MTA moves the message to the cc:Mail MTS-OUT queue, which is part of the private information store.

4. The Exchange Connector for cc:Mail then retrieves the message from MTS-OUT and converts the envelope, text, and any body parts into a structured format. During this conversion, the data is written into a .TMP file in the *\ccmcdata\submit* directory, which is then renamed with a .CCM extension and moved to *\ccmcdata\import*. If there are multiple messages to be transferred, each message is submitted individually.

5. The IMPORT.EXE program checks for messages every 15 seconds (default) and uses special parameters defined in the registry to bring a message into the cc:Mail postoffice and update the cc:Mail users' pointer file. IMPORT was written for MS-DOS and so an NTVDM (Windows NT Virtual DOS Machine) is spawned each time this process runs.

6. The cc:Mail Client polls the postoffice (default every 6 minutes) and retrieves the message header. If a message is destined for a downstream postoffice, a cc:Mail router MTA transfers the message.

Message Routing from cc:Mail to Exchange

A similar process is used to transfer messages sent from cc:Mail to a user on Exchange Server. The routing process is as follows:

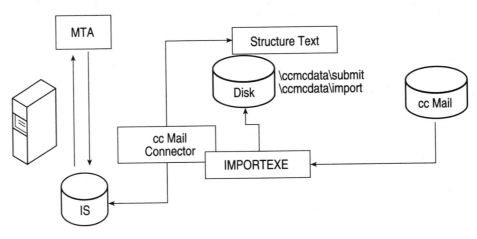

1. The cc:Mail user addresses a message to the Exchange user by choosing the name from the directory if dirsync has been implemented or by typing in the Exchange address, which usually involves selecting the postoffice entry that relates to Exchange (default is the Exchange site name). The user can then type in the cc:Mail proxy address of the Exchange user. To avoid undelivered messages, addresses should be entered in *Last, First* format with an additional comma before the last name (,Bowden, Paul). Messages will fail if the cc:Mail user enters the name in *Last, First* without two commas because cc:Mail will swing the name around to *First Last* format, which will not match the default cc:Mail proxy address generated for the Exchange user. Dirsync overcomes these problems by entering data into the foreign alias name (FAN) field for each Exchange user synchronized with cc:Mail.

2. The message resides in the postoffice queue for cc:Mail to Exchange until the EXPORT program executes, which is every 15 seconds by default. The Exchange Server will spawn a NTVDM to execute EXPORT.EXE.

3. The EXPORT process brings out the messages and writes them into a .CCM file in the *\ccmcdata\export* directory. Multiple cc:Mail messages can reside in the same .CCM file.

4. The Connector for cc:Mail will process the exported messages by converting them to an Exchange-compatible format and placing them in the MTS-IN queue within the private information store.

5. The Exchange MTA pulls out the message, looks at the header, replaces the information with Exchange directory information, and passes the message back to the store for local delivery. If the intended Exchange recipient is located on a different server, the Exchange MTA will route the message on.

Configuring Connector for cc:Mail

Before configuring the Connector for cc:Mail, understand the relationships within the cc:Mail network. In most circumstances, the default Connector for cc:Mail options can be used, although configuring directory synchronization may require custom tuning to avoid incorrect addressing between the two systems. It's recommended that you start by:

- Documenting the existing cc:Mail network—Note the number of postoffices, physical locations, which operating system they are on, gateways to other systems, etc.

- Documenting the message routing topology between the postoffices—Find out how many router MTAs there are (ROUTER.EXE) and how they connect with each postoffice (Type 1—Direct Drive mapping; Type 2—Native Protocol, Asynchronous, or X.25). Also, determine which postoffices are designated hubs. This information determines the optimum placement of Connectors for cc:Mail.

- Finding out how the automatic directory exchange ADE) topology has been configured, if at all—Here you will come across terms such as *Superior*, *Subordinate*, *Peer*, *Broadcaster*, *Division* and *Enterprise*. You can get this information by looking at the propagation type for each postoffice within the cc:Mail ADMIN program.

- Looking at the address structuring inside the postoffice to see if it based on *Last Name, First Name* or *First Name Last Name*—Many postoffices are based on the former, so you may want to change some Connector for cc:Mail entries in the registry on the Exchange Server (explained more thoroughly later). If the Connector for cc:Mail is executed in the default state, it may produce undesirable address formats after the dirsync process has completed.

The Connection Point

There are many ways to link Exchange Server with the cc:Mail environment. Some companies connect directly into a cc:Mail hub postoffice, while others take the more cautious approach and connect Exchange to a dummy postoffice, which is akin to a shadow postoffice in the Mail environment. Located on the Exchange server, the dummy postoffice can use the cc:Mail router program (the Windows NT version if possible) to route messages to the live cc:Mail environment. Separating Exchange and cc:Mail makes troubleshooting easier and allows testing of the cc:Mail directory on a dummy postoffice. Smaller companies with few postoffices may opt for a direct Connector for cc:Mail into the cc:Mail environment if they don't want to manage another postoffice.

Visibility of Exchange users to all of the cc:Mail postoffices in the ADE environment is another consideration. Many companies choose the *Broadcaster* ADE relationship because it provides the best fit for the majority of environments.

Avoid implementing dirsync with a cc:Mail subordinate postoffice because users will not be visible outside the local postoffice. Depending on where the postoffice resides in the ADE hierarchy, cc:Mail can be both a *Superior* and *Subordinate* at the same time.

Database Versions and Postoffices

The database version of the connected postoffice can impact performance and stability. For example, DB8 generally provides more stability than DB6 and enables online maintenance.

The version of the database in the connecting postoffice should match the rest of the postoffice infrastructure, particularly if the cc:Mail environment uses aliases extensively. Mixing two database versions can cause non-delivery reports from aliases. To overcome this issue, use the CCMC.EXE program from Exchange Server 5.0 SP2 or 5.5 SP1 and implement the *Use ANR* registry parameter.

Rules for the Connection

When implementing the Connector for cc:Mail, follow these guidelines:

- Each physical Exchange server can have one Connector for cc:Mail.

- In one site, you can implement as many Connectors for cc:Mail as there are servers.

- Don't have two Exchange servers in the same site connected to a single cc:Mail postoffice.

- Multiple send and receive Connectors for cc:Mail can be configured in a single site when multiple shadow postoffices are used and when the cc:Mail routing has been configured manually.

- Only one Connector for cc:Mail should have dirsync enabled; the rest should be pure messaging connectors (manually change the routing path in the cc:Mail environment).

- Implementing dual Connectors for cc:Mail for fault tolerance will work only if you are prepared to manually adjust the cc:Mail postoffice routes in the event of a failure. This is because cc:Mail cannot use alternate routes. In the event of one CCMC failure, Exchange users can still send messages to cc:Mail, but messages from cc:Mail can only be retrieved if messages are being routed to the dummy postoffice.

These guidelines are not iron clad, but *not* following them could mean changing some entries or adopting a nonstandard configuration. Make your choice carefully and document the connection strategy.

Enhancing Robustness and Performance

To increase robustness with the connecting cc:Mail postoffice, the Exchange server housing the Connector for cc:Mail should be running:

- Windows NT Server 3.51 Service Pack 5 or later
- Windows NT Server 4.0 Service Pack 3 or later

In certain situations, Windows NT Server may write to a cc:Mail data file when another process has an exclusive lock, resulting in postoffice corruption. A Lotus utility called CCREGMOD changes the way that Windows NT Server implements its record-locking mechanism and network redirector write cache. Newer releases of the cc:Mail Client program automatically adjust these parameters on workstations, but it is necessary to manually apply the CCREGMOD program or add the following registry parameters for each server running the Connector for cc:Mail:

```
HKEY_LOCAL_MACHINE/System/CurrentControlSet/Services/LanmanWorkstation/
    Parameters
```

```
Value: UseOpportunisticLocking
Type: REG_DWORD
Data: 0

Value: UseNtCaching
Type: REG_DWORD
Value: 0
```

If changing the above values results degrades Exchange Server system performance, run the Connector for cc:Mail on a dedicated machine. The CCREGMOD program is available on newer releases of the cc:Mail software CD-ROM or direct from Lotus at **http://www.ccmail.com.**

Improving Performance

An NTVDM (Virtual DOS Machine) is created to execute the DOS-based IMPORT and EXPORT programs, which enable message flow between Exchange and cc:Mail. The contents of CONFIG.NT and AUTOEXEC.NT are processed every 15 seconds, the default duration for executing the EXPORT utility.

To increase performance, remove unnecessary commands from the CONFIG.NT and AUTOEXEC.NT files, such as the virtual CD-ROM driver and virtual network protocol drivers. To decrease the load on the server, reduce the IMPORT and EXPORT polling period. In most circumstances, raising the EXPORT frequency from 15 to 60 seconds is acceptable. The IMPORT frequency can be left at 15 seconds because IMPORT will only run if there are messages to import into cc:Mail.

Setting Up a Test Connector

Run the Connector for cc:Mail on a test system to determine if there are any limitations, pitfalls, or gaps in your own knowledge. Two common problems can occur when setting up the test:

1. Creating a test cc:Mail postoffice "dynamically" by specifying all of the necessary parameters on the one command line could encounter a bug in version 5.12 of the cc:Mail ADMIN.EXE program used to setup up a DB6 postoffice. Instead, set up a postoffice interactively by running ADMIN.EXE on its own and then specifying the name, password, and directory when asked. Here's a sample command line that dynamically creates a postoffice:

    ```
    ADMIN /NTEST-PO /P12345 /Dc:\ccdata
    ```

    The bug in ADMIN.EXE (ver. 5.12) will automatically corrupt the postoffice name and password even though the postoffice was created successfully and new entries added. The result is that the Connector for cc:Mail won't run and the cc:Mail ADMIN program will no longer run against the postoffice after the initial creation.

2. On the Connector for cc:Mail **Postoffice** tab, the **Permit ADE to propagate entries synched to cc:Mail to downstream postoffices** checkbox is selected by default. To avoid errors, enable ADE on the test postoffice with the /DIRPROP/Y switch.

Connector for cc:Mail Configuration and IMPORT/EXPORT

Configuring Connector for cc:Mail involves nine tabs, only two of which need to be modified for simple messaging. The first thing to do is copy to the local Exchange server the IMPORT.EXE and EXPORT.EXE programs, which should be located in the \ccadmin directory on most cc:Mail systems. There are three options for placing these programs:

- In the path for Windows NT
- In a new directory and modify the existing path
- In a new directory and adjust the following registry entries:

  Export.exe—path to EXPORT.EXE

  Import.exe—path to IMPORT.EXE

For IMPORT/EXPORT version 6.0 (DB8), copy the IE.RI file to the system path. Place the required files in the path because this is where the Migration Wizard expects them when performing a migration.

It is possible to use the OS/2 versions of IMPORT and EXPORT by modifying the appropriate registry keys. Because these utilities are character-based, Windows NT can start the OS/2 subsystem to execute them. Avoid renaming the files from IMPORT2/EXPORT2 to IMPORT and EXPORT. Version 8.0 of the OS/2 utilities **will not run** on a Windows NT computer.

Postoffice Configuration Tab

The configuration information on the **Postoffice** tab allows you to specify the following, some of which are explained in more detail below:

- The cc:Mail postoffice to communicate with
- The version of IMPORT/EXPORT in use
- The language setting for the postoffice
- Exchange message tracking options
- Secondary ADE propagation options
- Preservation of forwarding information in messages

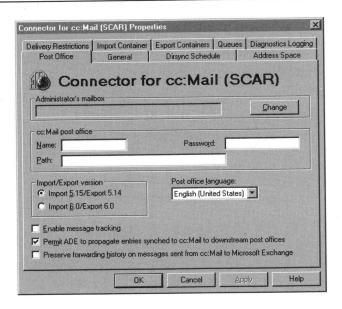

Postoffice Name and Path

Enter the postoffice name along with spaces and other punctuation used. Specify the path in universal naming convention (UNC) format. If the cc:Mail postoffice is located on a Novell NetWare server make sure that:

- Gateway services for NetWare are installed.

- The frame types have been set correctly.

- A NetWare account has been created for the Exchange site services account, and the password details have been configured correctly.

- The UNC path includes the NetWare server name and volume, such as\\Netware1\\sys\\ccmail\\ccdata.

Postoffice Password

The password field can cause problems if not completely understood. Here's a brief description:

When the Connector for cc:Mail is exporting from cc:Mail, the security context of the cc:Mail-to-Exchange queue is used instead of the context of the cc:Mail postoffice password. In addition, every local account in a cc:Mail postoffice has a password, including mailboxes, mobile users, and directly connected postoffices. If you manually create a postoffice (P) entry in cc:Mail, no password will be associated with it (null) by default. The first time the Connector for cc:Mail communicates with the postoffice, the password specified on the **General** tab is applied to that postoffice entry. Therefore, any subsequent attempt to access the postoffice under this context requires the same password.

If you want a global password change, you have to adjust the:

- **General** tab of the connector
- Postoffice password
- cc:Mail-to-Exchange postoffice entry

Postoffice Language

The postoffice language should match the language setting on a DB8 postoffice. Even if DB6 is used, the local language should still be specified to ensure correct codepage translation.

Import/Export Version

Select the correct IMPORT/EXPORT version for your postoffice:

- Select Import 5.15/Export 5.14 if you are working with DB6
- Select Import 6.0/Export 6.0 if you are working with DB8

Other Flags

- **Message Tracking**—The **Enable message tracking** option allows the Exchange server to track messages as they are flowing in and out of the connector. View these messages within the message tracking center.

- **Forwarding History**—The **Preserve forwarding history on messages sent from cc:Mail to Microsoft Exchange** box should be selected if you want to encapsulate the forward information generated by cc:Mail into a forward.txt file that will be seen by the Exchange Client.

- **Propagate Entries**—The box labeled **Permit ADE to propagate entries synched to cc:Mail downstream postoffices** is selected by default. When checked, Exchange directory entries pushed into the cc:Mail postoffice directory are re-propagated by the cc:Mail ADE to other postoffices if the necessary relationships have been established (ADE is discussed in more depth later). Clear the checkbox if the connecting postoffice does not have ADE enabled or if re-propagation is not desired. These diagrams illustrate the flag in both positions:

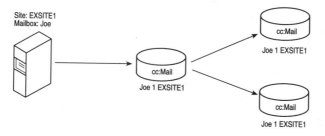

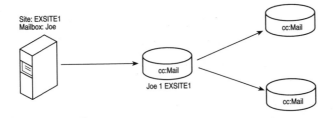

Note cc:Mail ADE supports a range of propagation relationships, some of which may interfere with the propagation flag. For example, ADE relationships of *Superior/Subordinate* and *Broadcaster* allow the Exchange directory to pass through, while other relationships such as *Peer* specify that non-local entries received from another postoffice should not be propagated.

General Configuration and Address Space Tabs

- **General configuration tab**—Used to enter information such as an administrative note and to set a message size limit on the Connector for cc:Mail.

Note Microsoft Exchange 5.x supports message size restriction only when sending messages from Exchange to cc:Mail.

- **Address space tab**—Used to define the routes from the Exchange Server network to each of the cc:Mail postoffices. Select **New General** and specify the Type (CCMAIL) and Address of the postoffices that are reachable using this connector. Examples of address space include:

```
CCMAIL:    *
CCMAIL:    * at P01
CCMAIL:    * at  *
CCMAIL:    * at P0??
```

Configuring the cc:Mail Postoffice

When configured for dirsync, the Connector for cc:Mail automatically creates the necessary queue entry on the cc:Mail postoffice. For non-dirsync connectors, cc:Mail-to-Exchange routing must be manually configured. The postoffice name for Exchange will be the same as the cc:Mail proxy on the **Site Addressing** tab. Because cc:Mail considers an Exchange site as one large postoffice, the default proxy postoffice name will be inherited from the Exchange site name. The location code will be P (directly connected postoffice), and the address type will be blank because the cc:Mail router is not involved.

Note The **Comments** field for the cc:Mail to Exchange postoffice entry should be set to "MSExchangeCCMC *<server name>*" so users deleted from the Exchange environment are propagated to cc:Mail. For example:

```
EXSITE1      P          MSExchangeCCMC PLUTO
```

If a space is part of the Exchange site name, ignore the warning when trying to create the cc:Mail queue.

Starting the Connector for cc:Mail

Before starting the Connector for cc:Mail, check the **Routing** tab under **Site Addressing** to verify that the new CCMAIL route has been incorporated into the GWART. If not, manually recalculate routing. After the routing has been established, start the Connector for cc:Mail (from **Control Panel**), pass messages between the two systems, and check the Event Log to view any connection errors.

Troubleshooting the Connector

If connection errors appear in the Windows NT Event Log or if there are problems starting the connector, execute the CCMC.EXE program manually from a Windows NT command prompt. The severity settings on Connector for cc:Mail Service's UI should be set to **Maximum** in the **Diagnostics Logging** page so you can view enough information to troubleshoot the connector.

Another troubleshooting technique is to view messages waiting to be exported in the cc:Mail postoffice queue and see if they disappear after a short time. Because directly connected postoffice (P entries) have associated USR files, it is possible to log on to the queue from a standard cc:Mail MS-DOS or Windows client. Instead of specifying a user name, specify the queue name for logon actions. The password is the same one used for the Connector for cc:Mail (located on the **General** tab).

Note Any messages you read will not be exported to the Exchange environment. To view the messages without affecting the queue, forward them to another account. You can use this trick to look at queues between cc:Mail postoffices as well.

If zero byte files are stacking up in the *\ccmcdata\export* directory, review the connector settings because the Connector for cc:Mail may be having problems contacting the postoffice. Check the Event Log to confirm. If the connector settings don't seem to be the problem, the connecting postoffice may be shut down for maintenance. In any case, remove the zero byte files manually.

Other Connector Results

Even without dirsync configured between the two systems, the Connector for cc:Mail will create a new directory called DIRSYNC in \exchsrvr\ccmcdata with two subdirectories called IMPORT and EXPORT. In addition, the act of starting the connector will create in \exchsrvr\ccmcdata an EXPORT.INI file that takes on the standard parameter-passing format used by the EXPORT program. The actual file may be similar to this example:

```
[export]
CMD = "/EXSITE1"  /D\\cpq-msg1\ccdata  /END/16  /ITEMSIZE /FORMAT/FAN
/BATCH  /FILES/MACBIN2  /DATE/1  /CODEPAGE/850

[export2]
CMD = "/EXSITE1"  /D\\cpq-msg1\ccdata  /END/16  /ITEMSIZE /FORMAT/FAN
/BATCH  /FILES/MACBIN2  /DATE/1  /CODEPAGE/850
```

Notice that the Export program pulls messages from the queue name that relates to the Exchange site.

Testing Message Connectivity

To send a message from an Exchange client, type [CCMAIL:Jim Watkins at PO1] on the TO: line. To send a message from a cc:Mail client:

1. Compose a new message and select the Exchange site name
2. Type in the cc:Mail proxy address of the Exchange user. If dirsync is not configured, enter the Exchange name in *,Last, First* format because cc:Mail normally changes the format to *First Last* upon pressing return.

When the first message has been sent from the Exchange client to a cc:Mail user, an IMPORT.INI file is created under \exchsrvr\ccmcdata. It should look something like this:

```
[import]
CMD = "/PO1"  /D\\cpq-msg1\ccdata  /ITEMSIZE  /PARTIAL  /BATCH
/FILES/MACBIN2  /DATE/1  /CODEPAGE/850

[import2]
CMD = "/PO1"  /D\\cpq-msg1\ccdata  /ITEMSIZE  /PARTIAL  /BATCH
/FILES/MACBIN2  /DATE/1  /CODEPAGE/850
```

Interoperability Levels

The Connector for cc:Mail retains most, but not all, of the message properties generated by both messaging systems. The following table outlines the conversion interoperability:

Exchange feature	cc:Mail interpretation
TO: CC: BCC:	Interpreted correctly
Importance (urgent, normal, low)	Urgent, normal, low
Message flags	Lost—no such feature in cc:Mail
Message sensitivity	Lost—no such feature in cc:Mail
Delivery receipt	Lost—no such feature in cc:Mail
Read receipt	Generated when message is read
cc:Mail forms	Imported as an .LFM file attachment that can be read if the application is loaded locally
File attachments	Correct—with associated file names
Shortcuts	Translated to absolute path
Embedded URLs	Appears as plain text
Embedded OLE objects	Separate attachment that can be launched with the appropriate viewer
Rich text (colors, fonts, etc.)	Lost
Text justification	Lost
Tabs	Converted to 5 spaces (can be adjusted in the registry)
Special characters ($, @, %, £)	Translated correctly
Bullet points	Converted to asterisks
Embedded messages	Attached as additional text items

Using Exchange Server as a Gateway

cc:Mail users can use the Exchange server as a gateway to other messaging worlds such as SMTP, X.400, and Fax. Typically, the biggest requirement is for cc:Mail users to have full outbound and inbound Internet mail, which is simply a matter of configuring the Internet Mail Service on the Exchange server.

However, multiple file attachments in a message sent by a cc:Mail user may fuse together once they have passed through the Internet Mail Service. The recipient will notice that the MIME type will be *Application/MS-TNEF*. The Internet Mail Service leaves the preservation of RTF information to the sender by default, but cc:Mail users have no way of specifying RTF preservation and so the Internet Mail Service assumes that it should be preserved.

The solution is to reconfigure the Internet Mail Service so that it *never* sends rich-text with the message. This makes file attachments readable for Internet recipients, but strips out rich-text information for all messages, including those sent from Exchange users. If rich-text is required, consider establishing two Internet Mail Services: one for cc:Mail users and another for Exchange users.

Implementing cc:Mail Directory Synchronization

Before tackling directory synchronization between Exchange and cc:Mail, it's important to understand how cc:Mail handles this natively. There are three ways to transfer directories in cc:Mail:

1. Manually enter the names and addresses into each postoffice—a tedious task at best and nearly impossible with large messaging environments.

2. Take a snapshot of the cc:Mail directory using the EXPORT command with the /DIRECTORY switch to place the cc:Mail directory into a structured format in a text file. The file will look like this:

   ```
   Name:     User's name (or postoffice queue name)
   Locn:     Location code (L, R, P, A)
   Addr:     Address (home postoffice or telephone number)
   Cmts:     Comments field (up to 126 characters)
   Name:
   Locn:
   Addr:
   Cmts:
   …etc
   ```

   These records are listed sequentially in a single file, which you can import into another postoffice with the IMPORT command and the /DIRECTORY switch. Even though L (Local) users do not have addresses, their home postoffice is placed on the Addr: line in the file when you perform an export. Through this process, a secondary postoffice recognizes this user as *local* on another postoffice rather than on this one.

3. Because manual imports and exports are time consuming, ADE (automatic directory exchange) is the third method of directory propagation and is recommended for all sizes of cc:Mail networks. ADE differs from the IMPORT/EXPORT directory method in that only changes are propagated and the cc:Mail routers make the adjustments to the directory. The Exchange Connector for cc:Mail does not use ADE, but does support the sending of changes to the cc:Mail directory instead of sending the whole directory. Exchange Server accomplishes this by comparing the current Exchange directory to the cc:Mail directory.

   To configure automatic directory propagation between cc:Mail postoffices:

   - The administrators of each postoffice must enable ADE by starting the ADMIN.EXE program with the /DIRPROP/Y switch. On DB6 postoffices this creates a special bulletin board called **##Directory Updates** (where all the updates are stored). On DB8 postoffices, this is created then the postoffice is installed.

- The administrators then define an ADE relationship with each other depending on their requirements. For example, *Superior/Subordinate* relationships could be used if one of the postoffices has the master directory and the other postoffices have a slave directory. All changes are fed from the *Superior*, even mailbox creation and deletion. The other common type of relationship is *Broadcaster*, which implies decentralized administration where only the local users of each postoffice are propagated. It is possible to create your own relationship by setting individual propagation flags.

- The router call lists are configured to exchange directory updates as well as messages.

▶ To propagate a directory entry

1. The administrator of one postoffice makes a change in the directory, such as creating a local user called "Bloggs, Fred".

2. When the administrator exits the Administrator program, there is a yes/no prompt for change propagation. If *no* is selected the user will exist but other postoffices will not receive the change. If *yes* is selected a specially formatted message is written into the local *##Directory Updates* bulletin board. The message is addressed to the postoffice administrator and consists of a single file attachment with this message (no text body). The file is called CCMUPDAT (with no file extension). The contents of the CCMUPDAT file look like this:

```
Name: Bloggs, Fred
Locn: L·
Addr: P01
Cmts: Extension 3459
```

3. When the cc:Mail router of this postoffice next connects to an adjacent router, it will search through the *##Directory Updates* bulletin board, looking for new entries.

4. All new messages (directory changes) are bundled into one CCMUPDAT file and filtered through the propagation relationship that has been set for the adjacent postoffice. This router determines what updates it is allowed to send across.

5. The CCMUPDAT file is passed between the two routers.

6. The adjacent cc:Mail router receives the incoming update and passes it through the propagation relationship filter set for the sending postoffice. This router works out what updates it should receive from this postoffice and, in effect, uses the propagation filters as a level of security.

7. The changes that are allowed through are then applied online to the postoffice directory.

The same process is used for deletions but the update message has the Locn: field set to *DL* (delete local user). All directory update messages remain in the ##Directory Updates bulletin board and have to be manually cleared down by the administrator or an automated process. A single bulletin board can hold up to 32,767 messages; they must be cleaned out periodically.

How the Connector for cc:Mail Performs Directory Synchronization

An Exchange server synchronizes its directory with cc:Mail through an automated IMPORT/EXPORT procedure that imports only changes into cc:Mail. The process for Connector for cc:Mail dirsync is:

1. Export the directory, mailing lists, and bulletin board from the connecting cc:Mail postoffice

   ```
   Directory = EXPORT\CCMDIR.EXP
   Mailing lists = EXPORT\CCMLIST.EXP
   Bulletin boards = EXPORT\CCMBB.EXP
   ```

2. Parse the CCMDIR.EXP file and calculate the number of Exchange entries and cc:Mail entries retrieved from the directory.

3. Parse the CCMLIST.EXP file and calculate the number of cc:Mail mailing lists.

4. Parse the CCMBB.EXP file and calculate the number of cc:Mail bulletin boards.

5. Search the Exchange directory and prepare a cc:Mail Import file.

6. Compare the Import file to the information extracted from the postoffice and conclude the alterations required.

   ```
   Exchange deletions = IMPORT\CCMDEL.IMP
   Exchange additions = IMPORT\CCMDIR.IMP
   ```

7. Delete any Exchange entries from cc:Mail by importing the CCMDEL.IMP file into the postoffice.

8. Add any Exchange entries to cc:Mail by importing the CCMDIR.IMP file into the postoffice.

9. Start updating the Exchange directory by making the necessary additions, deletions, and modifications.

10. Update the cc:Mail mailing lists in the Exchange directory.

11. Update cc:Mail bulletin boards in the Exchange directory.

A Pentium 166-MHz machine with 64 MB of RAM should be able to import:

- 8,500 new updates imported into Exchange per hour
- 2,500 unchanged imports per minute

Preparing to Synchronize Exchange and cc:Mail

Before configuring dirsync between the two messaging systems, investigate the current set up and requirements. By default, Exchange assumes that:

- Once imported, you want your cc:Mail users to appear on the global address list in *First Name Last Name* format.

- The Exchange alias (and therefore the Microsoft Mail and SMTP proxy names) should be built using the first name and one character from the last name.

SMTP Proxy Addresses

Using the connector to link Exchange Server and cc:Mail makes it possible for cc:Mail users to send and receive messages to and from the Internet. Consider the following when evaluating adding this capability.

Awkward address formats—To prevent awkward address formats, the directories of Exchange and cc:Mail should be synchronized. For example, a cc:Mail user would send a message to a user on the Internet by:

1. Selecting the postoffice queue name that relates to the Exchange site.

2. Typing in the SMTP address.

3. Sending the message.

If the originator is not a custom recipient on the Exchange server, the from and reply-to field would look like this:

```
IMCEACCMAIL-Jim+20Wilson+20at+20PO1@domain.com
```

Alias and address generation—If your company is large, consider changing the registry parameter that controls the generation of alias (and therefore SMTP) addresses for each cc:Mail user. By default, the Connector for cc:Mail generates alias addresses for cc:Mail users as follows:

```
First Name then first character from last name (e.g. JimW)
```

SMTP proxy addresses are generated from the alias by default, so if there are two JimWs the SMTP addresses will be JimW@domain.com and JimW2@domain.com. These addresses can be changed after creation, but not without some administration overhead and potential confusion.

To resolve this issue, change either the registry parameter called "Dirsync alias name rule" detailed at the end of this paper or adjust the SMTP proxy generation rules so that the address is built using other mailbox fields. For example, some companies have an SMTP naming convention of *First.Last@domain*. Because the cc:Mail dirsync process populates the *first name* and *surname* fields in the directory, there is flexibility for building other addresses.

The following SMTP site addressing rule could be set:

```
SMTP: %g.%s@microsoft.com
```

Note The Connector for cc:Mail does not populate the *First Name* and *Surname* fields of Exchange custom recipients if the cc:Mail directory is formatted in *First Last* instead of the usual *Last, First* format.

Any of the following variables can be used with the SMTP proxy generator (case sensitive):

Variable	Description
%d	Display Name
%g	Given Name
%I	Initials
%m	Mailbox (or alias) name
%s	Last Name
%r*xy*	Replace character *x* with *y*
%*nv*	Use *n* characters of the variable *v*

Note Not all proxy generators in Exchange support these variables. For instance, the cc:Mail proxy generator (CCMPROXY.DLL) does not support %r*xy* but does support all of the others.

Distinguished Names

Every object within Exchange requires an X.500 Distinguished Name (DN). For Exchange Mailboxes, this name is inherited from the hierarchy and alias, such as:

```
/o=Microsoft/ou=North America/cn=Recipients/cn=Paul.Bowden
```

The Connector for cc:Mail dirsync process allocates a DN for each cc:Mail custom recipient. The Relative Distinguished Name (RDN) is a calculated field and at first glance seems a random hex string, such as:

```
/o=Microsoft/ou=North America/cn=Users/cn=66688E05
```

This hex string is stamped on the header of messages sent from cc:Mail to Exchange users. If a cc:Mail user moves from an existing postoffice to another one (FUM), the next dirsync cycle removes the old custom recipient and creates a new one. Because the hex string is calculated from the cc:Mail user name and address, the new DN is different, so when messages previously received from the cc:Mail user are replied to from Exchange, the message bounces back as non-deliverable.

As a result, try to minimize the movement of cc:Mail users. If this is impossible, configure an *Enterprise* ADE relationship between the shadow postoffice and the downstream cc:Mail network, then change the *Use ANR* registry parameter (Exchange Server 5.0 SP2 and 5.5 SP1 or above) to ensure that the RDN for users stays constant regardless of postoffice. This change results in the Connector for cc:Mail always calculating the same DN for cc:Mail users, independent of their home postoffice name.

The Import Container Tab

When configuring the Connector for cc:Mail for dirsync, the desired environment should determine where the cc:Mail custom recipients are created:

- If Exchange is being deployed as a message-switching backbone, create a separate container to house these custom recipients.

- If cc:Mail connectivity is needed as a precursor to migrating all users over to Exchange, consider placing the entries in the standard *Recipients* container.

- Place all cc:Mail objects in the *Recipients* container because during the migration to Exchange, it is undesirable to relocate the custom recipients to a different container. If this occurs, the underlying DN for the cc:Mail user changes and that results in non-delivery messages for replies to existing messages in Exchange.

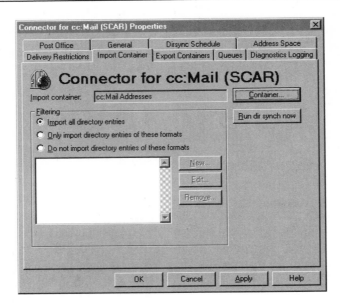

Import filtering is the next item to configure. By default, this imports every entry from the connecting cc:Mail postoffice, and you must change this setting if you want to import only certain entries or to exclude the importing of addresses from certain cc:Mail postoffices. The import filtering strings can be configured in much the same way as configuring the **Address Space** tab (for example: * at PO2).

Do not click the **Run dir synch now** button on the **Import** container tab until you have configured the **Export Container** tab (covered later).

If dirsync must be re-established after a major directory reconfiguration, mail messages could start backing up in the Exchange queues while the Connector for cc:Mail is down. Rather than starting the connector and letting it process the backlogged messages (which could result in non-deliveries if the directory is inconsistent), force directory synchronization from the command line by running "CCMC CCDIR" before starting the connector. The **Run dir synch now** button can be used only when the connector is active.

The Export Containers Tab

The **Export Containers** tab defines the containers of users to be exported to cc:Mail. This can provide great flexibility, allowing you to restrict certain groups of users from being visible in the cc:Mail environment. There is a downside to this flexibility; if a full global directory is required and the Exchange administrator creates another container or a new site comes on line, you must reconfigure the Connector for cc:Mail to export these as well.

The container housing the cc:Mail custom recipients can also be configured for export. The Connector for cc:Mail ensures that duplicate entries are not created in cc:Mail. It's also possible to use the trust level setting to control exactly which recipients are exported out of a container. For example, you may want to hide certain users from the cc:Mail environment instead of whole containers.

Note You cannot select the trust level assigned to cc:Mail custom recipient objects imported into Exchange: they all have trust level 0.

The Dirsync Schedule Tab

This tab defines when directory synchronization is performed (default **Never**). *Always* forces a full dirsync every 15 minutes, which is overkill for most configurations. **Selected times** (with whole hours blocked) initiates a dirsync only on the hour of each highlighted block.

When subsequent dirsync cycles run, the Exchange server does not re-replicate unchanged cc:Mail entries to other Exchange servers. For example, if a cc:Mail user already appears in Exchange, dirsync will not modify or increment the object's Update Sequence Number (USN).

After Dirsync

After the first dirsync, there are a few extra .INI files in the *exchsrvr\ccmcdata* directory:

File name	Controls
BBOARDS.INI	Command string parameters for exporting bulletin board names from a postoffice.
EXPORTDR.INI	Command string parameters for exporting the directory from a postoffice.
IMPORTDR.INI	Command string parameters for importing the directory into a postoffice.
LISTS.INI	Command string parameters for exporting mailing list names from a postoffice.

In addition, there are some new files in subdirectories beneath
\exchsrvr\ccmcdata\dirsync.

File path	Lists
EXPORT\CCMBB.EXP	Bulletin board names on the connecting cc:Mail postoffice.
EXPORT\CCMDIR.EXP	The directory on the connecting cc:Mail postoffice (includes cc:Mail and Exchange users).
EXPORT\CCMLIST.EXP	Mailing list names and users from the connecting cc:Mail postoffice.
IMPORT\CCMDEL.IMP	Exchange recipients deleted from the cc:Mail directory (because they no longer exist in Exchange) in the last directory synchronization cycle.
IMPORT\CCMDIR.UND	Exchange recipients that could not be added to the cc:Mail directory in the last directory synchronization cycle.
IMPORT\CCMDIR.IMP	Exchange recipients added to the cc:Mail directory in the last directory synchronization cycle.

Checking the cc:Mail Postoffice

All Exchange recipients should appear in the cc:Mail directory in this format:

Name:	Locn:	Addr:	Cmts:
Last, First	1	EXSITE1 Last, First	Notes

- The name in the cc:Mail directory is taken from the cc:Mail proxy e-mail address for the Exchange recipient, which defaults to *Last Name, First Name*.

- The location code of 1 indicates that this is a local user of another postoffice.

- The address field contains the name of the Exchange site where this user exists followed by the user's name. This method of addressing is known as a foreign alias name (FAN) and is implemented in this way so that messages sent from cc:Mail to Exchange are presented in *Last Name, First Name* format.

- The comments field is taken from the *Notes* attribute on the Exchange mailbox.

If users on other Exchange sites were also propagated through this connector, a new postoffice entry would have this format:

Name:	Locn:	Addr:	Cmts:
EXSITE2	p	EXSITE1	
Springer, Will	1	EXSITE2	

This informs cc:Mail that any messages sent to Will Springer should be directed at the EXSITE2 postoffice. cc:Mail then works out that the EXSITE2 postoffice is through EXSITE1 and queues the message for EXSITE1. cc:Mail always goes through this chaining effect to make sure that the outgoing message is placed in the correct queue.

Checking the Exchange Server

The import container should be populated with custom recipients that relate to the cc:Mail users. The display name for each cc:Mail custom recipient has been built in *First Name Last Name* format, which is the default way to build normal Exchange mailboxes. If your company has decided that display names should be built differently (such as in *Last Name, First Name* format), modify the registry entry called **Dir Synch display name generation rule**, detailed later in this chapter.

By default, addresses for cc:Mail users are generated in *First Name Last Name* format regardless of the format used in the cc:Mail directory. In Exchange Server 5.0 with Service Pack 1 (or later) you can change the generation format for addresses by adjusting the **Generate secondary proxy address** registry parameter. If you plan to backbone two or more cc:Mail networks through Exchange, set this parameter to 1 so that directory synchronization is handled correctly.

When cc:Mail alias names are synchronized, Exchange cannot associate the imported alias with the name of the postoffice where the user is located if the alias refers to a user downstream of the connecting postoffice. Therefore, Exchange Server appends the name of the connecting postoffice (derived from the connector's **General** tab). Generally, the import program can resolve the alias name into the name of the real user and send the message on to the destination postoffice.

However, a problem can arise if there is a version mismatch between the cc:Mail postoffices. For example, if the connecting postoffice is DB8 and the other postoffices are DB6, messaging to downstream aliases will fail because the message is addressed to the real user in *Last Name, First Name at downstream-PO* format instead of *First Name Last Name at downstream-PO*. This causes the cc:Mail router program to bounce the message.

There are two ways around this problem:

- Make sure the connecting postoffice version matches that of the downstream postoffices.

- Implement the *Use ANR* registry parameter with Exchange Server 5.0 SP2 or 5.5 SP1 and above.

Problems with the Second Synchronization Cycle

When the directory synchronization cycle occurs for the second time, Exchange users may appear twice on the global address list. One address refers to the real mailbox for the user and the other is a custom recipient, appearing in the *Import* container.

The problem is due to the way that Exchange differentiates between cc:Mail users and imported Exchange users and can be solved by adding **MSExchangeCCMC** *<server name>* to the comments field relating to the cc:Mail-to-Exchange postoffice name.

Bulletin Boards and Mailing Lists

Bulletin board and mailing list addresses are imported into Exchange as custom recipients, but Exchange does not automatically recognize these recipients as public folders and distribution lists. In addition, the home postoffice addresses for these BBs and MLs are not automatically assigned to these recipients so an NDR (non-delivery report) error will occur when Exchange users send messages to these recipients. Manually edit the cc:Mail address for these types of recipients to get around the problem or filter them out using the **Import** tab.

Maintaining Mailing and Distribution Lists

Both Exchange Server and cc:Mail use the concept of group lists, but call them different names: Exchange uses the term distribution lists (DLs) and cc:Mail refers to them as mailing lists (MLs). Exchange DLs are more functional than cc:Mail's equivalent because they can contain any type of recipient, including mailboxes, custom recipients, hidden recipients, public folders, and other distribution lists. cc:Mail Mailing Lists cannot contain the names of other mailing lists on the same postoffice and have a hard-coded limit of up to 200 names per mailing list and 4 kb size for the message header.

Achieving coexistence between cc:Mail mailing lists and Exchange distribution lists requires much care because of the cc:Mail limitations. For example, if an Exchange user sends a message to a DL defined in Exchange with cc:Mail users (>200 custom recipients) on the list, the Connector for cc:Mail would not even attempt to import the message for cc:Mail users and would return this message: "Error: Unable to deliver the message due to the number of specified recipients of the message."

To illustrate the options for coexistence, consider the following scenario: a cc:Mail mailing list called "#Sales Team" has to include both cc:Mail and Exchange users. The following four options are available and all include pros and cons:

- Add the l Exchange recipients to the current cc:Mail mailing list.

  PROs: Short-term ease and convenience.

  CONs: As the team expands, the 200-user limit may be reached. More work to do if the end goal is full migration to Exchange.

- Create an Exchange distribution list for the sales team and add this DL's l account to the existing cc:Mail mailing list.

  PROs: The sales team members on Exchange are controlled by the Exchange administrators and likewise for cc:Mail. Good solution if most of the members are on cc:Mail.

  CONs: There are two points of administration

- Create an Exchange distribution list for the whole the sales team and add Exchange mailboxes and the cc:Mail custom recipient account for the cc:Mail mailing list holding sales team members on cc:Mail .

  PROs: Scaleable solution that works if most of the members are on Exchange.

  CONs: Two points of administration. More work to do if the end goal is a full migration to Exchange.

- Create an Exchange distribution list for the whole the sales team and add Exchange mailboxes and cc:Mail custom recipients to this list. cc:Mail users would then send to the l account for the Exchange DL.

  PROs: All administration is performed on Exchange. Good solution if most users are located on Exchange. Less work to do if migrating to Exchange.

  CONs: The 4-KB header might be reached on cc:Mail and the message would be undeliverable, although this can be worked around by using nested DLs.

For some companies, the best solution is an adaptation of the last option. By creating a sales team distribution list in Exchange, this could act as a master to other DLs, which could hold the actual user accounts. The child lists would be nested under the master and would contain no more than 200—they may even be hidden from the directory. When a cc:Mail user sends a message to the list, the cc:Mail proxy address for the master would receive it, expand the DL, and send messages to the recipients. When the Connector for cc:Mail imports each message, only the names of the child lists appear in the header (on the BCC line) and so the message is not bounced back.

In addition, all cc:Mail mailing lists would be controlled through Exchange, which means that membership control could be delegated to Exchange clients. As users are migrated to Exchange and custom recipient objects are converted to mailboxes, which in turn keeps the DL membership intact. As the cc:Mail mailing lists have to be moved to Exchange at some stage, it is best to do this early on in the project to save administration overhead during the migration.

Maintaining Bulletin Boards and Public Folders

Both Exchange and cc:Mail have the concept of shared repositories for collaboration: cc:Mail uses bulletin boards (BB) and Exchange has public folders (PF). Because the two offer different administration and synchronization features, achieving coexistence is a challenge. The two most used approaches are:

- Make the cc:Mail bulletin boards the primary repository for user postings, and use Exchange public folders as a subordinate from cc:Mail.

- Make the Exchange public folders the primary repository for user postings and configure rules so that the cc:Mail bulletin boards receive updates.

Each strategy has its own pros and cons, and your choice depends on how your user community leverages bulletin boards today. Also you may decide to use one strategy for existing cc:Mail bulletin boards, but use public folders for any new requests for collaborative repositories. Neither solution handles deletes, so use age rules on public folders to remove older items.

Making Bulletin Boards the Primary Repository

The steps you must follow to have cc:Mail bulletin boards be primary for user postings and have Exchange public folders receive updates are:

1. Use the Exchange Migration Wizard to create the Exchange public folders for the corresponding cc:Mail bulletin boards.

2. Change the cc:Mail proxy address on each public folder to something that begins with a tilde (~). Because cc:Mail doesn't offer hidden address, adding the tilde places these addresses at the bottom of the list in cc:Mail to lessen the possibility of users accidentally mailing to them.

3. Add the addresses changed in step #2 above to the cc:Mail directory. To do this, un-hide the public folders and let dirsync add the addresses to the cc:Mail directory. Be aware that this exposes the addresses in the Exchange global address list.

4. Add each corresponding address to the propagation list for the respective bulletin board.

5. On the cc:Mail postoffice connected to the Connector for cc:Mail, create a create only (C/O) entry for the Exchange shadow postoffice name so that when the router runs against this postoffice it will create propagation messages for the Exchange public folders. Don't add the connected postoffice to the bulletin board propagation list because this can cause looping.

6. Change the age limit for the Exchange public folders to delete older content. Also advise administrators that when messages are removed from bulletin boards, they must be removed manually from the Exchange public folders.

7. Modify the target address on the custom recipient for the cc:Mail bulletin boards to add the *at PO* information so messages from Exchange reach the BB's postoffice. Users on cc:Mail will continue to send messages to the bulletin boards just as they always have, and users on Exchange will mail to the custom recipient for the cc:Mail bulletin boards.

Making Public Folders the Primary Repository

Follow these steps to have Exchange public folders be the primary repository for user postings and have cc:Mail bulletin boards receive updates:

1. Create the cc:Mail bulletin board.

2. Create the Exchange public folders with the Exchange Migration Wizard and un-hide them from the directory.

3. Create a rule on the public folder to forward all messages (untouched) to the cc:Mail address of the bulletin board.

4. Educate cc:Mail users to send their bulletin board messages to the address of the public folder.

Strategy Limitations

Although these strategies are simple, they are limited in two ways: Deletions aren't handled automatically and users *must* send their messages to the proper address. If users inadvertently send a message to the non-primary address, the message will only exist in that system.

Connector for cc:Mail: Implementation Best Practices

When deploying the connector, an organization must typically consider:

- **User requirements**

  Ensure that end-to-end delivery time between systems is equal to or better than delivery time within the native messaging environment.

  Support file attachments in both directions.

Maintain directory entries in their native systems' format: cc:Mail users see Exchange users in the directory as though they were cc:Mail users, and Exchange users see cc:Mail users as members in Exchange global address list (GAL).

Support message fidelity such as message priority and read-receipt in both directions.

- **Administration/operations requirements**

Administer Connectors for cc:Mail from a single computer.

Minimize hardware requirements to integrate the Exchange and cc:Mail environments.

Track messages sent between the Exchange and cc:Mail environments, and monitor the mail flow between them.

A planning team must consider the coexistence or migration path and the speed at which it will be traveled. Some organizations migrate slowly, working out coexistence issues as they go. Others migrate quickly, minimizing the coexistence timeframe and disruption to the business. Project planning is, of course, simplified by a quick migration with minimal time spent on coexistence issues.

The following are practices Microsoft has found to be helpful when implementing the connector.

Configure Directory Synchronization

The Connector for cc:Mail provides directory synchronization between Exchange and cc:Mail directories, greatly reducing the directory administration. After configuration, cc:Mail addresses appear in the Exchange GAL as custom recipients. Exchange addresses exported into the cc:Mail system appear as native cc:Mail addresses, and Exchange sites appear as cc:Mail postoffices.

The Connector for cc:Mail can also export Exchange addresses using the cc:Mail export "PROP" option. You can configure the attached cc:Mail postoffice to distribute addresses using cc:Mail Automatic Directory Exchange (ADE), propagating Exchange addresses throughout the cc:Mail environment. Enable ADE in a cc:Mail environment with multiple postoffices to automatically propagate Exchange addresses.

Locate cc:Mail Addresses in the Final Destination Container

When configuring directory synchronization, you must select a recipients container for imported cc:Mail directory entries. To simplify migration, select the import container that you will later use to migrate cc:Mail. You can select this container during migration, which automatically converts the custom recipient directory entries to Exchange mailboxes. Remember that cc:Mail users will appear in the Exchange GAL regardless of which container you import them into.

Install at Least One Exchange 5.5 Server in Exchange 4.0 Sites

For cc:Mail users to address Exchange 4.0 users, Exchange 4.0 users must have a cc:Mail proxy address, which the Connector for cc:Mail automatically generates when first installed in a site. Because Exchange Server 4.0 does not support the connector, you must install an Exchange 5.5 server in the site. This will generate cc:Mail proxy addresses for all users in the 4.0 site, including the 5.5 server, which are then exported to the cc:Mail environment during directory synchronization configuration.

Standardize Exchange Directory cc:Mail Proxy Address Format

The cc:Mail directory requires unique user names, regardless of which postoffice they reside in. For example, cc:Mail does not permit both "Joe User at NEWYORK" and "Joe User at NEWJERSEY," but Exchange allows these cc:Mail proxy addresses because they are unique. During directory synchronization, the cc:Mail directory will only accept one of the "Joe User" entries, leaving the other out.

▶ **To standardize addresses**

1. Ensure unique cc:Mail proxy addresses in the Exchange directory by appending display names with administrator-defined values for the site addressing rule, adding brackets [NJ] to each display name in the "NEWJERSEY" site. For example, the address generator format can read "%s.%g [NJ] at Trenton". The cc:Mail proxy address for "Joe User" becomes "User.Joe [NJ] at Trenton".

   Site addressing rules do not permit duplicate cc:Mail proxy addresses within the same site. If proxy addresses use display names and there are two users with the same display name, the second cc:Mail proxy will be appended with a number: "User.Joe [NJ]2 at Trenton" is the proxy address for the second user in the site with first name "Joe" and last name "User".

2. Create unique cc:Mail proxy addresses in the Exchange organization by adding administrator-defined text (brackets) to the site addressing rule *for the cc:Mail proxy*. This results in a unique identifier per site for display names.

3. Maintain unique cc:Mail proxy address for directory entries imported into an Exchange site from a foreign mail system that does not support directory synchronization with Exchange. When importing a large list of custom recipients into an Exchange site, the cc:Mail proxy generator creates addresses based on a single proxy generation rule. All of these addresses appear to be from the same postoffice to cc:Mail users.

Although the cc:Mail proxy generator appends duplicate proxy addresses with a number, you can directly import the cc:Mail proxy field in an import file, examining the file to discover and resolve duplicates. You can also generate the cc:Mail proxy addresses using information meaningful to your business to distinguish between duplicate names, such as including information in the *Notes* field as this will map to the cc:Mail *Comments* field.

Enable Message Tracking

The Connector for cc:Mail allows administrators to track messages that have been submitted to the connector for delivery. Although useful in troubleshooting scenarios, you might not want to enable message tracking all of the time because of the added overhead and disk space required for message tracking log files.

Consider Multiple Connectors for Load Balancing and Redundancy

In many cases, you can use a single Exchange server and Connector for cc:Mail to link Exchange and cc:Mail messaging systems. Configure multiple connectors and cc:Mail hub postoffices to achieve redundancy and load balancing. Within Exchange, you can use multiple connectors and allocated address space to configure automatic load balancing for Exchange mail sent to the cc:Mail system or deploy multiple connectors but define specific address spaces for each. The latter option requires manual intervention.

A cc:Mail environment with ADE routes all mail flowing to an Exchange environment through a single path. If the cc:Mail hub postoffice that connects to the Exchange system fails, you can restore it or make a routing change in the cc:Mail directory telling a new cc:Mail postoffice that the Exchange site is now directly attached (instead of indirectly attached through the cc:Mail hub postoffice). You must also point the connector to the newly designated cc:Mail postoffice.

Optimize Exchange for Connector Configuration

Properly tune Exchange servers that host Connectors for cc:Mail (and any other connector). Use the Exchange Performance Optimizer program and select the **Connector/Directory Import** setting to ensure proper system tuning to support the Connector for cc:Mail.

Avoid Setting Directory Synchronization Schedule to Always

A directory synchronization schedule configuration of **Always** will cause unnecessary processing on the Exchange server, occurring every 15 minutes. The connector uses both the cc:Mail IMPORT.EXE and EXPORT.EXE programs, exporting the entire cc:Mail directory from the cc:Mail postoffice and parsing it, but only importing changes into the Exchange directory. Changes to Exchange directory entries are exported into a file format understood by the cc:Mail import program and then imported into the attached cc:Mail postoffice.

Use the button on the Connector for cc:Mail import schedule page to request an immediate directory synchronization cycle. When scheduling selected times, you can view the page in 15-minute intervals, although a 3- to 6-hour interval provides acceptable synchronization. You can increase the interval during peak times.

Avoid Using Same Name for Exchange Site as Existing cc:Mail Postoffices

For messages to route from cc:Mail to Exchange, the Exchange site name must be defined in each cc:Mail postoffice directory. This happens automatically on the directly attached cc:Mail postoffice when you configure the connector and enable directory synchronization. The Exchange site name will also propagate throughout the cc:Mail system when ADE is used in the cc:Mail environment. Exchange site names and cc:Mail postoffice names must be unique. If a cc:Mail postoffice has the same name as the Exchange site, use the **Site Addressing** tab in the Exchange Administrator program to change the name of the default proxy addresses for these Exchange users. Then define the Exchange site using this customized proxy name.

Configure Link Monitor

Using the Exchange Administrator program, you can configure link monitor to regulate the connection between the cc:Mail and Exchange environments, sending a ping test message from the Exchange server system attendant service across the connector to an invalid cc:Mail address. When a non-delivery report (NDR) returns, the link monitor calculates the round trip message time and compares it to an interval defined during link monitor configuration. If the round trip time exceeds the interval, Exchange can send notification mail to administrators or a broadcast message to a Windows NT user group, or execute any program that you specify when configuring the link monitor.

Use the Windows NT Performance Monitor to Benchmark Load

Performance Monitor allows system administrators to see how well a server handles load, writing data to log files and an active screen and monitoring from a remote machine. Additionally, you can configure alerts so that when a specified threshold is reached, a program can be run automatically such as a custom pager service or other batch process. Configure these settings:

▶ **To configure % Processor Time for CCMC**

1. In Performance Monitor, click on the **Add Counter** button (plus sign), and select the object called **Process.**

2. In the **Counter** list make sure **% processor time** is selected.

3. Select **CCMC** in the **Instance** list. This shows the percentage of elapsed processor time that all threads of a given process (CCMC) used during execution.

▶ **To configure MSExchangeCCMC Object**

- In the **Add to Chart** dialogue box, select the object **MSExchangeCCMC** to set these counters:

Name	Explanation
Dirsync to cc:Mail	The number of directory updates sent to cc:Mail since the last dirsync started.
Dirsync to Exchange	The number of directory updates sent to Exchange since the last dirsync started.
Exchange MTS-IN	Messages awaiting delivery in the Exchange IN queue.
Exchange MTS-OUT	Messages awaiting delivery in the Exchange OUT queue.
Messages sent to cc:Mail	Number of messages sent to cc:Mail.
Messages sent to cc:Mail/hr	Number of messages sent to cc:Mail/hour
Messages sent to Exchange	Number of messages sent to Exchange
Messages sent to Exchange/hr	Number of messages sent to Exchange/hour
NDRs to cc:Mail	Number of NDRs sent to cc:Mail
NDRs to Exchange	Number of NDRs sent to Exchange

Perform Timely Maintenance on Connector for cc:Mail Postoffice

In Microsoft benchmark testing, the Connector for Lotus cc:Mail handled more than 10,000 randomly generated messages per hour on a Pentium 120-MHz server with 64 MB of RAM. However, the performance curve dropped significantly for subsequent test runs because of the fragmentation of the Connector for cc:Mail postoffice. Maintenance of the cc:Mail database restored performance.

Traffic through the connector hits a peak load when roughly 50% of the migration has been completed because half of the population is on Exchange while the other half remains on cc:Mail. Therefore, perform maintenance on the cc:Mail postoffice database, which requires stopping the connector service.

Migration from cc:Mail to Exchange Server

If your ultimate goal is to move all cc:Mail postoffice information to Exchange, you must make many business and technical decisions:

- Pre-design of the Exchange server network backbone
- Pre-design and specification of the Exchange servers
- Windows NT Server design and domain accounts for all users
- Existing postoffice architecture (DB6 or DB8)
- Tools for migrating cc:Mail mailboxes to Exchange
- When the migration can occur (downtimes, etc.)
- Consolidation of postoffices
- Methods available for moving cc:Mail mailing lists to Exchange
- Methods available for moving cc:Mail bulletin boards to Exchange
- Methods available for migrating cc:Mobile users to Exchange
- Methods of moving gateways to Exchange
- Rolling out the Exchange/Outlook client
- Roving user abilities
- Setting up remote access facilities
- Migrating diary information from Organizer to Exchange
- Training for support staff, help desks, and end users
- Introduction of new facilities available in Exchange
- Possible migration of SmartSuite to Microsoft Office

Exchange Site Design

Before any data can be migrated from cc:Mail, a well-structured, reliable Exchange backbone should be put in place. At this stage, the hardware and software requirements will have been determined and the backbone will have been fully tested with all necessary connectors in place to aid the migration. Users should not lose any functionality or data when moving to Exchange.

One impact on space should be noted: When the Migration Wizard extracts mailboxes from cc:Mail, it cannot retain the single-instance nature of cc:Mail, even though the Exchange server itself supports single-instance storage. Therefore, the data in a 500-Mb cc:Mail postoffice will potentially take up more space once migrated to Exchange. To quantify exactly how much disk space will be required to migrate the postoffice, run the CHKSTAT command with the /MESSAGES parameter (MSGMGR for DB8) to see the total message data space taken up by each mailbox without regard for the single-instance storage architecture.

Methods for Migrating Mailing Lists

As discussed previously, there are four ways to handle coexistence between cc:Mail mailing lists and Exchange distribution lists. They are:

- cc:Mail mailing lists with the Exchange recipients' lowercase "l" entries as members
- cc:Mail mailing lists with the Exchange distribution lists' lowercase "l" entries as members
- Exchange distribution lists with cc:Mail custom recipients as members
- Exchange distribution lists with cc:Mail mailing list custom recipient as members

Depending on how mailing lists are used within your cc:Mail environment and the requirements established for the migration, a blend of these solutions may be the best solution. In most cases it is best to migrate cc:Mail mailing lists to distribution lists before any users are migrated. Regardless of when you choose to move the mailing lists, a process will need to be devised to assist in the move. These different methodologies are discussed below.

Move Mailing Lists Before Migrating User Data

When you move Mailing Lists to Exchange distribution lists, the cc:Mail custom recipients are made members of the DLs. With these in place, the Migration Wizard can preserve DL membership when cc:Mail mailboxes are migrated to Exchange. This allows for all list membership to be administrated from Exchange, as well as allowing for nested mailing lists.

Move Mailing Lists After Migrating Users

Another method is to convert all the mailing lists to distribution lists after all the users in a list are migrated. This way, when users are migrated to Exchange, their cc:Mail directory entries are changed from a uppercase "L" entry to a lowercase "l" entry pointing to the Exchange postoffice, which in turn preserves the mailing list membership.

Process for Moving the Mailing Lists

Because the information on membership of mailing lists is already contained within cc:Mail, extract it into a format that can be imported into Exchange with the cc:Mail Export utility, Microsoft Access 95 or later, and the Exchange Administrator bulk import/export utility. The process begins by running the cc:Mail Export utility against the postoffice that contains the mailing list to be migrated. The command is:

```
EXPORT /Nponame /Ppassword /dpath /LIST /@ml.exp
```

This will produce a file named ML.EXP that lists each member of a mailing list in the following format:

```
Name: LIST"#All cc:Mail Users" " Bowden, Paul " "ccmpo"
Locn: +L
Addr:
Cmts:
```

All we are concerned with is the line for NAME because this lists the mailing list name, members of the list, and the PO on which those members are located. Parse this file to strip out the unnecessary information with the following command:

```
Type ml.exp | find "NAME:" > parsed.txt
```

Open the file named PARSED.TXT and, in Notepad, perform a search on the string *NAME: LIST* and replace it with a *NULL*. Now the file should contain entries for the members of the mailing lists in this format:

```
"ML NAME" "Lastname, Firstname" "PO"
```

These entries are defined as follows:

- *ML NAME* is the mailing list name
- *Lastname, Firstname* is the cc:Mail member's name
- *PO* is the member's postoffice name

This file can now easily be imported into a Microsoft Access table, which you should name *Mailing Lists* or something equally obvious. Next, create a comma-delimited (.CSV) export file for the cc:Mail custom recipients and import that into a separate Access table named something like *cc:Mail Recipients*. Use the **Get External Data/Import** command from the **File** menu to import files into MS Access. With this data in Access, run a joint query between the two tables to create a new .CSV file to create the distribution lists and add the members.

Create a query on the two tables using the *Lastname, Firstname* field as the key to match up between the two tables. The type of fields needed are:

```
Obj-Class, Mode, Display-Name, Directory Name, Members
DL, Update, #All cc:Mail Users, allccmail, 89E5B39
```

Note In the example, the *Members* field is set to the distinguished name (DN) of the cc:Mail custom recipient that is an 8-digit hex value included in the .CSV exported from Exchange.

After the query has been created with the correct fields, export that data to a .CSV file on the **File** menu by clicking **Save As** and **Export.** After saving this to a .CSV file, import the entries into the Exchange directory and then delete them from the cc:Mail directory. The next time directory synchronization runs, the cc:Mail proxy addresses of the distribution lists will be added as lowercase "l" entries in cc:Mail. Make sure these entries begin with a pound sign (#) to make it easier for users to find the new mailing lists in the directory.

Methods for Deploying the Outlook Client

An important part of migrating to Exchange is installing the Microsoft Outlook client on the users' desktops. In planning for your migration, take time to look at how to deploy the Outlook client in an unattended fashion. An overview of the unattended install process is described below. Study the detailed process in the *Microsoft Outlook 97 Administrator's Guide*, which can be found both in TechNet and on the Microsoft Web site at **http://www.microsoft.com/outlook /adminguide.**

- Install Outlook to a file server share by using USETUP.EXE from the Exchange Server 5.5 Client CD-ROM or by running "setup.exe /a" from the Win32 directory.

- Create a directory named CUSTOM under the root of the share.

- Copy the following files to the CUSTOM directory: PROFGEN.EXE from the *Exchange 5.0 Resource Kit* (part of the *BackOffice Resource Kit*) and CHNGINBX.EXE from the valuepack directory on the Outlook CD-ROM.

- Create a profile generator control file in the CUSTOM directory and name it OUTLOOK.PRF. Details for changing settings within .PRF files can be found in the *Microsoft Outlook 97 Administrator's Guide*.

- Use the Network Installation Wizard (NIW) to customize the .STF file used for the Outlook install. Make sure NIW version 2.1 is installed. Save the .STF as CUSTOM.STF in the CUSTOM directory created above.

- Write a batch file (Windows 95 only) that executes the following commands:

```
Echo Installing Outlook 8.03
start /w %0\..\setup.exe /b2 /Qn1 /S %0\..\custom\custom.stf
echo Changing Desktop Inbox icon to Outlook Icon
start /w %0\..\valupack\chnginbx.exe /Q
echo Running New profile Generator
copy %0\..\custom\outlook.prf %windir% /v
start /w %0\..\profgen %0\..\Office\WMS\Win95\newprof.exe -P
%windir%\outlook.prf -S -X -U -L
goto end
:END
Echo off
cls
@exit
```

- For Windows NT, you need administrator privileges to do this. When you are done, make sure users are logged on before you generate profiles.

To help end users adjust to a new mail client, alter Outlook to look more like cc:Mail by turning off the Outlook bar and turning on the folder view. If you choose to leave the Outlook bar on, consider turning on the folder view to make Outlook more familiar to cc:Mail users.

Instructions for installing Outlook 98 are included in the *Outlook Deployment Kit* (ODK). Outlook 98 has many new features and provides a more intuitive user interface. The drafts folder concept is also supported under this new client, which may help cc:Mail users adjust to Outlook.

Methods for Migrating cc:Mail Archives

Users tend to be electronic packrats when it comes to mail messages. This leads to poor message management and large archives of messages that may never be looked at again. Some material, of course, should be saved, and some must be. For instance, some government organizations must retain a copy of all e-mail messages to be compliant with laws such as the Freedom of Information Act.

Consider the situation and determine whether you should automate the cc:Mail-to-Exchange migration or perform it manually. There are three approaches:

- Move the cc:Mail archives back into the user's mailbox so it is migrated with the Migration Wizard tool.
- Harvest the cc:Mail archives to a central location, then convert the data to a PST in the user's home directory
- Use migration tools on the user's local workstation during or after the Outlook Client installation to convert the archived data.

The approach you choose will depend on what percentage of users have archives and how much volume is expected. Poll the cc:Mail user community on how many have archives and the size of those archives to determine the effect the archive migration will have on time and storage requirements.

For example, if there are few users, each with a small archive, have the users import the archives before migration. If there are a lot of users, each with a small archive, harvest to a central location. If there are high numbers of users, each with a large archive, use migration tools at the desktops to convert the data.

Some combination of these approaches might work best for you. The goal is to convert archive data directly to .PST files so that it does not touch the cc:Mail or Exchange message database. This creates the least impact on storage requirements for the old and new messaging system.

Importing Archives Back into the User's Mailbox

This approach is relatively easy. Inform users that any archives need to be re-imported into their mailbox before they are migrated. From there, the steps differ depending on the version of cc:Mail used. Consult the cc:Mail client documentation on how to import archives back into the mailboxes. When the Migration Wizard is used to move the user's mailbox to Exchange, it moves the archived data too. If you configure the Outlook client to run auto-archive on initial startup, it will move the older messages out to an auto-archive .PST file.

Harvesting to Central Location

This approach requires two processes: harvest the archive files to the central location, then convert the PST files in the user's home directory. You can include the harvest step in the automated setup of the Outlook client.

Basically, the harvest involves finding all files on the hard drive that end with .CCA and moving them to a drive letter or UNC share in a directory named for the user. If users have only one archive, you can rename the file USERNAME.CCA before moving it to the central location. There are many shareware and third-party utilities that can harvest and move the files to the central location. You can even write your own MS-DOS batch script or Visual Basic application to perform this task.

Step 2, converting the .CCA files to .PST files, can be done with existing cc:Mail utilities. Follow these steps:

1. Create a dummy cc:Mail postoffice at the central location, and create "fake" mailboxes for all the users with the export and import utilities

2. Use the cc:Mail MS-DOS client to import the archive file into the respective "fake" user mailbox.

3. Use the Exchange Migration Wizard from Exchange Server 5.5 to export the user's "fake" mailbox directly to a .PST file.

4. Move that .PST file to the user's home directory and have the Outlook client configured to use this .PST file as the auto-archive location.

This second task could be automated by using a MS-DOS keyboard stuffing program to feed the keystrokes to the cc:Mail MS-DOS client.

Local Migration with Tools

There are two cc:Mail archive migration tools that can convert directly to a .PST file: "Mail box Converter for cc:Mail" from The MESA Group (Error! Bookmark not defined.), and "ccAccess" from ComAxis (Error! Bookmark not defined.). Both run in interactive mode or unattended command-line mode. Other vendors probably offer similar products.

After the tool has been chosen, decide if it should run in automated mode or have the user do the import interactively. If users run the utility and import their own cc:Mail archives, they will decide what archived data is brought over to Exchange. This can work **if** they know that space is limited. If you do not convince them of this fact, expect your Exchange messaging database to grow quickly as they import everything. Explain to them that they need to determine the business value of the archived data.

If you automate the task, have it execute when the Outlook client installs on the user's workstation. You may have to script other features, such as moving all archive files to a single directory on the local hard drive or removing the archives after the process has run. The documentation that comes with the utility you choose will explain how to run in unattended mode.

Tools Available for Migration

The Migration Wizard (MAILMIG.EXE) is good tool for transferring cc:Mail data to Exchange Server but it cannot migrate everything. With Exchange Server 5.0, the Migration Wizard can migrate DB6 and DB7 postoffices. The wizard supplied with Exchange Server 5.5 can migrate DB6, DB7, and DB8 postoffices. The Exchange 5.5 MAILMIG tool also includes a one-step migration for cc:Mail and has the ability to migrate cc:Mail mailboxes directly to PST files.

The following data has to be moved manually:

- cc:Mail mailing lists (postoffice and private)
- cc:Mail rules
- cc:Mail private directory (PRIVDIR.INI)
- cc:Mail archive files
- Lotus organizer information

After migration, users will notice that the contents of their *Drafts* folder have been placed as special mail messages within their Inbox. They may also see a folder named *Clipboard*. cc:Mail uses this special folder for internal purposes, and so it is safe to delete it once migration is done.

Procedures Before Migration

Before transferring the data from cc:Mail, make sure support staff, help desks, and end users are fully trained. Next, send e-mail to users requesting that they:

- Delete unwanted e-mail in inboxes, messages logs, deleted bin, and private folders.
- Move any required archive messages to private folders (if a special tool is not going to be used).

Tell users that this information won't get migrated:

- Private mailing lists
- Local Internet addresses in the private directory (PRVDIR.INI file)
- Rules that the user has implemented in cc:Mail
- Lotus organizer diary

Also tell users to rename their cc:Mail personal folders if they are called **Calendar**, **Notes**, **Journaling**, **Tasks**, or **Contacts**. Such names can cause problems. For instance, if a personal cc:Mail folder called **Contacts** is migrated, Outlook will not create its own **Contacts** folder on initial startup.

Enforcing a policy on how much data can be migrated can cut down the time it takes to migrate. Consider using the CHKSTAT (or MSGMGR) tool to delete information from **Inboxes**, **Message Logs**, **Trash**, and **Private** folders.

A final step is to service the postoffices to ensure that there are no inconsistencies or corruption problems. Sometimes the Migration Wizard simply skips a corrupted message or attachment, and sometimes it halts. Run the following procedures:

- ANALYZE
- CHKSTAT (DB6 only)
- RECLAIM

Seconds Before Migration

If migrating a whole postoffice, halt the cc:Mail Router MTAs, Link gateways, Exchange Connector for cc:Mail, and any entity delivering information into the postoffice to be migrated. If it is not possible to halt the router MTA for a long period of time because it services more than one postoffice, remove the necessary entries out of the router call list. If messages are delivered while the Migration Wizard is running, the wizard may halt or it will not migrate new messages once it has passed the mailbox in question.

Make sure no Administrator programs are running against the postoffice and that all users are logged off. You can log them off by:

- Sending an e-mail
- Broadcasting a message over the telephone system
- Creating a CCPODOWN file in the \ccdata directory (only stops new users from logging on)
- Removing permissions from the directory
- Running NPODOWN (Novell networks only)

Run the Migration Wizard on either the fastest available PC or on the Exchange server to which you are migrating mailboxes. Minimize the migration time by running it on the same network segment of the server that has the cc:Mail postoffice.

How the Migration Wizard Works

The Exchange Migration Wizard is pre-installed on each Exchange server. With version 5.x you can use the tool to migrate information from Microsoft Mail, Lotus cc:Mail, Novell GroupWise, and Collabra Share.

For cc:Mail migration, copy over the appropriate version of EXPORT into the system path of the machine from which you are running the Migration wizard. You can boost performance and avoid some limitations (such as cc:Mail's 57-character mailbox name limit) by using the OS/2 version of the EXPORT program. To use this, manually rename EXPORT2.EXE to EXPORT.EXE

Migration Steps

1. Specify the path to the postoffice and supply the postoffice name and password.

2. When prompted on whether to perform a one- or two-step migration, choose two step: it gives better control over the migration process, allows you to use a new naming standard, and accommodates cc:Mail user names over 64 characters long. Specify a location for the migration data, which consists of one packing list file and many primary and secondary files.

3. Select the type of information to transfer:

   - Information to create mailboxes
   - Personal e-mail messages (all or date range)
   - Bulletin boards

4. Choose which local ("L") users should be migrated.

5. At this stage, the cc:Mail data is extracted from the postoffice and placed into a set of migration files.

6. These files are created under the migration directory specified:

File name	Purpose
Postoffice Name.PKL	Packing list file. Matches the primary and secondary files with the mailbox name.
Postoffice Name.PRI	Directory import file. Specifies how entries are going to appear in the Exchange directory once imported.
Xxxxxxxx.PRI	Sequentially numbered primary file. Holds the message headers and folder names for migrated messages.
Xxxxxxxx.SEC	Sequentially numbered secondary file. Holds the message bodies relative to the headers defined in the primary file.

7. If necessary, change the primary file for the postoffice at this point to dictate how imported entries are going to appear in the Exchange GAL. Because the cc:Mail messages have been exported at this point, there may be little time available to make your changes. If there are a lot of changes to be made, adjust the primary file for the postoffice and then save a copy. If you can be sure that no administration is going to take place on the cc:Mail postoffice, rerun the first stage again but use the old primary file. This method can buy you more time to make changes.

8. Run through the Migration Wizard for the second run and actually perform the migration.

Connector for cc:Mail and Migration in Different Sites

A problem can occur when the Connector for cc:Mail has been set up and the directory has been synchronized within one Exchange site, and the migration of postoffice data is being performed at another site. Such a scenario might involve companies that have not implemented many Connectors for cc:Mail or when connectors are part of a Exchange hub site.

Look for errors in the Windows NT Event Log that are similar to the following:

```
"Could not remove object xxxxxxxx because the directory service reported
the following error: Changes cannot be written to this directory object.
Try connecting to a Microsoft Exchange server computer in the same site
as this object."
```

The problem is that the Migration Wizard is trying to manipulate objects in this site when the objects belong to another site. The only workaround is to delete the cc:Mail custom recipients first and then go for the migration. Unfortunately, because the X500 DN name will have now changed, messages previously sent from the cc:Mail user to Exchange users can no longer be replied to. For this reason, it is recommended you migrate cc:Mail users to the same site as the Connector for cc:Mail.

Converting Lotus Organizer Information

Most organizations will not use Organizer as a group-scheduling tool. However, cc:Mail administrators usually allow users to install the Organizer product and there may be some diary sharing between managers and secretaries.

Microsoft Outlook can translate information from Organizer version 1.0, 1.1, and 2.1, but the Organizer program executables *must* be installed on the machine doing the translation and the support files for Organizer from the Outlook installation must also be present.

When users attempt to transfer their Organizer file to Outlook Calendaring, the last .OR2 file to be opened will be displayed as the file to import from. The user will also be prompted for the types of information (planner, diary, addresses, etc.) that should be transferred. Users have the ability of changing the field mappings, although this is not normally necessary. By accepting the default options, users will find that the following information transfers to Outlook:

- Diary items
- Recurring items
- Tasks list with priorities and due dates
- Contacts listing

Converting PRIVDIR.INI Information

cc:Mail personal addresses such as private SMTP addresses are held in a file called PRIVDIR.INI at the local workstation. The format of the PRIVDIR.INI file is as follows:

```
[Internet]
EntryCount=3
Entry1=Sue.Bowden@qatraining.com
```

```
Entry2=dstrange@microsoft.com
Entry3=Mark.Sunner@syrena.co.uk

[X400]
EntryCount=1
Entry1=c=gb;a=attmail;p=lotus;s=Honer;g=Mike
```

The file above indicates that the pseudo-postoffice used to access the Internet is called *Internet*. It is relatively easy to write a small Visual Basic application to parse the contents of this file and to reformat the data into an Outlook Contacts import format. Format the data this way:

First Name,Last Name,E-mail Address
Sue,Bowden,Sue.Bowden@qatraining.com
D,Strange,dstrange@microsoft.com
Mark,Sunner,Mark.Sunner@syrena.co.uk

Migrating a cc:Mobile User to Exchange

Starting with the assumption that remote users are using cc:Mobile for Windows and depending on time and requirements, there are two ways to migrate cc:Mobile users:

- Use the Migration Wizard to connect with the DB7 postoffice on the local hard disk of the cc:Mobile user and perform a direct migration transfer. The name of the mobile postoffice will be LOCALPO and the password will be the user's normal mailbox password.

- Get the cc:Mobile user to dock with the cc:Mail mailbox on the LAN, and transfer all messages. From here, perform the migration in the normal way. Make sure that the cc:Mobile user is defined within the postoffice directory as L before the migration. The Migration Wizard cannot migrate R accounts.

Note For more information on this subject, see the *Microsoft Exchange Migration Guide*.

Using Outlook Against a cc:Mail Postoffice

Another option worth considering is using the Lotus cc:Mail MAPI provider which is on the Office 97 CD-ROM. Two files exist in the VALUPACK directory; CCMAILSP.EXE (Windows 95 and Windows NT 4.0) and CCMAILNT.EXE (Windows NT 3.51).

This provider can be added to a new or existing MAPI profile and once configured cc:Mail messages can be accessed. One of the downsides of this logon method is that all cc:Mail messages are downloaded into a .PST file from the postoffice: you can't look directly at the postoffice mailbox.

Even if this provider does not give any direct benefit for your migration, it does allow users to convert their cc:Mail private mailing lists into Exchange personal address book entries. It is still a manual process to log on to the mailbox and tell Outlook that you want the information converted, but it may save many hours of retyping for those cc:Mail users who have previously created many private mailing lists.

Network Bandwidth Traffic Patterns

Because all users are converting to a new client, network administrators need to know what effect Exchange Server will have on the network. To calculate the amount of traffic seen between Exchange servers, refer to Chapter 8. You can also refer to Chapter 5, "Planning Exchange Architecture in a Bandwidth-Sensitive Environment."

The chart below is not definitive, but it should provide some guidance. The first figure shows the number of frames generated on the network and the second shows the actual amount of data passed between the client and server.

Function	DB6	DB8	Outlook 8.02
"9am" client startup	118f/38k	201f/91k	135f/21k
"Warm" client startup	112f/37k	111f/ 32k	133f/22k
Client logoff and exit	10f/1k	20f/6k	31f/3k
Compose message	0f/0k	0f/0k	4f/1644 bytes
Address book lookup	5f/510 bytes	0f/0k	4f/1046 bytes
Sending a 1k message	106f/22k	207f/65k	12f/3k
Reading a new message	50f/10k	32f/12k	4f/3k
Opening the address book	16f/4k	252f/138k	7f/6k
Attaching a 1.95-Mb file	0f/0k	0f/0k	2337f/2129k
Sending a 1.95-Mb message	2610/2182k	2729f/2261k	59f/40k
Checking for new messages	17f/3k	9f/5k	0f/0k

Connector for cc:Mail Registry Entries

This list details some of the more common registry entries that may need to be adjusted to get the desired interoperability between Exchange Server and cc:Mail. All of these parameters are held under:

```
HKEY_LOCAL_MACHINE\SYSTEM\CurrentControlSet\Services\MSExchangeCCMC\Para
meters
```

Note The Connector for cc:Mail service must be stopped and restarted after a change is made to any of these parameters.

Parameter name	Initial data value	Notes
Always delete IMPORT/EXPORT output	0x00000001 (1)	Not implemented in Exchange Server 5.x.
cc:Mail Administrator file path	" "	Not implemented in Exchange Server 5.x.
cc:Mail- to-Exchange queue size	0x00000040 (64)	Maximum number of messages that can be waiting for a worker thread. EXPORT will not run again until the number of messages waiting drops below this number. This prevents the thread from getting overloaded.
Connector store path	C:\exchsrvr\ccmcdata	Change value if there are more than eight characters in a directory name or if the path includes spaces.
Dirsync alias name rule	%F%1L	Rules for how Exchange should create aliases for directory entries that are synchronized.
Dirsync display name rule	%F %L	Rules for how Exchange should create display names for directory entries that are synchronized.
Dirsync export BB command line	/BBOARD /LIST /BATCH	Specifies that Exchange should extract the list of bulletin boards.
Dirsync export command line	/DIRECTORY/L/R/A/P /FORMAT /NOFAN /BATCH	Specifies that Exchange should extract local, mobile, alias users, and postoffice entries. Does not export foreign alias names.
Dirsync export ML command line	/LIST /BATCH	Specifies that Exchange should extract the list of mailing lists.
Dirsync import command line	/DIRECTORY/PROP /BATCH	(Specifies that this is a directory import, rather than mail message, and that entries should be repropagated to other postoffices.)
Exchange-to-cc:Mail queue size	0x00000040 (64)	Maximum number of messages that can be queued to wait for a worker thread. The connector will not retrieve more messages from MTS-OUT until the number of messages waiting drops below this number. This prevents the thread from getting overloaded.
Export command line	/ITEMSIZE /FORMAT/FAN /BATCH /FILES/MACBIN2	Messages should be exported with their byte sizes; also, the FAN should replace the cc:Mail names in the header and Macintosh file attachments should be exported in MacBinary II format.
Export.exe	Export.exe	Path to the EXPORT.EXE program.

Parameter name	Initial data value	Notes
Fixed width font	0x00000000 (0)	Specifies whether a fixed width font should be used or not.
Generate secondary proxy address	0x00000000 (0)	Specifies whether cc:Mail directory entries that have been synchronized in Exchange will have two proxy addresses or one. If set to "0," cc:Mail entries will be synchronized in *First Last* format. If set to "1," cc:Mail entries will have a primary proxy of *Last, First* and a secondary proxy of *First Last*.
Import command line	/ITEMSIZE /PARTIAL /BATCH /FILES/MACBIN2	Specifies that when mail messages are imported, the byte count is attached, the message is delivered even if there are unknown recipients, and Macintosh file attachments are in MacBinary II format.
Import.exe	Import.exe	Path to the IMPORT.EXE program.
Inbound conversion threads	0x00000002 (2)	Number of threads allocated for messages entering Exchange.
Locale date format	0x00000000 (0)	0 specifies that the date format of the IMPORT/EXPORT programs should be used. 1 = US format, 2 = UK format, 3 = Japanese format. **Note:** Levels 2 and 3 are supported only in Exchange 5.0 SP3 and 5.5 SP1 and above.
Maximum number of exceptions before shutdown	0x00000019 (25)	Number of connection errors that can occur on startup before the Connector for cc:Mail automatically shuts down.
Maximum number of messages to EXPORT	0x00000010 (16)	Number of messages that can be exported from cc:Mail in any one export session.
Maximum number of messages to IMPORT	0x00000005 (5)	Number of messages that can be imported into cc:Mail in any one import session.
Mutually exclude IMPORT and EXPORT	0x00000001 (1)	Whether Import and Export sessions run in separate time windows.
Outbound conversion threads	0x00000002 (2)	Number of threads allocated for messages leaving Exchange.
Save a copy of the exported files	0x00000000 (0)	Whether to keep copies of messages leaving cc:Mail. Copies are held in *\ccmcdata\export.bak*.
Save a copy of the imported files	0x00000000 (0)	Whether to keep copies of messages entering cc:Mail. Copies are held in *\ccmcdata\import.bak*.
Seconds to wait before Export	0x0000000f (15)	Polling interval for messages leaving cc:Mail.

(continued)

Parameter name	Initial data value	Notes
Seconds to wait before Import	0x0000000f (15)	Polling interval for delivering messages to cc:Mail. Import will only run if there are messages to import into cc:Mail. Also, import will execute before this time has elapsed if the number of messages waiting to be imported is equal or more than the value for the **Maximum number of messages to be imported** registry value.
Tab length	0x00000005	Number of spaces that account for one tab character.
Use ANR	0x00000000	Dictates whether messages are imported from the CCMC in "user at postoffice" format (default) or whether the postoffice portion should be stripped and cc:Mail's own automatic name checking routines should be used (1). This parameter is not present by default and can only be set when using the Exchange 5.0 SP2 or 5.5 SP1.
User settings	0x00000000	Should be set to 1 if any registry settings are manually modified.

Connector for cc:Mail Quick List

Run through this numbered checklist if you have problems with the Connector for cc:Mail. Look elsewhere in this chapter for detailed discussions of these points.

Connectivity

1. Use a shadow postoffice and locate it on the Exchange server itself.
2. Make sure that you have adjusted oplock and Windows NT caching registry entries or applied CCREGMOD.
3. Change the **Seconds to wait before Export** registry value to 60 or 120 seconds to relieve contention on postoffice files.
4. Check that the correct versions of IMPORT and EXPORT exist in the path of the Exchange server.
5. Check the Exchange GWART to ensure that the routing table is correct. If not, manually recalculate the routing.

6. If you receive NDRs from the Connector for cc:Mail with "Invalid date format" error messages, obtain the CCMC.EXE program from Exchange Server 5.0 SP3 or 5.5 SP1 and adjust the **Locale date format** registry entry appropriately.

7. Push diagnostics logging to maximum and then run the CCMC manually (from a command prompt) to get more information.

Directory Synchronization

1. Make sure that **MSExchangeCCMC** *<server name>* is located in the **Comments** field for the Exchange queue on the connecting postoffice.

2. Adjust Connector for cc:Mail registry entries to alter naming rules.

3. Adjust **Generate secondary proxy** registry parameter to perform backboning.

4. Use Exchange Server 5.0 SP2 or 5.5 SP1 and adjust the **Use ANR** registry parameter to **1** if working with a cc:Mail Enterprise ADE environment.

5. Push diagnostics logging to maximum and then run CCMC CCDIR manually to get more information.

cc:Mail Migration Best Practices

Exchange 5.5 provides a wizard tool that migrates cc:Mail mailboxes and data to the Exchange environment, using a graphical user interface. This section summarizes best practices and recommendations for migrating cc:Mail LAN attached and cc:Mobile clients to Exchange. Refer to the *Microsoft Exchange Administrator's Guide*, the README file, and the migration documents on the Exchange Server CD-ROM for more information.

Organizations migrating from cc:Mail to Exchange must consider:

- User requirements
  - Minimize the migration timeframe and disruption of the corporate mail system.
  - Support conversion of mail and file attachments.
  - Migrate cc:Mail archives
  - Preserve bulletin boards and private folders.

- Administration/operations requirements
  - Modify the user mailbox name and attributes (the directory) as part of the migration.
  - Conduct phased migration, first moving mailboxes and later importing user data.
  - Establish seamless coexistence during a longer term migration.

A planning team must consider the coexistence or migration path and the speed at which it will be traveled. Some organizations migrate slowly, working out coexistence issues as they go. Others migrate quickly, minimizing the coexistence timeframe and disruption to the business. Project planning favors quick migrations, optimized deployments, with minimal time spent on coexistence issues. Although the base services of the Migration Wizard meet some of user and administrative requirements, you'll need to implement specific configuration steps for others.

The rest of this chapter is a selection of practices Microsoft has found to be effective.

Consolidate cc:Mail Postoffices

Group users by communication requirements, consolidating multiple cc:Mail postoffices on one or more Exchange servers. This reduces the number of servers and keeps mail among users of an organizational or business unit on the same server, increasing delivery performance and reducing LAN traffic. Exchange easily accommodates thousands of users on a single server with sub-second response time.

Copy cc:Mail Databases to the Exchange Server

To increase migration performance, first copy cc:Mail databases to the Windows NT Server hosting the Exchange mailboxes. This approach requires additional disk space on the Exchange server, but reading data locally is more efficient in than reading it over the network. And if cc:Mail postoffices reside on a NetWare server, you can avoid having to support NetWare connectivity during the migration.

The Migration Wizard builds intermediate files, storing them in a subdirectory (\Migrate) and later using them while importing user data to Exchange. Increase performance by specifying a temporary migration directory on a dedicated physical disk drive, allowing the wizard to write intermediate files on this disk subsystem and store the data on another. Back up this directory after each migration pass in case you need the information later on.

Plan for Server Disk Space Requirements During Migration

There are four disk space requirements:

- Size of cc:Mail databases copied to the Exchange server.

- Size of the new Exchange database, increasing from a single-instance store to non-single-instance store. Migrated mailboxes receive a separate copy of single-instance stored messages. This is because of limitations in the tools supplied by Lotus for full mailbox moves.

- Size of the data files that the wizard temporarily stores in the *Migrate* subdirectory

- Disk space for transaction log files when you do not enable circular logging. (However, you should enable circular database logging during a migration if you do not have enough space to store the incremental log files until backup runs.)

Modify Migration Wizard Intermediate Files

Use the migration from cc:Mail as an opportunity to standardize directory names and user IDs. You have the choice of performing a user migration in a single step or exporting the cc:Mail directory, making modifications, and then completing the process. Remember that if you change user display names, replies to migrated messages will not resolve the destination mail address. Notify users to replace the address in the "To" field with the address from the Exchange GAL when responding to these messages.

Because of an issue in how Outlook 97 stores nicknames for cc:Mail custom recipients, you must disable the nickname cache during migration. Otherwise, when users compose new mail to a nickname, the message will return a non-delivery report (NDR) because the custom recipient no longer exists. See Knowledge Base article Q169259, Title: OL97: New Nickname Features in Outlook 8.02.

When consolidating several cc:Mail postoffices into a domain, e-mail aliases must be unique within the site and Windows NT accounts unique within the domain. Use the migration to standardize e-mail aliases, Windows NT account names, and user display names, making them unique throughout the organization across domain and site boundaries. This will ease administration later on. You can configure the directory synchronization process in the Connector for cc:Mail to build the alias and display name fields to your standard with a registry change. This will ease administration later on and make it easier to build user profiles with the PROFGEN utility when deploying the Outlook client in unattended mode.

To perform these two steps, edit the intermediate file DIRECTORY.PRI. This file contains the directory information for each user from the cc:Mail postoffice. Do not change the MIGRATE proxy field because this is used as a key field to map user data to an existing mailbox. You can change directory attributes in bulk after a migration by exporting the directory to a .CSV (comma delimited) file, modifying and then re-importing it. You cannot, however, change the actual "internal directory" name for the user after the migration.

Coordinate Directory Updates in External Systems

After you migrate cc:Mail users to Exchange, purge their cc:Mail directory entries in corporate directories and replace them with their Exchange directory addresses. You can grandfather old addresses in external system directories using Exchange proxy addresses. Messages sent to an old address route through Exchange, resolving to the proper destination mailbox. If automated directory synchronization is not set up for all mail systems, update these external mail system directories to include the new addresses of migrated users.

Convert Entire cc:Mail Postoffices in Bulk

Migrate entire cc:Mail postoffices instead of parts, leaving the cc:Mail directory intact and avoiding the maintenance of DLs for users in split postoffices. Change only the postoffice address for the migrated postoffice so that it is indirectly routed through the Exchange postoffice. Providing you maintain cc:Mail proxy addresses in the Exchange directory for cc:Mail users, Exchange will properly resolve the legacy address and deliver messages sent from remaining cc:Mail postoffices. This can only be done when performing a complete cc:Mail postoffice migration.

If you migrate all cc:Mail postoffices at the same time, you will not need to maintain connectors to the old environment. If you have a large cc:Mail environment, provide connectivity so that Exchange users can coexist with the cc:Mail users until you complete the migration to Exchange.

Change cc:Mail Entries When Migrating Partial Postoffices

If you need to migrate individuals or groups of users from a postoffice but not the entire postoffice, then change the capital "L" entries to lowercase "l" entries. This preserves the cc:Mail mailing list membership for the mailboxes that have been migrated. If you have migrated all your cc:Mail mailing lists to Exchange distribution lists before the migration, you can skip this step and just delete the mailboxes because the Migration Wizard will keep the custom recipient's DL membership intact.

Establish Public Folders for cc:Mail Bulletin Board Data

The cc:Mail Migration Wizard can convert cc:Mail bulletin board data to public folders, migrating bulletin board data to the Exchange public folder root (default). You can also choose to copy the cc:Mail bulletin board data to a cc:Mail mailbox and then use the Exchange 5.5 Migration Wizard to migrate the data to a .PST (Personal Storage File). Then you can add the .PST file to an Exchange client and copy the data to a new public folder structure.

If your migration requires data interoperability between cc:Mail bulletin boards and Exchange public folders, set up propagation from cc:Mail to Exchange. This involves creating a connect-only call list entry on cc:Mail for the Exchange postoffice, adding the address of the public folder to the bulletin board propagation list, and running a router instance against the connected postoffice to generate propagation messages. This solution is discussed in more detail in this chapter.

Use Bulk Import/Export and a Database for Manipulating Directory Information

The Exchange Administrator program allows you to import and export all Exchange directory information, including DL data and user directory attributes, using a .CSV ASCII file. Working with a database application such as Microsoft Excel or Microsoft Access, you can easily modify the .CSV file, adding, deleting, or updating user directory data. You can also create DLs, quickly formatting data in the .CSV export file and importing it into Exchange.

Use Transend Transport Drivers for Private Address List Migration

Although the cc:Mail data Migration Wizard does not migrate private address lists, the MAPI transport that ships with Microsoft Office 97 (in the *valuepack* subdirectory—provided by Transend) allows an Exchange or Outlook client to connect to a cc:Mail postoffice, including a local cc:Mobile postoffice. From the **Tools**, **cc:Mail Service Tools** menu of the Outlook client, users can import cc:Mail private address lists into a .PAB file.

Install Client Code in Advance and Test Client Connectivity

The greater proportion of risk and the work of migrating mail systems typically involve client installation. Install client systems in advance so that users can generate profiles and test drive server connectivity before the new system goes into production.

During pre-production staging, use the Migration Wizard to create Windows NT accounts and Exchange mailboxes for cc:Mail users. If you deploy a separate Exchange site for a business unit, configure a connector to the Exchange environment to test connectivity, but do not configure directory replication to avoid duplicate GAL entries for cc:Mail users. When you are ready for production, use the Migration Wizard to port user data to the respective Exchange mailboxes. Purge old cc:Mail addresses from the corporate directory and configure directory replication between the new Exchange site and the existing corporate production site.

If you deploy a very large Exchange site and add one or more new servers to a business unit, you can still deploy client software and test it in advance without incurring duplicate GAL entries (for legacy mail system IDs and one new Exchange IDs). Simply create a test mailbox in which clients can test connectivity. At a cutover time from the legacy mail system to Exchange, create the new production Exchange mailboxes and purge the legacy mailboxes.

Migrate User IDs in Advance

Use the data Migration Wizard to port user IDs and create mailboxes without migrating user data. Then run the wizard later to move user data into respective mailboxes. This offers the advantage of setting up and testing the back-end server environment, migrating user data in bulk. This solution works best when you deploy a new Exchange site in advance, but do not configure it for directory replication or synchronization with the legacy mail system. If directories are shared with the legacy system and mailboxes are created in advance, you might create duplicate GAL entries.

The Migration Wizard matches user data with correct mailboxes by using a "Migrate" proxy address. Refer to the migration documents on the Exchange Server CD-ROM for more information.

Perform Maintenance on cc:Mail Databases Prior to Migration

Prior to migrating user data, perform maintenance routines on the cc:Mail postoffice database files to ensure that the migration tool can successfully complete and avoid corrupted data. See the section cc:Mail: Implementation Best Practices in the middle of this chapter.

Account for Data Not Being Migrated

Notify users to print out and reconfigure private address lists if the migration team chooses not to provide another facility to do this. Note postoffice address lists, distribution lists, and client side rules that do not migrate.

Have Users Delete Old Mail in Advance or Migrate Mail Based on Age

Use the migration as an opportunity for users clean out old mail in advance, reducing migration time and reserving server disk space for new data. The cc:Mail Migration Wizard allows you to select messages for migration based on a date range. You can also use the cc:Mail reclaim tool to purge mail based on age prior to running the Exchange Migration Wizard to port over data. When you do run the migration tool, you can select all mail. Many users will move these old messages to archive files, so you must establish a policy on how to migrate this data. See the following section for more information.

Establish a Policy for cc:Mail Archive Files

You cannot directly migrate cc:Mail archive files (.CCA) into Exchange with the Migration Wizard because .CCA file export APIs are not been exposed in the cc:Mail export command. To migrate cc:Mail archive file data, you must use one of three different methods:

- Move the cc:Mail archives back into the user's mailbox so it migrates with the Migration wizard tool.

- Harvest the cc:Mail archives to a central location, then convert the data to a .PST with the Migration wizard and place them on the user's home directory.

- Use third-party migration tools on the user's local workstation during or after the Exchange client installation to convert archived data.

Instruct Users to Replace Names When Replying

When users reply to migrated messages and the sender's display name does not match the sender's migrated display name, the reply fails. If you modify the display name field upon migration, migrated users must replace the address in the *To* field with the new address from the GAL.

Plan for cc:Mobile Users

You can bulk migrate remote user data only if it is first copied to a cc:Mail postoffice. Remote user migration options include:

1. Instructing users to copy all data from laptops to cc:Mail postoffices.

2. Allowing cc:Mobile users to copy their databases to a predefined file subdirectory that you then export to a central cc:Mail postoffice with a batch file. Run the migration wizard against this postoffice.

3. Running the Migration Wizard against individual laptop cc:Mobile postoffices.

4. Using the Transend cc:Mail transport drivers to connect Exchange or Outlook clients to local cc:Mobile postoffices, importing data into local .PST files (**cc:Mail Service Tools** on the **Tools** menu).

C H A P T E R   1 2

Microsoft Mail for PC Networks

This chapter describes how to deploy the MS Mail Connector for Exchange for coexistence and migration, including directory synchronization implementation. It assumes that you have thorough experience with and knowledge of Microsoft Mail messaging systems, Windows NT, and Exchange Server. You should also be familiar with the information in:

- Chapters 1–4 of the *Microsoft Exchange Migration Guide* (included on the Exchange Server CD-ROM).

- "MS Exchange Server Migration and Coexistence: Planning Considerations and Components" on Microsoft TechNet.

- "Microsoft Exchange Mail Coexistence and Migration with LAN and Host Mail Systems" also on Microsoft TechNet.

MS Mail Connector for Exchange Planning Guidelines

The Microsoft Mail Connector provides seamless messaging connectivity to Microsoft Mail for PC Networks, AppleTalk Networks, and PC Networks gateways. It has four components:

PC MTA   Similar to the Microsoft Mail 3.x MTA, this routes mail between a Microsoft Mail postoffice, the connector postoffice, a Microsoft Mail gateway, and the computer running Microsoft Exchange Server.

AppleTalk MTA   This performs the same sort of routing, but for Microsoft Mail for AppleTalk Networks.

Connector postoffice   This is the data file structure used to store messages in transit between users of Microsoft Exchange, Microsoft Mail 3.x, and gateways.

Microsoft Mail Interchange   This transfers and translates messages between the connector postoffice to the Microsoft Exchange MTA.

These components allow Microsoft Exchange users to send and receive messages and files, and to exchange directories, meeting requests, and free/busy information with users on other systems. After the connector is in place and directory synchronization has taken place, these components allow Microsoft Exchange administrators to use the Migration Wizard to migrate Microsoft Mail users easily.

Prepare to Implement MS Mail Connector

Before you connect to Exchange and synchronize directories, you should first document, evaluate, and clean up any existing problems within the MS Mail environment:

- Document the current MS Mail routing topology, dirsync configuration, and each postoffice's current user population.
- Evaluate if any routing changes are required to improve coexistence with Exchange Server.
- Have all users clean up their MS Mail inboxes to 20 to 30 MB to help ensure a smooth migration.
- Repair any existing problems with the MS Mail postoffice data, message delivery, or directory systems.

Why Document the Microsoft Mail Environment?

Good question. Many MS Mail administrators see little value in documenting the existing system, especially because they are about to migrate over to a new one. It takes a lot of time to document all postoffices, MTAs, configuration files, etc., and the job is difficult to pursue and complete during a fast-moving Exchange migration.

So why bother? Because consultants, solution providers, and customers all have found that documenting and cleaning up the existing MS Mail messaging system saves substantial time and effort during coexistence and migration phases. Complete infrastructure information can help you configure Microsoft Mail Connectors of Exchange Server. And documentation of all MS Mail hubs, gateway postoffices, and MTA instances of MS Mail (whether Exchange Server–based or Microsoft Mail–based) can make it much easier to troubleshoot message transport problems—within the Microsoft Mail system or between Microsoft Mail and Exchange.

For best results during coexistence and migration, update and maintain the MS Mail environment and routing documentation until all MS Mail postoffices have been migrated to Exchange.

You can determine the routing structure by saving routing tables from hub and downstream postoffices with the Microsoft Mail Administrator program (ADMIN.EXE). From the menu select "External-Admin, Report, Setup, All Postoffices, File."

Check for Existing MS Mail Database Problems

The Microsoft Mail Postoffice Diagnostics utility (PODIAG.EXE) includes a set of tools that check the database and fix prevalent problems. You can get PODIAG from the Microsoft Mail for PC Networks version 3.5 installation software or in application note WA0883. For information on how to obtain this and other MS Mail (P) appnotes, see Knowledge Base article Q114119, Title: PC Gen: Application Notes and Replacement Files for PC Mail.

PODIAG is best used in "report-only" mode. After it identifies a problem, you can either use TechNet to get repair instructions or contact Microsoft Technical Support for assistance. Microsoft does not recommend using PODIAG to fix database problems because of several known issues. For a list of them, search the Knowledge Base for keyword **PODIAG**.

If you want try it on your own, make sure to back up the entire MS Mail postoffice before attempting any repairs.

Change Existing MS Mail Routing Configuration?

Another good question. If you have documented the current environment, you can study the overall plan and consider these criteria:

- Are there issues or problems with the existing MS Mail environment that reconfiguration would resolve?

- Does the existing routing configuration correlate to the network topology? For example, are MS Mail hubs defined on either side of a slow WAN link?

You can sometimes resolve performance issues by relocating hubs between postoffices located across slower links or different physical locations. Possibilities include configuring a dedicated Microsoft Mail hub postoffice, configuring the Exchange Server connector postoffice as a hub postoffice (which allows you to configure multiple instances of Connector (PC) MTAs), or using an Exchange Server MS Mail connector server as the routing hub.

For more information on optimizing the existing MS Mail messaging system, see *Recommendations for Better Performance* on TechNet (search on **WA0940**) or on Microsoft's FTP site (search on **WA0940.EXE**). This application note explains how to improve the performance of large implementations of Microsoft Mail for PC Networks by decreasing delivery time and making the standard deviation of delivery times predictable and closer to the median.

Existing Microsoft Mail MTAs

Using a Mail EXTERNAL.EXE or multitasking MTA process to connect directly to the Exchange Connector postoffice is not supported, primarily because this configuration was not tested during development.

Microsoft Mail for PC Networks uses message transfer agents (MTAs) to move mail between Mail for PC Networks postoffices. This is either an MS-DOS–based application that resides on a dedicated computer or a process that runs as a Windows NT service (the Windows NT multitasking message transfer agent, or NTMMTA). The Microsoft Mail Connector (PC) MTA is a more robust, efficient MS Mail MTA. After the connector is configured, this MTA can take over the function of moving mail between the Microsoft Mail postoffices. It runs as a service, is easier to administer, and has few problems associated with it.

The Exchange MTA services only postoffices that are defined as direct connections. For indirect postoffices, it deposits mail in the outbound mailbag of the hub postoffice, expecting a different MTA to pick up the mail and move it. Define postoffices as direct to avoid this issue.

Configure the Microsoft Exchange Connector postoffice to be a dirsync requestor to receive and send directory updates between Microsoft Mail and Exchange. If you configure it as a dirsync server, you will have to do more configuring on the Microsoft Mail side.

Plan the Number of PCMTA Instances per Connector

There are practical limits to how many instances of Microsoft Mail Connector PCMTA can run on the same Exchange Server. The limit (in most cases) is seven combined instances of the PCMTA, MSMI, IMC, Schedule+ Free & Busy Connector, MTA, or Directory Synchronization on a system running Windows NT 4.0 (or Windows NT 4.0 SP1) and Microsoft Exchange Server 4.0.

The eighth instance fails to start and generates this error message:

```
Initialization of the dynamic link library D:\WINNT\system32\USER32.dll
has failed.
The process is terminating abnormally.
```

Followed by a second message:

```
Could not start the <%insert service name here%> on <%computername%>.
Error 2186: The service is not responding to the control function.
No event log errors are reported (with logging at maximum for Microsoft
Exchange).
```

This occurs because the system does not have enough remaining memory to create a new desktop heap for the service being started.

The limit can be raised, but doing so requires changing registry entries to allow more but smaller desktop heaps for Windows NT services. The best solution is to limit MS Mail connector instances to seven or less.

For more information see Knowledge Base article Q158308, Title: XFOR: Err Msg: Initialization of Dynamic Link Library Failed [exchange].

Plan the Number of MS Mail Postoffices per PCMTA Instance

In addition to limiting PCMTA instances, you should also carefully control the number of MS Mail postoffices served by any one PCMTA instance. There are no specific numbers, but you should consider hardware and network capabilities when you add connections to MS Mail postoffices to each PCMTA instance.

You can get a feel for the limits within your system by monitoring the following MSMI and PCMTA Performance Monitor counters after implementing the MSMail connector, then fine-tuning as needed.

Object	Counter	Description
MSExchange MSMI	Messages received	Measures the number of messages received by Exchange Server from the MS Mail Connector. If this number is increasing, the connector is receiving mail. If this number is not changing, there could be either no mail to transfer or a problem.
MSExchange PCMTA	File contentions/hour	Some file contentions are normal while the MS Mail Connector (PC) MTA, any other MS Mail (PC) MTA, and MS Mail clients try to read and write exclusively to key files in MS Mail and MS Mail Connector postoffices. If too many occur, maybe a file is locked open or too much traffic is going through a particular postoffice.
MSExchange PCMTA	LAN/WAN messages moved/hour	Use this to check MS Mail Connector (PC) MTA performance. It should show similar numbers day to day for any given hour, as long as there are no configuration changes in it or in other MS Mail (PC) MTAs. Investigate any strong deviance from the normal value.

Monitor the MSExchangePCMTA counters on any PCMTA instance that handles heavy messaging traffic (either by connecting to a larger number of postoffices or connecting to postoffices containing 200 or more mailboxes).

If monitoring shows...	Then...
Increasing demand or decreasing performance on a particular server	Create a dedicated Mail Connector server by moving other Exchange Server functions (such as the Internet Mail Connector or Directory Replication Connectors) to other Exchange Servers.
A PCMTA's messages/hour or bytes/hour is growing.	Consider reconfiguring the PCMTA instance to connect to fewer postoffices.
Message queues are backing up within the postoffices directly serviced by the PCMTA or within the MSMI itself (and messages are still flowing).	Consider adding a connector instance or a dedicated MS Mail connector server.

MS Mail Connector Physical Location

Typically, you should implement the MS Mail Connector at the first Exchange server being introduced into an existing Microsoft Mail network. This should result in delivery speeds comparable to those users had on the Microsoft Mail Network.

Prepare to Implement Directory Synchronization

Directory synchronization (dirsync) should already be functioning properly within the Microsoft Mail environment. Resolve any dirsync issues before attempting Mail/Exchange coexistence or trying to migrate Mail users to Exchange.

One of the best resources for MS Mail directory synchronization is the application note WA0725 *Directory Synchronization* [dirsync] on TechNet (search on **WA0725**) or the Microsoft Web at **http://support.microsoft.com/support/kb/articles/q96/0/60.asp**. Below, two extracts from this application note describe the most common MS Mail dirsync problem and its resolution, and offer guidelines for resolving any dirsync issues that cause abnormal termination of dirsync process executables.

Common Problem: Dirsync Not Working Due to Fatal 203 Rebuild Error

This is usually caused by older versions of the MS Mail client locking open certain global address list (GAL) files on an MS Mail postoffice, specifically the MS Mail Windows client files MSSFS.DLL (prior to 3.2.4079) or AB.DLL (prior to 3.2.4048).

Make sure you have the latest updates and versions for all clients. For more information see Knowledge Base article Q108831, Title: PC DirSync: Err Msg: Fatal [203] GAL Rebuild Problem, and Q99117, Title: PC DirSync: Err Msg: Fatal [203] GAL Rebuild Problem.

Diagnosing and Repairing an Existing MS Mail Dirsync Problem

Check the current DISPATCH.LOG files on each MS Mail postoffice for any errors similar to the following (from: Knowledge Base article Q148705):

- INST1 02/02/96 13:18 Checking the process table on NET1\PO1
- INST1 02/02/96 13:18 Running NSDA - xx
- INST1 02/02/96 13:18 "NSDA - xx" terminated abnormally with exit code 65 where -xx could be -RT, -S, or -RR. This error occurs if some portion of the NDSA.exe dirsync process does not complete.

The dirsync process, DISPATCH.EXE, consists of three phases: T1, T2, and T3. The three phases are spawned by NSDA -RT, NSDA -S, and NSDA -RR, respectively. NSDA will in turn spawn another process, as follows:

- T1: NSDA -RT will spawn reqmain.
- T2: NSDA -S will spawn srvmain.
- T3: NSDA -RR will spawn reqmain, import, and rebuild.

▶ **To determine the source of the exit code 65, follow these steps**

1. Check several lines above the exit code to find the postoffice responsible for the error. Note the PO and the time stamp.

2. Go to the postoffice that reported the error and check the DIRSYNC.LOG file. Locate the entries with the same date and time stamp. There may be a more specific error listed that will help you locate the problem.

For example, if the Mail Administrator program (ADMIN.EXE) is running against NET1\PO1, import will not be able to complete, and you will see the following entries in the DIRSYNC.LOG on the DS server:

```
02/02/96 13:18 | 1 -1 Microsoft Mail DirSync Requestor V3.5.12
02/02/96 13:18 | 1 105 36
02/02/96 13:18 | 2 91 ADMIN
02/02/96 13:18 | 2 -1 Mailbox name: Admin.
02/02/96 13:18 | 2 -1 Full name: Administrator.
02/02/96 13:18 | 2 -1 FLAG.GLB is locked open.
02/02/96 13:18 | 1 -1 Import is finished
```

In the DSSERVER.LOG on the requestor, you will see the following entries:

```
02/02/96 13:18 | Status Microsoft Mail DirSync Requestor V3.5.12
02/02/96 13:18 | Status Requestor updates received: 36
02/02/96 13:18 | Fatal [91] The database is locked by another
   process: ADMIN
02/02/96 13:18 | Fatal [ ] Mailbox name: Admin.
02/02/96 13:18 | Fatal [ ] Full name: Administrator.
02/02/96 13:18 | Fatal [ ] FLAG.GLB is locked open.
02/02/96 13:18 | Status Import is finished
```

To correct this problem, close ADMIN.EXE on the problem postoffice and let dirsync run again.

If there are no associated error messages in the DIRSYNC.LOG, go to the following steps.

1. Determine at which stage the error occurred:

   - NSDA -RT (T1 time)
   - NSDA -S (T2 time - runs only on DS server)
   - NSDA -RR (T3 time)

2. If the error occurs in T1 (NSDA -RT), make sure that:

   - REQCONF.GLB is 512 bytes only and accessible.
   - REQTRANS.GLB is accessible (not locked).
   - REQMAIN.EXE is in the correct location and accessible by the machine running DISPATCH.EXE.

3. Only the dirsync server should be running T2. If the error occurs in T2 (NSDA -S), make sure that:

   - RVCONF.GLB is divisible by 1024 and accessible.
   - MSTTRANS.GLB is accessible.
   - SYSTEM.KEY is 560 bytes only.
   - SYSTEM.MBG is divisible by 116 bytes and accessible.
   - SRVMAIN.EXE is in the correct location and accessible by DISPATCH.EXE.

If the two SYSTEM files do not divide evenly, or if the SYSTEM.MBG file is very large (quotient larger than 100), you may want to reset the two SYSTEM mailbag files. Refer to *Directory Synchronization (DirSync)* on TechNet (search on **WA0725**) for the resetting procedures.

4. If the error occurs in T3 (NSDA -RR), make sure that:

- SRVTRANS.GLB is 0 bytes after T3 completion; if it is not, reset it with this command:

```
TYPE NUL > SRVTRANS.GLB
```

- USRTRANS.GLB should be in the same state as SRVTRANS.GLB (above)
- NMETRANS.GLB same conditions as SRVTRANS.GLB applies
- GWTRANS.GLB same conditions as SRVTRANS.GLB applies
- IGWTRANS.GLB is not present; if it is delete it
- INMETRAN.GLB is not present; if it is delete it
- IUSRTRAN.GLB is not present; if it is delete it
- SRVUPDS.GLB is not present; if it is delete it
- REQUPDS.GLB is not present; if it is delete it
- Any SORTxxxx.GLB where xxxx is a number is not present; if it is delete it
- REQMAIN.EXE is in the correct location and accessible by DISPATCH.EXE.
- IMPORT.EXE is in the correct location and accessible by DISPATCH.EXE.
- REBUILD.EXE is in the correct location and accessible by DISPATCH.EXE.

Because the REBUILD.EXE process in T3 is the most time- and resource-consuming process, the exit code 65 error may also be caused by:

- Lack of disk space on postoffice server.
- Ownerless files (Novell only) on postoffice server.
- Lack of available memory on Dispatch computer.

This section provides a defined starting point for troubleshooting generic dirsync exit code errors. Other factors may be at work. For additional information, see Chapter 14 in the *Microsoft Mail for PC Networks Administrator's Guide*. See also the DIRSYNC.TXT file on Disk 1 of the Microsoft Mail for PC Networks server setup diskettes.

MS Mail Coexistence and Dirsync

Before implementing the MS Mail Connector and any of the dirsync components, make sure the latest Microsoft Exchange server version and service pack are installed.

After you have documented, evaluated, cleaned up, and repaired the existing MS Mail environment, you need a plan for implementing the Exchange MS Mail connector. The online Exchange server books and product documentation have complete setup instructions.

Reserved Network Names

These network names for common Microsoft and third-party Mail gateways are reserved. Do not use them:

ATTMAIL	GTE	SMTP
COMPUSERVE	MCI	SNADS
DISOSS	MHS	SOURCE
EASYLINK	MSMAIL	VMGATE
ENVOY	OV	X400
FAX	PROFS	*EMS

If one of these names is used to set up the MS Mail connector, this error occurs:

```
<network name> is a reserved network name. Enter a different name.
```

Backboning MS Mail over Exchange

The Microsoft Mail Connector supports pass-through routing, which enables postoffices to use Exchange as a backbone. This can be used for migration by having existing gateways route mail to the migrated mailboxes as if they were on the existing system. For more information on backboning, see Knowledge Base article Q148389, Title: XFOR: How to Backbone MSMail 3.x over Exchange.

Planning Around Unstable Connections

If an existing network connection is known to be unstable, minimize its impact by:

- Checking for other physical connection options between the existing MS Mail system and Exchange Server.

- Using link monitors to watch for delays in traffic across the gateway and server monitors to watch the Exchange Server with the gateway installed. Windows NT Server Performance Monitor can watch the Exchange Server computer's queue size for the gateway. Use the monitor in alert view to warn administrators if the queue grows too large.

- Minimizing message traffic across this connection.

Planning for Exchange Link Monitors

During coexistence and migration, use Exchange link monitors to keep tabs on connectivity and message issues.

Configuring a link monitor to a Microsoft Mail postoffice entails configuring a nonexistent custom recipient (also known as a bounce recipient) so that delivery to the postoffice can be monitored. The link monitor sends messages at regular intervals to this "bounce" recipient. When the Microsoft Mail MTA determines that the user does not exist, it sends a non-delivery report (NDR) back to the link monitor, which then confirms that the link is up and working properly. If the link monitor does not receive an NDR within the configured time frame, it signals that the link is down.

Adding a bounce or custom recipient to the dirsync stream (or removing one) can result in a Replace transaction being generated and added to the list of pending dirsync transactions. During the next T2 cycle, the Directory Synchronization server processes this transaction and effectively instructs all other participating postoffices to remove this postoffice's entire list from their global address lists (GALs). You can resolve this by doing a full export from the postoffice that is not currently in the GAL and completing the dirsync manually. After performing a full export from the missing postoffice, the normal dirsync cycle should restore the missing addresses.

To avoid this problem, create link monitor recipients in their own container and do not export them into the dirsync process. Or you can set the trust level of the custom recipient container to 100, which prevents recipients from exporting to Microsoft Mail. For more information on link monitors, review Chapter 16 of the *Microsoft Exchange Administrator's Guide*. For more information on directory synchronization with Microsoft Mail, review Chapter 14 of the *Microsoft Exchange Server Administrator's Guide*.

Messaging Clients Interoperability

During coexistence, there is a mix of MS Mail and Outlook clients. The white paper *Interoperability with Outlook, MS Mail 3.x, MS Schedule+ 95 and 1.0* answers most user questions on coexistence and addresses the key interoperability scenarios so administrators can evaluate and manage their organization's move to Exchange and Outlook. Read it at the Microsoft.com Outlook site **http://www.microsoft.com/outlook/documents/ot97inwp/default.htm.**

Scheduling Interoperability

One of the most important aspects to consider when planning client interoperability is calendaring.

Microsoft Mail for PC Networks 3.x clients use Schedule+ 1.0, Microsoft Windows Messaging clients will run Schedule+ 7.0, and Outlook has its own calendaring mechanism. Here's a breakdown of the interoperability between these clients:

When a user running this client:	Opens the calendar or views free/busy details of a user or resource that is running Outlook	Opens the calendar or views free/busy details of a user or resource that is running Schedule+ 7.0 / 95	Opens the calendar or views free/busy details of a user or resource that is running Schedule+ 1.0
Outlook 8.x	Complete interoperability.	Complete interoperability.	Complete interoperability.
Schedule+ 7.0 or Schedule+ 95 (Windows Messaging clients, Exchange clients 4.0 and 5.0, or Office 95)	No interoperability because Schedule+ 7.0/95 cannot read Outlook format (see note below).	Complete interoperability.	Complete interoperability.
Schedule+ 1.0 (MS Mail)	No interoperability.	No interoperability.	User can open the other user's calendar only.

Note Outlook users on Exchange Server can view the free or busy details of Schedule+ 7.0/95 and Schedule+ 1.0 users who are also on Exchange Server but cannot view the details of those on Microsoft Mail Server. Users of Win32 Schedule+ 7.0/95 can view the free or busy details of Outlook users when all users are on Exchange Server and the Win32 driver is installed. This free driver is available for download from the Microsoft Outlook Web site: **http://www.microsoft.com/outlook/.** Schedule+ 1.0 and non-Win32 Schedule+ 7.0/95 users cannot view Outlook users' free/busy details. Outlook users who have at least Read permission to another user's calendar can see when that user is free or busy and can view the description (details) of that user's scheduled appointments and activities in the Meeting Planner.

During a multiphase migration, you must consider interoperability of calendaring clients, especially when migrating delegates, conference rooms, and resources. You may want to migrate conference rooms last so that all clients can continue to access these resources.

Schedule Free/Busy Connector

The MS Mail Connector of Exchange Server includes a free/busy connector. This allows current MS Mail (PC) 3.x users with Schedule+ 1.0 and Exchange Server users with Schedule+ 7.0 to view each other's free/busy information for calendaring purposes. For more information on free/busy connector setup and requirements, see Knowledge Base article Q147698,Title: XADM: Configuring the Schedule+ Free/Busy Connector.

A free/busy folder is automatically created on the first server installed in a site. Like any public folder, this one can be replicated to other site servers. The Microsoft Mail Administrator must run the SCHDIST program on the Microsoft Mail 3.x side to transfer MS Mail (PC) users' free/busy updates into Microsoft Exchange Server and to receive free/busy updates from Microsoft Exchange Server users. If a large number of users run Schedule+ 7.0, you should replicate the hidden folder that contains the Schedule+ 7.0 free and busy times.

Optimizing Interoperability Between Schedule+ 1.0 and 7.0 and Outlook

- Upgrade users in delegate relationships at the same time, regardless of their workgroups. Delegate relationships require that the members can open each other's calendar information, and this is possible only if both use the same client and the same back end.

- Upgrade all members of a workgroup at the same time.

- Upgrade resource accounts, such as conference rooms, after upgrading the users who use those resources. If you upgrade resource accounts to Outlook while users are running Schedule+, those users will not be able to open the resource accounts' Calendar folders, and so will not be able to book those resources. In a typical case, users could invite each other to a meeting, but could not reserve a conference room because their Schedule+ client software couldn't directly book the meeting in the Calendar folder for the conference room's account.

- During an Outlook upgrade, choose the option to continue using Schedule+, rather than using Outlook for scheduling. Users typically migrate to Outlook in phases for messaging, and after the messaging migration is complete, everyone migrates at the same time from Schedule+ to Outlook.

- Make sure users do not delete their Schedule+ files until everyone is ready to migrate to Outlook for scheduling. Outlook cannot export its calendar data back to Schedule+ files, so if Schedule+ files are deleted they must be retrieved from backup copies, or the data must be reentered by hand into Schedule+.

- If you use a Microsoft Mail back end, users in delegate relationships should not upgrade to Outlook for scheduling; instead, they should continue using Schedule+. Outlook works with MS Mail back ends by storing both messaging and calendar information locally. However, Outlook clients cannot access other Outlook clients' local data stores. With a Microsoft Mail back end, Outlook cannot participate in delegate relationships. For instructions on using Schedule+ with Outlook, see Knowledge Base article Q155897, Title: OL97: Using Schedule+ as the Primary Calendar in Outlook 97.

- Each resource account, such as those for conference rooms, should have a delegate account, and that delegate account should be signed on to Outlook on a continuously running computer. Outlook does not support direct booking, so users cannot book a resource by directly altering its Calendar folder. Instead, a user sends the resource's account a message requesting a meeting, and it (or its delegate) must be running Outlook to receive the message and act on it.

Electronic Forms Designer 1.0 Compatibility with Exchange or Outlook Forms

E-forms developed for the Microsoft Mail environment using Electronic Forms Designer (EFD) version 1.0 will work within the context of simple MAPI support. Exchange Server clients who decide to can use these forms because the Microsoft Outlook client is compatible. E-forms or messaging applications that adhere to simple MAPI specifications can continue to function under 32-bit desktop environments regardless of whether the system continues to use Microsoft Mail for PC Networks version 3.x or is upgraded to the Microsoft Exchange Client/Microsoft Mail service provider. The MAPI.DLL included with Microsoft Exchange Server supports simple MAPI.

Currently, no migration tools or procedures are available to migrate a Microsoft Mail/EFD 1.0 form to a Microsoft Exchange or Outlook form project.

For more information on EFD 1.0 compatibility, see pages 66–67 in Chapter 4 of the *Microsoft Exchange Server Migration Guide* (located on the Microsoft Exchange Server CD-ROM).

Directory Synchronization for Exchange to MS Mail for PC Networks

The Microsoft Exchange Directory Synchronization Agent (DXA) automatically circulates updated directories to all postoffices in the messaging system, whether on the same LAN, linked together asynchronously, or connected by a gateway. DXA enhances directory synchronization with flexible scheduling, which improves time zone management and update scheduling. Its multithreaded design allows for high-capacity performance with better error reporting and logging. The DXA can be a directory synchronization server and/or a requestor. Because of the multithreaded design, the DXA can make a more robust directory synchronization server by reducing address list maintenance, increasing security, and providing a more efficient process.

Dirsync for a computer running Microsoft Exchange Server can be configured at the same time as the Microsoft Mail Connector. The Exchange Connector postoffice can be defined as a remote Microsoft Mail postoffice and as a requestor on the current dirsync server. After this is configured, directory updates will be sent to the Exchange server when dirsync takes place.

The MS-DOS dirsync agent, DISPATCH.EXE, still needs to run against the existing Microsoft Mail for PC Networks postoffices, but should not be run against the Microsoft Exchange Connector postoffice. Microsoft Exchange services will handle their own sending and receiving of updated directory lists.

Exchange Dirsync/MS Mail Dirsync Comparison

Here are the key similarities and differences between the Exchange Server dirsync and Mail for PC Networks dirsync:

- Exchange Server dirsync can be run as frequently as hourly; a Mail for PC Networks postoffice can schedule only one dirsync a day, although an administrator can perform a dirsync manually.

- Exchange Server DXA servers and requestors apply changes immediately. The Exchange Server DXA server immediately applies T1 changes from a Mail (PC) requestor to a local directory (it queues them for remote directories) and the Exchange Server DXA requestor immediately applies T2 updates from a MS Mail (PC) dirsync server.

- Exchange Server DXA servers and requestors use the same dirsync protocol as is used in MS Mail (PC).

- Exchange Server can have more than one DXA server or requestor, one for each Mail for PC Networks system if there is more than one.

- Exchange Server does not use DISPATCH.EXE against the Mail Connector postoffice, although it must still be run against the Mail (PC) POs.

- The Mail (PC) files MSTTRANS, SRVTRANS, REQTRANS, REQCONF, and SRVCONF are not used by the Exchange Server Mail Connector postoffice.

- Exchange Server DXA server and requestors do not auto-create new definitions in a Mail Connector. Exchange Server, which has no direct equivalent, uses the "Update Routing" feature instead.

Exchange as a Dirsync Server or Dirsync Requestor

Generally, you should maintain the current Microsoft Mail directory synchronization configuration and set up Microsoft Exchange as a dirsync requestor to export:

- Exchange users into the dirsync stream.
- Other custom recipients (non-Microsoft Mail) into the shared file system (SFS) dirsync stream.

The advantage in migrating the dirsync server role to Microsoft Exchange is that the Exchange dirsync server runs as a Windows NT service, so it can run the T2 process in the background more or less continually. Many administrators configure T2 to run hourly, keeping dirsync requestors tightly synchronized to the server.

The disadvantage is that you have to reset the dirsync configurations for the Microsoft Mail postoffices, reset the current MS Mail dirsync requestor numbers, and change the dirsync server definitions. For additional information on resetting dirsync configurations, see the *Dirsync Application Note* on TechNet (search on **WA0725**).

Changing the dirsync server is a lot of work: too much work, probably, if you plan to move from Microsoft Mail to Microsoft Exchange soon, but not too much, probably, if you plan to leave a significant number of users on Microsoft Mail for a while.

Template Information

The postoffice migration tool does not migrate MS Mail custom template information to the Microsoft Exchange Server directory. There are three ways to migrate it:

- Use dirsync with directory export and import.
- Use dirsync with custom recipient conversion.
- Export the data from the postoffice, convert the format, then import.

Dirsync and migration methods affect which method you can use. For example, the first two options won't work for single-phase migration unless you set up the MS Mail Connector and directory synchronization first. For more information see Knowledge Base article Q158694, Title: XFOR: DirSync: Map Template Info Between MSMail & Exchange.

Custom Recipients

By default, new Exchange mailboxes are created in the site's recipient container, but you can create new containers specifically for MS Mail custom recipients.

When defining the dirsync requestors on Microsoft Exchange, you can specify where the Mail usernames will be stored. MS Mail custom recipients usually are created and tracked in separate recipient containers. When you create custom recipient containers, simplify administration and replication control by documenting which containers will be imported and exported, as well as the source MS Mail postoffice from which the recipients originate.

Import and Export: Microsoft Mail Custom Recipients Containers

When an Exchange Server system is functioning as a requestor to the MS Mail dirsync server, do not allow the MS Mail custom recipients to be exported from Exchange to MS Mail. Only the originating MS Mail postoffices hosting these users should be sending updates or modifications about their users to the dirsync server, so hide them or raise the trust level raised to 100 to prevent their being exporting.

Exporting custom recipients or removing their containers from the list of exported recipients can add Replace transactions for the SFS users' postoffices to the list of pending dirsync transactions. Inappropriate addition or removal of recipient containers on the dirsync stream can generate unnecessary dirsync transactions and cause the temporary loss of MS Mail (PC) address information from global address lists (GALs). Recovery can also require large numbers of dirsync transactions.

Troubleshooting Dirsync Between MS Mail and Exchange

Sometimes you have to reset the dirsync sequence numbers when troubleshooting Microsoft Mail dirsync problems with an Exchange Server participating as a requestor or as the dirsync server. Don't just reset dirsync numbers to smooth over a problem: do it as part of a systematic approach to troubleshooting dirsync. For comprehensive information on how the MS Mail dirsync process works and a description of all dirsync sequence numbers, see *Directory Synchronization [DirSync]* on TechNet (search on **WA0725**). See also Knowledge Base article Q152231, Title: XFOR: How To Reset Microsoft Exchange DirSync Numbers.

How To Avoid Potential Dirsync Problems and Excessive Transactions

Streamline your dirsync configuration on the Exchange server side by setting up separate custom recipient containers and disallowing any exports from them.

For administrative and organizational purposes, you can group various recipients (for instance, all users within a site or all custom external SMTP recipient addresses) into specific recipient containers, which you can add to or remove from the Microsoft Mail dirsync this way:

1. Start the Microsoft Exchange Administrator program, and expand the site, configuration, and connections containers.

2. Double-click the dirsync requestor object, click the **Export Containers** tab, and modify the **Export these Recipients** field.

Altering the Microsoft Mail dirsync stream by adding or removing recipient containers generates a lot of transactions. Messages sent to the dirsync server contain the standard dirsync transactions (add, modify, delete, or replace) but may combine them in unexpected ways.

Identical Display Names

When Microsoft Exchange Server is included in the MS Mail environment dirsync process, some display names are appended with 001. This happens whether the Exchange Server acts as dirsync server or requester.

All display names (friendly names) must be unique at the MS Mail postoffice level, but not at the global address list (GAL) level. For example it is OK for there to be Bob Smiths on separate nets:

```
Bob Smith NET1/PO1/BSMITH
Bob Smith NET2/PO2/BSMITH
```

But not in the same postoffice:

```
Bob Smith NET1/P01/BSMITH
Bob Smith NET1/P01/BSMITH2
```

Neither ADMIN.EXE nor IMPORT.EXE would allow the second Bob Smith to be created.

Exchange Server allows multiple objects to have the same display name, so the Exchange Directory Synchronization Service (DXA) must ensure that it does not send a second instance of a display name to any one MS Mail postoffice.

Exchange Server versions 5.0 with SP1 and above have a registry value that change this behavior, but it is a good idea to leave it in place. For one thing, it avoids name conflicts. For another, using the Registry Editor incorrectly can cause serious, system-wide problems that may require you to reinstall Windows NT to correct them. Microsoft cannot guarantee that any problems resulting from the use of Registry Editor can be solved. Use this tool at your own risk.

▶ **To set the registry value**

1. Run the Registry Editor (Regedt32.exe).
2. Under the HKEY_LOCAL_MACHINE subtree, go to the following subkey:

   \SYSTEM\CurrentControlSet\Services\MSExchangeDX
3. Add the following case-sensitive DWORD value of 0:

   Unique Display Names
4. Quit Registry Editor.

After setting the registry parameter above, the following steps **must** be performed.

1. Stop the Exchange dirsync service.
2. Delete the contents of the DXADATA subdirectory. Do not delete the directory, only the contents of the directory.
3. If the DXA is acting as the dirsync server, using the Microsoft Exchange Administrator utility, choose each remote requester object one by one and select **Export on next cycle** on the **General** tab. This forces a full dirsync export to be sent to each remote requester.
4. If the DXA is acting as a dirsync requester, using the Microsoft Exchange Administrator utility, choose the dirsync requester object and select **Export on next cycle** on the **Settings** tab. This forces a full dirsync export to be sent to the dirsync server.
5. Start the Microsoft Exchange Directory Synchronization Service.

For more information, see the *Microsoft Exchange DirSync Troubleshooter*, available on Microsoft's Web site: **http://support.microsoft.com/support /tshoot/DirSync.asp**. It lists steps in order, beginning with greatest benefit and least cost.

Migration from MS Mail to Exchange

After the coexistence logistics have been finalized and implemented (message delivery and directory synchronization is stable), the final step is to begin migrating MS Mail user mailboxes into the Exchange organization. After configuring, testing, and validating the message transport and directory synchronization configurations, focus on migrating Microsoft Mail data and clients to Microsoft Exchange Server.

Build a Detailed Migration Project Plan

When planning a migration, give careful thought to which postoffices will migrate, and the order and timeframe in which they will migrate. Don't forget the users' client machines. Maintain this plan in a project management program, spreadsheet, database, or word processor. It should include:

- Type of migration (full or partial).
- Postoffices being migrated (NETNAME/PO-NAME).
- Expected date of a postoffice migration.
- Actual date of a postoffice migration.
- Number of users being migrated with a postoffice.
- The Exchange Server to which the postoffice will be migrated.
- The classification of postoffice (hub, directory synchronization server, gateway, or user postoffice).
- The required prerequisites, such as other tasks, migrations, or events that must be completed before the postoffice migration can take place.
- The post-migration dependencies, such as other migrations or key events that require this migration.

Migration Prerequisite Reading

For best results, make sure all migration technical staff read Chapters 1–4 of the *Microsoft Exchange Migration Guide*. This book helps administrators plan the conversion from Microsoft Mail to Microsoft Exchange Server. A soft copy is on the Microsoft Exchange Server installation CD-ROM. Chapters 1 through 4 provide information on converting from Microsoft Mail to Microsoft Exchange Server. Other chapters cover other third-party and legacy messaging systems.

Migration Phases

You can break the migration process into five components (see below) by correlating migration order to messaging function or role:

- Migrate hub postoffices
- Migrate dirsync components
- Migrate gateways to connectors
- Migrate user postoffices
- Migrate clients

This view allows you to leverage Exchange server's more powerful messaging abilities for Microsoft Mail users during the coexistence period.

Validating the Migration Process

Before migrating all MS Mail users from a server postoffice, run a trial migration of at least one backup Microsoft Mail postoffice to a test computer running Exchange Server. This can help you identify issues unique to your environment or things you simply failed to anticipate.

Other preliminary steps:

- Document specific procedures for migrating a Microsoft Mail postoffice to Exchange Server.
- Step through the migration procedures against a backup or "dummy" postoffice.
- Document any unexpected results or newly needed migration procedures.
- Update the original migration plan with the results of the test.

Single-phase vs. Multi-phase Migration

Single-phase migration moves everyone at once; multi-phase moves users in groups at different times. For obvious reasons, smaller companies usually prefer to go single-phase and get it over in one shot. Larger companies often prefer multi-phase because their environment is more complex and extensive so that:

- Not all departments *can* upgrade at once.
- Hardware must be freed up in early phases so it can be redeployed in later phases.
- The Exchange Server implementation group can't migrate everyone within an acceptable downtime.

Refer to chapters 1–4 of the *Microsoft Exchange Server Migration Guide* (on the CD-ROM) for an in-depth discussion of migration practices and scenarios.

Avoiding Potential Bottlenecks

Messaging traffic between Microsoft Mail and an Exchange Server often increases in the middle of a multi-phase migration, when some users are on one system and the rest are on the other. A migration plan can avoid this by:

- Configuring multiple gateways to move mail between systems.
- Identifying de facto workgroups (groups who typically send mail primarily to each other) and migrating them over together.
- Restricting the size of messages sent on Exchange Server and the existing system.
- Connecting new sites to each other quickly to avoid sending mail between Exchange Server sites that are backboned over the existing system.
- Dedicating fast, high-powered computers to the MS Mail connector processes.

Offline Address Books and User Migrations

Offline address books allow users to address messages while disconnected from a server and to reduce the number of entries in their personal address books. A current address book helps to ensure that users are sending to the appropriate e-mail address.

To make sure offline address book information is current, users should generate their books regularly, especially during conversion and after a Microsoft Mail postoffice has been converted. You can schedule address book generation with the Microsoft Exchange Administrator program.

Client Migration

Microsoft Exchange provides two utilities to migrate users' data: the client-side conversion program and the server-side migration wizard. Because of the amount of data that is usually processed during the conversion, Microsoft usually recommends using the client-side utility.

Users can convert their individual MMFs to Microsoft Exchange personal information store (PST) files, completing the entire process at their workstations. The server can then deliver new messages and come online quicker. Client-side conversion requires that the user have free disk space equal to twice the size of the MS Mail *.MMF file.

If users store most of their mail on the MS Mail postoffice server, the server migration wizard is a better tool. Before you use it, make sure:

- Users clean their inboxes thoroughly. Set guidelines on acceptable message age, size, etc., to help streamline this process.

- The postoffice is in good health. (See the first section in this chapter for more information.)

- That you copy the MS Mail postoffice directories to another location and use a nonproduction Exchange server to perform a test migration.

Client Migration Order from MS Mail to Exchange

Some organizations may need to upgrade hardware or software before upgrading user messaging clients. If you have to do this, upgrade in this order:

1. **Hardware**—Upgrade client hardware to at least a 486 computer with 32-MB RAM.
2. **Operating System**—Upgrade client computers to the latest Windows 32-bit OS along with any released service packs.
3. **Outlook Client**—Install the latest Outlook client.

This order prevents having to do multiple installations of the same component.

Personal Address Books and Migrated Mailboxes

Often, users still on Microsoft Mail get non-delivery reports (NDRs) when they send messages by means of their personal address books (PABs) to recipients already on Microsoft Exchange. This is because the sender's PAB references the recipient's old Microsoft Mail address rather than the new Exchange address and the PABs of "non-migrated" Microsoft Mail users aren't updated every time a user or group of users is migrated to Exchange.

You can minimize or control the number of NDRs, but the available methods have drawbacks. Below is a table of the existing workarounds for this issue.

Approach	Description	Advantages	Disadvantages
Migrate complete postoffices.	When moving users from Microsoft Mail to Microsoft Exchange, migrate complete Microsoft Mail postoffices at a time.	The Microsoft Mail proxy address created for the migrated users is the same as their old Microsoft Mail 10x10x10 address. Thus, the addresses retained in the PABs are **not** invalidated. Migration does not invalidate PAB entries. You have to change the routing definitions to the migrated postoffice on the remaining Microsoft Mail postoffices, making them indirect using the Microsoft Exchange connector postoffice. In a "hub-and-spoke" Microsoft Mail system, the number of routing changes are minimized.	May not be feasible to migrate entire postoffices at once if the number of users per postoffice is very large, if multiple workgroups are spread across single postoffices, or if single workgroups are spread across multiple postoffices.
Use the global address list (GAL) rather than the personal address book (PAB).	Microsoft Mail users should be able to address the migrated recipients using the GAL instead of their PABs.	Because directory synchronization is configured and functioning between Microsoft Exchange and Microsoft Mail, each postoffice's GAL will be updated after each set of users is migrated. Addressing is now governed by a process that can be centrally controlled rather than using user's local address books.	Users are required to switch their primary address book from their PAB to their GAL. For Microsoft Exchange Client users: On the **Tools** menu, click **Options,** click **Addressing,** and click **Show this address list first.** For Microsoft Mail client users: On the **Compose** menu, click **Address** and select the **Global Address List** from the list of address lists. For Microsoft Mail client users, personal groups will not be updated because they must reference PAB recipients. Thus, messages sent to personal groups will continue to NDR unless manually updated by the sender.

(continued)

Approach	Description	Advantages	Disadvantages
Synchronize the PABs with the GAL.	Use a utility such as PABCHK or PABSYNC to synchronize the users' PABs with the GAL.	PABCHK will list those personal recipients that must be updated. PABSYNC will try to synchronize these recipients with the GAL. Users can manually update their PABs with the GAL. By running the utility, users ensure that their PAB is updated to the existing GAL, which correctly resolves the addresses of migrated recipients. Process should eliminate NDRs because the GAL should contain the most recent and correct addresses.	Requires users to run the utility after each migration to ensure their PAB is synchronized with the GAL. Although PABSYNC is contained within TechNet, Microsoft Technical Support does not officially support it. There are some potential problems with PABSYNC, which are documented in TechNet.
Create a message forwarding scheme.	Instead of deleting the migrated mailboxes from their Microsoft Mail postoffices, retain them and use a third-party or custom utility to forward all messages from the old Microsoft Mail mailbox to the new Microsoft Exchange mailbox.	Instead of creating NDRs, messages addressed to "old" mailboxes are delivered to the respective mailbox and then forwarded to migrated user's Microsoft Exchange mailbox.	Requires that mailboxes be maintained in both Microsoft Mail and Microsoft Exchange until all users are migrated to Microsoft Exchange. May require users to monitor both their new Microsoft Exchange mailbox and old Microsoft Mail mailbox. Both mailboxes can be accessed from the Microsoft Exchange client by configuring both the Microsoft Mail and Microsoft Exchange information services within the same user profile. Generates more mail to be processed within the entire messaging system.

Full postoffice migrations with the Microsoft Exchange Migration Wizard save time and effort over partial migrations. Refer to the *Microsoft Exchange Server Migration Guide* for a comparison of the methods.

You can further simplify administration by getting all clients to use the global address list (GAL) as their default address book rather than personal address books (PABs) during the coexistence and migration phases. How you accomplish this is up to you.

Microsoft Mail recipients and personal distribution lists retained in Microsoft Mail PABs are not automatically updated to Exchange Server recipients during migration. Users may have to rebuild personal distribution lists from the new GAL. Clients can continue to use PABs for recipients not hosted on Microsoft Mail or Exchange Server (such as SMTP Internet mail addresses).

In general, clients do not need PABs to send e-mail to users who are provided in the GAL. A PAB is intended to provide recipients (such as Internet recipients outside of the organization) who are *not* provided by the GAL. Still, some users maintain GAL addresses in their PAB to minimize search time or so they send e-mail while working offline.

Remote Client Migration

Microsoft Exchange provides two utilities to migrate users' data: the client-side conversion program and the server-side migration wizard. Because of the amount of data that is usually processed during the conversion, Microsoft usually recommends the client-side utility.

Because remote clients typically use a local MMF as their primary message store, they can use the client conversion tool to convert their individual MMF files to Microsoft Exchange Server personal information store (PST) files, completing the entire process at their workstation. This frees up the server to deliver new messages and generally come online faster. Client-side conversion requires that the user's disk have free space equal to about twice the size of the current MMF file.

Migrate an Entire Postoffice Using the Migration Wizard

Migrating all users on a postoffice at the same time has some compelling advantages. The Microsoft Mail Network and postoffice name can be logically assigned to the computer running Microsoft Exchange Server, so that messages destined for users on a particular postoffice can be routed to the computer running Microsoft Exchange Server and delivered through the proxy addresses. This requires only a couple of changes to the routing of the Microsoft Mail network.

Perhaps more important is the fact that migrating an entire postoffice at once preserves the validity of non-migrated users' personal address books. A single Microsoft Exchange Server can assume the network or postoffice name for an unlimited number of Microsoft Mail postoffices.

It is also quicker and involves fewer contingencies than migrating a subset of the entire postoffice. Completing full postoffice migrations with the Exchange Migration Wizard will save time and effort. See the *Microsoft Exchange Server Migration Guide*, pages 49–52, for a comparison of partial and full post-office migrations.

Migration Wizard—Known Issues

When you migrate an entire MS Mail postoffice that contains shared folders, the Wizard for Microsoft Mail for PC Networks fails to migrate shared folders from Mail for PC Networks postoffices. All other postoffice data is migrated successfully.

The application log in the Event Log reads:

```
Could not migrate shared folders Event 168
```

This happens when the Information Store *Site Configuration* properties in the Microsoft Exchange Administrator program does not have the Microsoft Exchange Service Account specified under the **Top Level Folder Creation** permissions tab.

▶ **To resolve**

1. Start the Microsoft Exchange Administrator program.
2. Under **Configuration,** double-click the **Information Store Site Configuration** tab.
3. Select the **Top Level Folder Creation** tab.
4. Change the **Allowed to Create Top Level Folder** radio button to **All.**
5. Finish the migration.

When you complete the migration, change the setting back.

More Information

- Q166545, Title: XFOR: DXA Appends 001 Only When Needed [Exchange]
- Q156545, Title: XFOR: How to Set Up a 2nd MS-type Proxy Address for MSMail Users
- Q149284, Title: XADM: PC Mail Shared Folders not Converted To Public Folders
- Q175978, Title: XFOR: List of Reserved Microsoft Mail Network Names
- Q152231, Title: XFOR: How To Reset Microsoft Exchange DirSync Numbers

C H A P T E R   1 3

Fisher EMC2/TAO—SNADS Systems

This chapter explains how to configure the Exchange Connector for SNADS, which provides a direct messaging connection between Microsoft Exchange Server and SNADS-compliant messaging systems such as:

- IBM OfficeVision/MVS
- IBM OfficeVision/400
- IBM JustMail/400
- ICOM OfficePath
- Fisher International EMC2 TAO
- Verimation Memo
- Soft-Switch Central and LMS
- NB Systems TOSS
- Software AG Connect

The Connector for SNADS uses Microsoft SNA Server to provide an SNA connection to the host through standard SNA facilities, including SDLC, Token Ring, Ethernet, and X.25. It also provides transparent e-mail delivery between the Exchange and SNADS systems, using the native interfaces of each system to map the e-mail architectures. It handles all mail object conversions and maps status information, which are different in the two environments. It also provides:

- **Multiple host routing**—Supports simultaneous connections to multiple SNA hosts, routing messages to their destinations.
- **Internet integration**—Works with Exchange Internet Mail Service to allow SNADS users to send and receive messages over the Internet.
- **Automatic generation of temporary e-mail addresses**—Places temporary e-mail address in the Exchange directory for foreign e-mail system users sending mail to SNADS users. Addresses are then added to host directories during synchronization, allowing SNADS users to reply.

To get the most out of this chapter, you must understand Exchange architecture thoroughly and have access to the Exchange Connector for SNADS documentation on the Exchange 5.5 CD-ROM so that you can, if necessary, find details on configuration aspects that are mentioned but not explained in detail.

SNADS Addressing

SNADS is a proprietary architecture developed by IBM for mail, document, and object distribution. It is a store-and-forward communication with its own defined rules. SNADS is closely tied to SNA because it exploits services for program-to-program communication (APPC, LU6.2) to communicate to peer "nodes." It also has design affinities that allow it to work with IBM office architecture Document Interchange Architecture (DIA) and Document Content Architecture (DCA).

The header in SNADS distributions contains two important values:

- **DSU—Distribution System Unit** composed of two parts:
    - RGN—Routing Group Name (usually is blank)
    - REN—Routing Element Name
- **DUN—Distribution Unit Name** composed of two parts:
    - DGN—Distribution Group Name (sometimes called Node ID)
    - DEN—Distribution Element Name (sometimes called User ID)

Each of these can contain up to eight characters.

The SNADS routing application uses the DSU to decide which link to use for communications with the partner application. It must be unique within a SNADS network. The DUN defines the user who will receive the distribution and has to be unique within a SNADS node. The DGN/DEN pair must be unique, not the individual values. This diagram illustrates a message's path through a SNADS-compliant e-mail system:

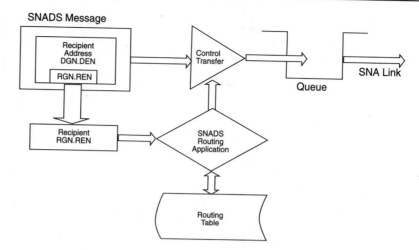

The only value used for routing is the DSU=RGN.REN. The DUN=DGN.DEN is passed with the message to the next system; if this is the recipient's e-mail system, it deposits the message in the proper mailbox based on the DUN value.

SNADS-Compliant E-mail System Architecture

Most e-mail systems that use SNADS as a transmission protocol have these components:

- E-mail application with a directory and mailbox database
- SNADS routing application
- SNA communication application

In the IBM mainframe, the SNA communication application is Virtual Telecommunications Access Method (VTAM). This diagram below shows a SNADS configuration with VTAMs and one Logical Unit (LU).

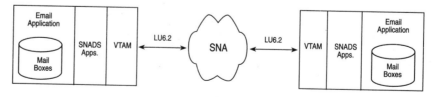

The SNADS application has to use the internal API to communicate with the e-mail system, so each host e-mail application has its own SNADS component (supplied by the host system manufacturer) that must be installed and configured before the Exchange Connector got SNADS can be implemented. All SNADS applications emulate the SNA Advanced Program-to-Program Communications (APPC) protocol for communication over an SNA network using LU6.2 (Logical Unit Type 6.2 defined for APPC protocol). The Exchange Connector for SNADS follows the same architecture except that it does not have a SNADS routing system and it works as a peer-to-peer connection.

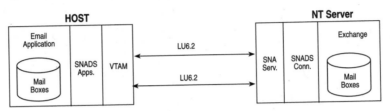

This figure shows the most common host e-mail system configuration with one LU for receive and one for transmit. Some systems use one independent LU to provide bi-directional communication. The use of one or two LUs depends on the SNADS application and VTAM version. For more information on SNA architecture, see the SNA Server documentation.

Host Configuration

VTAM Configuration

VTAM is the IBM host application that provides SNA connectivity.

The VTAM configuration presented in the Exchange 5.5 documentation is valid for any of these e-mail systems. See that documentation for details; here are the basic requirements:

Hardware

- Physical support—Token Ring, Ethernet, Synchronous Data Link Communication (SDLC), X.25)
- Communication Controller—3174, 3745 with the required TIC

Software

- Network Control Protocol (NCP)/VTAM release levels (to implement independent LUs in the host environment): IBM ACF/VTAM version 3.2 and IBM ACF/NCP version 5 release 2.1 or later.

The VTAM administrator must define a LINK (determined by physical link type) and a PU (physical unit) 2.0 with two dependent LUs. It is a good idea to define an additional LU for 3270 emulation so that it can be used to check the initial connection and to log on to the mainframe and test the mail transfer after the installation is finished.

See the VTAM Configuration Example and SNA Server Mapping section for examples of VTAM definitions for two LUs.

TAO SNADS Configuration

The EMC2/TAO SNADS gateway software allows EMC2/TAO to communicate with other SNADS-compliant systems, including the Exchange Connector for SNADS. The SNADS connector functions as a distinct DSUN system to an EMC2/TAO system and must be configured as a secondary LU (SLU) when communicating with the EMC2/TAO system. Because EMC2/TAO restricts all partner systems to communicate with the EMC2/TAO LU in single-session mode, configuring the connector as an SLU also allows it to communicate with the EMC2/TAO system.

The EMC2/TAO system serves as a SNADS routing node for the connector. Thus, for another remote SNADS system to communicate with users served by the SNADS connector via EMC2/TAO, the DSUN of the connector must be registered in the routing table of the remote system. The routing entry defined for the SNADS connector (and implicit for the Exchange users) at these remote systems shares the connection and routing queue with the DSUN entry of EMC2/TAO. Similarly, the other connected SNADS system users can send mail to Exchange users as if they are in the EMC2/TAO domain, which automatically stores and forwards messages sent between Exchange and the remote SNADS network. No additional LU configuration is needed at these remote SNADS systems.

Before an LU6.2 connection and mail session can begin between EMC2/TAO and the SNADS connector, you must:

- Configure EMC2/TAO to define the Exchange Connector for SNADS.
- Configure SNA Server and the SNADS connector to match the EMC2/TAO configuration.

TAO-SNADS Application Configuration Parameter File Updates

After the application is loaded, the TAO-SNADS application configuration file (which acts as a routing table) must be updated to include the SNADS connector parameters. These parameters control TDSRD, TDSQS, and TDSQR application programs. Here is an example of this file:

```
TDSRD    DB_APPID=TAOSERV,
    DB_XMNAME=TAO,
    DB_ACBNAME=TAO,
    RGN=TAORGN, <- RGN of the EMC2/TAO system. It can be blank
    REN=TAOREN, <- REN of the EMC2/TAO system.
    DOMAIN=.SNADS,
    PASSWORD=SNADSPW,
    PROCESS_INTERVAL=180,
    DEFAULT_DGN=TAODGN, <-DGN of the EMC2/TAO system.
    ADMINISTRATOR=SNADS.ADMIN,
    CONNECTION=(DSVHOST;DSVHOST),
    CONNECTION=(EXCHANGE;EXCHANGE),
TDSQS    CONNECTION_NEXT_DSUN=DSVHOST,
    MODE=LU62MODE,
    PROCESS_INTERVAL=300,
    HOP_COUNT=2
TDSQS    CONNECTION_NEXT_DSUN=EXCHANGE
    MODE=LU62MODE
    PROCESS_INTERVAL=600
    HOP_COUNT=2
```

TDSRD statement defines characteristics of the local (EMC2) SNADS system.

The TDSRD CONNECTION parameter defines the route information to other connected SNADS systems including the SNADS connector.

Each additional CONNECTION statement is defined as follows:

```
CONNECTION=( Partner RGN.REN ; connect_next_dsun-id )
```

The *Partner RGN.REN* defines the connector RGN.REN. Although the RGN is not normally used, the REN is mandatory. If the RGN is not used, simply define the REN without the dot (.). The *Partner RGN.REN* definition must match the SNADS connector page LOCALRGN and LOCALREN fields. In the above example EXCHANGE is the REN for the SNADS connector and RGN is not used. The *connect_next_dsun-id* defines the routing identifier that will be used in the next statement.

Each CONNECTION statement has a TDSQS statement of this form:

TDSQS CONNECTION_NEXT_DSUN=*connect_next_dsun-id*,
    MODE=*lu6.2_mode*,

PROCESS_INTERVAL=*process_interval_in_seconds*,
HOP_COUNT=*hop_count*

The *connect_next_dsun-id* must match the identifier in the CONNECTION statement.

The *lu6.2_mode* is the mode name used by the EMC2/TAO SNADS gateway and the SNADS connector to communicate with each other. This mode is defined in VTAM for the connector LUs and the name must match.

The *process_interval_in_seconds* defines the frequency of the host SNADS queue servicing interval in seconds.

The *hop_count* defines the maximum number of nodes a document can pass through before being rejected. A value of 10 is typical.

TAO-SNADS LU6.2 Communication Parameters

The SNADS connector uses two dependent connector LUs against one host LU: one connector LU receives mail from EMC2/TAO and the other sends mail to EMC2/TAO.

The TAO-SNADS does not support independent LUs. The TAO-SNADS gateway LU6.2 communication parameter definitions control the characteristics of VTAM communications between network nodes. It can use one or two LUs to communicate with other systems. The LOCALLU statement defines the VTAM application EMC2/TAO uses when communicating with other logical units using LU6.2.

```
LOCALLU LOCALNAME=label,
APPLID=EMC2tao_applid,
SESSIONLIMIT=number_sessions
```

The APPLID parameter defines the EMC2/TAO application. This value should be assigned to the uninterpreted LU name defined in the partner LU definition in the SNA Server.

To avoid confusion, it is a good idea to use the value of the APPLID parameter as the PARTNERLU Alias. If TAO-SNADS uses two LUs to communicate, there are two LOCALLU statements with different APPLIDs. In this case EMC2 will use the first defined LU to send mail and the second one to receive.

Two PARTNERLU statements must be added in the TAO-SNADS LU6.2 file for the SNADS connector. The first defines the Exchange Connector receive LU and the second defines the Exchange Connector send LU. These match the LOCAL LU definitions entered in the VTAM and SNA Server that were allocated for this link. Use this format:

PARTNERLU LOCALNAME=*connect_next_dsun-id*,
  NETWORKNAME=*exhconnr_lu_name*,
  PARSESS=NO,
  SESSIONTYPE=SLU

The *connect_next_dsun-id* is not presently used by EMC2/TAO but you should set it equal to the CONNECT_NEXT_DSUN parameter in the TDSQS statement of the TAO-SNADS file presented in the previous section above.

The *exhconnr_lu_name* defines the SNADS connector receive LU. This must match the LOCALLU value from the configuration page in SNADS connector page in Exchange.

Set the PARSESS to NO (only single session used) as specified in the *EMC2/TAO Gateway Guide*, Chapter 6.

The SESSIONTYPE parameter defines the LU characteristics.

Because the SNA server assumes a host connection with the EMC2/TAO system, a secondary LU (SLU) must be specified for the SNADS connector. Use this format:

PARTNERLU LOCALNAME=*label*,
  NETWORKNAME=*exhconns_lu_name*,
  PARSESS=NO,
  SESSIONTYPE=SLU

This statement is similar to the first except that the NETWORKNAME addresses the SNADS Connector send LU.

This section also requires the addition of a MODE statement. The MODE name definition must be consistent with the MODE parameter assignment of the TDSQS statement. Format:

MODE MODENAME=*lu6.2_mode*,
  SESSIONLIMIT=1

lu6.2_mode must be the same as the TDSQS MODE parameter.

This is an example of the TAO-SNADS LU6.2 file using two LUs for EMC2. The bold, italicized letters that match indicate corresponding lines.

```
LOCALLU LOCALNAME=TDSLU, < This is the EMC2 Send LU (Connector Receive)
    APPLID=TDSLU,   (A)    <- PARTNER LU when EMC2 has one APPLID
    SESSIONLIMIT=10
LOCALLU LOCALNAME=TDRLU, < This is the EMC2 Receive LU (Connector Send)
APPLID=TDRLU,   (B)    <- PARTNER LU when EMC2 has two APPLID's
    SESSIONLIMIT=10
PARTNERLU   LOCALNAME=EXCHANGE,
        NETWORKNAME=EXCHLUR,    (A)
```

```
            PARSESS=NO,
            SESSIONTYPE=SLU
PARTNERLU    LOCALNAME=EXCHANGE,
            NETWORKNAME=EXCHLUS,    (B)
            PARSESS=NO,
            SESSIONTYPE=SLU
MODE        MODENAME=LU62MODE,
      SESSIONLIMIT=1
```

The arrows show how the LUs communicate with each other and how sessions are established. If EMC2 uses one LU (only one LOCALLU statement), both SNADS connector sessions are established with it.

The section TAO Configuration File Mapping to SNA Server Panels has screen shots of the applications' GUIs to help you match fields with values from the above example.

The NCP/VTAM must be configured according to the PU, LU, and MODE definitions. See the Exchange 5.5 documentation for details.

SNA Server and SNADS Connector Configuration

SNA Server Configuration

Use the Exchange 5.5 CD-ROM documentation to configure SNA Server. The connector uses two LUs, so you must define two local dependent LUs in the SNA Server that match the VTAM definitions obtained from the SNA administrator. When TAO-SNADS is using two APPLIDs, the partner LU is the APPLID defined for the second LOCALLU from the TAO-SNADS LU6.2 configuration file. You must also define a MODE in your SNA Server that matches the name from VTAM and TAO-SNADS configuration file.

SNADS Connector Property Page Values Mapping at the end of the chapter shows how to associate these values.

SNADS Connector Configuration

The SNADS connector is configured using the connector property page from the Exchange Administrator. In this template, you must edit these fields:

- **PARTNER RGN**—has the RGN defined in the TDSRD statement of the TAO-SNADS configuration file (usually is blank)

- **PARTNER REN**—Has the REN defined in the TDSRD statement of the TAO-SNADS configuration file.

- **LOCAL RGN**—The RGN of the SNADS connector (usually is blank).

- **LOCAL REN**—The REN of the SNADS connector.

- **PARTNER LU**—The alias of the remote APPC LU defined in the SNA Server, corresponding to the APPLID defined in TAO-SNADS LU6.2 configuration file for receive. When there is only one LOCALLU, this is its APPLID value; when there are two, this is the APPLID of the second LOCALLU statement.

- **Local LU Alias**—The alias of the LU defined in the SNA Server for onnector send that matches the **second** PARTNERLU defined in the TAO-SNADS LU6.2 configuration file.

- **Receive Local LU Alias**—The alias of the Local LU from the SNA Server that matches the first PARNERLU from the TAO-SNADS LU6.2 file.

- **Mode Name**—The mode defined for the SNADS connector definitions in VTAM and in the TAO-SNADS files.

The section SNADS Connector Property Page Values Mapping at the end of this chapter provides an example of how to map the above description.

User Registration

After the connection is established, users from either system can send mail. Proper addressing format, of course, is essential. In this case both systems use a SNADS-type address for the recipient. Users can enter addresses manually when they edit the message or can enter them in their personal address book for later reference, or the Administrator can register addresses in the e-mail system directory.

Exchange User Registration in EMC2

As soon as the SNADS proxy generator is loaded, SNADS addresses are generated for Exchange users according to the rule defined by the administrator in the Site Addressing. The address format for EMC2 users sending mail to Exchange users is:

DGN.DEN@RGN.REN.SNADS

Where:

- **DGN.DEN** is the SNADS address generated by the SNADS proxy generator for the Exchange users.

- **RGN.REN** is the value for the Exchange connector as defined in the TAO-SNADS configuration file (RGN can be blank).

- **SNADS** shows that this entry is a SNADS-type address and must be routed accordingly. For example, Dave Smith is a user on an Exchange server that has a SNADS connector with the configuration from the above examples. His SNADS address is:

- **EXCHANGE.SMITHD@EXCHANGE.SNADS** (The RGN is not present because it is blank.)

In EMC2 directory, the ALIAS identifies each user. The administrator can register external SNADS users under aliases in the EMC2 directory, specifying them as "shadow" users and setting the "Forward Address" field with the full SNADS address as it shows in the above example. If Exchange users are registered in the EMC2 directory, an EMC2 user can send mail to them by simply typing the ALIAS in the TO: field. Exchange users registered in the EMC2 directory can also be part of distribution lists.

EMC2 User Registration in Exchange

In Exchange all EMC2 users are registered as customer recipients with an address type of SNADS. Their SNADS address have this format:

SNADS:DGN.ALIAS

Where:

- **DGN** is the value for the EMC2 system as defined in the TDSRD statement of the TAO-SNADS configuration file.
- **ALIAS** is the ALIAS name of that user from the EMC2 directory (*ALIAS is the equivalent of DEN from the SNADS standards*).

EMC2 directory ALIASes must be unique, so keep an eye on the SNADS proxy generator, which can cause conflicts by generating equivalent DENs. Compare values before starting user registration in either system, especially before a large registration.

VTAM Configuration Example and SNA Server Mapping

This example illustrates the configuration for a Token-Ring connection to an IBM 37x5 Token-Ring interface controller (TIC). The bold, italicized letters in the table columns correspond to property values in the screen shots included below the tables.

LNK02	LINE ADDRESS=(131,FULL),
	LOCADDR=400037450001,
	PORTADD=01,
	ANS=CONT,
	CLOCKING=EXT,

		DUPLEX=FULL,

(continued)

LNK02		**LINE ADDRESS=(131,FULL),**

		MAXPU=1,
		RETRIES=(7,1,7),
		SERVLIM=32,
		NRZI=NO,
		ISTATUS=ACTIVE
		SERVICE MAXLIST=1
(A)	**EXCHPU**	ADDR=C1,
		PUTYPE=2,
		IBBLK=05D, *(B)*
		IDNUM=000C1, *(C)*
		PASSLIM=7,
		MAXOUT=7,
		MAXLU=2,
		DATMODE=HALF,
		MAXDATA=1033,
		PACING=7, VPACING=7,
		SSCPFM=FSS,
		ISTATUS=ACTIVE,
		IRETRY=NO

LNKPATHPATH		**DIALNO=0104400000000001**

EXCHLUR LU	*(D)*	LOCADDR=01, *(E)*
		USSTAB=,
		LOGAPPL=,
		LOGMODE=LU62MODE
		SSCPFM=FSS
EXCHLUS LU		LOCADDR=02,
		USSTAB=,
		LOGAPPL=,
		LOGMODE=LU62MODE
		SSCPFM=FSS

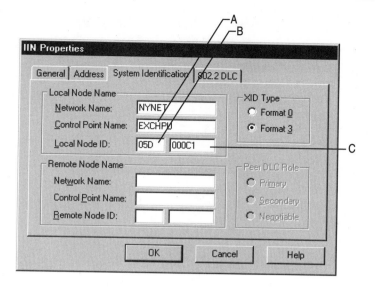

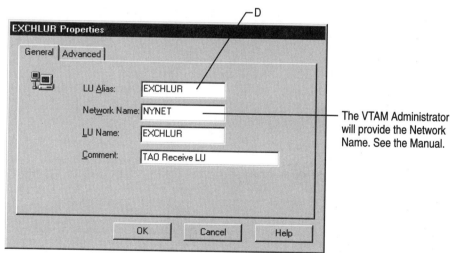

The VTAM Administrator will provide the Network Name. See the Manual.

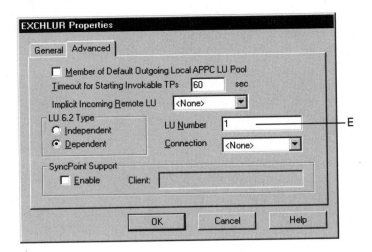

TAO Configuration File Mapping to SNA Server Panels

The bold, italicized letters in the table columns correspond to property values in the screen shots included below the table.

LOCALLU	LOCALNAME=TDSLU,	
	APPLID=**TDSLU**,	
	SESSIONLIMIT=10	
LOCALLU	LOCALNAME=TDRLU,	
	APPLID=**TDRLU**,	*(A)*
	SESSIONLIMIT=10	
PARTNERLU	LOCALNAME=EXCHANGE,	
	NETWORKNAME=**EXCHLUR**,	
	PARSESS=NO,	*(B)*
	SESSIONTYPE=SLU	
PARTNERLU	LOCALNAME=EXCHANGE,	
	NETWORKNAME=**EXCHLUS**,	
	PARSESS=NO,	
	SESSIONTYPE=SLU	

MODE	MODENAME=LU62MODE,
	SESSIONLIMIT=1

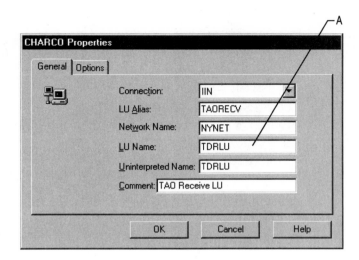

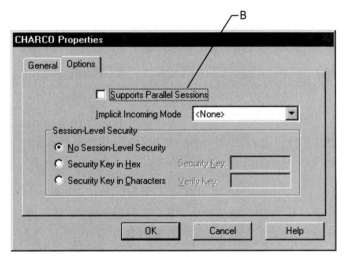

SNADS Connector Property Page Values Mapping

The bold, italicized letters in the table columns correspond to property values in the screen shots included below the tables.

TDSRD	DB_APPID=TAOSERV,
	DB_XMNAME=TAO,
	DB_ACBNAME=TAO,

RGN=TAORGN,　　*(A)*

(continued)

TDSRD	**DB_APPID=TAOSERV,**

REN=TAOREN, *(B)*　　(DGN for EMC2 users when registered as SNADS custom recipients)

DOMAIN=.SNADS,

PASSWORD=SNADSPW,

PROCESS_INTERVAL=180,

DEFAULT_DGN=TAODGN,　　(DGN for EMC2 users when registered as SNADS custom recipients)

ADMINISTRATOR=SNADS.ADMIN,

CONNECTION=(DSVHOST;DSVHOST),

CONNECTION=(EXCHANGE;EXCHANGE),　　*(C)*

TDSQS	**CONNECTION_NEXT_DSUN=DSVHOST,**

MODE=LU62MODE,

PROCESS_INTERVAL=300,

HOP_COUNT=2

TDSQS	**CONNECTION_NEXT_DSUN=EXCHANGE**

MODE=LU62MODE

PROCESS_INTERVAL=600

HOP_COUNT=2

LOCALLU	**LOCALNAME=TDSLU,**

APPLID=**TDSLU**,

SESSIONLIMIT=10

LOCALLU	**LOCALNAME=TDRLU,**

APPLID=**TDRLU**,　　*(D)*

SESSIONLIMIT=10

PARTNERLU	**LOCALNAME=EXCHANGE,**

NETWORKNAME=**EXCHLUR**,　　*(E)*

PARSESS=NO,

SESSIONTYPE=SLU

PARTNERLU	LOCALNAME=EXCHANGE,	
	NETWORKNAME=**EXCHLUS**,	*(F)*
	PARSESS=NO,	
	SESSIONTYPE=SLU	
MODE	MODENAME=**LU62MODE**,	*(G)*
	SESSIONLIMIT=1	

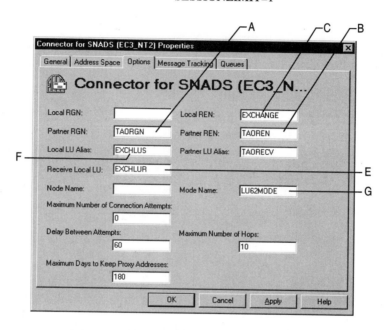

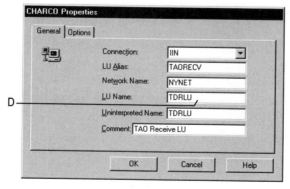

C H A P T E R   1 4

AppleTalk Quarterdeck/StarNine Mail Systems

Often systems administrators of large organizations must manage a heterogeneous network, including a number of mail environments that support a specific department or business unit local area network (LAN) and connect over the corporate wide area network (WAN). Planning coexistence and migration in these environments is challenging. The Microsoft Exchange Server 5.5 Connector for AppleTalk integrates both AppleTalk 3.*x* and Quarterdeck/StarNine 3.*x* and 4.*x* mail systems with Microsoft Exchange. The connector:

- Allows Microsoft Exchange Server 5.5 to function as a message switch for AppleTalk and Quarterdeck/StarNine mail going to Lotus cc:Mail, Lotus Notes, MS Mail, PROFS, SNADS and other SMTP mail systems.

- Supports scheduled full directory synchronization.

- Supports full migration from AppleTalk and Quarterdeck/StarNine mail systems.

- Routes Internet mail inbound to and outbound from AppleTalk and Quarterdeck mail systems through Microsoft Exchange Server 5.5.

Written for Exchange administrators in charge of integrating AppleTalk and Quarterdeck mail systems, this chapter outlines coexistence considerations, migration procedures, and step-by-step instructions on running the Source Extractor utility.

Coexistence Test Plan

Before you connect the Exchange messaging system with the AppleTalk or Quarterdeck/StarNine environment, build a test lab that represents the legacy AppleTalk or Quarterdeck/StarNine environment and the Exchange production environment. You can also refer to Chapter 3 for guidelines on setting up a test environment. A thorough test plan helps ensure a smooth coexistence and migration, exposing issues and anomalies so that you can resolve them before rolling out the system to users. Create a plan that uses the AppleTalk/Quarterdeck coexistence lab to test:

- Connections between AppleTalk or Quarterdeck/StarNine and Microsoft Exchange.
- Compatibility with Macintosh business productivity applications, mail attachments, and message formatting.
- Coexistence with Macintosh group and Microsoft Exchange distribution lists.
- Step-by-step migration from the AppleTalk/Quarterdeck system, including documenting the process.
- AppleTalk directory synchronization configuration from T1 to T3.

Coexistence Considerations

Prior to connecting Exchange with an existing AppleTalk/Quarterdeck messaging system, create a strategy for:

Hyper-card electronic forms Currently there is no migration path for AppleTalk or Quarterdeck/StarNine HyperCard e-forms to Exchange Server forms. Depending on resources, you can develop a cross-platform solution using Exchange Collaboration Data Objects (CDO) or Web-based technologies.

E-mail-enabled applications Identify all business applications that use AppleTalk or Quarterdeck/StarNine mail and develop a workaround or alternate solution. Exchange does not support a migration path for applications written with Quarterdeck/StarNine libraries. You can build a similar application with CDO or Internet-based technologies.

Quarterdeck/StarNine 411 directory services Although Exchange Server 5.5 supports these directory services, you could experience some (documented) incompatibilities when attempting to route Internet mail through Exchange. Contact Quarterdeck/StarNine support for more information on this issue.

End-user and client support communication   Create a frequently-asked-questions (FAQ) document, citing known coexistence anomalies, and make it available to all users. Here are some key issues:

- Remind users not to send mail from Macintosh personal address books during migration because of changes to the global address list.

- Inform users up-front about what you will and will not migrate from AppleTalk or Quarterdeck/StarNine.

- Document and communicate lost functionality, such as HyperCard forms or Macintosh personal address books, and what workarounds or solutions you have planned.

- Talk about new client functionality using Macintosh client terminology.

Local mail storage   Estimate users' local mail file size before allowing them to move to the server. Overloading the AppleTalk or Quarterdeck/StarNine server can result in system failure and lost mail.

Moving to distribution lists or maintaining Macintosh groups   Develop a coexistence strategy for Exchange distribution lists and Macintosh groups, deciding whether to maintain Macintosh groups or to migrate them to distribution lists after the first directory synchronization with the AppleTalk or Quarterdeck/StarNine mail system.

If you keep all Macintosh groups until you complete the migration, you lose the ability to decentralize distribution list administration with Exchange and to view distribution list members from Exchange. You must also add migrated Exchange users back into Macintosh groups. If you move Macintosh groups to distribution lists prior to the first migration phase, legacy users can no longer view distribution list members and some legacy mail users may receive duplicate messages if they belong to a list nested within another list.

Migration Steps

Carefully plan your migration from AppleTalk or Quarterdeck/StarNine to Exchange, following these steps:

1. Develop a migration checklist (sample):

   PRE-MIGRATION

   Obtain list of users you will migrate.

Verify the following information for each user:

- Windows NT domain
- Exchange recipient container membership
- Operating system
- Current mail client
- Postoffice location
- Types and numbers of clients needed

If a user has multiple mail accounts, determine migration order (PC, Macintosh, Notes).

Verify that Windows NT accounts have been created for each user.

Determine user's Macintosh group membership(s).

Determine size of Macintosh mail data files.

Request/verify that user has uploaded mail file to server.

Verify that user understands that Macintosh personal address books will not be migrated if moving to an Exchange client for Macintosh.

MIGRATION

Verify that all Macintosh post offices have been backed up.

Perform MS Mail (AppleTalk) migration.

- Migrate remote postoffices.
- Migrate local postoffices.

POST-MIGRATION

Change Exchange user Information with the Administrator program.

- Fill in the General tab with the appropriate information.
- Select Windows NT account.
- Verify user's SMTP address.

Verify the number of migrated messages by selecting Mailbox resources object in the Exchange Administrator program.

Delete user legacy mail account(s).

- Delete user Macintosh post office account(s) in the legacy environment.

Force server replication.

- Run the legacy directory synchronization.

Select Export on Next Cycle after 7:00 p.m.

Perform directory synchronization.

- Run legacy directory synchronization.
- Verify there are no duplicate entries in the global address list.

Update Exchange distribution lists and Macintosh groups.

- Determine migrated user's distribution list membership(s).
- Update Exchange distribution lists.
- Update Macintosh groups.

Verify addresses are accurate in legacy systems.

Send test welcome message to migrated users through the Internet.

POST-MIGRATION FOLLOW-UP

Call the key contact for the migrated group.

2. Determine which users to migrate.

You can migrate users by division, geographic workgroup, or postoffice. A rule of thumb: identify geographic workgroups that communicate and port them together; this most often ensures everyone is on the same mail system at the same time, and it helps eliminate coexistence anomalies for roughly 70% of communications. If this is not an option, migrate users by postoffice.

3. Schedule which users to migrate.

Determine each geographic workgroup's schedule to minimize interference with business routines. Schedule Exchange Client or Microsoft Outlook deployment and end-user training before user postoffice migration.

Using the Source Extractor

The Exchange Source Extractor for AppleTalk or Quarterdeck/StarNine is the only tool that extracts users, schedules, and messages from these messaging environments. Here's how to use it:

▶ **To get the source extractor from the Exchange Server 5.5 CD-ROM**

1. Open the Server\Migrate\Tools\Macmail\ directory.
2. Move the MACMAIL.SIT file to a Windows NT Macintosh Volume accessible from all Macintosh clients.
3. Connect to the Macintosh Volume from Chooser on the Macintosh.
4. Obtain Stuffit Expander for the Macintosh platform and install it on the Macintosh.
5. Double-click on the MACMAIL.SIT to expand the files.

▶ **To run the source extractor**

1. From a Macintosh client, open the **Microsoft Source Extractor**. An empty **Microsoft Source Extractor** window opens.

2. Click **Migrate** from the menu bar. Click **Migrate Users**.

3. Select **Last <COMMA> First** (or whatever your new naming convention will be) under **Generate First and Last Names**.

4. Make sure to select **E-mail messages**.

5. Select **Schedule + Information**. Click **All**.

6. Select **Personal Address Books**. (Only check this if you migrate users from a Macintosh to a PC-based Exchange client. Otherwise, users will receive a migrated personal address book that they cannot import into Exchange.)

7. Select **Log System Group Membership**.

8. Click the **Continue** button when finished.

9. The **Select User Accounts to Migrate** window opens. Scroll down the list to select the user(s) to migrate. Hold the shift key down to select more than one user.

10. Click the **Add** button. The users are now listed under the **Select Accounts** window. Click **Continue**.

11. Save the data file into the migration folder that was created (for example, MG11/21/PORMCRMT). Name the file POSTOFFICE (for example, PORMCRMT). Click the **Save** button. This folder contains the data files to be imported into Exchange.

12. The users you selected are now migrated as documented in the **Microsoft Source Extractor** window.

13. After you finish the migration, on the **File** menu, click **Save As** to save the log file and save it in the same migration folder as POSTOFFICEDATE.LOG. Click **Save**.

14. Click **File**, then **Quit** or **File**, then **Restart** to exit the Source Extractor.

15. Close all open windows.

To help complete the last step of the migration, transfer the source-extracted folder to a directory or sharepoint reachable from where you will run the Exchange AppleTalk Migration Wizard. For an easy method to get the extracted files to the PC environment, use Chooser on the Macintosh to map a network drive to the maildata directory on the Exchange server running the Exchange Connector for AppleTalk. Copy the extracted data folder temporarily to the \maildata\log directory on the Exchange server. From the Windows NT machine hosting Exchange, move the folder from the temporary log directory to a permanent designated migration folder.

Troubleshooting Tips

You must enable the *Pause* button on the Exchange directory synchronization service to allow for a manual T2 cycle during the AppleTalk/Quarterdeck dirsync process:

Warning Using the Registry Editor incorrectly can cause serious, system-wide problems that may require you to reinstall Windows NT to correct them. Microsoft cannot guarantee that any problems resulting from the use of Registry Editor can be solved. Use this tool at your own risk.

---

1. Start Registry Editor (REGEDT32.EXE) and locate the following registry key:

   HKEY_LOCAL_MACHINE\SYSTEM\CurrentControlSet\Services \MSExchangeDX

2. On the **Edit** menu, click **Add Value**.

3. Enter:

   Value Name: PauseKicksDX

   Data Type: REG_DWORD

   Value: 1

4. Click **OK** and quit Registry Editor.

5. In **Control Panel Services**, stop and restart the Exchange directory synchronization service.

You can also perform a manual directory synchronization process with AppleTalk or Quarterdeck/StarNine systems:

1. To force a manual T1, select the Macintosh DER, click **file, export complete directory**, and **Import complete directory**.

2. Wait for the dirsync names to populate the Exchange global address list.

3. To force a manual T2, click the **Pause** button on the Exchange directory synchronization service (which requires editing the registry key in the previous section). Expect error message 2140 after pausing the service.

4. Verify that the Macintosh administrator receives a SRVTX message in the subject line. **Do not read it**.

5. To force a manual T3, exit and restart the Macintosh DER.

More Information

- Q154619, Title: XFOR: Export Menu Disabled on Exchange Connection DER
- Q156961, Title: XFOR: Mac Connection Gateway Will Not Install on System 7.5.3
- Q160664, Title: XFOR: Cannot Configure Microsoft Mail Connector (AppleTalk)
- Q169659, Title: XFOR: Err Msg: AppleTalk Mail Connector Service Not Created
- Q152477, Title: XFOR: Handshake Files Moved to BADMAIL Directory
- Q171259, Title: XFOR: How to Move the Microsoft Mail Connector Postoffice

CHAPTER 15

The Deployment Auditing Process

During any large Exchange deployment, especially when multiple subcontractors are involved, you must audit the deployment in progress and assess it against the deployment plan. An audit makes sure that all the design work completed as you worked through in Part 1 of this book, "Planning for Exchange," has been incorporated into the deployment. A deployment is a complicated process, and simply reviewing project documentation is not enough. This chapter provides a framework to organize the review and assessment and to identify and address potentially troublesome items.

The Auditing Process

You can use this chapter's template as the vehicle to drive your audit. And as is often the case, your mileage may vary. Client implementation specifics may make some issues moot while increasing the importance of others. No audit template can ever be 100% accurate for all cases, even ones with identical configurations and deployment plans, so use this document to help outline the auditing efforts in a particular case, not as the final deliverable.

A deployment for a large product such as Exchange in a large organization entails specific work items. The audit group identifies these items, assesses them against the template in this document, and adds job-specific issues to calculate the time and resources needed to complete the audit and to define the final deliverables.

Each segment contains an italicized section that describes what you should document:

What should be in this section:

Summary of the documentation that you should produce at this stage of the audit.

Areas of Focus

Technology Documentation Review Analysis of documentation to ensure that the deployed architecture matches the design. This includes comparing several customer-supplied documents with the observed deployment: Architecture Requirements, High-Level Design Requirements, Server Design, Public Folder Design, Site Design, Directory Synchronization, Windows NT Server Domain and Server Design, Windows WINS Design, DNS, and Windows NT DHCP Design.

Deployment and Migration Review Analysis of documentation detailing Server Build and Deployment Process Review, Desktop Deployment Process Review, Data Migration Process Review, and other customer-supplied implementation-related information.

Staffing Review and Skills Inventory Including Organization Chart, Development/Engineering Personnel, Deployment Personnel, Operations Personnel, Administration Personnel, Help Desk Personnel, and User Education Personnel.

Project Planning Review Including Services, Change Management, Functional Specification, Server Release Strategy, Development/Engineering, Testing, Deployment and Retrofit, Deployment Schedule, and Site Discovery.

Operations Tools and Processes Including Backup and Recovery, Maintenance, Service Packs, Status Monitoring, Message Routing, Server Services, Event Logs, Performance Trending, Service Level Agreements, Metrics, Reporting, Incident Tracking and Escalation, Capturing Problems, Internal Escalation, External Escalation, Remote Operation Capabilities, and Network Monitor Agent.

Server Inspection Onsite and remote access inspection of Windows NT and Exchange servers to determine if they meet the documented specifications, congruent with the High-Level Design.

Audit Process Deliverables

- Detailed Exchange Technical Solution Readiness Review, which identifies outstanding technical issues with the specific design of systems in the deployment.

- Checklist from those servers inspected, which demonstrates adherence to or variance from the system designed.

- Recommendations on how to proceed if differences are found between the High-Level Design and the deployed system. Identification of any areas of improvement in the design, implementation, or operations systems already in place should also be stated.

Key Assumptions

These documents are completed:

- Architecture Requirements
- High Level Design Requirements
- Server Design
- Public Folder Design
- Site Design
- Directory Synchronization
- Windows NT Server Domain and Server Design
- Windows WINS/DHCP Design or DNS Design
- Server Build Process
- Deployment Process
- Desktop Deployment Process
- Data Migration Process
- Personnel listings for: Development/Engineering; Deployment; Operations; Administration; Help Desk; and User Education
- Deployment Plan for Exchange: Services, Change Management, Functional Specification, Server Release Strategy, Development/Engineering, Testing, Deployment and Retrofit, Deployment Schedule, Site Discovery
- Operations documentation, including: Backup and Recovery, Maintenance, Service Packs, Status Monitoring, Message routing, Server Services, Event Logs, Performance Trending, Service Level Agreements, Metrics, Reporting, Incident Tracking and Escalation, Capturing Problems, Internal Escalation, External Escalation, Remote Operation Capabilities, Network Monitor Agent

By this stage, documentation should be in its final, deliverable format (that is, not a collection of notes and e-mail).

System Documentation Review

To assess readiness, the consultant should review all supplied customer documentation and any recommendations made in customer architecture documents and the High-Level Design documents. The review may also include implementation details to help derive the best known solution for the deployment, based on the design goals set forth in earlier documents.

The following sections are templates for the review summaries that would be completed against each of the functional areas, including recommendations for changes where appropriate.

Documentation Versions Reviewed

What should be in this section:

Record the list of documentation received from the customer as part of the audit process. If documents are not available from the customer, issue action items to the respective parties to supply the documentation or initiate a project to complete the documentation. If either of these steps is needed, stop the audit process until it is completed.

In many deployment projects, the documents will be split into two categories: design and implementation specific. If this is the case, two audit processes can be started. One would be the audit of the high-level design to ensure that the design is feasible; the other could be started after the initial design audit has been completed to evaluate the feasibility of the implementation details regarding Exchange at the company.

Exchange High-Level Design Review

What should be in this section:

Review the top-level definition of the Exchange organization with respect to the company's WAN architecture. If Exchange is being deployed in a distributed and disconnected fashion, you must ensure that these conditions are met:

- *Same organization name on every Exchange site*
- *Unique site names to prevent duplication of directory name space*
- *Unique server names to prevent duplication within the flat NetBIOS name space*
- *Mailbox display name standards*
- *Unique top-level public folder names*
- *Unique Exchange message class ID*

Companies with available bandwidth should consider a connected Exchange deployment, in which each server is added to an Exchange site that knows about each of the other Exchange sites in the organization. This configuration also requires attention to the considerations listed above, but if the machine is connected to the rest of the organization some of the values are checked upon installation:

- *Unique site names to prevent duplication of directory name space*
- *Unique server names to prevent duplication of the flat NetBIOS name space*
- *Mailbox display name standards*

- *Unique top-level public folder names*
- *Unique exchange message class ID*

In addition to these conditions, create standard Address Book views. These views are replicated across all Exchange sites and that includes each site that replicates directory information within the organization. To ensure that mailbox and custom recipient directory objects appear in the standard views correctly, you should minimize these object attributes.

The public folder hierarchy is shared across all Exchange servers in the organization, so there must be guidelines for public folder usage and integration with NNTP newsgroups.

Exchange Site Review

What should be in this section:

Review the agreed-upon site topology. Document the security, replication schedule, site routing costs, and a clear relationship between each of the sites within the organization as well as the rationale for defining their boundaries. This allows you to diagram the overall organization, provide for the predictable creation of new sites, and define necessary items for sites added later. Maintaining this information during the course of the deployment simplifies future expansion of the Exchange topology by reducing problems and missed configuration items that affect operation.

Exchange Server Specification Review

Server configurations vary greatly for different implementations, but a few generic recommendations can be made for servers within any topology.

What should be in this section:

Review the server configuration details. Each topology has several distinct server types:

- *User servers*
- *Site DS bridgehead servers*
- *Site MTA/connector bridgehead servers*
- *Public folder servers*
- *Distribution list expansion servers*

And with Exchange 5.5:

- *Event scripting servers*
- *Clustered servers*
- *Very large user servers (servers with private or public data stores larger than 16 GB)*

If OWA is to be used in the configuration, you must decide if the OWA ASPs will be offered from the same server that houses the user mailboxes they are accessing, or a different one. In either case, configurations for IIS servers must be defined.

Internet Protocols Support Review

What should be in this section:

Review Exchange server support for WWW (OWA), POP3, NNTP, and LDAP accesses in the Exchange organization. If POP3 is to be used as a client access protocol, the server build document may need additional detail regarding the configuration for SMTP forwarding. If LDAP is used as an access protocol for the directory, the document may need more on its configuration details, namely, maximum number of results returned for a specific query and access permissions through LDAP.

Public Folders Design Review

What should be in this section:

Review Exchange Server public folder architecture, security, replication partners, and replication schedules. It can also comment on time-sensitive recovery and administration processes that are exceptions or specialized implementations for specific business processes or GroupWare functions. Regardless of the implementation of Exchange 5.5, there should also be discussion of the use of public folders as a semi-structured repository for business data used in conjunction with the messaging system to implement GroupWare or Workflow applications. Exchange 5.5, also requires addressing the use of the scripting agent on public folders, the definition of which servers will execute Event Script, the maintenance and administration associated with the authoring of Event Script, and the use of COM objects from Event Script.

External Mail System Connectivity Review

What should be in this section:

Describe how the Exchange System connects to other foreign systems that currently exist in the architecture or are planned for later deployment. Outline directory synchronization and operational procedures for each system and how it will connect into the Exchange architecture, if it needs to be based on a third-party component.

One of the most compelling reasons for a company to deploy Exchange is to join multiple mainframe and disparate LAN-based mail systems into a single unified system. With the recent addition of various connectors, Exchange offers simple and robust connectivity options. Typically, when connecting foreign mail systems to Exchange, two types of connections can be maintained: directory synchronization and message transfer.

Directory Synchronization with Foreign Mail Systems

Exchange 5.5 offers two methods of synchronizing the Exchange directory with foreign systems: DAPI-based operations (bulk export, and import operations) and programmatic operations based on LDAP and ADSI. With architectures based on Exchange 5.0 and earlier, DAPI operations are the only option for directory synchronization with foreign hosts.

When deciding on a directory synchronization strategy, consider:

- Service level for replication of changes from one directory to others.
- Fields (including custom fields) that must be replicated. Some organizations may need to replicate a number of custom properties or specific descriptive fields.
- Relevant field mapping for Exchange descriptive fields to foreign system directories.
- Distribution list management processes and procedures. Keep in mind that some foreign mail systems expand distribution lists based on where they are created. In the case of a bulk import process, this distribution list expansion server will always be the import server, which may or may not be desirable.
- Pilot strategy for the update process.
- End-to-end directory replication time for change rippling through the Exchange and foreign directories and its relationship to the established service level for directory replication.

Core Network Services

Several core network services are required for the efficient and effective operation of the Exchange product inside of an organization:

- Windows NT Server domain topology
- WINS/DHCP/DNS/Name service topologies
- Time synchronization topologies and processes

In an ideal situation, these core network services will be documented and in place before Exchange deployment begins. These services can be deployed along with Exchange, but it then takes much longer to generate the Exchange architecture overall.

Windows NT Server Domain

What should be in this section:

Document the architecture of Windows NT, which provides all Exchange environment security services. Include:

- *Base network topology information*
- *Protocol varieties and their prevalence on the documented network topologies above*
- *WAN link speed documentation*
- *Windows NT Server domain model*
- *Administrative policies including details on maintenance of user accounts, global/local groups, and machine accounts*

Name Resolution Services (WINS or DNS)

What should be in this section:

Describe administrative policies for deploying proper name resolution services for the Exchange architecture. Name resolution services are essential for any client server application and are typically provided with two primary services for networks using TCP/IP as an underlying protocol: DNS and WINS/DHCP. All other major network protocols predominantly rely on some type of broadcast name resolution, which in a larger topology may become prohibitive because of excessive name resolution traffic generation. Include:

- *Description of the base name resolution services. If these services are based on DNS, construct a tree of DNS primary, secondary, and caching servers that makes the most of the underlying network topology.*
- *Name database update and modification procedures.*

- *Name database backup and recovery processes.*
- *Name database administrators or administrative groups.*

Dynamic Host Configuration Protocol (DHCP)

What should be in this section:

If name resolution is to be using DHCP/WINS, document relevant parameters for the creation of a viable DHCP/WINS architecture. Include:

- *Scope definitions for the organization*
- *Update policies, including lease duration*
- *Policies for static address allocation*
- *DHCP/WINS database backup policies*
- *Service levels for address propagation and renewal*
- *Designated push/pull replication partners in the organization as well as the rationale for assigning this function to each of the servers for easier future expansion*

System Clock Synchronization

What should be in this section:

Outline the strategy for synchronizing the system clock on messaging servers.

Exchange servers must be time synchronized to ensure proper message delivery and simplify troubleshooting. Within Exchange or when connecting foreign mail systems to Exchange, unsynchronized time stamps can delay or prevent delivery. Synchronization becomes even more important if foreign hosts act as the gateway for a particular transport, such as the outgoing or incoming SMTP message transfer host.

There are several ways to synchronize. One is to use a central Exchange Server Administrator console with multiple server monitors that identify and synchronize clocks. Another is to use a central Network Time Protocol (NTP)-enabled node to synchronize with an external time host, such as the atomic clock. Another is to synchronize with Windows NT, using the "net time /domain:domainname /set" command.

Physical Network Topology

What should be in this section:

Review any existing physical network fault tolerance. Identify processes or components that provide redundant links or other failure-tolerant services and consider them so that the Exchange design avoids unnecessary efforts.

An Exchange deployment offers several fault-tolerance alternatives. Some are exposed as core functionality, such as the creation of multiple connectors between sites within the organization or the establishment of a least-cost routing architecture that uses multiple bridgehead servers in each physical site. Others are external to Exchange, such as building tolerance into the underlying WAN. The degree of failure tolerance achieved may be dictated by the costs of providing redundancy or by issues such as the reliability of the WAN link connecting the remote site or any service level agreements (SLAs) in effect for that link.

Deployment Process Review

Server Deployment Process

What should be in this section:

Describe suggested areas and relevant values in the documents relating to the construction, configuration, and server version management procedures. This documentation should be complete before deployment begins. The key areas depend on many customer and project details, so the list below is not complete, just a good starting place for the review.

The server build and deployment schedule and process must be extensively documented to ensure quick, smooth completion. Thorough documentation also helps eliminate duplicate efforts, and provides clear steps for recreating failed servers and configuring servers uniformly. Document the following components at a minimum:

- Build/deployment scheduling—This should include detail about the deployment of Exchange servers within the organization as well as the schedule for building the servers, indicating the interdependence and subordinate relationship between specific tasks in the process of building the server.

- Basic server capacity management (when new servers are required based on users/server)—This should include a process that regional site project managers can use to request servers or user capacity and ownership of capacity planning.

- Server build template with information necessary to build and ship specific servers including name, TCP/IP address, DNS servers, WINS servers, server role, hardware configuration, physical location of installation, and SA contact information.

Note any specific, defined policies for server or site naming.

Platform Release Strategy

A concise, clear explanation of the Exchange platform release strategy helps introduce servers successfully into a production environment and makes sure that the server configurations and problems are quantifiable and resolvable. The strategy document must provide, at a minimum, information on:

- Version control—verification that there is a common version of all software packages on all built servers.
- Quality assurance/control process documentation—before the server enters deployment, it should be inspected and its configuration and version verified.
- Release milestones.
- Timelines for milestone achievement.

Desktop Deployment

What should be in this section:

Detail the plans for the release of desktops and for the iterative sequence if the deployment is phased (several defined installation groups in sequence). At a minimum, this desktop deployment plan should cover deployment scheduling, site discovery, desktop software deployment, data migration, and a planned feedback loop for improving the process.

Review all of this documentation at this phase in the audit process. Below are summaries of the suggested content and recommendations for areas to document. Far from comprehensive, this list will vary with configuration and deployment scenario.

Deployment Scheduling

When developing a deployment schedule, take these steps to ensure smooth operation:

- Contact affected business units *before* setting the deployment timeframe to avoid posing significant risks to business operations.
- Regional site project managers should use feedback from the business units to develop a detailed schedule for each location based on the existing desktop deployment plan.

Site Information Inventory

Site information inventory involves acquiring and recording the information needed to deploy Exchange at each site: site contact information, ship-to information, names of file server, address, and onsite support personnel information.

Desktop Software Deployment

This section of the desktop deployment plan should include all client deployment steps that must be performed by field installation specialists. Wherever possible, use automated scripts to reduce labor and minimize human error. To optimize the installation of Exchange and the Windows NT Workstation operating system, use unattended installation scripts or provide a document detailing installation process choices.

Data Migration

If data is being migrated from the existing messaging client to the Exchange client, include in this section a strategy for this process. Answer these questions:

- Are existing filters for the data migration available?

- Are there size considerations with the migration? (Some conversions require additional space.)

- Have you stated a maximum age for messaging items on the client desktop?

- Is the client responsible for deleting items that are beyond that maximum age? If so, has this been communicated to the client, and if so, how?

- Does the data to be migrated exist at the client or on a network server? Using desktop data migration rather than server-based migration typically requires more desktop deployment resources. The difficulty of staffing sufficient resources is influenced by how many desktops are ready for Windows NT Workstation in addition to Exchange.

Desktop Deployment Process Feedback

A deployment project manager's feedback is required so that deployment lessons learned and best practices can be quickly disseminated to all deployment project managers. To see if the deployment manager's feedback necessitates any engineering changes, personnel from Exchange engineering and deployment should be involved in this feedback loop. During deployment, hold regular status meetings to discuss upcoming migrations and any lessons learned. This is an effective way to transfer knowledge between engineering, operations, deployment, and help desk organizations.

Customer feedback is also a necessary component to the deployment success. To monitor satisfaction and discover necessary actions, it is recommended that you formally survey deployment customers twice: during migration to evaluate satisfaction with the deployment process, then 2 to 4 weeks after migration to evaluate satisfaction with the new messaging system.

Staffing Review

Organizational Review

What should be in this section:

Describe the relevant team member responsibilities and the relationship between titles and team members, and associate each of the team roles with a project member.

Project team roles should be clearly defined to prevent imposing overlapping responsibilities on deployment team members. Generally speaking, a successful team should contain the following roles (all or some of which may be occupied by internal personnel):

Position title	Position role
Product Manager	Sets objectives and manages external relationships budget.
Program Manager	Designs and implements the Exchange network and identifies the functional requirements for the Exchange messaging system.
Exchange Engineering	Determines the technical configuration of the Exchange Servers. This includes all components of the servers including the message transfer agents, directory synchronization, interaction with other messaging systems, ability to act as an SMTP gateway, etc.
Testing/Quality Assurance	Ensures the conformance of the Exchange system to functional requirements and corporate standards.
Operations Development	Develops procedures, policies, and programs to monitor and control aspects of the Exchange network.
Technical Consulting, Third-Level Technical Support	Provides consulting services and problem resolution for internal business units, as the system goes into initial pilot and then deployment.
Training Development	Develops training materials and documentation targeted for both end users and technical support personnel.
Rollout Planning	Determines the most efficient way to roll out Exchange and Windows NT Servers so as to minimize cost and implementation time.
Migration Planning	Determines what work must be performed to migrate from an existing messaging system to Exchange. This may include porting mail-enabled applications and the translating users' existing data.
Implementation Management	Manages the implementation of the Exchange Server and associated components.

(continued)

Position title	Position role
End User Technical Support	Provides technical support for end users and solves problems and answers questions about Exchange.
Messaging Transport Operations	Maintains, operates, monitors, and repairs the Exchange environment after it is in place.
ID Administration	Maintains the user database for Exchange users.
Marketing–Customer Relations	Develops and executes marketing programs for implementing Exchange. This includes product demonstrations, newsletters, and pilot site coordination. Acts as the client advocate in design meetings.
Financial Control	Monitors financial aspects of the project. Tracks expenditures versus budget.

If a proper deployment team is not constructed, some resources may be over-used, jeopardizing the deployment.

Wherever possible, the person in each role should be dedicated to fulfilling that role's responsibilities and not tasked with others. If a shortage of bodies means you have to combine project roles, the table below shows which combinations offer the lowest possible risk.

Project role	Could be combined with
Product Manager	Testing Q/A , Technical Consulting, Training Development, Implementation Management, End-User Technical Support, Marketing–Customer Relations
Program Manager	Exchange Engineering, Operations Development, Technical Consulting, Training Development ,Rollout Planning, Migration Planning
Exchange Engineering	Program Manager, Technical Consulting, Training Development, Implementation Management, End-User Technical Support, Messaging Transport Operations, ID Administration
Testing Q/A	Product Manager, Technical Consulting, Training Development, Implementation Management, End-User Technical Support, Messaging Transport Operations
Operations Development	Product Manager, Exchange Engineering, Technical Consulting, Training Development, Rollout Planning, Migration Planning
Technical Consulting	Product Manager, Program Manager, Exchange Engineering, Testing Q/A, Operations Development, Training Development, Rollout Planning, Migration Planning, Implementation Management, Messaging Transport Operations, ID Administration

Project role	Could be combined with
Training Development	Product Manager, Program Manager, Exchange Engineering, Testing Q/A, Operations Development, Technical Consulting, End-User Technical Support, Marketing–Customer Relations
Rollout Planning	Operations Development, Technical Consulting, Migration Planning, Implementation Management, Messaging Transport Operations
Migration Planning	Operations Development, Technical Consulting, Rollout Planning, Implementation Management, End-User Technical Support
Implementation Management	Product Manager, Exchange Engineering, Testing Q/A, Technical Consulting, Rollout Planning, Migration Planning, Messaging Transport Operations
End User Technical Support	Product Manager, Exchange Engineering, Testing Q/A, ID Administration, Marketing–Customer Relations
Messaging Transport Operations	Exchange Engineering, Testing Q/A, Technical Consulting, Rollout Planning, Implementation Management, ID Administration
ID Administration	Exchange Engineering, Technical Consulting, End User Technical Support, Messaging Transport Operations
Marketing–Customer Relations	Product Manager, Training Development
Financial Control	None

Training Plan and Implementation Schedule

What should be in this section:

Develop a schedule to ensure that personnel satisfactorily complete training. Thorough training plans for engineering, administrative, and operations staff must be in place, but without an implementation schedule, it is impossible to assess their readiness at any point in the process.

End User

What should be in this section:

Clear training documentation and schedules for end users who will use the messaging client is one of the most effective mechanisms for reducing the overall support burden and cost of ownership associated with the system. Review the following focus areas and suggest ways to improve the end-user training plan. Identify additional deliverables, those based on different or additional media, or the delivery of training at different or additional times. Include a risk analysis of training delivery.

There are many ways to provide training to end users: hands-off training by installation personnel after the installation of the client has completed, Getting Started documents customized to the user's environment, or computer based training (CBT) for client operation.

End users should also receive references to resources such as Microsoft Press books (Step by Step, Field Guide, etc.) that support varied experience levels. Other resources include publications delivered to the end-user community through electronic mail and FAQs available on the Web or in public folders (Exchange Server ships with a Getting Started public folder). FAQs educate the user on a variety of best practices and can reduce help desk calls and administrative overhead. Some possible best practices are using .PST and/or .OST files, archiving old messages, or emptying sent items folder.

The auditing process does not stop here. It continues when you hand off the Exchange messaging system to operations and develop daily administration procedures. This assessment is covered in the companion book *Managing and Maintaining Microsoft Exchange 5.5*.

CHAPTER 16

Deploying Outlook Clients and Exchange Servers

This chapter begins with a discussion of general deployment stages. It then defines principles and planning in the context of rolling out Microsoft Outlook clients. The second half of the chapter details how to implement an unattended installation of Exchange servers and connectors.

Overview of Deployment Stages

Deployment has four stages.

Deployment Planning The most important step, but many IT organizations do not schedule enough time to plan the deployment adequately. Time spent here can save more time later, can ensure that servers and client workstations receive a stable, functionally correct installation, and can reduce support issues for the deployment team. During this phase the project team should develop a formal and complete plan for the entire deployment process, one that gives the deployment team the big picture. Planning should define needs, restraints, desired functionality, etc., and should be as specific and thorough as possible or practical.

Development Here the project team uses the information gathered during planning to create server and client configurations that match the organization's requirements.

Pilot Deployment *aka Testing*. The deployment team verifies all aspects of the deployment process. Initial testing should first be conducted in a lab to isolate the production environment from adverse effect. After initial testing is complete, a pilot deployment generates system and user information needed for final deployment. Refer to Chapter 3, "Setting Up a Test Environment."

Production deployment Deploying to the entire organization. If planning was insufficient, you will find out about it here.

Client Deployment Planning

Most large organizations consider the deployment of client components a minor aspect of an Exchange deployment, but it is in fact very important. Done well, it can ensure a smooth overall deployment, allowing users to reap the benefits of the new technology while avoiding problems and setbacks. During planning, the deployment team defines the client configuration and the deployment method. The next few sections describe the planning process, outline a framework for it, and provide an example deliverable—a completed plan including the features and requirements to be deployed.

Planning is *critical*. Inadequate planning can retard or derail the deployment process with any number of problems. Final deployment is not the time to find out that the proposed client configuration does not match your business needs. Redesigning at this stage would cost enough money, time, and effort to jeopardize the entire project.

Deployment Audience

The deployment audience is composed of the target workstations to which you are going to deploy the Outlook client. Determine and document their number, locations, general functional needs, and specific configurations.

Client Functional Specification

This describes audience requirements and the client features and functions that will be delivered to the workstations. It is used throughout the project to verify that the deployed Outlook client matches the original specification.

Pilot Group

This is the group of workstations and users that will test the Outlook client and provide feature and deployment feedback necessary to plan the production deployment. The group should mirror the overall deployment audience, including at least one representative of each type of user and one from each department or division. For example, if your company produces computer software, the pilot group would include at least one representative from each of these groups:

- Executive
- Executive secretary
- Sales representative
- Accountant
- General administrative secretary
- Software developer
- Software tester

Assemble a group that gives the project team a good test bed in which to verify Outlook client features and functions. If the pilot group contains only one type of user, testing will verify the client only against that group and may lack important information on users' levels of expertise or features they rely on or require.

The project team must set the pilot users' expectations to help ensure that feedback is balanced and usable. For example, don't force the pilot group to rely solely on the piloted software. Allow participants to send mission-critical mail by some means in addition to the test software (leave their old e-mail operational and accessible). Inform pilot users that the software is being tested, so workstations probably will require multiple reloads or reconfigurations. Pilot group members must accommodate changes and allow the project team access to their workstations when necessary. If the pilot group does not understand all of this going in, look for less than favorable (and less than usable) feedback.

Deployment Method

Planning also defines the Outlook client deployment method. This information is used to develop the client packages and other aspects of the project.

The deployment method can range from individual manual installations to a fully automated process using Microsoft Systems Management Server. The size of the deployment audience is the determinant here. If you have hundreds or thousands of users, a manual process requires a lot of time and can introduce numerous installation errors. On the other hand, if you plan to use an automated process, you have to add time to the development stage—for building the process. Decide on an automated or a manual process during planning, then alter the deployment timeline accordingly.

Deployment Timeline

The planning process develops the deployment timeline by estimating the time required to complete each task and phase. By the end of the planning stage it should be possible to determine overall project effort and time and to see the proposed schedule fits the deployment deadline, if there is one. If the schedule requires too much time, examine the proposal for possible changes and trade-offs. For example, if the timeframe and features are fixed, perhaps you can add resources. If you can't, then consider scaling back the feature list or the deployment. As a rule, it is better to add time or resources than to cut features or reduce the scope of the deployment.

Example Deliverable

Here is an example of the deliverables at this stage of the project. Complete documents would have much more detail; these offer examples of types of content.

Deployment Audience

The company is a manufacturing organization with 10 administrative offices and 5 factories located throughout the U.S. The network infrastructure is Windows NT Server. The client population is 40% Microsoft Windows 95 and 60% Microsoft Windows NT Workstation 4.0. Outside of a few general-use workstations, every client workstation will require the new messaging infrastructure. Typical usage scenarios follow.

The administrative offices use stationary desktop workstations with either Windows 95 or Windows NT Workstation. Users have dedicated workstations and do not need to "roam" to different ones. Workstations will be connected to the network infrastructure through a shared 10-MB Ethernet segment. There are 150 to 400 workstations per administrative office for a total of 2,800.

Administrative office personnel use the standard office productivity tools such as Microsoft Office. Levels of expertise vary, but all users are familiar with the general tools and concepts. The more advanced use Windows NT Workstation as their corporate desktop.

The executive team from each office use laptop workstations with Windows NT Workstation. Executives' office workstations connected to the network over a shared 10-MB Ethernet segment. There are between 10 and 50 members of the executive team per administrative office for a total of 300.

Executives also use Microsoft Office as their standard office productivity tools. They are of average computer expertise or below, relying mostly on e-mail and specific business-related software. For security reasons, the entire team uses Windows NT Workstation.

Sales team members are based out of home offices. They use laptops, of which 60% use Windows 95 and 40% use Windows NT Workstation. There are 450 laptops in the organization, accessing the corporate network over a 28.8-bps modem. Sales team members visit the corporate office at least once a month for staff meetings, and while there they hook up to general-use docking stations connected to the corporate network through a 10-MB Ethernet segment.

Sales team members are skilled computer users, troubleshooting their own support issues when they can and using the corporate help desk when they cannot. They also use the standard productivity tools including Microsoft Office. Away from the office most of the time, they rely heavily on e-mail.

Each factory has a small administrative support department using 20 workstations (for a total of 100) with the same configuration and use as the administrative office workstations.

Each factory floor has between 100 and 250 workstations, running the manufacturing process application and used by task-based employees. For example, the stockroom team uses the workstations to track inventory and place orders. They do not use any of the standard productivity tools. Currently, there is one workstation for every four factory employees.

A few general-use workstations serve as kiosks or information centers for the general public. To maintain security, these workstations will not be included in the deployment of the Outlook client.

Client Functional Specification

The project team, based on the information gathered during the Define Deployment Audience phase, has determined the need to develop three Outlook configuration packages:

- General use
- Laptop workstations
- Factory floor

Pilot Group

As identified by the planning team, the pilot group users provide an evenly dispersed testing environment for the deployment. These users have agreed to participate and they understand the commitment required to assist the project team.

Here are the numbers and groups selected:

- 10 executives—One executive from each office. Each executive performs a different job function, so the mix provides a good cross-section.

- 20 administrative staff—Two members from each office: one using Windows 95 and the other using Windows NT Workstation. Each staff member performs a different job function, so the mix provides a good cross-section.

- 20 sales representatives—Ten of the sales workstations will use Windows 95 and the other ten will use Windows NT Workstation. Sales representatives function independently, so 20 provides a good cross-section.

- 20 factory employees—A cross section of employees chosen based by job function. Each workstation is used by a pair of employees, providing the project team with an example of a shared workstation.

Deployment Method

For this large client population, the project team will use Microsoft Systems Management Server to automate the Outlook client package deployment. The SMS infrastructure is currently implemented and functioning. The development and pilot stages will identify configuration or tuning parameters that require alteration, and an infrastructure department representative on the project team will handle them.

SMS Installer, a tool that uses snapshot (imaging) technology, will be used to create Outlook configuration packages in both Windows 95 and Windows NT Workstation for each of the three proposed configurations.

Any additional configuration that cannot be completed with the above tools will be addressed using Wilson Windowware's WinBatch utility.

Developing an Outlook Package

This discussion of the development process, tools, and packages assumes that the user community runs either Microsoft Windows NT Workstation 4.0 or Windows 95 and that SMS is the deployment infrastructure. The deliverable for this stage is a client configuration package for each operating system.

Developing the client configurations and the deployment process requires solid information gathered during the planning stage. Numerous factors drive Outlook client development, the most important being the type of operating system currently used by the deployment audience.

Unattended Installation

Microsoft Outlook provides a number of unattended installation methods. The most basic is providing command line switches that tell the Outlook setup program to perform various types of installations. For example, the command line

```
SETUP.EXE /Q1 /B1
```

installs Microsoft Outlook using the Typical installation with no user interaction. Although this method requires little or no up-front work, most organizations require additional configuration.

The Outlook setup program uses a number of different files during the setup process. OUTLOOK.STF tells setup how to install the client software and defines, among other things, the default destination directory. Microsoft's Network Installation Wizard (NIW), which you can use to modify default settings, provides a GUI method of modifying the *.STF files for Outlook.

You can also use the NIW to modify the behavior of the Custom installation. When these modifications are complete, save the modified *.STF file under a different file name. You could name the three installation types in this example:

- STANDARD.STF
- REMOTE.STF
- SPECIAL.STF

Create a share-point on a network server, then copy all required installation files to it using the setup program's /A command line parameter. You can now set up a custom version of Outlook by specifying a command line such as:

```
SETUP.EXE /Q1 /B2 /S \CUSTOM\SPECIAL.STF
```

This installs Outlook with a Typical installation using the new SPECIAL.STF file for the defaults.

This solution is discussed in detail in the *Microsoft Outlook 97 Administrator's Guide* found on the Microsoft Web at **http://www.microsoft.com/outlook /adminguide**.

SMS Installer Installation

The SMS Installer is an add-on to Microsoft Systems Management Server 1.2, available on the Microsoft Web at **http://backoffice.microsoft.com/downtrial**. (This is the BackOffice download site. Look under **Other Downloads**.) It requires that an SMS 1.2 or higher site be installed before it can uncompress the SMS Installer utilities.

The SMS Installer is a snapshot-type installation utility: it repackages applications by taking a snapshot before and after the software installation and recording only the differences.

When the SMS Installer repackages an application, it automatically generates a default script that contains all of the steps that the setup process completes during installation on a reference machine. The SMS Installer can compile a single executable (for example, "MyApp.EXE") that includes a compressed version of all files and changes to be installed, as well as the installation script.

Windows NT Security

Windows NT Workstation can provide a secure workstation by limiting access to parts of the file system and registry. Although this benefits network administrators, it produces some software distribution challenges. If software is distributed to a workstation and installed in the user's context, the user may not have the necessary permissions to replace files or make registry settings There are ways around this issue, but each has drawbacks.

For example, granting everyone administrative privileges on the workstations eliminates software distribution concerns but introduces numerous security and support issues. Users with administrative privileges can modify workstation configuration information, significantly increasing support call frequency and complexity. It is not a good idea to give users administrative privileges.

The SMS Package Command Manager (PCM) service for Windows NT helps with these software distribution concerns. PCM runs on the workstation in an administrative security context. Software distributed to workstations through PCM is installed in the background with administrative privileges. This eliminates the need to grant everyone administrative privileges, but it can create some problems when you have to modify user profiles.

Windows NT Workstation partitions configuration information into registry hives. Information relative to the workstation is stored in HKEY_LOCAL_MACHINE; user-specific information in HKEY_CURRENT_USER. Each user is logged into a Windows NT workstation that has a distinct configuration or profile. If roaming profiles are enabled, users' profiles follow them to whichever workstation they use. Similarly, a Windows NT service running on a workstation also has a user profile or configuration, a fact normally of little consequence. But when software is distributed using PCM, any changes the installation package makes to the user's configuration affect only the PCM service user profile—the user's profile is unaffected.

The solution is to split the software package into two parts. The machine part, sent using PCM, contains all configuration and file changes except user profile changes. The second part, containing only the changes required for the user profile, is sent to the workstation using the interactive version of PCM. The interactive version uses the same security context as the logged in user when it runs on a Windows NT Workstation. When the second part of the software package is executed, the changes are made to the currently logged-in user.

This solution for distributing software to Windows NT workstations is discussed in detail in the March 1998 Microsoft TechNet article titled *Advanced Techniques of Software Distribution with the SMS Installer*. This article will come in useful if you are deploying to Windows NT workstations; you may want to print out a copy for reference.

Outlook 97 Example

Here are the steps used to create the Outlook 97 deployment package. The procedure is based on the example company above and as such is representative, not exhaustive. Your organization will have its own requirements, and steps may vary.

The Outlook 97 client deployment package can be divided into three parts. The first develops the unattended setup features to be used in setup. This information is used by both Windows 95 and Windows NT Workstation. The second part demonstrates how to complete the installation package for Windows 95 only. This includes a number of tools and batch file utilities. The third part provides an example of the complete Windows NT Workstation installation package. As described above, Windows NT Workstation maintains a tighter security model and requires additional development. Normally Outlook 97 requires the Windows NT Workstation user to possess administrative privileges.

Unattended Installation Package

1. From the Exchange 5.5 client CD-ROM, run SETUP /A from the OUTLOOK.W32 directory.

2. Select a directory for the shared installation location.

3. When asked for the location of the *Microsoft Shared Components*, select the **Local Hard Drive** option.

4. Click **OK** to complete the administrative installation of Outlook.

5. Start the Network Installation Wizard.

6. Open the SETUP.LST file from the administrative installation of Outlook. This automatically opens the OUTLOOK.STF file.

7. The *Primary Location* for Outlook will be **<ProgramFilesFolder>\Microsoft Office**. Click the **Next** button to continue.

8. The *Document Location* for Outlook will be **C:\My Documents**. Click the **Next** button to continue.

9. The *Shared Files* location will be on the **Local Hard Drive**. Click the **Next** button to continue.

10. To assist in troubleshooting installation issues, name the *Installation Log* file as **C:\OUTLOOK.LOG.** Click the **Next** button to continue.

11. For *Installation Type* select **Custom**. This allows the custom configuration of the Outlook client. Click the **Next** button to continue.

12. Deselect the **Office Assistant, Holidays and Forms**, and **MS Info** components. Click the **Next** button to continue.

13. On the *Yes/No Questions* dialog box, select **Yes** for the Schedule+ conversion and **No** for the unused MS Mail files. Click the **Next** button to continue.

14. Select the **Prevent users from changing groups during installation** check box. Click the **Next** button to continue.

15. Leave the defaults on the *Start Menu and Desktop Items* dialog. Click the **Next** button to continue.

16. Enter **CUSTOM** for the *Setup Files SubFolder*. Click the **Next** button to continue.

17. Select **No Exit or Progress dialogs; no system restart even if necessary** on the *Select Quiet Mode* dialog box.

18. Change the custom setup files as **SPECIAL.*** on the *Save Changes* dialog box.

The unattended portion of setup is now complete. The custom setup files have been saved on the network installation point in the CUSTOM directory.

Windows 95 Installation Package

To complete the installation process for the Windows 95 client workstations, you must develop a process to perform the unattended installation and create the user's MAPI profile. Here is a list of example steps in this process:

1. Copy the CHNGINBX.EXE utility from the VALUPACK directory on the Outlook CD-ROM to the CUSTOM directory. This utility changes the Inbox icon on the user's desktop to the Outlook-style icon.

2. Copy the PROFGEN.EXE utility from the Exchange 5.0 Resource Kit to the CUSTOM directory.

3. Create a profile generator control file in the CUSTOM directory named SPECIAL.PRF. For details, see *Microsoft Outlook 97 Administrator's Guide* available on the Microsoft Web site at **http://www.microsoft.com/outlook /adminguide**.

4. Create a batch file on the network installation point similar to the following:

```
ECHO Installing Outlook 8.03
START /W %0\SETUP.EXE /L %0\..\CUSTOM\SPECIAL.LST /B2 /QTN
ECHO Changing Desktop Inbox icon to Outlook Icon
START /W %0\..\CUSTOM\CHNGINBX.EXE /Q
ECHO Running New profile Generator
COPY %0\..\CUSTOM\SPECIAL.PRF %WINDIR% /v
START /W %0\..\CUSTOM\PROFGEN %0\..\OFFICE\WMS\WIN95\NEWPROF.EXE -P
%WINDIR%\SPECIAL.PRF -S -X -U -L
```

This batch file installs the Outlook client with the customized setup files, changes the Inbox icon on the desktop, and generates the user's MAPI profile.

Windows NT Workstation Installation Package

To complete the installation process for the Windows NT Workstations, you must develop a process to perform the unattended installation and create the user's MAPI profile. Here is a list of example steps for this process.

1. Copy the CHNGINBX.EXE utility from the VALUPACK directory on the Outlook CD-ROM to the CUSTOM directory. This utility changes the Inbox icon on the user's desktop to the Outlook-style icon.

2. Copy the PROFGEN.EXE utility from the Exchange 5.0 Resource Kit to the CUSTOM directory.

3. Create a profile generator control file in the CUSTOM directory named SPECIAL.PRF. For details see the *Microsoft Outlook 97 Administrator's Guide* available on the Microsoft Web site at **http://www.microsoft.com/outlook/adminguide**.

4. Create a SMS Installer package on the network installation point using the following example steps:

5. Start the SMS Installer

6. Click the **Repackage** button.

7. In the **Executable** field enter: **C:\SOURCE\MSOFFICE\SETUP.EXE**

8. In the **Command Line** field enter: **/L CUSTOM\SPECIAL.LST /B2**
   Do not enter the /QTN parameter.

9. Click the **Next** button. The SMS Installer will scan the directory structure and the registry hives.

10. When the Outlook setup program finishes, click the **Next** button. The SMS Installer will rescan the directories and registry.

11. When the SMS Installer finishes rescanning, it displays the **Expert** window.

12. Under **Application Files** verify that the installer captured all of the files. Depending on what was happening on the workstation at installation time, there may be extra files that are not required by Outlook.

13. Under **User Configuration** verify that the installer captured all of the registry changes. Again, depending on what was happening on the workstation at installation time, there may be extra registry changes that are not required by Outlook.

14. Switch the Installer into **Script View**.

15. Using the "Advanced Techniques of Software Distribution with the SMS Installer" article (TechNet March 1998) as a guide, split the registry information into the machine and user components. Add script commands to enable the package to be used in both machine and user mode. Below are portions of an example script, explaining the changes: normal text is the original script, **BOLD** denotes additions.

Enable the package to accept command-line parameters.

```
Stop writing to installation log
If CMDLINE Does Not Contain "-U" then
 If CMDLINE Does Not Contain "-M" then
    Display Message "Invalid Syntax"
    Text: %CMDLINE% You must provide either a -U, -M, or both to
    install the Machine/User components of this package. Note: You
    must be an administrator...
 End Block
End Block
Check If Directory not writable %SYS% Start Block
 Set Variable SYS to %WIN%
End Block
Set Variable APPTITLE to
Set Variable GROUP to Microsoft Outlook.lnk
Set Variable DISABLED to !
Set Variable MAINDIR to
```

If –M is specified, install the machine components.

```
Rem If the command line contains a -M then update the machine
components.
If CMDLINE Contains "-M" then
 Install All Files (actual script removed)
 Create Shortcuts (actual script removed)
 Edit 945 registry keys (Only Machine Components)
End Block
```

If –U is specified, install the user configuration changes.

```
Rem If the command line contains a -U update the user configuration
changes.
If CMDLINE Contains "-U" then
  Edit 17 registry keys
  Execute %INST%\..\CUSTOM\CHNGINBX.EXE /Q (Wait)
  Install File %INST%\CUSTOM\SPECIAL.PRF to %WIN%\SPECIAL.PRF
  Execute %INST%\..\CUSTOM\PROFGEN.EXE
%INST%\..\OFFICE\WMS\WINNT\NEWPROF.EXE -P %WIN%\SPECIAL.PRF -S -X -U
-L
End Block
```

16. When the manual configuration of the script is complete, click the **Compile** button. This creates a self-extracting .EXE file that is used to perform the installation.

Included in the User Configuration section of the Installer script are the necessary command lines to change the Inbox icon and create the user's MAPI profile. When this SMS Installer script is run, it performs the normal program installation plus the special configuration for the user's MAPI profile.

You can expand the User Configuration section to include more configuration processes. For example, if a user is migrating to Outlook from a different messaging system, you can add a step that converts the older mailbox files to the Outlook format.

Outlook 98 Example

Here are the steps used to create the Outlook 98 deployment package. The procedure is based on the example company above and as such is representative, not exhaustive. Your organization will have its own requirements, and steps may vary.

Microsoft Outlook 98 has a tool called Outlook Deployment Kit (ODK) that helps you deploy the client. Like Outlook 97's NIW, the ODK is used to customize installations. ODK supports more customizations than the NIW. For example, you can use the ODK to define a user's MAPI profile, eliminating the need for custom tools and scripts.

Another major difference is that Outlook 98 no longer requires the user to have administrative privileges on Windows NT Workstations. Both Windows 95 and Windows NT Workstation can use the same deployment package, reducing development time.

▶ **To deploy OL98 with the ODK**

1. Install the ODK by running SETUP.EXE from the CD-ROM and clicking on the **Install Outlook 98 Deployment Wizard** icon. This automatically installs the files in the C:\Program Files\odk directory on your hard drive and places some shortcuts on your start menu.

2. Run the ODK to build your customized version of Outlook 98 and Internet Explorer 4.0. This consists of 5 stages:

   Stage 1: Gather Information about the company name, the language preference, and destination folder.

   Stage 2: Specify Active Setup Parameters such as what components to install, the custom components to include, and information about trusted publishers.

   Stage 3: Customize Active Setup settings such as destination folder on the user's hard drive, customize the setup screen, and set installation options.

   Stage 4: Customize Outlook 98 Setup Options and Internet Explorer setup options (from the IEAK)

   Stage 5: Customize user settings such as server names, LDAP settings, and additional registry settings.

3. After you create the customized package, you must sign the following files:

   BRANDING.CAB

   CHL<XXXX>.CAB

   DESKTOP.CAB

   FOLDER<N>.CAB

   OUTCIF.CAB

   SETUP.EXE

   Any custom components such as EXE files, if added

4. To sign your custom files you first must obtain a digital certificate, then use the MAKECERT.EXE, CERT2SPC.EXE, and SIGNCODE.EXE programs to sign the files. You can obtain a digital certificate from a CA; for more information, see "Certificate Authorities Providing Services for Microsoft Products" at **http://www.microsoft.com/security**. You can find the signing programs in the \Program Files\ODK\Reskit\Addons\Tools folder that was created when you installed the ODK.

5. You should now create a batch script to wrap around the installation process. This is similar to the procedure above for Outlook 97 except this does not require running many of the custom tools such as CHNGINBX.EXE and REGEDIT.EXE. Because the profile generation process in the ODK does not currently support environmental variable substitution for parameters such as username or servername, you will probably still need to use PROFGEN.EXE with a custom .PRF file to build the user's WMS profile. This is the same process used for Outlook 97, except it is necessary to substitute the newer version of NEWPROF.EXE. Here's an example batch file:

```
@ECHO OFF
%0\..\SETUP.EXE /Q
COPY %0\..\CUSTOM\OL98.PRF %WINDIR% /v
START /w %0\..\PROFGEN.EXE %0\..\OFFICE\WMS\WIN95\NEWPROF.EXE -P
%WINDIR%\OL98.PRF -S -X -U -L
```

6. Depending on how you will deploy the Outlook 98 client, your next step will be either to create an SMS package or to document the instructions of how to run the customized setup from the server location. You could also use third-party tools to perform an unattended installation.

The SMS Installer can also repackage the Outlook 98 package could. Although this is no longer required because of Windows NT Workstation security issues, the project team can still use other SMS Installer features such as rollback or versioning.

The same steps that were used to repackage Outlook 97 can be used to produce both the machine and the user components for Outlook 98.

Outlook 98 Tips

If your previous installations of Outlook 97 have the automatic upgrade registry switch enabled, you can just copy all the files created with the ODK to that location, and the next time users restart Outlook it will prompt them to upgrade their version of Outlook. The Outlook automatic upgrade feature upgrades Windows 95 and Windows NT Workstation clients to the latest version of Outlook, if the version of Outlook installed on the client is older than the one at the installation point. If you use a shared installation point for Outlook, you can enable the automatic upgrade feature by adding the following registry key on the Add Registry Entries screen (Stage 5) of the wizard:

```
[HKEY_LOCAL_MACHINE\SOFTWARE\Microsoft\Office\8.0\Outlook\UpgradePath]
"serverpath" = "<\\\\server\\share\\subdir>"
where "<\\\\server\\share\\subdir>" is the Outlook directory on the
server that contains Outlook.stf.
```

If you use SMS Installer or another snapshot utility to perform the installation, make sure to place the HKEY_CURRENT_USER information in a separate package for distribution to users.

You should create a batch script to perform the signing process every time you do a new build of Outlook 98. Otherwise, while you are testing your custom setups you will get errors about applications not being signed. You could do this by using SourceSafe to create the builds and have the signing programs run at the end of the build process.

Known Issues with the OL98 ODW from the README.TXT File

- Windows NT version 4, Service Pack 3 and Internet Explorer 4.*x* required.

  Outlook 98 Deployment Kit requires Microsoft Windows NT version 4, Service Pack 3 and Internet Explorer 4.*x*.

- Must Install Internet Explorer (minimal install) and Microsoft Outlook Express.

  Outlook 98 is integrated with Internet Explorer and Outlook Express, so you cannot remove these programs from an Outlook 98 installation. However, using the ODW, you can turn on a setting to prevent Internet Explorer icons from appearing on users' desktops.

- Run from network server not supported by Outlook 98.

  The Outlook 98 setup engine, Active Setup, does not allow you to run setup from network installations.

- OUT98PRF.ADM should not be used with POLEDIT.EXE.

  Don't use OUT98PRF.ADM with the Microsoft Policy Editor (POLEDIT.EXE) to set system policy. It should be used only in conjunction with the ODW.

- ODK contains most recent list of setup command line switches.

  After finalizing the ODW help files, a few changes were made to the list of setup command line switches. The list in the ODK is up to date.

- Adding DWord registry keys without value name does not work

  In Stage 5 of the ODW, if you create a DWord registry value without entering a Value name, the item attempts to write itself to the 'Default' item in the new registry key. While the registry key will be written, registry keys you added after that point will not be.

- Certificate authorities settings not set on Windows NT 4, if package was built on Windows 95.

  If you change the default certificate authorities information as part of the Internet Explorer customizations, you must build the customized Outlook 98 package on a computer running Windows NT 4.

- English Outlook 98 will not install on Far East operating systems.

  The English (EN) version of Outlook 98 will not install on Far East operating systems, such as Japanese, Korean, Chinese Simplified, and Chinese Traditional.

- Setting Mail Editor in Stage 5 prevents user from changing the editor.

  Setting one of the Outlook 98 Mail Editors in Stage 5 (Customize User Settings) sets the editor as policy and does not allow the user to change it.

- Language limitations for Microsoft LDAP Directory Service for Corporate/Workgroup Configurations

  The Microsoft LDAP Directory Service for Corporate/Workgroup Configurations might not be available for all language versions of Outlook 98. Look for the Valupack\CorpLDAP directory on the Outlook 98 CD-ROM to see if it is available.

- Office maintenance mode reinstall and setup /y.

  After installing Outlook 98, if you perform a Microsoft Office 97 maintenance mode reinstall or a "setup /y" command from Office setup, you may encounter object ID warnings or .SRG warning messages. These warnings can be safely dismissed and Office "setup /y" or maintenance mode reinstall will complete successfully.

- Windows Desktop Update must be turned on when deploying customized Internet Explorer channels.

  To deploy customized Internet Explorer channels with Outlook 98, you must turn on the Windows Desktop Update in the ODW.

Pilot Deployment

During this stage, the team tests and verifies all the pieces of the process. This section describes the process, using SMS as deployment mechanism. The deliverables from this stage are a verified deployment mechanism and complete client configuration packages.

Testing is critical: inadequate testing can jeopardize the entire project. Verify every aspect of the deployment process and the process as a whole. Evaluate the deployment mechanism and infrastructure to ensure that each client receives the Outlook package and that all error reporting features are working. Client workstations are dynamic, so verify the installation package on various workstations. As this stage completes, collect the pilot users' feedback and verify that the deployed client matches user community and business needs. If data collected now shows that the package is incorrect or enhancements are needed, the project team must go back to the development stage and redesign the package, after which the team must start back in at the beginning of the pilot stage.

Evaluating Deployment Mechanism

Verify the deployment mechanism and infrastructure during this stage to ensure a successful deployment of the Outlook client software. If you are using SMS, monitor the process to verify that the software packages are arriving at the workstations, that they are executing in a timely fashion, and that the error reporting features are working correctly.

If the deployment mechanism or infrastructure is not yet implemented, test and verify it by implementing it in a lab just as you would in the production environment. Use the installation packages as the verification tool for the lab.

After the mechanism is verified in the lab, implement it in the production environment and reverify it (to make sure no anomalies were introduced) before deploying the first pilot group.

Verifying Client Installation

Because client workstations are dynamic, check various workstations in the pilot group manually to verify that the installation was successful and the client software is functioning correctly. Choose a few workstations from each type of pilot group member. For example, if the deployment includes executives, administrative staff, sales representatives, and factory employees, verify several workstations from each group. The more you test, the more meaningful your results will be.

Collecting User Feedback

Software packages often behave differently on paper than they do on workstations. The feedback you gather in this stage can help you fine tune the existing software deployment package.

Create a standard feedback form to ensure that you get the same types of information from each user, although specific questions on the form depend on the Outlook features implemented. Make sure that the form captures the user's location and job function because this information helps analyze responses. For example, if all of the pilot users in one building have the same problem, it may be caused by an anomaly in the building rather than by the client software. Some general questions for the form:

- What operating system are you using?
- Are you a laptop user?
- What issues have you had with the Outlook client?
- What is your favorite feature?
- What is your least favorite feature?
- What would you like to see implemented differently?

Be sure to include a general *comments* section at the end of the form—this is always useful for getting users to say exactly what is on their minds and address issues not covered by the form.

After you have it all, categorize the responses then rank items in order of importance. For example, responses can be categorized this way:

- Top installation issues
- Top usability issues
- Most requested features
- Most unwanted features

If the pilot group is large, consider entering the information in a database (or having respondents submit it in a database) to simplify compilation and manipulation.

Revising Installation Package (if necessary)

Nobody wants to, but you may *have* to revise the software installation package if installation issues or feedback say you must. If so, you must return to the development stage and reconfigure the package, then start back in on all the steps for the development and pilot stages.

Deploying Outlook Clients

Once the pilot stage is complete and verified, you can start deploying the Outlook client to the entire user community. The deliverables of this stage are a completed deployment timeline and a successful client deployment.

You can use several approaches for a large deployment. One of the most successful is a staged or incremental process, wherein you divide your user base into segments and deploy incrementally. The first segment is relatively small and as the process is verified you increase the size of the groups. If issues crop up, you can scale back the group size until the issues are resolved. This approach allows the deployment team to catch issues relatively quickly without affecting a large number of users. If you set out to deploy across the organization at one time, a small problem can sometimes quickly derail the entire process.

Initial Deployment Group

The first group is the pilot group. Deploying again to them verifies that the production deployment processes are implemented correctly and that no new variables have been introduced.

Verifying Client Installation

As you did in the pilot stage, manually verify some workstations to ensure that the client software is properly installed and functioning. You can scale back manual verifications as the deployment progresses. But don't scale it all the way back to zero: you still should spot-check some workstations periodically to keep an eye on things at that level.

Deploying Incremental Groups

As each deployment group is verified and you start to increase group size, increase modestly. For example, if you verify deployment for a group of 100 workstations, increase the next group to 120. Keep the groups manageable in case an issue crops up.

Unattended Setup and Configuration of Servers and Connectors

The second half of this chapter discusses how you can install and configure Exchange servers in unattended mode, saving time, reducing deployment costs, and eliminating potential setup and configuration errors. It describes ways to use a SETUP.INI file, controlling the setup process, and how to use bulk importing to configure connectors and create user mailboxes. If you plan to deploy many Exchange servers in your enterprise, set aside time to automate the process, which should take approximately 24 to 48 development hours. If you plan to deploy a small number of servers in a central location, don't take the time to automate the installation process. If your organization has remote sites with no technical staff, automating the process should cost less than sending an administrator to set up each site.

Evaluate and review the following to determine how to use an unattended server setup in your organization:

- Source file storage location for unattended setup, and whether to distribute this on CD-ROM for field locations.

- Level of technical experience needed for those who will install and configure Exchange servers.

- If deploying to existing servers, whether to use SMS or a similar application to install Exchange services.

- If building and deploying new servers, how to integrate Exchange server deployment into the process.

- If a vendor builds servers, how to plan for and specify connectivity requirements so that new servers can communicate with existing servers for first-time replication.

- A rigorous change control process to track changes with older build versions and to upgrade them to new requirements.

- A test pilot on 1% of the sites to identify and resolve setup issues before finalizing the build process.

- Using an application such as Microsoft SourceSafe to manage and provide setup file version control.

You cannot upgrade existing Microsoft Exchange 4.0 or 5.0 servers in unattended mode because you must convert information store and directory databases to the new version 5.5 format during the upgrade. Although you cannot use the built-in unattended setup for upgrading existing servers, you should still standardize the process. You can find out more about the upgrade process in Appendix C: "References and Resources."

Exchange Setup in Unattended Mode

To run an unattended setup of Microsoft Exchange Server 5.5, you must create setup control (SETUP.INI) files. You can build these using the three examples found on the Exchange 5.5 CD-ROM (under \SERVER\SUPPORT\BATSETUP \SETUP). Or you can build them from scratch using the information contained in the Exchange 5.5 Setup Parameters table.

If you will roll out just a few servers using an unattended installation, you can build these files specifically for each server and assign unique filenames, for example, SERVERNAME.INI. Store these files in a separate directory where you will run the setup. Add a command line in the setup batch file (which the Windows NT setup will call through a "boot1" registry key) to run setup unattended. If you must roll out thousands of Exchange servers, build the .INI and .BAT files using a database application such as Microsoft Access or Microsoft Excel to handle server data for various parameters. Access and Excel can also export data into comma-delimited file (.CSV) format necessary to build these setup control files.

The example batch script (below) uses the "%0\..\" command to make it nonspecific to any server or share location, but this requires the script to run from the SETUP.EXE location. It also uses the %servername% environmental variable to choose the correct control file. Therefore, you must set this pointer before this script is called. Using environmental variables in setup script parameters allows you to standardize scripts and then use another process to gather specific setup information and propagate those environmental variables. The section called Configuring Connectors and Creating User Accounts (below) discusses the two commands that run ADMIN.EXE to import data .

```
@Echo off
Echo Setting up Exchange server %servername% in unattended mode >
%temp%\exsetup.log
%0\..\setup.exe /Q %0\..\custom\%servername%.ini
If errorlevel 1 goto failed
c:\exchsrvr\bin\admin.exe /I %0\..\custom\%servername%.con /O
%0\..\custom\%servername%con..txt
c:\exchsrvr\bin\admin.exe /I %0\..\custom\%servername%.usr /O
%0\..\custom\%servername%..txt
Goto end

:failed
Echo Exchange server installation did not complete successfully >>
%temp%\exsetup.log
```

```
:end
Echo Finished with install >> %temp%\exsetup.log
cls
@exit
```

Exchange Server 5.5 Setup Parameters

Entry	Description	Value
Section = [Product ID] (Optional if running setup from select CD-ROM)		
Cdkey	The Exchange CDkey	In the format of xxx-xxxxxxx
Section = [Paths] (All entries are optional)		
ServerDest	Location to install the server component.	Local path, that is: c:\exchsrvr
AdminDest	Location to install the administrative component.	Local path, that is: c:\exchsrvr
Section = [Components] (All entries are optional)		
Services=	Whether to install the services for the system attendant, the directory, the information store, and the MTA.	True or False
Administrator	Whether to install the Administrator program.	True or False
MSMailConnector	Whether to install the Microsoft Mail Connector.	True or false
X400	Whether to install the X.400 Connector.	True or false
Sample Applications	Whether to install the sample applications clients can use.	True or false
Books Online	Whether to install online documentation.	True or false
Active Server Components	Whether to install the Active Server Components.(OWA—Microsoft Outlook Web Access.).	True or false
cc:Mail	Whether to install the Connector for cc:Mail.	True or False

Entry	Description	Value
Event Service	Whether to install the event service.	True or false
Section = [Site]		
SiteName	Name of new site, if one is being created.	Site name
SiteProxyName	Site proxy name for new site. Used to determine the site proxy address for connectors such as the MS Mail Connector postoffice name.	Site proxy name
Section = [Organization]		
OrganizationName	Organization name, if a new one is being created.	Organization name
OrganizationProxy Name	Organization proxy name for new site. Used to determine the organization proxy addresses for connectors such as the MS Mail Connector network name.	Organization proxy name
Section = [ServiceAccount]		
AccountName=	Service account name, if a new site is being created.	Windows NT service account name in the format "domain\account"
AccountPassword	The service account password is required.	Service account password for the account in the value "AccountName"
Section = [Licensing]		
PerSeat	Whether to set up licensing on a per-seat basis.	True or False

(continued)

Entry	Description	Value
Section = [SitePermissions]		
Account1 through Account4	Account that will be granted site administrator permissions. Specify up to four accounts in addition to the service account.	Windows NT account name in the format "domain\account"
Section = [X.400] (This section is optional if no X.400 connector will be needed)		
Organization	X.400 attribute for organization.	X.400 Org value
OrgUnit1	X.400 attribute for organizational unit one.	X.400 OU1
OrgUnit2	X.400 attribute for organizational unit two.	X.400 OU2
OrgUnit3	X.400 attribute for organizational unit three.	X.400 OU3
OrgUnit4	X.400 attribute for organizational unit four.	X.400 OU4
PrivManDomName	X.400 attribute for the private management domain (PRMD).	X.400 PRMD
AdminManDomName	X.400 attribute for the administrative management domain (ADMD).	X.400 ADMD
Country	X.400 attribute for country.	X.400 Country

Configuring Connectors and Creating User Accounts

Installing Exchange Server and its components is pretty straightforward, but configuring connectors and creating new user accounts involves planning. This section outlines the process to configure installed connectors, install new ones, and create user mailboxes and associated Windows NT accounts. Although this section doesn't provide specifics on every type of connector, you can use it to determine what information you will need. (You should also read Chapter 17, "Deploying Specialized Directories with ADSI," which describes how to use ADSI to automatically associate mailboxes and Windows NT accounts.)

Warning This section requires you to edit Windows NT Registry and use the Microsoft Exchange Administrator program in raw mode. Entering invalid data in the registry or the directory can corrupt the system and force you to re-install.

While developing and testing these import files, use a machine in a controlled "sandbox" environment (test lab), that is, isolate the machine from the production environment and configure it so that you can easily rebuild it.

Installing and Configuring Connectors

You can view mail connectors in the Exchange directory as objects with properties that you can configure using the bulk import/export process built into the Administrator program. Because the bulk import/export process uses recipient containers as the basepoint location for objects (default), you must use an optional file (*.TXT) to specify a different location. The Internet Mail Service and Connector for cc:Mail store some values in the Windows NT registry, which you will configure using an import file and the REGEDIT.EXE program. Here's an example of how to set up and configure an X.400 connector—other connectors will follow this process but will differ in their properties.

Preliminaries:

- Configure a machine with an X.400 connector and a directory replication connector.

- See the Configuring and Tuning the MTA section in Chapter 6. Assume the connector is on a remote server, connecting to a central bridgehead server. (All remote servers use the same destination host name, MTA name, and password.)

▶ **To generate the .CSV file for importing**

1. On the test server run the Exchange Administrator program in raw mode (admin.exe /r).

2. Set up both an MTA transport stack and an X.400 connector with the information for the central bridgehead server, including connected sites.

3. Set up the directory replication connector for this server only, configuring it to replicate with the central site.

4. Using the Administrator program in raw mode, view properties for the three newly created objects, then cut and paste the property names for all the configured (default) values in a .CSV file. Use the property names that show up on the list when you first open in raw mode.

   - **MTA Transport Stack**: Obj-Class,Mode,Directory Name,Admin-Display-Name,Instance-Type,N-Address,N-Address-Type

- **X.400 Connector**: Obj-Class,Delivery-Mechanism,Admin-Display-Name,N-Address,N-Address-Type,Gateway-Local-Desig,MTA-Local-Desig,Supporting-Stack,Directory Name,Home-MTA,Home-Server,Activation-Schedule,Activation-Style,ADMD,Can-Preserve-DNs,Computer-Name,Connected-Domains,Country-Name,Deliv-Ext-Cont-Types,Deliverable Information Types,Diagnostic-reg-key,Encapsulation-Method,Obj-Container,PRMD,Routing-List,Supported-Application-Context,Transfer-Retry-Interval,Transfer-Timeout-Non-Urgent,Transfer-Timeout-Normal,Transfer-Timeout-Urgent,Association-Lifetime,Incoming message size limit,RTS-Checkpoint-Size,RTS-Recovery-Timeout,RTS-Window-Size,Num-Of-Open-Retries,Num-Of-Transfer-Retries,Open-Retry-Interval,Session-Disconnect-Timer,Temp-Assoc-Threshold,Two-Way-Alternate-Facility,Incoming message size limit

- **Directory Replication Connector**: Obj-Class,Mode,Admin-Display-Name,Common-Name,Local-Bridge-Head,Local-Bridge-Head-Address,Outbound-Sites,Remote-Bridge-Head,Remote-Bridge-Head-Address,Remote-Site,Activation-Style,Activation-Schedule

5. Using directory export on the three .CSV files, one for each object, export the settings of the existing object properties. You need to set the basepoint with an option file for each of the three objects because they are in different directory locations. See the example files for details on how to do this.

You can then import the information in the three .CSV files and additional option files (found on the sample CD-ROM) into another Exchange server, creating an identical MTA transport stack, X.400 connector, and a directory replication connector. For the MTA transport stack and X.400 connector, N-Address contains either an IP address or a hostname, and N-Address-Type has a value of 0 for an IP addresses and 1 for a hostname. Other connectors will have properties with specific formats or values. Look up the property in the Schema help file (Microsoft Exchange Server CD-ROM) to find specific property information.

Use these definitions with the sample files:

- LOCALSRV = local server name
- LOCALSITE = local site name
- LOCALORG = local organization name
- REMOTESRV = remote server name
- REMOTESITE = remote site name
- REMOTEORG = remote organization name

MTA Transport Stack
Options file (MTA.TXT):

```
[Export]
DirectoryService=LOCALSRV
HomeServer=LOCALSRV
Basepoint=/o=LOCALORG/ou=LOCALSITE/cn=configuration/cn=servers/cn=LOCALS
RV
ExportObject=All
InformationLevel=Full
RawMode=Yes
HiddenObjects=Yes
Subcontainers=Yes

[IMPORT]
DirectoryService=LOCALSRV
Basepoint=/o=LOCALORG/ou=LOCALSITE/cn=configuration/cn=servers/cn=LOCALS
RV
container=
InformationLevel=Full
OverwriteProperties=Yes
RawMode=Yes
```

CSV file:

(Locate MTA.CSV on the sample CD.)

X.400 Connector
Options file (X400.TXT):

```
[Export]
DirectoryService=LOCALSRV
HomeServer=LOCALSRV
Basepoint=/o=LOCALORG/ou=LOCALSITE/cn=configuration/cn=connections
ExportObject=All
InformationLevel=Full
RawMode=Yes
HiddenObjects=Yes
Subcontainers=Yes
```

```
[IMPORT]
DirectoryService=LOCALSRV
Basepoint=/o=LOCALORG/ou=LOCALSITE/cn=configuration/cn=connections
container=
InformationLevel=Full
OverwriteProperties=Yes
RawMode=Yes
```

CSV File:

(Locate X400.CSV on the sample CD.)

Directory Replication Connector

Options File (REPLICATOR.TXT):

```
[Export]
DirectoryService=LOCALSRV
HomeServer=LOCALSRV
Basepoint=/o=LOCALORG/ou=LOCALSITE/cn=configuration/cn=Dir-Repl
ExportObject=All
InformationLevel=Full
RawMode=Yes
HiddenObjects=Yes
Subcontainers=Yes

[IMPORT]
DirectoryService=LOCALSRV
Basepoint=/o=LOCALORG/ou=LOCALSITE/cn=configuration/cn=Dir-Repl
container=
InformationLevel=Full
OverwriteProperties=Yes
RawMode=Yes
```

CSV File:

(Look for REPLICATOR.CSV on the sample CD-ROM.)

To import these files, use the command line: **admin.exe /I** *import***.csv /O** *options***.txt.** To build an Exchange server in unattended mode, expand this command line in the batch script, using variable names and current path commands, allowing the script to be used on any server:

```
c:\exchsrvr\bin\admin.exe /I %0\..\custom\%servername%.con /O
%0\..\custom\%servername%con.txt
```

Other connectors, such as the Internet Mail Service, Connector for cc:Mail, and MS Mail connector, store some values in the Windows NT Registry. For those connectors, follow the steps outlined above and use Regedit to export the registry entries to a file. Because Exchange Server automatically creates many of the registry entries when you set up the connector *during* the import process, you need only to include registry entries to change in a .REG file. Then add the following command to the batch script for the unattended server installation:

```
%systemroot%\system32\regedit.exe %0\..\custom\%servername%.reg
```

Specific registry values vary depending on the connector, so refer to that connector's documentation for explanations of registry values. For more information on the Connector for cc:Mail, see Chapter 11, "Lotus cc:Mail."

Configuring User Mailboxes and Windows NT Server Domain Accounts

You can use the bulk import/export process to configure Exchange mailboxes and Windows NT user accounts. You can specify in a .CSV file attributes for a mailbox object that you want (documented in the Schema Properties and Attributes, Microsoft Exchange books online). These are the only required properties in your .CSV file to create new mailboxes:

```
obj-class,mode,display-name,given-name,initials,surname,alias name
```

Mailbox,Create,"Nixon, Toby",Toby,P,Nixon,tobynix
Mailbox,Create,"Dodge, Gregory",Gregory,H,Dodge,gregdod

You can also use the utility HEADERS.EXE from the *BackOffice Resource Kit* to write the headers in an import file that creates mailboxes. If you want the recipients to go into a container other than Recipients, add the setting "container=" to the import option file (described later in this section). You can automatically create and associate Windows NT accounts with the appropriate mailboxes in the options file or you can associate previously created Windows NT accounts by adding the "Assoc-NT-Account" property to your .CSV file.

Here's the command line to run in the setup script:

```
c:\exchsrvr\bin\admin.exe /I %0\..\custom\%servername%.usr /O
%0\..\custom\%servername%usr.txt
```

Where "%servername%.usr" is the .CSV file containing the user information and the %servername%usr.txt is the options file to specify the recipients container in which the mailboxes will be created, as well as other options. With this same procedure you can also create users on a remote server, but you must specify the server in the OPTIONS.TXT file or as a property in the .CSV file. The following is a list of the options available for the import control file.

```
[Import]
DirectoryService=<DS server name> ;(default=NULL)
Basepoint=<DN of basepoint object> ;(default=NULL for the local site)
Container=<RDN of container object> ;(default=Recipients)
InformationLevel=[None, Minimal, Full] ;(default=Minimal)
RecipientTemplate=<DN of default recipient object> ;(default=none)
NTDomain=<NT domain where accounts will be created> ;(default=none)
OverwriteProperties=[Yes, No] ;(default=No)
CreateNTAccounts=[Yes, No] ;(default=No)
DeleteNTAccounts=[Yes, No] ;(default=No)
ApplyNTSecurity=[Yes, No] ;(default=Yes)
GeneratePassword=[Yes, No] ;(default=No)
RawMode=[Yes, No] ;(default=No)
CodePage=[-1,0,code-page-ID] ;(default=0)
```

Creating the .CSV and options files for each server for a large deployment can be a daunting task. Use Microsoft Access as your repository to ease standardizing and creating these files, extracting data from an existing source, such as an HR database or phone directory, and then generating the .CSV files. Name the fields to match the Exchange properties so that you can easily export query results into the .CSV file. You can also use separate tables in Access to manage the options files, but you might find it easier to work from a template and modify it for each import.

More Information

For more information regarding Microsoft Exchange unattended setup, consult these Knowledge Base articles:

- Q181864, Title: XADM: Setup /Q Prompts for Service Account
- Q175115, Title: XADM: Err Msg: There is Something Wrong with the INI File
- Q180404, Title: XADM: Silent Mode Setup Does Not Support Upgrade Mode
- Q176243, Title: XADM: Batch Setup-Setup /r /q Options Combined Unsupported
- Q168490, Title: XADM: Unattended Exchange Server Setup

C H A P T E R   1 7

Deploying Specialized Directories with ADSI

Organizations with large distributed computing environments commonly deploy a number of specialized directories for network operating systems, messaging systems, workgroup software applications, and human resource databases. These directories provide security (initial authentication and access control) and customized property associations for specific applications. They often contain overlapping information, including phone number, location, job title, and so forth. Managing and synchronizing redundant information in disparate directories can increase administrative costs. And redundant data can increase the risk of directories lagging behind updates made to "authoritative" source directories.

You can consolidate and simplify regular administrative processes such as creating, modifying, and deleting mail users with scripts that can update multiple directories and manipulate existing directory information while performing routine changes or adding new properties in bulk. This section provides a simple scenario and script sample using Active Directory Service Interfaces (ADSI, formerly known as OLE-DS) to create a Windows NT Server domain account and a Microsoft Exchange mailbox, and associate the two. It also includes another sample to add users, customized recipients, or a distribution list to a distribution list.

Using ADSI

ADSI provides a *single set of interfaces* for managing multiple directory services, including Windows NT Directory Services, Novell NetWare Directory Services, and Lightweight Directory Access Protocol (LDAP). Because standard ADSI objects include typical namespaces for various network operating systems, administrators can use it to manage Exchange directories. The *Microsoft Exchange Server Resource Guide,* pp. 165–183 (Chapter 9, "Collaboration"), details available object classes in the Exchange Server directory schema and their properties. It also provides sample ADSI code (using Active Data Objects—ADO) to create a distribution list and populate it, and modify the phone number property of a mailbox.

You can also find more information on the TechNet sampler CD-ROM:

- "Active Directory Service Interfaces—The Easy Way to Access and Manage LDAP-Based Directories (Windows NT 4.0)"
- "Active Directory Services Interface in the MS Exchange 5.5 Environment"

The Benefits

Prior to the release of ADSI, when administrators wanted to script changes against a directory they wrote a proprietary application using vendor-provided application programming interfaces (APIs). Or they wrote a script using a vendor-supported proprietary scripting language. The process of updating records in a directory usually required administrators exporting all directory information, running the script or proprietary application against the data, and then importing it back into the directory.

In a messaging environment where servers regularly replicate directories, such as Exchange, frequent changes can generate a great deal of network traffic, possibly overloading the underlying network. Using ADSI scripts, organizations can update multiple directories and implement as few new specialized directories as possible, reducing the administrative burden of maintaining multiple copies of identical data in multiple directories. By using ADSI to access directory information, you can minimize the risk of copying data from one directory to another and reduce out-of-sync data.

With ADSI script, network administrators can write a single code module that can access data in disparate directories, maintaining uniformity of namespaces and referring to objects and their properties in the same way each time. An ADSI application is also portable—you can reuse its logic.

Limitation with Windows NT Security Identifier

When an organization has multiple network operating systems, each supporting its own specialized interface for accessing, creating, modifying, or deleting objects such as users, administrators must often use a variety of tools. Using an ADSI script to create user accounts can provide these advantages:

- Creating users across systems with the same script.
- Setting specialized directory attributes for users in one directory without having to set them on all user definitions.

A common challenge for Exchange Server administrators is associating newly created domain accounts with their newly created mailboxes. ADSI version 2.0 cannot manipulate Windows NT Server 4.0 Access Control Lists (ACLs), containing security information on user permissions, or a Windows NT security identifier (SID), a user's account name binary representation. When administrators create a new Windows NT domain account and an Exchange mailbox, they cannot automatically associate the two using ADSI because a mailbox requires the Windows NT account SID. The sample below provides a workaround to this.

Associating a New Domain Account and Mailbox

This sample uses a simple user interface (a Web form—DEFAULT.HTM) that you can view with an Internet browser such as Microsoft Internet Explorer 4.01 or later. The form calls an Active Server Pages file (PROCESS.ASP) to create the Windows NT Server domain account and Exchange mailbox, *and associate* the two. This Web application—the PROCESS.ASP file—has these features:

- Uses ADSI with the Windows NT provider to create the Windows NT Server domain account and the LDAP provider to access the Exchange Server directory.

- Associates the newly created domain account with the new mailbox by instantiating a small Microsoft Visual Basic component (ExAdmin.DLL) to look up the Windows NT SID.

- Works off the security context of the viewer, using Windows NT LAN Manager (NTLM) authentication.

The administrators or support staff using this script must have Administrator authority on the Exchange Server and in the Windows NT Server domain where they create accounts and mailboxes.

DEFAULT.HTM Code

You can find this file on the sample CD-ROM included at the back in this book.

```
<html>

<head>
<title>Home Page</title>
</head>

<body>

<h4><font face="Tahoma"><big><big><strong>Windows NT / Exchange User
Creation</strong></big></big></font></h4>
```

```
<form method="GET" action="http://<server>/<share>/process.asp">
  <table border="0" width="100%">
    <tr>
      <td width="25%"><font face="Tahoma">New Alias/Account
ID:</font></td>
      <td width="74%"><font face="Tahoma"><input type="text"
name="Alias" size="20" tabindex="1"></font></td>
    </tr>
  </table>
  <p><font face="Tahoma"><strong>Windows NT Domain Account
Information</strong></font></p>
  <table border="0" width="100%">
    <tr>
      <td width="25%"><font face="Tahoma">Domain:</font></td>
      <td width="74%"><font face="Tahoma"><input type="text"
        name="NTDomain" size="20" tabindex="2"></font></td>
    </tr>
    <tr>
      <td width="25%"><font face="Tahoma">Account Description:
        </font></td>
      <td width="74%"><font face="Tahoma"><input type="text"
        name="NTDescription" size="20" tabindex="3"></font></td>
    </tr>
    <tr>
      <td width="25%"><font face="Tahoma">Account Password:</font></td>
      <td width="74%"><font face="Tahoma"><input type="text"
        name="NTPassword" size="20" value="NewUserPW"></font></td>
    </tr>
  </table>
  <p><font face="Tahoma"><strong>Exchange Mailbox Information
      </strong></font></p>
 <table border="0" width="107%">
    <tr>
      <td width="19%"><font face="Tahoma">Server</font></td>
      <td width="23%"><font face="Tahoma"><input type="text"
        name="ExServer" size="20" tabindex="4"></font></td>
      <td width="21%"><font face="Tahoma">First Name:</font></td>
      <td width="37%"><font face="Tahoma"><input type="text"
        name="ExFirstName" size="20" tabindex="8"></font></td>
    </tr>
    <tr>
      <td width="19%"><font face="Tahoma">Organization (/o):</font></td>
      <td width="23%"><font face="Tahoma"><input type="text"
        name="ExOrg" size="20" tabindex="5"></font></td>
 <td width="21%"><font face="Tahoma">Last Name:</font></td>
      <td width="37%"><font face="Tahoma"><input type="text"
        name="ExLastName" size="20" tabindex="9"></font></td>
    </tr>
    <tr>
      <td width="19%"><font face="Tahoma">Site (/ou):</font></td>
```

```
        <td width="23%"><font face="Tahoma"><input type="text"
          name="ExSite" size="20" tabindex="6"></font></td>
        <td width="21%"><font face="Tahoma">Display Name:</font></td>
        <td width="37%"><font face="Tahoma"><input type="text"
          name="ExDisplayName" size="20" tabindex="10"></font></td>
      </tr>
      <tr>
<td width="19%"><font face="Tahoma">Container (/cn):</font></td>
        <td width="23%"><font face="Tahoma"><input type="text"
          name="ExContainer" size="20" value="Recipients"
          tabindex="7"></font></td>
        <td width="21%"></td>
        <td width="37%"></td>
      </tr>
    </table>
    <div align="center"><center><table border="0" width="100%">
      <tr>
        <td width="100%"><div align="left"><p><input type="submit"
          value="Submit" name="B1"> <input type="reset" value="Reset"
          name="B2"></td>
      </tr>
    </table>
    </center></div>
  </form>
  </body>
  </html>
```

PROCESS.ASP Code

You can find this file on the sample CD-ROM included at the back of this book.

Note   There are four additional lines to the PROCESS.ASP code that *are not in the sample file* on the CD-ROM. Please add these lines to the sample code when adapting it. These lines are represented in **bold** text below.

```
<%@ LANGUAGE="VBSCRIPT" %>

<html>
<head>
<meta NAME="GENERATOR" Content="Microsoft Visual InterDev 1.0">

<title>Document Title</title>
</head>
<body>

<%
stop
```

```
        Dim strExServer
        Dim strExSite
        Dim strExContainer
        Dim strAlias
        Dim strExDisplayName
        Dim strNTDescription
        Dim strNTDomain
        Dim strExOrg

    '---------------------------------------------------------------
    ' Get data elements from the form
    '---------------------------------------------------------------
        strAlias = Request.QueryString("Alias")
        strDomain = Request.QueryString("NTDomain")
        strDescription = Request.QueryString("NTDescription")
        strPassword = Request.QueryString("NTPassword")

        strServer = Request.QueryString("ExServer")
        strOrg = Request.QueryString("ExOrg")
        strSite = Request.QueryString("ExSite")
        strContainer = Request.QueryString("ExContainer")

        strFirstName = Request.QueryString("ExFirstName")
        strLastName = Request.QueryString("ExLastName")
        strDisplayName = Request.QueryString("ExDisplayName")

    '---------------------------------------------------------------
    ' Present information to the User
    '---------------------------------------------------------------
%>
Your Request:<br><br>

Microsoft Windows NT Information:<br><br>

Alias:          <% = strAlias %> <br><br>

Domain:         <% = strDomain %> <br>
Description:<% = strDescription %> <br>
Password:       <% = strPassword %> <br><br>

Microsoft Exchange Information:<br><br>
```

```
Server:         <% = strServer %> <br>
Organization:   <% = strOrg %> <br>
Site:           <% = strSite %> <br>
Container:      <% = strContainer %> <br><br>

First Name:     <% = strFirstName %> <br>
Last Name:      <% = strLastName %> <br>
DisplayName:<% = strDisplayName %> <br>

<%
'------------------------------------------------------------
' Create Accounts
'------------------------------------------------------------

    Dim strPath
    Dim objContainer
    Dim objUser


'------------------------------------------------------------
' Create Microsoft Windows NT Domain Account
'------------------------------------------------------------

    ' build ADSI WinNT provider path to the target domain
    strPath = "WinNT://" + strDomain

    ' create ADSI container object (IADsContainer)
    Set objContainer = GetObject(strPath)

    ' create new user via ADSI container object
    Set objUser = objContainer.Create("user", strAlias)

    ' set user properties
    objUser.FullName = strDisplayName
    objUser.Description = strDescription

    ' flush ADSI creation buffer to underlying directory
    objUser.SetInfo

    objUser.SetPassword(strPassword)
    objUser.SetInfo

    ' cleanup
    Set objContainer = Nothing
    Set objUser = Nothing
%>
```

```
<br>Windows NT Domain Account Created!<br><br>

<%
'-----------------------------------------------------------
' Create Microsoft Exchange Mailbox
'-----------------------------------------------------------
    Dim strMTA
    Dim strMDB
    Dim objExAdmin
    ' build ADSI LDAP provider path to the target Exchange container
    strPath = "LDAP://" + strServer + "/cn=" + strContainer + ",ou=" +
strSite + ",o=" + strOrg

    ' build default MTA path
    strMTA = "cn=Microsoft MTA,cn=" + strServer +
",cn=Servers,cn=Configuration,ou=" + strSite + ",o=" + strOrg

    'build default MDB path
    strMDB = "cn=Microsoft Private MDB,cn=" + strServer +
",cn=Servers,cn=Configuration,ou=" + strSite + ",o=" + strOrg

    ' create ADSI container object
    Set objContainer = GetObject(strPath)

    ' create new Exchange mailbox ("organizationalPerson") via ADSI
    Set objUser = objContainer.Create("organizationalPerson", "cn=" +
strAlias)

    ' set mailbox properties
    objUser.Put "cn", CStr(strDisplayName)
    objUser.Put "uid", CStr(strAlias)
    objUser.Put "Home-MTA", CStr(strMTA)
    objUser.Put "Home-MDB", CStr(strMDB)
    objUser.Put "mailPreferenceOption", 0
    objUser.Put "givenName", CStr(strFirstName)
    objUser.Put "sn", CStr(strLastName)

    ' flush ADSI creation buffer to underlying Exchange directory
    objUser.SetInfo

    ' we have a new Windows NT Domain account now and a new Exchange
    ' account that need to be matched up.
    ' Since ADSI cannot directly manipulate NT SID (Security IDs) in its
    ' current version, the following object does exactly that.

    ' ExAdmin.Lookup contains code to search the NT Directory for a user
    ' SID and assigns the SID to the Exchange mailbox
    Set objExAdmin = CreateObject("ExAdmin.Lookup")
    objExAdmin.SetSecurity CStr(strDomain), CStr(strAlias),
CStr(strServer), CStr(strOrg), CStr(strSite), CStr(strContainer)
```

```
            ' cleanup
            Set objExAdmin = Nothing
            Set objContainer = Nothing
            Set objUser = Nothing
%>

Exchange Mailbox Created!

</body>
</html>
```

EXADMIN Visual Basic Project Code

You can find the Visual Basic project (EXADMIN.VBP) and the compiled
EXADMIN.DLL and accompanying files on the sample CD-ROM included with
this book. Copy the EXADMIN program (EXADMIN.DLL) to a folder on the
computer that will run the Web application (IIS Server), and then register the
component using the following command: **regsvr32 exadmin.dll**. This allows the
Web application (PROCESS.ASP) to instantiate and use the component.

Declarations

```
' Private constants and data structures for use with Win32 API functions

' Mailbox rights for Exchange security descriptor
Private Const RIGHT_MODIFY_USER_ATTRIBUTES = &H2
Private Const RIGHT_MODIFY_ADMIN_ATTRIBUTES = &H4
Private Const RIGHT_SEND_AS = &H8
Private Const RIGHT_MAILBOX_OWNER = &H10
Private Const RIGHT_MODIFY_PERMISSIONS = &H80
Private Const RIGHT_SEARCH = &H100

' Win32 constants for security descriptors
Private Const ACL_REVISION = (2)
Private Const SECURITY_DESCRIPTOR_REVISION = (1)
Private Const SidTypeUser = 1

Private Type ACL
        AclRevision As Byte
        Sbz1 As Byte
        AclSize As Integer
        AceCount As Integer
        Sbz2 As Integer
End Type
```

```
Private Type ACE_HEADER
        AceType As Byte
        AceFlags As Byte
        AceSize As Long
End Type

Private Type ACCESS_ALLOWED_ACE
        Header As ACE_HEADER
        Mask As Long
        SidStart As Long
End Type

Private Type SECURITY_DESCRIPTOR
        Revision As Byte
        Sbz1 As Byte
        Control As Long
        Owner As Long
        Group As Long
        Sacl As ACL
        Dacl As ACL
End Type

' Private declarations of Win32 API functions
Private Declare Function LookupAccountName Lib "advapi32.dll" Alias
"LookupAccountNameA" _
        (ByVal IpSystemName As String, _
         ByVal IpAccountName As String, _
         pSID As Byte, _
         cbSid As Long, _
         ByVal ReferencedDomainName As String, _
         cbReferencedDomainName As Long, _
         peUse As Integer) As Long

Private Declare Function NetGetDCName Lib "NETAPI32.DLL" _
        (ServerName As Byte, _
         DomainName As Byte, _
         DCNPtr As Long) As Long

Private Declare Function NetApiBufferFree Lib "NETAPI32.DLL" _
        (ByVal Ptr As Long) As Long

Private Declare Function PtrToStr Lib "kernel32" _
        Alias "lstrcpyW" (RetVal As Byte, ByVal Ptr As Long) As Long

Private Declare Function GetLengthSid Lib "advapi32.dll" _
        (pSID As Byte) As Long
```

```
Private Declare Function InitializeSecurityDescriptor Lib "advapi32.dll" _
        (pSecurityDescriptor As SECURITY_DESCRIPTOR, _
        ByVal dwRevision As Long) As Long

Private Declare Function SetSecurityDescriptorOwner Lib "advapi32.dll" _
        (pSecurityDescriptor As SECURITY_DESCRIPTOR, _
        pOwner As Byte, _
        ByVal bOwnerDefaulted As Long) As Long

Private Declare Function SetSecurityDescriptorGroup Lib "advapi32.dll" _
        (pSecurityDescriptor As SECURITY_DESCRIPTOR, _
        pGroup As Byte, _
        ByVal bGroupDefaulted As Long) As Long

Private Declare Function SetSecurityDescriptorDacl Lib "advapi32.dll" _
        (pSecurityDescriptor As SECURITY_DESCRIPTOR, _
        ByVal bDaclPresent As Long, _
        pDacl As Byte, _
        ByVal bDaclDefaulted As Long) As Long

Private Declare Function MakeSelfRelativeSD Lib "advapi32.dll" _
        (pAbsoluteSecurityDescriptor As SECURITY_DESCRIPTOR, _
        pSelfRelativeSecurityDescriptor As Byte, _
        ByRef lpdwBufferLength As Long) As Long

Private Declare Function InitializeAcl Lib "advapi32.dll" _
        (pACL As Byte, _
        ByVal nAclLength As Long, _
        ByVal dwAclRevision As Long) As Long

Private Declare Function AddAccessAllowedAce Lib "advapi32.dll" _
        (pACL As Byte, _
        ByVal dwAceRevision As Long, _
        ByVal AccessMask As Long, _
        pSID As Byte) As Long

Private Declare Function GetSecurityDescriptorLength Lib "advapi32.dll" _
        (pSecurityDescriptor As SECURITY_DESCRIPTOR) As Long
'-------------------------------------------------------------
```

BuildSD

```
' BuildSD

' This routine uses Win32 API functions to create a security descriptor,
access control
' list and corresponding access control entries.
```

```
Public Sub BuildSD(strServer As String, strDomain As String, pSID() As
Byte, pSD() As Byte)

    Dim sdNew As SECURITY_DESCRIPTOR
    Dim aclNew As ACL
    Dim aaaNew As ACCESS_ALLOWED_ACE
    Dim pACL() As Byte
    Dim Length As Long
    Dim AccessMask As Long
    Dim bError As Boolean
    Dim i As Integer

    bError = InitializeSecurityDescriptor(sdNew,
SECURITY_DESCRIPTOR_REVISION)
    bError = SetSecurityDescriptorOwner(sdNew, pSID(0), 0)
    bError = SetSecurityDescriptorGroup(sdNew, pSID(0), 0)
    Length = Len(aclNew) + GetLengthSid(pSID(0)) + Len(aaaNew) -
Len(aaaNew.SidStart)
    ReDim pACL(Length)
    bError = InitializeAcl(pACL(0), Length, ACL_REVISION)
    AccessMask = CLng(RIGHT_MAILBOX_OWNER + RIGHT_SEND_AS +
RIGHT_MODIFY_USER_ATTRIBUTES)
    bError = AddAccessAllowedAce(pACL(0), ACL_REVISION, AccessMask,
pSID(0))
    bError = SetSecurityDescriptorDacl(sdNew, 1, pACL(0), 0)

    Length = GetSecurityDescriptorLength(sdNew)
    ReDim pSD(Length)
    bError = MakeSelfRelativeSD(sdNew, pSD(0), Length)

End Sub

'------------------------------------------------------------
```

GetPrimaryDCName

```
' GetPrimaryDCName

' This routine calls the Win32 function "NetGetDCName()" to return the
name of the
' PDC (Primary Domain Controller) computer.

Private Function GetPrimaryDCName(ByVal MName As String, ByVal DName As
String) As String

    Dim Result As Long
    Dim DCName As String
    Dim DCNPtr As Long
```

```
    Dim DNArray() As Byte
    Dim MNArray() As Byte
    Dim DCNArray(100) As Byte

    MNArray = MName & vbNullChar
    DNArray = DName & vbNullChar

    Result = NetGetDCName(MNArray(0), DNArray(0), DCNPtr)

    If Result <> 0 Then
        Exit Function
    End If

Result = PtrToStr(DCNArray(0), DCNPtr)
    Result = NetApiBufferFree(DCNPtr)
    DCName = DCNArray()
    GetPrimaryDCName = DCName

End Function
'------------------------------------------------------------
```

SetSecurity

```
' SetSecurity

' This routine will associate an NT Domain account with an Exchange
' mailbox. It requires information specifying the Windows NT Domain
' account and the Exchange mailbox.

' ADSI is used to set the "Assoc-NT-Account" and "NT-Security-
' Descriptor" properties
Public Sub SetSecurity(strNTDomain As String, strNTAccount As String,
strServer As String, _
                        strOrg As String, strSite As String, strContainer
As String)

    Dim pDomain(512) As Byte
    Dim pRawSID(512) As Byte
    Dim pSID(1024) As Byte
    Dim pRawSD() As Byte
    Dim pSD() As Byte
    Dim strPath As String
    Dim objUser As IADsUser
    Dim objContainer As IADsContainer

    ' Build the ADSI Path to the Exchange mailbox that's been passed
    ' in...
    strPath = "LDAP://" + strServer + "/cn=" + strNTAccount + ",cn=" +
strContainer + ",ou=" + strSite + ",o=" + strOrg
```

```
        ' Retrieve the IADsUser object encapsulating the Exchange mailbox
        Set objUser = GetObject(strPath)

        ' Lookup the SID for the Windows NT Domain account that's been
        ' passed in...
        Dim lReturn As Long
        lReturn = LookupAccountName(GetPrimaryDCName("", strNTDomain),
strNTAccount, pRawSID(0), 512, pDomain, 512, 1)

        ' Build the security descriptor for this new mailbox object
        BuildSD strServer, strNTDomain, pRawSID, pRawSD

        ' encode sid
        For i = 0 To GetLengthSid(pRawSID(0)) - 1
            pSID(2 * i) = AscB(Hex$(pRawSID(i) \ &H10))
            pSID(2 * i + 1) = AscB(Hex$(pRawSID(i) Mod &H10))
        Next i

        ' encode sd
        ReDim pSD(2 * UBound(pRawSD) + 1)
        For i = 0 To UBound(pRawSD) - 1
            pSD(2 * i) = AscB(Hex$(pRawSD(i) \ &H10))
            pSD(2 * i + 1) = AscB(Hex$(pRawSD(i) Mod &H10))
        Next i

        ' Set the owner of the Exchange mailbox to the Windows NT Domain
account that's been passed in...
        objUser.Put "Assoc-NT-Account", pSID
        objUser.Put "NT-Security-Descriptor", pSD
        objUser.SetInfo

        Set objUser = Nothing

End Sub

'------------------------------------------------------------
```

Adding a Recipient to a Distribution List

This sample (ADDUSER.VBS) offers a command line option for adding a
predefined user to distribution lists, adding distribution lists to other distribution
lists, or adding Exchange custom recipients to a distribution list. This script can
be called from within the sample for creating Exchange users accounts (provided
above), and can add them to multiple distribution lists at the same time their
accounts are created, bypassing additional administrative work later. This script
has these features:

- Uses ADSI with the LDAP provider to access the Exchange Server directory.
- Works off the security context of the viewer, using NTLM authentication.

The administrators or support staff using this script must have Administrator authority or be the distribution list owner for them to modify distribution lists if the list is not open for anonymous modification.

```
Dim strOrg
Dim strSite
Dim strContainer
Dim strServer
Dim strDLAlias
Dim strUserAlias
Dim strLDAPPath

Dim objArgs
Dim objIADsGroup

strOrg = "<your org>"
strSite = "<site name>"
strContainer = "Recipients"
strServer = "<site name-server name>"

Set objArgs=Wscript.Arguments

strDLAlias = objArgs.Item(0)
strUserAlias = objArgs.Item(1)

' build ADSI LDAP path
strLDAPPath = "LDAP://" + strServer + "/cn=" + strDLAlias + ",cn=" +
strContainer + ",ou=" + strSite + ",o=" + strOrg

' get group object
Set objIADsGroup = GetObject(strLDAPPath)

' add user
strLDAPPath = "LDAP://" + strServer + "/cn=" + strUserAlias + ",cn=" +
strContainer + ",ou=" + strSite + ",o=" + strOrg
objIADsGroup.Add(strLDAPPath)

' cleanup
Set objArgs = Nothing
Set objIADsGroup = Nothing
```

Extending the Process/Script for Your Organization

The scripts presented here are very simple and do not cover all of the possibilities that you can exploit by enhancing or integrating it with other directory resources. For example, you could:

- Populate new mailbox properties while creating or modifying a particular recipient.
- Prompt script users with set options (values) to fill in directory properties or fields.
- Import data from authoritative directory sources, such as enterprise HR databases and organizational hierarchy, or phone number and location information.
- Automatically add newly created mailboxes to office, departmental, or organizational distribution lists.
- Create domain accounts and mailboxes, and associate them *in bulk*.

You should develop administrative policies and standard processes for creating new objects and modifying information in multiple directories and implement scripts in the absence of a directory replication connector between systems. As your organization looks toward future computing technology, using standards-based directory replication connectors will facilitate the mailbox creation and directory synchronization process with less administrative intervention. Messaging system connectors can also support security principles and map properties from one directory to another.

APPENDIX A

Configuring the Dynamic Remote Access Service (RAS) Connector

This appendix details how to configure Microsoft Windows NT Server and Microsoft Exchange Server, implementing an Exchange Server Dynamic RAS Connector over TCP/IP. It also provides troubleshooting steps to isolate configuration issues or breakdowns in the functionality of the underlying components needed by the connector.

Configuring the Dynamic RAS Connector

Microsoft Premier Support has found the following method of configuring the Dynamic RAS Connector to be the most reliable:

1. Confirm that you have selected the correct modem device and port usage options.
2. Confirm that RAS is configured to support TCP/IP for both incoming and outgoing connections.
3. Create a pool of IP addresses for RAS.
4. Confirm Exchange Server is using a static IP address for its network interface card.
5. Confirm DNS is enabled for Windows Name Resolution (WINS).
6. Create or modify the local HOSTS file.
7. Generate a RAS phone book entry.
8. Configure the phone book entry to use only TCP/IP.
9. Configure the phone book entry not to use the remote network as the default gateway.
10. Ensure that the current user name and password are not used for authentication.
11. Create a RAS Connector account in User Manager for domains.
12. Grant the RASCON account dial-in access.
13. Give the RASCON account Exchange Server permissions.

14. Create a RAS MTA transport stack.

15. Create a Dynamic RAS Connector.

16. Create an X.400 custom recipient.

17. Stop and restart services.

18. Send a test message.

Preliminaries

Disable LAN connectivity Computers that run Exchange Server and connect through the Dynamic RAS Connector should not be connected to each other over the LAN: it hinders name resolution. If a LAN connection exists, disable it, and restart the servers to purge any cached connectivity information.

Install latest service pack Update Windows NT Server and Exchange Server with the latest service packs. Specifically, install Service Pack 3 (or later) on Windows NT Server 4.0, and Service Pack 5 on Windows NT Server 3.51.

Install the TCP/IP protocol Exchange Server computers connected dynamically through RAS must have TCP/IP installed and properly configured, as shown in the following steps.

RAS Server Configuration

Step 1: Confirm that you have selected the correct modem device and port usage options.

▶ **Windows NT Server 4.0**

1. In Control Panel, double-click the Network icon, and click the Services tab.

2. Select Remote Access Service and click the Properties button to open the Remote Access Setup window. (If Remote Access Service is not listed, install it by clicking the Add button.)

3. Verify that you have selected the correct COM port and modem device, then click the Configure button, and verify that Port Usage is set to Dial out and Receive calls in the Configure Port Usage window (assuming you want bi-directional connectivity).

▶ **Windows NT Server 3.51**

1. In Control Panel, double-click the Network icon.

2. Under Installed Network Software, select Remote Access Service and click the Configure button. (If the Remote Access Service is not listed, add it.)

3. Verify that the correct COM port is selected, click the Configure button, and verify that the correct modem is selected in the Attached Devices list box of the Configure Port window. Also verify that Port Usage is set to Dial out and Receive calls (assuming you want bi-directional connectivity).

Step 2: Confirm that RAS is configured to support TCP/IP for both incoming and outgoing connections.

▶ **Windows NT Server 4.0**

1. In Control Panel, double-click the Network icon.

2. Click the Services tab, select Remote Access Service, and click the Properties button.

3. Click the Network button, taking you to the Network Configuration window, and verify that TCP/IP is selected under Dial out Protocols.

4. Verify that TCP/IP is also selected under Allow remote clients running.

▶ **Windows NT Server 3.51**

1. In Control Panel, double-click the Network icon.

2. Under Installed Network Software, select Remote Access Service and click the Configure button.

3. Click the Network button and verify that TCP/IP is selected under Dial out Protocols.

4. Verify that TCP/IP is also selected under Allow remote clients running.

Step 3: Create a pool of IP addresses for RAS.

The address pool must contain at least two IP addresses. If your organization uses multiple modem lines, the number of addresses in the pool must be at least one greater than the number of ports. For example, if you use a four-port DigiBoard, you must have at least five addresses in the pool. The local server uses the first address, and the others are assigned to the servers that dial in.

Only the computers at each end of the active RAS connection use the IP addresses you select for address pools. However, these IP addresses should not duplicate any addresses used on the local network. If your organization uses DHCP or another method of assigning IP addresses on the LAN, exclude the RAS pool addresses or keep them outside the scope of normally assigned addresses.

Assign IP addresses for the RAS pool from the same subnet as the network card. For example, the pools for three Exchange Servers connecting through Dynamic RAS can contain the following information.

Server name	Domain	NetCard IP		RAS IP pool
SEATTLE	WASHINGTON	131.107.10.10	4 modems	131.107.10.201 to 131.107.10.205
PORTLAND	OREGON	207.68.151.151	1 modem	207.68.151.201 to 207.68.151.202
DALLAS	TEXAS	204.95.110.110	1 modem	204.95.110.201 to 204.95.110.202

▶ **Windows NT Server 4.0**

1. In **Control Panel**, double-click the **Network** icon.
2. Click the **Services** tab, select **Remote Access Service**, and click the **Properties** button.
3. Click the **Network** button and click the **Configure** button directly to the right of the **TCP/IP** check box. This takes you to the **RAS Server TCP/IP Configuration** window.
4. Select the **Use static address pool** option and type in the **Begin** and **End** values.

▶ **Windows NT Server 3.51**

1. In **Control Panel**, double-click the **Network** icon.
2. Under Installed Network Software, select Remote Access Service, and click the Configure button.
3. Click the **Network** button and then the **Configure** button directly to the right of the **TCP/IP** check box.
4. Select the **Use static address pool** option and type in the **Begin** and **End** values.

TCP/IP Configuration

Step 4: Confirm Exchange Server uses a static IP address for its network interface card.

▶ **Windows NT Server 4.0**

1. In **Control Panel**, double-click the **Network** icon.
2. Click **Protocols**, select the TCP/IP protocol, and click the **Properties** button. This brings up the **Microsoft TCP/IP Properties** window.
3. On the **IP Address** tab, verify that **Specify an IP** address is selected and that the **IP Address** and **Subnet Mask** values have been filled in.

▶ **Windows NT Server 3.51**

1. In **Control Panel**, double-click the **Network** icon.
2. Select the TCP/IP protocol in the **Installed Network Software** section, and click the **Configure** button, taking you to the **TCP/IP Configuration** window.
3. Verify that the **Enable Automatic DHCP Configuration** check box is cleared and that the **IP Address** and **Subnet Mask** values have been filled in.

Step 5: Confirm DNS is enabled for Windows Name Resolution.

Setting this allows the HOSTS file to be used for Windows name resolution.

▶ **Windows NT Server 4.0**

1. In **Control Panel**, double-click the **Network** icon.
2. Click the **Protocols** tab. Select the TCP/IP protocol and click the **Properties** button, which takes you to the **Microsoft TCP/IP Properties** window.
3. Click the **WINS Address** tab and verify that the **Enable DNS for Windows Resolution** check box is selected.

▶ **Windows NT Server 3.51**

1. In **Control Panel**, double-click the **Network** icon.
2. Select the TCP/IP protocol in the **Installed Network Software** section, and click the **Configure** button.
3. Click the Advanced button and verify that the Enable DNS for Windows Name Resolution check box is selected in the Advanced Microsoft TCP/IP Configuration window.

Step 6: Create or modify the local HOSTS file.

Locate the Winnt\System32\Drivers\Etc directory. If the directory already contains a HOSTS file, edit it to include the server names and IP addresses for each Exchange Server you connect with a Dynamic RAS Connector. If there is no HOSTS file, create one. If you're unfamiliar with HOSTS files, take a look at the Hosts.sam sample file provided with Windows NT Server.

Modify the HOSTS file to include the server name and the IP address of the network interface card from the participating Exchange Server computers. In the three-server example cited in Step 3, Seattle's HOSTS file contains these lines:

```
207.68.151.151   PORTLAND
DALLAS
```

Portland's HOSTS file contains:

```
131.107.10.10    SEATTLE
204.95.110.110   DALLAS
```

Dallas' HOSTS file contains:

```
131.107.10.10    SEATTLE
207.68.151.151   PORTLAND
```

Follow these guidelines with HOSTS files:

- Before saving the file, scroll to the bottom of the file and add a few hard returns to create blank lines.

- Save the HOSTS file as a text file, without any extension. (Applications such as Notepad automatically append filenames with .TXT. If you use Notepad to create the file, do not select UNICODE format in the Save As dialog box).

- Make sure the file name HOSTS is spelled correctly (note the need for the final "S").

RAS Client Configuration

Step 7: Generate a RAS phone book entry.

▶ **Windows NT Server 4.0**

1. On the computer running Exchange Server, start Dial-Up Networking

2. On the **Start** menu, point to **Programs**, then **Accessories**, and click **Dial-Up Networking**

3. Create a phone book entry to dial.

4. Type a description and the phone number of the other RAS server.

▶ **Windows NT Server 3.51**

- On the computer running Exchange Server, open the Remote Access program and add a phone book entry containing a description and the phone number of the RAS server (in the **Edit Phone Book Entry** window).

Step 8: Configure the phone book entry to use only TCP/IP.

▶ **Windows NT Server 4.0**

- With **Phone Book Entry** open, click the **More** button, select the **Edit entry and modem properties** option, and then click the **Server** tab of the **Edit Phone Book Entry** window. Of the three network protocols, only **TCP/IP** should be selected.

▶ **Windows NT Server 3.51**

1. In the (**Add** or) **Edit Phone Book Entry** dialog box, click the **Network** icon. If it is not displayed, click the **Advanced** button.

2. After the **Network Protocol Settings** dialog box is displayed, make sure **PPP** is selected and that **TCP/IP** is the only one of the three network selected.

Step 9: Configure phone book entry so that the remote network is not used as the default gateway.

▶ **Windows NT Server 4.0**

1. With **Phone Book Entry** open, click the **More** button, select the **Edit entry and modem properties** option, and then click the **Server** tab.

2. Click the **TCP/IP Settings** button, bringing up the **PPP TCP/IP Settings** dialog box. Make sure the **Use default gateway on remote network** check box is cleared.

▶ **Windows NT Server 3.51**

1. In the (**Add** or) **Edit Phone Book Entry** dialog box, click the **Network** icon. If it is not displayed, then first click the **Advanced** button.

2. After the **Network Protocol Settings** dialog box displays, click the **TCP/IP Settings** button, bringing up the **PPP TCP/IP Settings** dialog.

3. Make sure the **Use default gateway on remote network** check box is cleared.

Step 10: Ensure the current user name and password are not used for authentication.

Windows NT Server RAS services support two authentication mechanisms. The first applies the user's own logon credentials to establish the connection to the remote server. The second uses credentials that the user supplies manually. In Windows NT Server 4.0, the method applied depends on whether the **Use current user name and password** check box is selected. In Windows NT Server 3.51, the method applied depends on whether the **Authenticate using current user name and password** check box is selected.

If the **Use current username and password** (or **Authenticate using current user name and password**) check box is selected, Exchange Server uses the credentials of the local Exchange Server service account. If the local service account has full Administrator permissions within the remote Exchange Server site, authentication works properly. However, the Exchange Server message transfer agent (MTA) requires a duplex communication link between the two systems. This means that the remote MTA also attempts to bind back to the local computer over RPC. To do this, the credentials from the remote system to access the local system must also be present and validated.

If the check box is not selected, authentication credentials are provided when the Exchange Server MTA attempts to connect to the remote server over RAS. At that time, the local MTA uses the account information provided in the RAS Override dialog box of the RAS Connector. The information supplied here must be an authorized account in the remote system that can both log on to the remote system over RAS and access the Exchange Server directory database with full permissions.

▶ **Windows NT Server 4.0**

1. In the Edit Phone Book Entry dialog box, click the Security tab. Select Accept only Microsoft encrypted authentication.

2. Make sure the **Use current username and password** check box is *not* selected. This allows the information from the RAS Connector Override page to be passed to the other system as the connector's security credentials.

▶ **Windows NT Server 3.51**

- In the (Add or) Edit Phone Book Entry dialog box, make sure the Authenticate using current user name and password check box is not selected.

Configuring the Override Account

Step 11: Create a RAS Connector account in User Manager for domains.

Open User Manager for domains and create an account that the other servers' RAS Connectors will use. Provide the *identical* user name and password (case sensitive) on each domain. In the three-server example above, you would create these accounts:

Domain	UserName	Password
WASHINGTON	RASCON	ras
OREGON	RASCON	ras
TEXAS	RASCON	ras

Step 12: Grant the RASCON account dial-in access.

▶ **Windows NT Server 4.0**

1. In User Manager for Domains, open the User Properties for the RAS Connector (RASCON) account.

2. Click the **Dialin** button to go to the **Dialin Information** window, and make sure the **Grant dialin permission to user** check box is selected.

▶ **Windows NT Server 3.51**

1. Open the Remote Access Administrator program.

2. On the **Users** menu, click **Permissions**, taking you to the **Remote Access Permissions** dialog.

3. Select the RAS Connector (RASCON) account and select the **Grant dialin permission to user** check box.

Step 13: Give the RASCON account Microsoft Exchange Server permissions.

1. Open the Microsoft Exchange Administrator program.

2. Select your server name in the left pane (*OrgName*/*SiteName*/Configuration /Servers/*ServerName*).

3. On the **File** menu, click **Properties**.

4. Click the **Permissions** tab, and add the RASCON account with a role of Service Account Admin. Granting only a User, Admin, or Permission Admin role on the server object will *not* work.

If you don't see a **Permissions** tab when you click **Properties** on the **File** menu, you need to do one of the following:

- Log on with an account that has either a Permissions Admin or a Service Account Admin role in Exchange Server.

  – Or –

  On the Microsoft Exchange Administrator **Tools** menu, click **Options**, then the **Permissions** tab, and select the **Show Permissions page for all objects** and the **Display rights for roles on Permissions page** check boxes.

Now you should be able to perform Step 13.

RAS Connector Configuration

Step 14: Create a RAS MTA transport stack.

(See the *Microsoft Exchange Server Administrator's Guide* for more information.)

1. In the Exchange Administrator program, click **New Other** on the **File** menu. Select **MTA Transport Stack**.

2. In the **Type** dialog box, select **RAS MTA Transport Stack** and in the **Server** dialog box select the Microsoft Exchange Server where RAS is installed.

3. Click **OK**. When the RAS MTA Transport Stack property pages display, click **OK** to finish. No additional configuration is needed.

Step 15: Create a Dynamic RAS Connector.

(For more information, see *the Microsoft Exchange Server Administrator's Guide*.)

1. In the Microsoft Exchange Administrator program, click **New Other** on the **File** menu.

2. Choose **Dynamic RAS Connector**. If prompted to switch to the Connections container, click **OK**.

3. Fill in the various property pages as needed (in the **RAS Connector to** *ServerName* **Properties** window), following the instructions below.

Note Unless you need to fill in a field, leave it blank or leave in the default value.

- **General** tab

  The contents of the Remote Server Name box must match exactly (including case) the Local MTA name of the other server (Message Transfer Agent Properties page). To display this on the other server, open the property pages on the OrgName/SiteName/Configuration/Servers/ServerName/Message Transfer Agent object. You can find the Local MTA name on the General tab.

The Local MTA name is the same as the Windows NT Server name by default and is in all uppercase letters.

- **RAS Override** tab

Under Connect as, type the information for the other domain's RAS Connector (RASCON) account that you created earlier. Use uppercase letters for the user name and domain name.

- **Address Space** tab

Leave this blank for most configurations and use the Connected Sites tab instead.

- **Connected Sites** tab

Click the New button and add the organization and site information from the other Exchange Server computer to the General tab (SiteName Properties window).

Click the Routing Address tab. All the boxes should match the X.400 e-mail address information from the other server exactly (including case, spaces, and so forth). To view this on the other server, open the OrgName/SiteName /Configuration/Site Addressing object's properties, select the Site Addressing tab, then the X.400 e-mail address, and click the Edit button.

Some of the characters in an Exchange Server organization or site name may not be valid in an X.400 address. Question marks ("?") appear in their place. Do not confuse an Exchange Server organization name with the X.400 organization (o). A typical X.400 address in Exchange Server looks like this:

```
c=US;a= p=ExchangeOrgName;o=ExchangSiteName;s=LastName;g=FirstName
```

If the other site has modified display names of the organization or sites, that administrator must open the properties of each object and give you the directory names. Usually the names are the same, but if not, use directory names in the connected site's configuration. Names must match exactly, including case, spaces, and special characters.

Testing Configuration

Step 16: Create an X.400 custom recipient.

Create a new custom recipient with an X.400 address type on your server for one of the mailboxes on the other computer running Exchange Server. You will use two custom recipients (one on each of the computers running Exchange Server) to test the RAS Connector.

Caution: Do not add a Directory Replication Connector until mail capabilities have been fully confirmed.

If the RAS Connector is not working, the Directory Replication Connector quickly clogs the queue and error logs. Also, you can get directory replication to work only if both sites have the identical organization names.

If you do not find a Site Addressing object or the **New Custom Recipient** menu option and **E-mail Addresses** tab needed in the next procedure, you must install the Microsoft Mail Connector, the X.400 Connector, or the Internet Mail Connector. After that, you can immediately remove it if you want. Installing any of these components makes changes to the server that persist even if you remove the components.

▶ **To create a correctly addressed custom recipient, do the following:**

1. Start the Exchange Administrator program on both Server1 and Server2.
2. On Server1, click **New Custom Recipient** on the **File** menu.
3. If prompted to select the correct container, click **OK**.
4. Select **X.400 Address** and click **OK**.
5. On Server2, select a local mailbox in either the global address list or the recipients containers, click **Properties** on the **File** menu.
6. Click the E-mail Addresses tab.
7. Select the X.400 e-mail address and click the **Edit** button.
8. On Server1, type the information in each box exactly as it is displayed on Server2 (including case and spacing). Watch for a space in the **ADMD (a)** box of Server2. If the **ADMD (a)** text box appears blank, it probably contains a space. You can check by moving the cursor to the text box and using the LEFT ARROW and RIGHT ARROW keys to move within the box. Server1's address must exactly match Server2's mailbox.
9. When you have finished filling out all boxes on Server1, click **OK**.
10. You are presented with a set of property pages similar to what you see when you create a new mailbox. Fill in at least the **Display** and **Alias** boxes. The display name and alias you choose at this point can be whatever you want. They can match the information from Server2, but they do not have to. After you have filled in the boxes, click **OK**.

You have now created a custom recipient on Server1 for a mailbox on Server2. To allow for testing in both directions, repeat Steps **a** through **j** above, switching Server1 and Server2.

Step 17: Stop and restart services.

Stop and restart the Exchange Server MTA if you have added or modified a transport stack or connector.

If you have made changes to TCP/IP or RAS, you should also stop and restart the RAS service or restart the server.

Step 18: Send a test message.

Send a test message to the custom recipient created above to confirm that the RAS Connector works. If messages can be successfully sent in both directions, the RAS Connector installation is finished. If mail cannot be sent in one or both directions, move on to the Troubleshooting section below.

Troubleshooting

The troubleshooting steps below are presented in four phases, from the most basic to the most complex. Most reported problems with the Exchange Server Dynamic RAS Connector are caused by a basic configuration issue, a failure in the RAS connectivity, or an underlying problem with network functionality over RAS (especially name resolution or RPC problems). Most reported failed connections show these symptoms:

- Local modem dials and connects to the remote modem.
- Some data is exchanged, but then the modem hangs up.
- This pattern repeats over and over.
- No e-mail is sent.

When you have gone through the troubleshooting steps in phases 2 and 3, but have been unable to resolve the problem, proceed to Phase 4, which provides steps to try before you escalate the problem to Microsoft Support.

Phase 1: Initial Troubleshooting

1. Walk through the step-by-step Configuring Dynamic RAS Connector method and double-check everything in the order listed. Look for steps you missed, values or strings you entered incorrectly, and so forth.

2. Remotely access Server2 from Server1 directly using either dial-up networking or the RAS client to test whether you have basic RAS functionality, outside Exchange.

   If you do not, then review your RAS and Windows NT configuration. If the modem dials, but cannot connect to the other modem, turn up PPP logging. You can enable the PPP.LOG file by setting the following registry entry to a value of 1.

   ```
   HKEY_LOCAL_MACHINE\SYSTEM\CurrentControlSet\Services\RasMan
   \PPP\Logging: 1
   ```

3. Check the *RemoteListen* parameter setting under the following registry key:

   ```
   HKEY_LOCAL_MACHINE\SYSTEM\CurrentControlSet\Services \RemoteAccess
   \Parameters\NetbiosGateway
   ```

It should be set to 2. A value of 0 or 1 indicates that after the Exchange RAS MTA Transport stack was added something unusual occurred, such as the removal or re-installation of the RAS server. You can try simply resetting the value to 2, but given the unknowns in this situation, you might need to remove and reinstall the Exchange RAS Connector and RAS MTA Transport stack as well.

4. If you attempt to send a message, but quickly receive a non-delivery report (NDR) before the server even attempts to dial, there is likely an addressing problem on the local server. Double-check the exact spelling in all text boxes in the custom recipient, and on the connector's **Connected Sites** tab. (Verify any addresses on the **Address Space** tab.)

5. If the server does connect to the other server, but you get an NDR, carefully read the NDR to determine if it originated from your server or the other server.

   If it comes from the other server, the recipient may not exist on the other server or there may be a spelling or typing error in the custom recipient entry.

   If the NDR comes from your server, it could indicate too many failed connection attempts or that the message was deleted from the queue through the Exchange Administrator program. If so, send a new test message.

Phase 2: Troubleshooting Basic Network Functionality over RAS

1. Connect from Server1 to Server2 using the same phone book entry the RAS Connector uses.

   Be sure to use the same account and password used on the **RAS Override** tab to connect.

   If you first log on locally to both servers with the RASCON account, you won't have to specify the security context in Step 4 (of this phase). You will also be able to use the **Run with Security** check box while testing RPC in Step 8.

   To log on as RASCON, you first have to give the account permissions to log on locally using User Manager for Domains. Click **User Rights** on the **Policies** menu, select **Log on locally** from the **Rights** list, and add the RASCON account.

2. Check the IP addresses Server2 supplied to Server1 for the connection.

   If Server2 (the server receiving the call and assigning the IP addresses from its static pool) has only one modem and two addresses in its pool, the IP address assigned to Server1 for this connection will be the second address in Server2's pool. If Server2 has more than one modem or two addresses in its pool, you need to verify the assigned address.

- Windows NT Server 4.0

  From Server1 (dialing server), double-click the Dial-Up Network Monitor icon on the right side (or bottom) of the taskbar. In the Dial-Up Networking Monitor dialog box, click the Details button on either the Status or the Summary tab. The IP address displayed is the one that Server2 (dialed server) assigned to Server1 from its static IP address pool for the connection.

- Windows NT Server 3.51

  From Server1 (dialing server), open the Remote Access client and click the Status button on the right side of the toolbar. The IP address displayed near the bottom of the Port Status dialog box is the one Server2 (dialed server) assigned to Server1 from its static IP address pool for the connection.

3. Ping IP addresses in both directions over the RAS connection.

- From Server1 (dialing server), ping the first IP address in Server2's pool.

- From Server1, ping Server2's network card IP address.

- From Server1, ping Server2 by its server name.

- From Server2, ping the IP address assigned to Server1 for this connection (from Server2's pool).

Pinging Server1's network card IP or host name will not work from the RAS server to the RAS client.

With the three-server example, if Seattle called Portland, send the following pings:

```
From Seattle:
PING 207.68.151.201          (RAS Pool IP)
PING 207.68.151.151          (NetCard IP)
PING PORTLAND                (Host Name)
From Portland:
PING 207.68.151.202          (RAS Pool IP)
```

4. Carry out a **net use** command from Server1 to connect to IPC$ on Server2. This establishes the proper security context to the other server's domain.

   net use *target_server***\ipc$ /user:***domain******user_name user_password*

   In the three-server example, if Seattle (Server1) connected to Portland (Server2), the command issued on the Seattle server would be:

   net use \\portland\ipc$ /user:oregon\rascon ras

Be sure to allow the command to complete successfully or to give a specific error message.

If there is any failure at this point, carefully check your command line syntax, server name, domain name, RAS Connector account name, and password (including case). Then check the security information for the RAS Connector account on the other domain.

If you receive this message:

```
System error 53 has occurred
```

followed by:

```
The network path was not found
```

and you were able to ping successfully by host name, then there is either a misspelling or the "Confirm DNS is enable for Windows Name Resolution" step (described earlier in this appendix) was not performed.

5. Carry out a **net use** command in the other direction (from Server2 to Server1), using the IP address that was assigned from the Server2's pool (see Step 2 in this phase).

   This works only if Server2 operates on Windows NT Server 4.0. The Windows NT Server 3.51 object manager doesn't support device lookup by IP address. If Server2 uses Windows NT Server 3.51, skip this step.

   If Seattle (Server1) connected to Portland (Server2), use this command on the Portland server:

   net use \\207.68.151.202\ipc$ /user:washington\rascon ras

   Allow the command to complete successfully or to give a specific error message.

   If there is any failure at this point, carefully check the command line syntax, IP address, domain name, RAS Connector account name, and password (including case). Then check the security information for the RAS Connector account on the other domain.

6. Carry out a **net view** command from Server1 to view the shares on Server2:

   net view server2

   When Server1 initiates the RAS call, Server 2 supplies the IP addresses. Server1 should have an entry in its HOSTS file that allows it to resolve Server2's name to an IP address so the standard **net view** *servername* command works.

   If Seattle (Server1) connected to Portland (Server2), use this command on the Seattle server:

   net view portland

If name resolution works, you should see a list of the shares on the other server (Portland).

7. Carry out a **net view** command in the other direction (from Server2 to Server1), using the IP address assigned from Server2's pool (see Step 2).

The **net view** command only works if Server2 operates on Windows NT Server 4.0. The Windows NT Server 3.51 object manager doesn't support device lookup by IP address. If Server2 uses Windows NT Server 3.51, skip this step.

Because Server1 acts as a RAS client and not a RAS server, the HOSTS entry that Server2 has for Server1 will not work. That entry is based on an IP address from the RAS pool on Server1, which is not used when Server1 is in the role of a client. As a result, a **net view** *servername* command does not work. However, in Windows NT Server 4.0, you can still test functionality by performing a **net view** command directly on the IP address.

If Seattle (Server1) connected to Portland (Server2), the command issued on the Portland server would be:

net view 207.68.151.202

If name resolution works, you should see a list of the shares on the other server (Seattle).

The **net use** in Step 5 and the **net view** in Step 7 mimic closely what happens when the MTA over RAS attempts a Bindback (the most common potential problem area).

8. Perform RPC Ping tests in both directions over the established connection. Be sure to configure the client half to use the TCP/IP protocol sequence. If you have logged on to both servers as the RASCON account (suggested in Step 1), select the **Run with Security** check box. If your test fails with Security selected, try again without it, clearing the check box.

The RPC Ping utility and documentation is on the Exchange Server CD-ROM.

- Run RPINGC32.EXE on Server1 and RPINGS.EXE on Server2, and ping Server2 by name.

- Run RPINGS.EXE on Server1 and RPINGC32.EXE on Server2, and ping Server1 by IP.

If the RPC Ping client does not report successful pings, there may be a problem with RPC.

In this example, with Seattle connecting to Portland, Seattle sends RPC ping messages to the server PORTLAND, and Portland sends RPC ping messages to server IP address 207.68.151.202.

Only Windows NT 4.0 supports sending RPC Ping messages by IP address.

9. Hang up the connection and connect Server2 to Server1, using the same phone book entry that you set the RAS Connector to use.

10. Repeat Steps 2 through 8 over the new connection.

If you complete all the steps in Phase 2 troubleshooting and have problems with connections in either direction, there could be underlying Windows NT Server problems that you must correct before continuing with Exchange Dynamic RAS Connector configuration.

Phase 3: Intermediate Troubleshooting

1. If no problems were uncovered in Phase 2, go to the Exchange Server MTAs on both servers and increase the logging for the X.400 Services and Field Engineering categories to Maximum. Log another failed connection.

2. Check the system logs on both servers for any reported RAS errors or warnings and the application logs on both servers for Exchange Server errors or warnings. Check the details of any Exchange Server errors for embedded Windows NT Server or RAS errors. The MSExchangeMTA 9311 Field Engineering event, in particular, often contains useful embedded RAS errors, such as a 9311 warning from the application log:

```
Source: MSExchangeMTA
Category: Field Engineering
Type: Warning
Event ID: 9311

Description: A RAS communications error has occurred for gateway
/o=MS/ou=PSS/cn=Configuration/cn=Connections/cn=DR. RAS error code
returned: 718. RAS Table index: 0. The MTA will attempt to recover
the RAS connection. [BASE IL PIPE RAS 35 230] (12)
```

The RAS error code embedded in bold letters above is documented in the RASPHONE.HLP file. To find the RAS error messages, open the Help file, click the **Find** tab, and search for "Error Messages." The Help file states that the RAS 718 error is a PPP time-out error:

```
A PPP conversation was started, but was terminated because the remote
computer did not respond within an appropriate time. This can be
caused by poor line quality or by a problem at the server.
```

Embedded RAS codes along with the error messages in the RAS Help file are useful tools in identifying initial problems.

If you encounter Event ID 9316, double-check the remote server name field on the RAS Connector's **General** tab (including case) and verify the information on the **RAS Override** tab.

```
Source: MSExchangeMTA
Category: Interface
Type: Warning
Event ID: 9316
```

```
Description: An RPC communications error occurred. No data was sent
over the RPC connection. Locality table (LTAB) index: <x>. Windows NT
error: 9301. The MTA will attempt to recover the RPC connection.
[BASE IL PIPE RAS xxxxx] (12)
```

3. Confirm that both modems are on the Windows NT Hardware Compatibility List and have modem scripts that were included with Windows NT Server, or that they are the most recent scripts from the manufacturer.

4. If the modem is a higher-speed modem, try using the generic Hayes-compatible 9600 script instead.

5. Disable any software (in the phone book entry) or hardware compression and retest.

Phase 4: Steps Before Escalating to Microsoft Support

1. Clear the application and system logs.

2. Start a Network Monitor trace.

▶ **To capture a trace over RAS with Network Monitor:**

1. Locate Network Monitor, found on the Microsoft Systems Management Server disks (or compact discs). Premier customers can get a dated copy directly from Microsoft Premier Support.

2. Run the Setup program and install Network Monitor on one of the computers running Exchange Server.

3. Open Network Monitor and click **Networks** on the **Capture** menu.

4. Select the network with the Current Address beginning with 5241 or 000000 and click **OK.**

5. On the **Capture** menu, click **Start**.

6. Perform a RAS Connector test. (You should see activity in Network Monitor at this point.)

7. On the **Capture** menu, click **Stop**.

8. Save a *.CAP file by clicking **Save As** on the **File** menu.

3. Send a test message (while X.400 Service and Field Engineering are still logging at Maximum).

4. Perform an Admin Dump:

1. Open the Exchange Administrator program in raw mode by typing:
   c:\exchsrvr\bin\admin /r

2. If a C:\Exchsrvr\Bin\Admindmp.txt file exists, delete or rename it.

3. Select the object you want to dump the raw properties from (in this case, the RAS Connector object).

4. Press and hold down the CTRL key.

5. On the **File** menu, click **Raw Properties**.

6. Release the CTRL key after the raw properties are displayed.

7. Click **Cancel** to exit the **Raw Properties** dialog box.

8. Rename the newly created ADMINDMP.TXT file to match the object it was dumped from. (Each new dump re-creates or appends to an existing ADMINDMP.TXT file.)

9. Quit the Exchange Administrator program.

5. Collect the following seven files (preferably zipped into one file).

- Server1 application log
- Server1 system log
- Server2 application log
- Server2 system log
- Network Monitor *.CAP trace of the RAS attempt
- ADMINDMP.TXT file for the RAS Connector object on Server 1
- ADMINDMP.TXT file for the RAS Connector object on Server 2

6. Contact Microsoft Support.

A P P E N D I X   B

Using ShivaRemote with Microsoft Exchange

Users of Microsoft Exchange under Windows 95 or Windows NT operating systems have a built-in underlying transport for remote connectivity: Dial-Up Networking (DUN) and Remote Access Service (RAS), respectively. To provide full remote connectivity for MS-DOS, Windows 3.*x*, and Windows for Workgroups (which doesn't support the Exchange remote APIs), the Exchange Client includes ShivaRemote version 3.59.

This appendix explains how to configure ShivaRemote 3.59.

ShivaRemote for MS-DOS allows for remote mail retrieval, but because the Exchange Client for MS-DOS doesn't support offline operation, the remote connection must be maintained throughout transmission. Exchange communicates with the Shiva dial-up adapter using the standard remote access software APIs, which Shiva supplies through the RASC16.DLL installed in the \Windows\System directory: RASC16.DLL communicates with the CONNAPI.DLL (also installed in the \Windows\System directory), which contains the connection APIs for Shiva.

Note ShivaRemote can connect to any Point-to-Point Protocol (PPP)–compatible server. However, for Exchange and Schedule + operation, ShivaRemote is supported only when connecting to a Windows NT RAS server or a Shiva LanRover. Exchange does not support Shiva Remote 4.0 (although it may work if the connection is established first). Exchange can initiate dialing only when configured specifically with ShivaRemote 3.59.

ShivaRemote must be set up and configured differently depending on the operating system and connection protocols; each combination has a section below. For more information (including updated modem scripts for use with ShivaRemote) see Shiva's Web page, **http://www.shiva.com**.

Supported Protocols

Operating System	Desired Protocol for connectivity	Notes	KnowledgeBase Article(s)
DOS	NetBEUI	Not Supported	
	IPX	Real mode IPX (obtain from Novell)	ID: Q158074
	TCP/IP	LanMan TCP/IP (Install from Windows NT 3.51 Server CD)	ID: Q157740
Windows 3.1x	NetBEUI	LanMan NetBEUI (Install from Windows NT 3.51 Server CD)	ID: Q158095
	IPX	Real Mode IPX (obtain from Novell)	ID: Q158077
	TCP/IP	LanMan TCP/IP (Install from Windows NT 3.51 Server CD) or a 3rd Party TCP stack - see Shiva's confighlp file installed with Shiva for setup information	ID: Q159904
Windows for Workgroups 3.11	NetBEUI	NetBEUI (from WFW 3.11)	ID: Q158111
	IPX	WFW IPX not supported, Real mode IPX setup per ID: Q158077	ID: Q158077 (for real mode IPX ONLY)
	TCP/IP	TCP/IP (3.11B for WFW 3.11)	ID: Q158111

With Exchange—RAS Server

Summary

ShivaRemote software can be used with an Exchange Client to allow users remote access to an Exchange Server (using either a Windows NT RAS Server or Shiva LanRover). This section discusses the server settings necessary to connect an Exchange Client over Shiva.

Note   Shiva version 3.59 connects to any PPP dial-up server, but an Exchange Client over a ShivaRemote connection is supported only when it dials in to either a Shiva LanRover or a Windows NT RAS Server.

Setup

Before testing ShivaRemote from a client computer, it is a good idea to make sure the RAS server is fully functional by test dialing into it from either a Windows NT Workstation (with RAS) or from a Windows 95 client (with DUN). You may also need updated modem scripts for Windows NT, depending on which modems the server and client computers use. If you are unable to connect from Windows 95 or Windows NT, see the Microsoft Knowledge Base for information on setting up RAS under Windows NT or contact Windows NT Product Support for assistance.

For an Exchange Client to connect properly over ShivaRemote through a Windows NT RAS Server, you must:

1. Grant access to all remote users using the Remote Access Admin utility. To do this, start the utility from the **Remote Access** program group, click **Permissions** on the **Users** menu, select each user you want to have dial-in capabilities, and check the **Grant Dial-in Permission to User** checkbox.

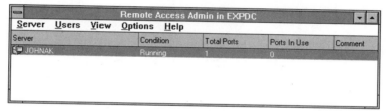

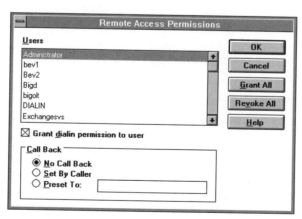

2. Verify that **Require Microsoft Encrypted Authentication** is cleared in the Network Configuration of Windows NT RAS:

A. Open Control Panel.

B. Double-click the Network icon.

C. Click the **Services** tab.

D. Select **Remote Access Service**.

E. Click the **Properties** button.

F. Click the **Network** button.

You can select either of two alternatives:

- Select **Any Authentication Including Clear Text**.

- Select **Encrypted Authentication**.

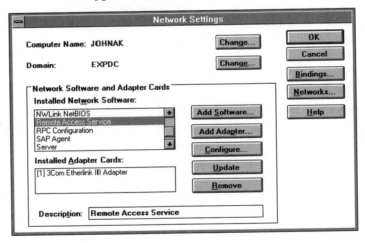

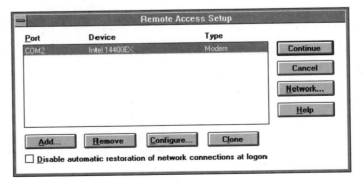

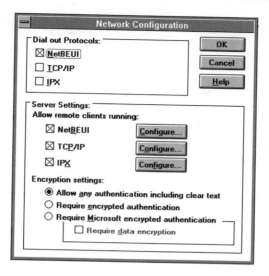

If you select **Require Microsoft Encrypted Authentication**, you receive this error message when you attempt to connect:

```
Unable to negotiate LCP connection. Please check that remote device
is installed and configured, and that dial-in is enabled.
```

3. Ensure that the Windows NT account does **not** have **User Must Change Password at Next Logon** selected.

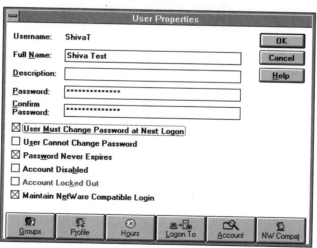

4. If you want to use IPX as the protocol for connectivity over ShivaRemote, you must configure either Microsoft File and Print Services for NetWare (FPNW) or a NetWare server to respond to the find_nearest_server query. For FPNW, this option is set through control panel/FPNW, respond to Find_Nearest_Server request.

```
┌─────────────────────────────────────────────────────────────┐
│ ─  │     File and Print Services for NetWare on JOHNAK        │
├─────────────────────────────────────────────────────────────┤
│ ┌─File Server Information─────────────────────┐  ┌─────────┐ │
│ │ Software Version:    File and Print Services │  │   OK    │ │
│ │                      for NetWare v3.51       │  └─────────┘ │
│ │ Connections Supported:              10000    │  ┌─────────┐ │
│ │ Connections In Use:                     1    │  │ Cancel  │ │
│ │ Available Volumes:                      1    │  └─────────┘ │
│ │ Number of Users:                        0    │  ┌─────────┐ │
│ │ Number of Open Files:                   0    │  │  Help   │ │
│ │ Number of File Locks:                   0    │  └─────────┘ │
│ │ Network Address:                69930DD3     │              │
│ │ Node Address:                000000000001    │              │
│ └──────────────────────────────────────────────┘             │
│                                                               │
│ FPNW Server Name:        JOHNAK_FPNW                          │
│ Description:             ┌────────────────────────────┐       │
│ Home directory root path: SYS:                               │
│ Default queue:          ┌────────────────────────┐ ▼│        │
│ ☒ Allow new users to login                                   │
│ ☒ Respond to Find_Nearest_Server requests                    │
│        ┌────────┐  ┌────────┐  ┌────────┐                     │
│        │ Users  │  │Volumes │  │ Files  │                     │
│        └────────┘  └────────┘  └────────┘                     │
└─────────────────────────────────────────────────────────────┘
```

5. ShivaRemote 3.59 requires that a local account be granted dial-in access (version 3.59 does not understand domains). A RAS Server PDC or BDC is recommended.

If the RAS Server is not a PDC or BDC, you must grant dial-in access to a local account on it. To do this, start the User Manager for Domains, create a local account with the same username and password as the domain account, double-click on the user, click on the **Dial-in** tab, and select the **Grant Dial-in Permissions to User** checkbox.

A Windows NT computer set up as a PDC or BDC has only one set of accounts—its *local* accounts are also its *domain* accounts; a Windows NT Server computer maintains local and domain accounts as separate accounts. Because of this, you should set up the Windows NT RAS Server as a PDC or BDC.

With Exchange (MS-DOS/real-mode IPX)

Summary

With Exchange Clients for MS-DOS, ShivaRemote allows remote access of Exchange Servers, using either a Windows NT RAS server or a Shiva LanRover. This section shows how to install and configure the ShivaRemote software that ships with Exchange to work over IPX.

When you use ShivaRemote, you must run CONNECT.EXE from the Exchange Client directory, establish the remote connection, and then start the Exchange

Client. This is necessary because the Exchange Client for MS-DOS has no built-in remote functionality, so there is no way to download only the message headers.

Installing the Software

The MS-DOS version of ShivaRemote has no setup program, but you can install it while you are installing the Exchange Client for MS-DOS. If you do not install it then and want to install it later, you must reinstall the Exchange Client for MS-DOS. For MS-DOS, all ShivaRemote files are copied into the Exchange Client directory.

▶   **To configure Shiva for dial-in:**

1. Configure (you must do it manually) your AUTOEXEC.BAT, CONFIG.SYS, and NET.CFG files as follows:

   CONFIG.SYS

   ```
   device=c:\dos\setver.exe
   device=c:\dos\himem.sys
   device=c:\dos\emm386.exe noems
   shell=c:\dos\command.com /p
   dos=high,umb
   lastdrive=z
   ```

   AUTOEXEC.BAT

   ```
   c:\<path>\lsl.com
   c:\exchange_dir\dialodi.exe
   c:\<path>\ipxodi
   c:\<path>\vlm (or netx)
   set exchange=c:\exchange_dir
   set RPC_Binding_Order=ncacn_np,ncalrpc,ncacn_spx,netbios
   ```

   NET.CFG (nwclient directory)

   ```
   preferred server=servername
    Link Driver DIALODI
   ```

2. Verify that you don't receive any error messages when you reboot with the newly configured files.

3. Start CONNECT.EXE in the Exchange install directory.

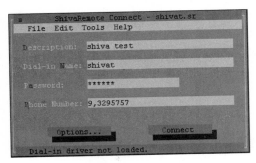

4. Open the **Tools** menu, click **Port Setup**, and select the appropriate modem and communications port.

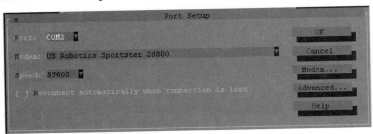

5. Click the **Options** button and verify that the **IPX Enabled** checkbox is the only one selected.

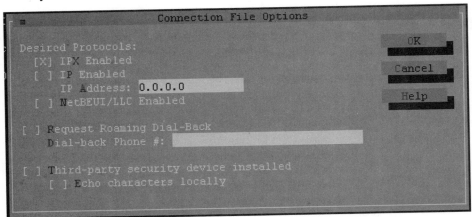

6. Specify a Description, Dial-in-Name (Windows NT account that has been granted dial-in access on the server), Password (Password for the Windows NT Account you are dialing in on), and Phone number. Please note that the account does not necessarily have to be the Exchange Mailbox Primary Windows NT account.

7. Click the **Connect** button to connect to the RAS Server. Exchange supports dial-in connection to Windows NT RAS servers and Shiva LanRovers only.

8. Once connected, exit CONNECT.EXE by clicking **Exit** on the **File** menu. Please note that the connection will be maintained until you restart CONNECT.EXE and click **Disconnect**.

9. Start the Exchange Client for MS-DOS, enter the User Name (Exchange Mailbox Name), the Password (Windows NT Domain Password), and the Domain (Windows NT Domain Name that your account is in).

With Exchange (DOS/LAN Man TCP/IP)

Summary

This section describes the steps required to use ShivaRemote with the Exchange Client for MS-DOS and LAN Manager V2.2c with TCP/IP.

The Exchange Client for MS-DOS does not provide remote functionality, so you must run CONNECT.EXE to establish the connection before starting Exchange or accessing network resources.

This configuration requires optimized memory and will not work if Doublespace or Drvspace are implemented because of their conventional memory requirements. Use the CONFIG.SYS, AUTOEXEC.BAT, and PROTOCOL.INI files listed below as models.

Server Considerations

Configure the Remote Access Server (either Windows NT or a Shiva LanRover) to allow remote clients to request a predetermined IP address. Under Windows NT:

1. Open Control Panel.
2. Double-click the Network icon.
3. Click the Services tab.
4. Select Remote Access Service.
5. Click the Properties button.
6. Click the Network button.
7. Click the Configure button to the right of TCP/IP and select the Allow Remote Clients to Request a Predetermined IP Address checkbox.

Client Configuration

Install LAN Manager V2.2c software on the client computer. This is located on the Windows NT 3.51 Server CD-ROM in Clients\Lanman\Disks\Disk1\Setup.

> **Note** If Microsoft LAN Manager (LAN Man) has already been installed, run SETUP.EXE from the LAN Man installation directory (LANMAN.DOS by default).

1. Configure LAN Man with these options:
    -   TCP/IP (only) bound to the network card driver.
    -   A static IP address, subnet mask, and default gateway.
    -   DHCP disabled.
2. Add entries for the Exchange Server computername and IP address in the HOSTS file. This file is located in the \Lanman.dos\Etc directory.
    -   Username and HostName in the Advanced dialog.
    -   Windows Sockets enabled in Advanced.
    -   Computername, Username, and Domain in the Workstation Settings dialog.
3. Install the Exchange Client for MS-DOS. By default, it installs the ShivaRemote files into the same directory as the Exchange Client.
4. In the CONFIG.SYS file, add this line:

    ```
    DEVICE=C:\EXCHANGE\DIALNDIS.EXE(after DEVICE=...\PROTMAN.DOS
    /i:C:\LANMAN.DOS)
    ```

5. In the CONFIG.SYS file, remark out or remove the line that loads the network card driver.
6. In the \Lanman.dos\Protocol.ini file, make these changes:

    ```
    [TCPIP_XIF]
     BINDINGS = "LAN Card Driver" Remark out this line
     BINDINGS = SDIALIN$ Add this line

    [SDIALIN$] Add this line
    DriverName = SDIALIN$ Add this line
    ```

7. Reboot the computer and press F5 when the "Starting MS-DOS" text is displayed. This bypasses the CONFIG.SYS and AUTOEXEC.BAT files if you are using MS-DOS 6.*xx*.
8. Start CONNECT.EXE in the Exchange Client installation directory to bring up the ShivaRemote Connect window.

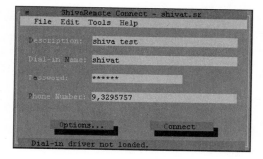

9. Select the **Port Setup** option from the **Tools** menu to configure the modem port. You might receive an Out of Memory message if you attempt to select a port/modem without first booting with F5.

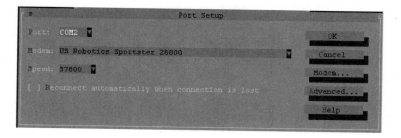

10. Click the **Options** button to select the IP protocol and type the static IP address of the client computer. For more information on creating and saving a connection file, refer to the *ShivaRemote Online Guide*.

11. Save the new connection information and exit the CONNECT.EXE utility.

12. Reboot the computer again. If you receive any errors during startup, resolve them before continuing.

13. Start the Connect utility again, open the connection file you want, and click the **Connect** button. After the connection has been established, exit the Connect program. You should see the message regarding the static IP address. Verify that this is the same IP address that was statically assigned to the client computer.

14. Next, attempt to ping the Exchange Server computer's IP address and host name. The PING.EXE utility is located in the \Lanman.dos\Netprog directory. If pinging the host name fails, but pinging the IP address works, the HOSTS file must be modified (see Step 1 above: Username and HostName in the Advanced dialog). You have to ping the machinename to "prove" that TCP/IP name resolution is working; this step is necessary for the Exchange Client to connect to the Exchange Server.

15. Start the Exchange Client.

To disconnect, either run CONNECT.EXE again and select Disconnect or run "connect /d" at the command line.

Example Configuration Files

CONFIG.SYS

```
device=c:\dos\himem.sys /testmem:off
device=c:\dos\emm386.exe noems
devicehigh=c:\win95\command\drvspace.sys /move
LASTDRIVE=Z
DOS=HIGH,UMB
DEVICEhigh=C:\LANMAN.DOS\DRIVERS\PROTMAN\PROTMAN.DOS /i:C:\LANMAN.DOS
devicehigh=c:\doscln\dialndis.exe
rem DEVICE=C:\LANMAN.DOS\DRIVERS\ETHERNET\DEPCA\DEPCA.DOS
DEVICEhigh=C:\LANMAN.DOS\DRIVERS\PROTOCOL\tcpip\tcpdrv.dos
/i:C:\LANMAN.DOS
DEVICEhigh=C:\LANMAN.DOS\DRIVERS\PROTOCOL\tcpip\nemm.dos
```

AUTOEXEC.BAT

```
@REM ==== LANMAN 2.2a == DO NOT MODIFY BETWEEN THESE LINES == LANMAN
2.2a
SET PATH=C:\LANMAN.DOS\NETPROG;%PATH%
C:\LANMAN.DOS\DRIVERS\PROTOCOL\tcpip\umb.com
NET START WORKSTATION
LOAD TCPIP
SOCKETS
rem NET LOGON shivat *
@REM ==== LANMAN 2.2a == DO NOT MODIFY BETWEEN THESE LINES == LANMAN
2.2a
set EXCHANGE=C:\DOSCLN
set RPC_BINDING_ORDER=ncalrpc,ncacn_np,ncacn_spx,ncacn_ip_tcp,netbios
```

PROTOCOL.INI

```
[PROTMAN]
 DRIVERNAME = PROTMAN$
 DYNAMIC = YES
 PRIORITY = NETBEUI
```

[TCPIP_XIF]

```
 DRIVERNAME = TCPIP$
 IPADDRESS0 = 200 200 200 201
 SUBNETMASK0 = 255 255 255 0
 DEFAULTGATEWAY0 =
 NBSESSIONS = 6
; the following two parameters were added after documentation was
completed
```

```
TCPSEGMENTSIZE = 1450
TCPWINDOWSIZE = 1450
LOAD = tcptsr[c],tinyrfc[c],emsbfr[cr]
UNLOAD = "unloadt /notsr[dc]"
; BINDINGS = "DEPCA_NIF"
BINDINGS = SDIALIN$
NETFILES = C:\LANMAN.DOS\ETC
DISABLEDHCP = 1
LANABASE = 0
```

[SDIALIN$]

```
DRIVERNAME=SDIALIN$
```

[DEPCA_NIF]

```
; PROTOCOL.INI section for the DEC EtherWORKS (MC, LC, Turbo & DEPCA)
Adapters

DriverName = DEPCA$
MaxMulticast = 12
MaxTransmits = 32
AdapterName = DE200
RamAddress = 0xD000
Interrupt = 3
; use Interupt = 5 for turbo board
```

With Exchange (Windows 3.x/LAN Man NetBEUI)

Summary

ShivaRemote software can be used with the Exchange Client to remotely access an Exchange Server (using either a Windows NT RAS server or Shiva LanRover). This section explains how to install and configure the ShivaRemote software that ships with Exchange to work over LAN Man NetBEUI version 2.2c.

Setup

1. Install MS-DOS on the computer.
2. Install Microsoft LAN Manager 2.2 (LAN Man software is located on the Windows NT 3.51 Server CD-ROM in the Clients\Lanman\disks directory).
3. Install Windows 3.1.
4. Install the Exchange Client for Windows 3.x.
5. After Exchange is installed, run the ShivaRemote Setup program from the Exchange program group.

6. When ShivaRemote Setup is complete, restart the computer to install the configuration changes.

7. When the computer restarts, make these changes to CONFIG.SYS and PROTOCOL.INI:

CONFIG.SYS

```
DEVICE=C:\SHIVA\DIALNDIS.EXE <- Add this line.
```

PROTOCOL.INI

Note The name of the NetBEUI section below might vary. The T1 entry specifies the main NetBEUI time-out value; 8000 specifies 8 seconds.

```
[NETBEUI]
; BINDINGS = "UBNEITP_NIF" <- Make this line a comment.
BINDINGS=SDIALIN$ <- Add this line.
T1=8000 <- Add this line.
[SDIALIN$] <- Add this line.
DriverName=SDIALIN$ <- Add this line.
```

8. Your computer should now be configured for ShivaRemote dial-in. Restart your computer again and watch for error messages as the computer starts.

9. You must log on to the network before starting the Exchange Client. If you are not connected to the network when you start the Exchange Client, LAN Manager displays this message:

    You are logged on, but have not been validated by a server. Therefore, you may not have permission to use some network resources.

10. Click **OK** and proceed.

▶ **To configure LAN Manager to prompt you to log on to the network when you start Windows:**

1. Run the LAN Manager Setup program (SETUP.EXE) in the LAN Manager directory (\Lanman.dos).

2. From the Configuration menu, select Workstation Settings.

3. In the **Workstation Settings** dialog box, click **OK**.

4. In the **Support for Windows Environment** dialog box, select **Yes** and click **OK**.

5. In the Windows Directory dialog box, type the directory where Windows is installed (by default, \Windows) and click **OK**.

6. In the **Memory Management** dialog box, choose memory management settings and click **OK**.

7. From the **LAN Manager** menu, click **Exit Setup**.

8. Reboot.

9. You can add the following commands to AUTOEXEC.BAT file (or type them at the MS-DOS prompt):

```
net start workstation
load networking_protocols
net logon username
```

10. After you have done this, reboot and verify that you don't receive any error messages when booting with the new AUTOEXEC.BAT and CONFIG.SYS files.

11. Install the Exchange Client software (run Setup from the Exchange Client CD-ROM or from the network install point). Select **Custom Install** and verify that Shiva is selected. Setup creates a ShivaRemote Setup icon in the Exchange program group.

12. If possible, verify that a valid Exchange mailbox/account exists while connected to the LAN. To do this, start the Exchange Client, create a profile, log on to your mailbox, and send a message to yourself.

13. Run ShivaRemote Setup from the Exchange Program group.

14. Select OK to Install ShivaRemote.

15. Select the port and the specific modem manufacturer/model.

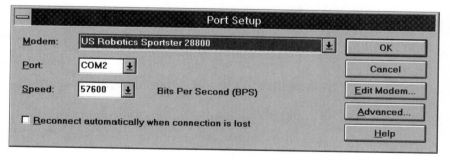

16. Specify a Description, Dial-in Name (Windows NT account that has been granted dial-in access on the server), Password (Password for the Windows NT Account you are dialing in on), and Phone Number.

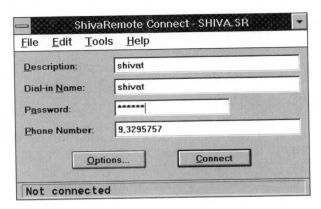

17. Dial the RAS Server (Exchange is supported dialing into either a Windows NT RAS server or a Shiva LanRover).

18. Once connected, minimize ShivaRemote Connect.

19. Start the Exchange Windows 3.*x* client (ONLINE as a test), Enter the User Name (Microsoft Exchange Mailbox Name), the Password (Windows NT Domain Password), the Domain (Windows NT Domain Name that your Account is in), and verify you can be properly logged in.

If these steps allow you to properly send and receive mail, Shiva and Exchange are configured correctly.

You can now configure the Exchange Client remote capabilities (Remote Mail or offline folders).

▶ **To configure the Exchange Client to automatically dial while working offline:**

1. Double-click the **Mail-Fax** icon in the **Control Panel**.

2. Click the **Show Profiles** button.

3. Select the profile.

4. Click the **Properties** button.

5. Select the Microsoft Exchange Server service.

6. Click the **Properties** button.

7. Click the Dial-up Networking tab.

8. Enter the Connection name, the user name, password, and domain name.

9. Click **OK**, click **OK**, and click **Close**.

You can now start the Exchange Client offline and select either remote mail/connect or Sync This Folder. Shiva will dial and transmit necessary information that depends on whether offline folders (.OST) or (.PST) files are being used.

For more information about specific remote options with the Exchange Client, see Knowledge Base article Q139934, Title: XCLN: The Microsoft Exchange Client and Mobile Users.

With Exchange (Windows 3.x/Real-mode IPX)

Summary

You can use ShivaRemote with the Exchange Client for Windows 3.x to allow remote access of Exchange Servers (using dial-in to a Windows NT RAS server or Shiva LanRover). This section explains how to install and configure the ShivaRemote software that ships with Exchange to work under Windows 3.x.

To install ShivaRemote on Windows 3.x, select the ShivaRemote component during the Exchange Client installation. This does not install Shiva: it installs the Shiva Setup program, which you should run from the icon located in the Exchange program group. Setup modifies the AUTOEXEC.BAT, WIN.INI, and SYSTEM.INI files. Next, install and configure ShivaRemote Dial-In Driver and protocols (See Shiva's software configuration notes (CONFIG.HLP) for more information.)

Please note that the ShivaRemote Setup icon added to the Exchange program group adds only the DIAL.386 driver to SYSTEM.INI; some manual steps are necessary. ShivaRemote Setup copies all of its files into the directory in which ShivaRemote is installed, except for VNB.386 and CTL3D.DLL, which are copied to the \Windows\System directory.

Setup

1. Test the modem connection using TERMINAL.EXE to verify that the modem itself is able to dial out and to verify the proper communications port. For more information about using Terminal to test your modem, see Knowledge Base article Q105940, Title: Troubleshooting Serial Port Problems in Windows [win3x].

   Set up your AUTOEXEC.BAT and CONFIG.SYS as follows (**Note:** the Novell client software must be licensed from Novell):

   CONFIG.SYS

   ```
   device=c:\dos\setver.exe
   device=c:\dos\himem.sys
   device=c:\dos\emm386.exe noems
   shell=c:\dos\command.com /p
   dos=high,umb
   lastdrive=z
   ```

   AUTOEXEC.BAT

```
lsl
c:\exchange_dir\dialodi.exe
ipxodi
vlm (or netx)
```

NET.CFG (nwclient directory)

```
preferred server=servername
Link Driver DIALODI
```

Verify that there are no error messages when booting with the newly configured AUTOEXEC.BAT and CONFIG.SYS files.

2. Install the Exchange Client software (run setup from the Exchange Client CD-ROM or from a network install point). Select **Custom** install and verify that Shiva is selected. Setup will create a ShivaRemote Setup icon in the Exchange program group.

3. If possible, verify that a valid Exchange mailbox/account exists while connected to the LAN. To do this, start the Exchange Client, create a profile, log on to your mailbox, and send a message to yourself.

4. Run ShivaRemote Setup from the Exchange program group.

5. Select **OK to Install ShivaRemote**.

6. Select the port and your specific modem manufacturer/model.

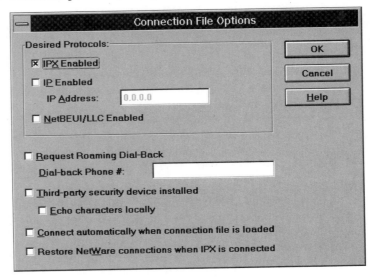

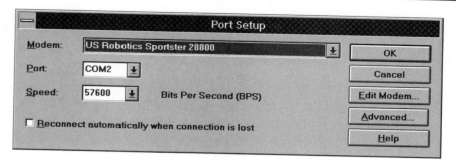

7. Specify a Description, Dial-in-Name (Windows NT account that has been granted dial-in access on the server), Password (Password for the Windows NT Account you are dialing in on), and Phone number.

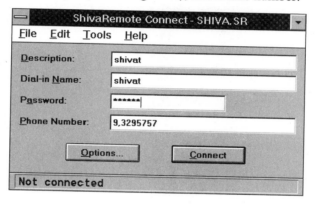

8. Dial the RAS Server (Exchange only supports dialing into either a Windows NT RAS server or a Shiva LanRover).

9. Once connected, minimize ShivaRemote Connect.

10. Start the Exchange Client for Windows 3.*x*, enter the User Name (Microsoft Exchange Mailbox Name), the Password (Windows NT Domain Password), the Domain (Windows NT Domain Name that your Account is in), and verify you can logon properly.

If the above step allows you to properly send and receive mail, Shiva and Exchange are configured correctly.

The Exchange Client remote capabilities can now be configured (remote mail or offline folders).

▶ **To configure the Exchange Client to automatically dial:**

1. Double-click the **Mail-Fax** icon in the **Control Panel**.

2. Click the **Show Profiles** button.

3. Select the profile.

4. Click the **Properties** button.

5. Select the **Microsoft Exchange Server** service.

6. Click the **Properties** button.

7. Click the **Dial-up Networking** tab.

8. Enter the Connection name, the user name, password, and domain name.

9. Click **OK**, click **OK**, and click **Close**.

The Exchange Client can be started offline. Whenever you select remote mail/connect or Sync This Folder, Shiva dials and transmits the information required by the option you select.

For more information about specific remote options with the Exchange Client, please see Knowledge Base article Q139934, Title: XCLN: The Microsoft Exchange Client and Mobile Users.

With Exchange (Windows for Workgroups 3.11/Windows for Workgroups TCP/IP or NetBEUI)

Summary

ShivaRemote software can be used with the Exchange Client to allow full remote mail functionality with Exchange for Windows NT RAS server and Shiva LanRover users. This section explains how to install and configure the ShivaRemote software under Windows for Workgroups 3.11 that ships with Exchange and either Microsoft NetBEUI or Microsoft TCP/IP version 3.11b.

Please note that Windows for Workgroups RAS can be used to access an Exchange Server. However, the remote mail features of Exchange (offline folders and remote mail) cannot be used with Windows for Workgroups RAS (it does not support the APIs necessary for remote mail). Also, if you use Windows for Workgroups RAS, you must connect with it before you start the Exchange Client.

Setup

1. Test the modem connection using TERMINAL.EXE to verify that the modem itself is able to dial out and to verify the proper comm port. For more information about using Terminal to test your modem, please see Knowledge Base article Q105940, Title: Troubleshooting Serial Port Problems in Windows [win3x].

2. Install the Exchange Client software (run Setup from the Exchange Client CD-ROM or from a network install point). Select **Custom** install and verify that the Shiva component is selected. Setup will create a ShivaRemote Setup icon in the Exchange program group.

3. If possible, verify that a valid Exchange mailbox/account exists while connected to the LAN. To do this, start the Exchange Client, create a profile, make sure you can log on to your mailbox, and send a message to yourself.

4. Run ShivaRemote Setup from the Exchange program group.

5. When prompted to Install ShivaRemote Dial-in Software and Update Windows for Workgroups files, select both and click **OK**.

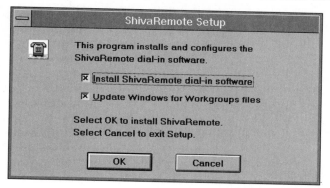

6. Select the port and your specific modem manufacturer/model.

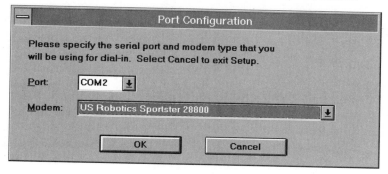

See **http://www.shiva.com/prod/ccl/modemstr.html** for updated scripts for many modems.

7. In the **Protocol Configuration** dialog, select either **Enable NetBEUI** or **Enable IP**, or both, but not **Enable IPX**. The Microsoft IPX/SPX protocol is not compatible with Shiva.

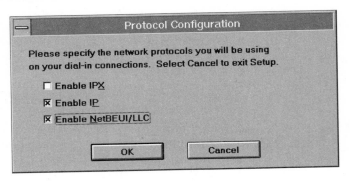

You can install TCP 3.11b from the Windows NT 3.51 Server CD-ROM under Clients/TCP32WFW/netsetup.

8. Configuration files will be changed (backups are saved).

9. Click **OK** for each.

10. Click **OK** for the message explaining to configure your network.

11. Click **No** to rebooting.

12. Add the Shiva Remote Dial In Adapter to Windows for Workgroups.

    A. Open the Network program group in Windows for Workgroups.

    B. Click the **Network Setup** icon, click the **Drivers** button, and then click the **Add Adapter button**.

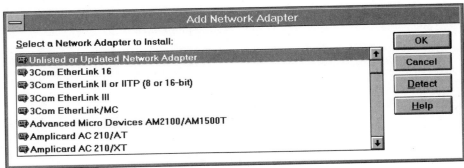

    C. Select Unlisted or Updated Network Adapter and click OK.

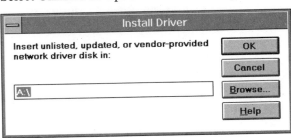

D. Click **Browse** and change to the directory where the Exchange Client was installed.

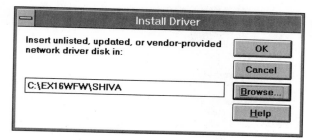

E. Select the Shiva subdirectory and click **OK**.

F. Click **OK** in the **Install Driver** dialog. ShivaRemote Dial-in Driver should then be an option under Network Adapters.

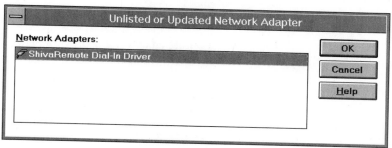

G. Click **OK** and then click **Close**. You can safely remove IPX/SPX as a protocol and leave only NetBEUI. Click **OK**.

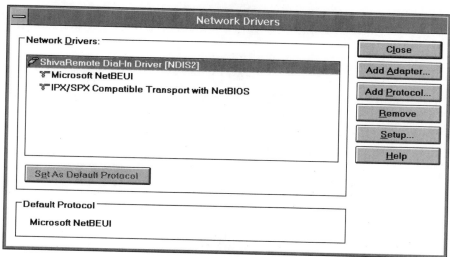

H. In the dialog that states "The files for enhanced mode protocol manager and currently installed on your computer," click **Yes to All**.

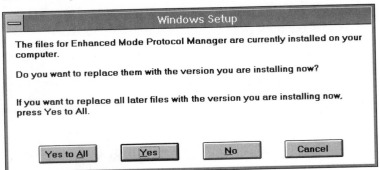

I. When prompted to insert the appropriate Windows for Workgroups disks, do so.

J. When prompted to insert the ShivaRemote Dial-In Software Disk or a disk with the updated or vendor-provided DIALNDIS.EXE file in, click the **Browse** button, change to the directory where you installed Exchange, and click **OK**.

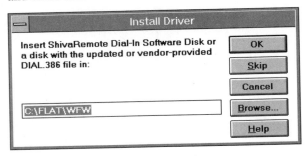

K. Click **OK**.

L. Click Restart Computer.

13. Verify that the NDIS2SUP.386 and NETBEUI.386 files are properly extracted from the Exchange CAB files during setup. The correct dates and sizes should be:

```
NDIS2SUP.386 dated 3/4/96, size 23736
NETBEUI.386 dated 3/4/96, size 37043
```

Note If these files are not updated by Shiva, Windows for Workgroups appears to hang for about two minutes when booting.

---

14. To manually extract the above files, from the Eng\Win16 directory on the Exchange Client CD-ROM run the following commands, where windows_dir is your Windows for Workgroups directory:

```
extract /a /l c:\windows_dir\system exchng1.cab netbeui.386
extract /a /l c:\windows_dir\system exchng1.cab ndis2sup.386
```

If you prefer, you can use Cabview or another extraction utility instead.

Note EXTRACT.EXE is not on the Exchange CD-ROMs. You will have to copy EXTRACT.EXE either from a Windows 95 or a Microsoft Office installation.

---

15. After you have finished this, reboot the computer and verify that you don't receive any error messages when booting with the new AUTOEXEC.BAT and CONFIG.SYS files.

16. Specify a Description, Dial-in Name (Windows NT account that has been granted dial-in access on the server), Password (Password for the Windows NT Account you are dialing in on), and Phone Number in the Shiva connect utility.

17. Connect to the RAS Server (Exchange is supports dialing into either a Windows NT RAS server or a Shiva LanRover).

18. Once connected, minimize ShivaRemote Connect.

19. Before you start Exchange, verify that the Shiva connection is providing network access—try to connect to a network share on the Exchange Server from File Manager (if using NetBEUI) or try to ping the machine name of the Exchange Server (if using TCP).

20. If using TCP/IP, edit the local HOSTS file and add the Exchange Server name and IP address. For more information on the HOSTS file, see Microsoft Knowledge Base article Q105997, Title: Differences Between the HOSTS and LMHOSTS Files in Windows NT [Winnt].

21. Start the Exchange Client for Windows 3.*x* (ONLINE as a test), enter the User Name (Microsoft Exchange Mailbox Name), the Password (Windows NT Domain Password), the Domain (Windows NT Domain Name of your Mailbox Account), and verify that you can properly log on to Exchange and send a message to yourself.

If the above steps allow you to properly send/receive mail, Shiva and Exchange are configured correctly.

You can now configure the Exchange Client remote capabilities (remote mail or offline folders).

▶ **To configure the Exchange Client to automatically dial while working offline**

1. Double-click the **Mail**-Fax icon in the **Control Panel**.
2. Click the **Show Profiles** button.
3. Select the profile.
4. Click the **Properties** button.
5. Select the Microsoft Exchange Server service.
6. Click the **Properties** button.
7. Click the Dial-up Networking tab.
8. Enter the Connection name, the user name, password, and domain name.
9. Click **OK**, click **OK**, and click **Close**.

The Exchange Client can be started offline. When you select remote mail/connect or Sync This Folder, Shiva dials and transmits the information required for offline folders (.OST) or (.PST) files.

For more information about specific remote options with the Microsoft Exchange Client, see Knowledge Base article Q139934, Title: XCLN: The Microsoft Exchange Client and Mobile Users.

ShivaRemote Error Messages

Error: Warning: Your IPX number changed during connection. The IPX protocol will no longer function properly. Please exit Windows, reload your IPX software, then restart Windows

Resolution: The IPX network number assigned to your computer changed while you were connected to the remote access server. This can happen if you dial in to two different remote networks in one session without restarting your computer between connections.

If you are using the Novell NetWare VLMs Version 1.2 or later and ShivaRemote 3.5, you can ignore this error message and your IPX-dependent software will function without errors. The later versions of the VLMs have been designed to handle this problem better than earlier versions. This warning message can be turned off by editing the SREMOTE.INI file and changing the following line.

```
[Options]
NotifyIPXAddress=No
```

If you are not using the NetWare VLMs or if you are using VLMs earlier than Version 1.2, close the dial-in connection and restart your computer, then dial in to the remote network again

Error: The MS Exchange directory service could not be opened. You must change your password before logging on for the first time. Microsoft Exchange for MS-DOS ID no:5866-80040120

Resolution: Start the User Manager for Domains on a Windows NT computer and select the Windows NT account that you are attempting to log on to. Clear the **User Must Change Password at Next Logon** checkbox.

A P P E N D I X   C

References and Resources

This list contains references to Microsoft support offerings and other sources of information on Exchange Server found through Microsoft Press, on the Microsoft Web site, or on TechNet.

Support and technical resources	Where found
Microsoft Support: Pointer to Support Online and support options	http://www.microsoft.com/support/
Microsoft Support Online: Access to Microsoft Technical Support's entire collection of problem-solving tools and technical information, including the Knowledge Base, troubleshooting wizards, service packs, and other downloads	http://support.microsoft.com/support /a.asp?M=F
Microsoft Enterprise Services: Worldwide services and support for large organizations	http://www.microsoft.com/Enterprise /support.htm
Premier Technical Support	http://www.microsoft.com/Enterprise /support/techsupport.htm
Premier Technical Account Management	http://www.microsoft.com/Enterprise /support/TAM.htm
Basic and Enhanced Supportability Review	Consult your Microsoft Consulting Services liaison or Technical Account Manager for additional information
Microsoft Certified Solution Providers	http://www.microsoft.com/mcsp/
Microsoft Certified Professional (MCP) training	http://www.microsoft.com/mcp/
Microsoft Training and Certification	http://www.microsoft.com/train_cert/
Microsoft Authorized Training Centers (ATECs)	http://www.microsoft.com/train_cert /train/atec.htm

(continued)

Support and technical resources	Where found

Microsoft Press:
Look for the following titles:
 	
   Microsoft Exchange Connectivity Guide
   Microsoft Exchange 5.0 Step by Step
   Field Guide to Microsoft Exchange
   BackOffice Resource Guide: Part One
   Microsoft Exchange
   BackOffice Resource Guide, Second
   Edition
	1-800-MSPRESS (677-7377)
	http://mspress.microsoft.com/

Microsoft BackOffice Web site	http://www.backoffice.microsoft.com
Microsoft Windows NT Web site	http://www.microsoft.com/ntserver/
Microsoft Exchange Web site	http://www.microsoft.com/exchange/
Microsoft Exchange 5.5 Routing Objects	http://www.backoffice.microsoft.com /downtrial/default.asp
Sample application download	http://www.microsoft.com/ithome /resource/exchange/default.htm
Microsoft Security Advisor Web site	http://www.microsoft.com/security
Microsoft Outlook 97 Administrator's Guide	http://www.microsoft.com/outlook /adminguide/
Microsoft Developer Network (MSDN)	http://www.microsoft.com/msdn/
Microsoft TechNet: Technical information, including recent sample application information on Microsoft Exchange	http://www.microsoft.com/technet/
Worldwide Exchange Connectivity Competency Center (EC3): Microsoft Consulting Services (MCS) group that works with other MCS offices and key partners, assisting enterprise customers with Exchange connectivity and migration	E-mail EC3@microsoft.com

General information	Where found
Microsoft Solutions Framework: To help you plan an enterprise architecture that adapts to (or drives) industry change, consistently build business-driven applications, and manage your computing environment	http://www.microsoft.com/msf/ You can also find an overview article on TechNet.
MS Exchange Server 5.5 Reviewer's Guide	Search TechNet
Managing Infrastructure Deployment Projects	Search TechNet

(continued)

General information	Where found
Q163537, Title: XGEN: Exchange Whitepapers Available on WWW	Query TechNet using the "Q" number, or search: http://support.microsoft.com /support/a.asp?M=F
Microsoft Exchange Installation Guide	Microsoft Exchange Server documentation (on the Exchange Server CD-ROM)
Microsoft Exchange Concepts and Planning Guide	Exchange Server CD-ROM
Microsoft Exchange Server Migration Guide	Exchange Server CD-ROM
Microsoft Exchange Administrator's Guide	Exchange Server CD-ROM
Microsoft Exchange Server 5.5 Resource Guide	*(Microsoft BackOffice Resource Kit, Second Edition)*
	For more information: http://mspress.microsoft.com/
	Available on TechNet
Microsoft Exchange Books Online	Exchange Server CD-ROM
Microsoft Outlook 97 Administrator's Guide	http://www.microsoft.com/outlook /adminguide/
Microsoft Outlook 98 Deployment Kit	On TechNet, May 1998 issue or later
"MS Exchange Server Migration and Coexistence: Planning Considerations and Components"	Search TechNet
"MS Exchange Server Host-Based Migration and Coexistence"	Search TechNet
"MS Exchange and Mail Coexistence and Migration with LAN and Host Mail Systems"	Search TechNet
"Module 5: Post Office Protocol 3 (POP3) Service"	Search for this title on TechNet, and then use **Sync Contents** (CTRL+S) to see the table of contents.
"Module 6: Lightweight Directory Access Protocol (LDAP)"	Search for this title on TechNet, and then use **Sync Contents** (CTRL+S) to see the table of contents.
"MS Exchange Forms Designer Fundamentals"	Search TechNet
"Extending MS Exchange Forms"	Search TechNet
"Introduction to Collaboration Data Objects"	Search TechNet
"Active Directory Services Interface in the MS Exchange 5.5 Environment"	Search TechNet

(continued)

General information	Where found
"Active Directory Service Interfaces—The Easy Way to Access and Manage LDAP-Based Directories (Windows NT 4.0)"	Search TechNet
"Integrating Client Applications with MS Exchange"	Search TechNet
"Interoperability with MS Exchange, MS Mail 3.*x*, MS Schedule+ 95 and 1.0"	Search TechNet

Exchange traffic analysis	Where found
"MS Exchange Performance: Concurrent Users Per Server"	Search TechNet
Q149217, Title: XCLN: Microsoft Exchange Message Size Limitations	Query TechNet using the "Q" number.
	For the most up-to-date collection of Knowledge Base articles, search Microsoft Technical Support online: http://support.microsoft.com/support /a.asp?M=F
Q163576, Title: XGEN: Changing the RPC Binding Order	
Q136516, Title: XCLN: Improving Windows Client Startup Times	
Q167100, Title: XCLN: Out of Memory Errors with Microsoft Exchange 5.0 16-Bit Client	
Q155048, Title: XCLN: Troubleshooting Startup of Windows Client	
Q161626, Title: XCLN: Troubleshooting IPX/SPX Connections	

Key Management server and security	Where found
Basic security and algorithm information	http://www.rsa.com
Q177492, Title: XADM: Key Management Server Fails to Reissue Key	Query TechNet using the "Q" number.
	For the most up-to-date collection of Knowledge Base articles, search Microsoft Technical Support online: http://support.microsoft.com/support /a.asp?M=F
Q148432, Title: XADM: Location of the Key Management Server Software	
Q177309, Title: XADM: Setup Cannot Initialize the Key Management Database	

(continued)

Key Management server and security	Where found

Q177734, Title: XADM: KM Server Features Not Supported in Exchange 5.5 release

Q176737, Title: XADM: Key Management Server Fails to Start and Logs Event 5060

Q174743, Title: XADM: Cannot Install 4.0/5/0 KMS After Installing 5.5 Server

Q156713, Title: XADM: KM Server Stops Intermittently on Alpha Servers

Q154531, Title: XADM: Moving the KM Server to Another Server in the Site

Q153394, Title: XADM: Error When Selecting Security Tab for Mailbox

Q152849, Title: XADM: How to Recover from a Lost Key Management Server

Q151689, Title: XADM: Error Starting Key Management Server

Q149333, Title: XADM: The Basics of Advanced Security

Q152498, Title: XADM: Unable to Enable Advanced Security on User Account

Q169519, Title: XADM: Exchange 5.5 Remove All Option Removes Database Files

Q146464, Title: XCLN: Err Msg: Unable to Obtain a Valid…Revocation List

Q152686, Title: XCLN: How Expired Encryption Key Pairs Work

Q154089, Title: XCLN: Cannot Send Sealed Message when Offline

Q147421, Title: XFOR: How Exchange Encryption is Disabled on French Servers

Q176681, Title: XGEN: Description of Microsoft Exchange Server 5.5

Q146463, Title: XGEN: KMS Cannot Write Certificate Revocation List

Q143380, Title: XGEN: Exchange Server Services and Their Dependencies

Q170908, Title: INFO: Key Management Server Functions not Exposed to Developers

Information and resources for cc:Mail	Where found
Microsoft Outlook 97 Administrator's Guide	http://www.microsoft.com/outlook/adminguide/
Q169259, Title: OL97: New Nickname Features in Outlook 8.02	Query TechNet using the "Q" number, or search: http://support.microsoft.com/support/a.asp?M=F
CCREGMOD program	Look on the cc:Mail software CD-ROM or search: http://www.ccmail.com
MESA MailBox Converter for cc:Mail	http://www.mesa.com
ComAxis Technology Web site	http://www.comaxis.com

More information on Microsoft Mail	Where found
Microsoft Exchange Server Migration Guide, pp. 49–52	Exchange Server CD-ROM
Exchange Forms Designer (EFD) 1.0 compatibility	Chapter 4, "Microsoft Exchange Server Migration Guide," pp. 66–67 (Exchange Server CD-ROM)
Microsoft Mail for PC Networks Administrator's Guide, Chapter 14	Microsoft Mail for PC Networks server setup diskettes
DIRSYNC.TXT	Microsoft Mail for PC Networks server setup diskettes
Q114119, Title: PC Gen: Application Notes and Replacement Files for PC Mail	Query TechNet using the "Q" number.
	For the most up-to-date collection of Knowledge Base articles, search Microsoft Technical Support online: http://support.microsoft.com/support/a.asp?M=F
Q158308, Title: XFOR: Err Msg: Initialization of Dynamic Link Library Failed [exchange]	
Q108831, Title: PC DirSync: Err Msg: Fatal [203] GAL Rebuild Problem	
Q99117, Title: PC DirSync: Err Msg: Fatal [203] GAL Rebuild Problem	
Q148389, Title: XFOR: How to Backbone MSMail 3.x over Exchange	
Q147698, Title: XADM: Configuring the Schedule+ Free/Busy Connector	
Q155897, Title: OL97: Using Schedule+ as the Primary Calendar in Outlook 97	
Q158694, Title: XFOR: DirSync: Map Template Info Between MSMail & Exchange	

(continued)

More information on Microsoft Mail	Where found
Q152231, Title: XFOR: How To Reset Microsoft Exchange DirSync Numbers	
Q166545, Title: XFOR: DXA Appends 001 Only When Needed [Exchange]	
Q156545, Title: XFOR: How to Set Up a 2nd MS-type Proxy Address for MSMail Users	
Q149284, Title: XADM: PC Mail Shared Folders not Converted To Public Folders	
Q175978, Title: XFOR: List of Reserved Microsoft Mail Network Names	
Q152231, Title: XFOR: How To Reset Microsoft Exchange DirSync Numbers	
PODIAG.EXE	Microsoft Mail for PC Networks version 3.5 installation software, or in application note WA0883 (see Q114119)
	You can download this from: ftp://ftp.microsoft.com/Softlib/Mslfiles
WA0940.EXE	In application note WA0940 (see Q114119)
	Download this from ftp://ftp.microsoft.com/Softlib/Mslfiles
Application note WA0725 on directory synchronization	Query TechNet using "WA0725".
	Download the executable from: ftp://ftp.microsoft.com/Softlib/Mslfiles

AppleTalk/Quarterdeck/StarNine Connectivity	Where found
Q154619, Title: XFOR: Export Menu Disabled on Exchange Connection DER	Query TechNet using the "Q" number.
	For the most up-to-date collection of Knowledge Base articles, search Microsoft Technical Support online: http://support.microsoft.com/support/a.asp?M=F
Q156961, Title: XFOR: Mac Connection Gateway Will Not Install on System 7.5.3	
Q160664, Title: XFOR: Cannot Configure Microsoft Mail Connector (AppleTalk)	
Q169659, Title: XFOR: Err Msg: AppleTalk Mail Connector Service Not Created	

(continued)

AppleTalk/Quarterdeck/StarNine Connectivity	Where found
Q152477, Title: XFOR: Handshake Files Moved to BADMAIL Directory	
Q171259, Title: XFOR: How to Move the Microsoft Mail Connector Postoffice	

More information on Lotus Notes	Where found
Migrating from Lotus Notes to Microsoft Exchange Server	You can find an abstract of this service guide on TechNet, April 1998 issue or later: "Migrating from Lotus Notes to MS Exchange Service Guide Abstract". MCSPs can order service guides by calling 1-800 SOL PROV. Other customers can order by calling 1-800-255-8414. For more information about service guides, e-mail SGQuest@microsoft.com.
"Connector for Lotus Notes"	Search TechNet
"MS Exchange Server Migration and Coexistence: Planning Considerations and Components for Lotus cc:Mail"	Search TechNet
Q175746: Title: XFOR: Specifying the Container for Propagated Users	Query TechNet using the "Q" number. For the most up-to-date collection of Knowledge Base articles, search Microsoft Technical Support online: http://support.microsoft.com/support /a.asp?M=F
Q180517, Title: XFOR: Customizing Dirsync Between Exchange and Notes	
Q174207, Title: XFOR: Notes Proxy Domain Name Over 31 Characters Stripped	
Q169393, Title: XFOR: Messages Containing Doclinks Are Getting Stuck in Exchange	
Q174730, Title: XFOR: Lotus Notes Invitations Result in NDR	
Q179057, Title: XFOR: Exchange-Notes Dirsync Fails with Truncated Person Doc	
Q177597, Title: XFOR: Delivery and Read Reports Do Not Appear in Lotus Notes	

(continued)

More information on Lotus Notes	Where found
Q177598, Title: XFOR: RTF Always Sent from Exchange Server to Lotus Notes	
Q175836, Title: XFOR: Lotus Notes Low Delivery Priority Message Not Delivered	
PROFGEN.EXE	*Microsoft Exchange 5.0 Resource Kit* (BackOffice Resource Kit)
CHNGINBX.EXE	Valuepack directory on the Outlook CD-ROM

Information on SMS and unattended setup	Where found
SMS Installer download	http://backoffice.microsoft.com /downtrial
"Advanced Techniques of Software Distribution with the SMS Installer"	Search TechNet
Microsoft Outlook 97 Administrator's Guide	http://www.microsoft.com/outlook /adminguide/
Q181864, Title: XADM: Setup/Q Prompts for Service Account	Query TechNet using the "Q" number.
	For the most up-to-date collection of Knowledge Base articles, search Microsoft Technical Support online: http://support.microsoft.com/support /a.asp?M=F
Q175115, Title: XADM: Err Msg: There is Something Wrong with the INI File	
Q180404, Title: XADM: Silent Mode Setup Does Not Support Upgrade Mode	
Q176243, Title: XADM: Batch Setup-Setup /r /q Options Combined Unsupported	
Q168490, Title: XADM: Unattended Exchange Server Setup	
Schema properties and attributes	See Microsoft Exchange Books Online (Exchange Server CD-ROM)

Knowledge Base articles on upgrading to Exchange 5.5	Where found
"Microsoft Exchange Server 5.5 Upgrade Procedures"	Query TechNet using the "Q" number.
	For the most up-to-date collection of Knowledge Base articles, search Microsoft Technical Support online: http://support.microsoft.com/support /a.asp?M=F

(continued)

Knowledge Base articles on upgrading to Exchange 5.5	Where found
Q179258, Title: XADM: Considerations When Upgrading to Exchange Server 5.5	
Q170280, Title: XADM: Upgrading From Exchange Standard Edition to the Enterprise	
Q152659, Title: XADM: Importing Exchange Accounts from Another Organization	
Q153121, Title: XADM: Migrating from WGPO to Exchange	
Q170337, Title: XADM: User Manager Can Cause File in Use Errors	
Q174254, Title: XADM: GroupWise Users must Grant Access Rights to be Migrated	
Q174729, Title: XADM: Err Msg: No Mapping Between Account Names and Security IDs	
Q175098, Title: XADM: Unexpected Error Occurs During Upgrade or Installation	
Q175100, Title: XADM: Unexpected Error 0xc0040000 Upgrading to Exchange 5.5	
Q176757, Title: XADM: Administrator Program Column Settings Lost After Upgrade	
Q177221, Title: XADM: Errors Occur During Exchange Service Pack Upgrade	
Q177735, Title: XADM: Unable To Access Exchange Administrator Program	
Q177959, Title: XADM: Information Store Does Not Start, Error -1022	
Q178302, Title: XADM: Upgrade to Exchange 5.5 Fails If Virus Software Is Enabled	
Q178303, Title: XADM: Chat 5.5 Err Msg: Unable To Start Microsoft Chat Service	
Q178779, Title: XADM: Exchange 5.5 Upgrade Fails with -1011 (Out of Memory)	
Q178857, Title: XADM: Setup.exe Not Found On Premier Select CD-ROM	
Q178919, Title: XADM: Exchange Event Service Not Installed During Upgrade	

(continued)

Knowledge Base articles on upgrading to Exchange 5.5	Where found
Q179927, Title: XADM: KCC Site Teardown Blocked by Site-Proxy-Space Attribute	
Q180009, Title: XADM: Exchange 5.5 Upgrade Fails With ID No: c106fdda	
Q180403, Title: XADM: Error Message Trying to Install Exchange 5.5 Upgrade Only	
Q180404, Title: XADM: Silent Mode Setup Does Not Support Upgrade Mode	
Q180876, Title: XADM: Err Msg: Invalid Home Server Definition in User List File	
Q182320, Title: XADM: Unable to Upgrade from Exchange Server 4.0 to 5.5	
Q182665, Title: XADM: Exchange Migration Wizard Fails with 7026 error	
Q182903, Title: XADM: Eseutil Utility Replaces Edbutil from Earlier Versions	
Q183105, Title: XADM: Dr. Watson While Upgrading from 4.0 SP4 to 5.5	
Q183312, Title: XADM: SFS Mail Not Migrated When Custom Recipient Is Converted	
Q145964, Title: XCLN: Upgrade Fails; Err Msg: Application(s) Are Running	
Q168182, Title: XCLN: Wizard Doesn't Migrate Schedule+ Info to Outlook Calendar	
Q173597, Title: XCLN: Migrating PAB Entries From Microsoft	
Q178124, Title: XCLN: Microsoft Outlook for Macintosh and Windows 3.1x	
Q181694, Title: XCLN: How to Upgrade Shared Workstation Installations of Exchange	
Q181939, Title: XCLN: Macintosh Mail Migration Fails to Import SMTP PAB Entries	
Q183531, Title: XCLN: How to Update Exchange Forms Designer Forms	
Q166567, Title: XCON: How to Enable Lowest Cost Routes Only	
Q164456, Title: XFOR: Migrated MS Mail Users May Not Receive Messages in Inbox	

(continued)

Knowledge Base articles on upgrading to Exchange 5.5	Where found
Q169130, Title: XFOR: MS Mail Migration Fails When User List File Is Specified	
Q169659, Title: XFOR: Err Msg: AppleTalk Mail Connector Service Not Created	
Q173895, Title: XFOR: Migration Process is Faster on an Intel Processor	
Q174037, Title: XFOR: OLE Objects Larger Than 1 MB Not Migrated into Exchange	
Q174153, Title: XFOR: Incorrect Character Mappings when MSFS32.DLL Doesn't Match	
Q174167, Title: XFOR: Forum Password Security Lost After Collabra Migration	
Q174168, Title: XFOR: GroupWise Messages Missing After Migration	
Q174253, Title: XFOR: MAC Binary Attachments not Migrated from GroupWise	
Q174725, Title: XFOR: Packing List Code Page 10000 or 437 May Cause Mismatch	
Q174738, Title: XFOR: Migrated Users Assigned Random PST Password	
Q174740, Title: XFOR: Error When Migrating Version 6 cc:Mail Post Office	
Q174749, Title: XFOR: cc:Mail Migration Does Not Create PST File	
Q175103, Title: XFOR: Migration Wizard Contains Inaccurate Help File Option	
Q176740, Title: XFOR: Migrated GroupWise Users Cannot See Migrated Messages	
Q177998, Title: XFOR: IMAP/POP3 Clients Cannot Reply to Migrated Messages	
Q179980, Title: XFOR: DBCS Messages Not Migrated Correctly from GroupWise	
Q180907, Title: XFOR: Unable to Send Bitmap in Body of Message	
Q181125, Title: XFOR: Bcc Recipients Visible in Migrated cc:Mail Messages	
Q181130, Title: XFOR: Additional Characters Appear in Migrated cc:Mail Messages	

(continued)

Knowledge Base articles on upgrading to Exchange 5.5	Where found
Q181636, Title: XFOR: Rule For Forwarding To Internet Address Does Not Work	
Q182279, Title: XFOR: Incorrect Cc: List When Resending or Forwarding From PROFS	
Q166349, Title: XGEN: Microsoft Exchange Version Numbers	
Q168735, Title: XGEN: README.TXT: Microsoft Exchange 5.0 U.S. Service Pack 2	
Q175203, Title: XWEB: Pine 3.96 Cannot Handle IMAP DRAFT Flag	
Q179895, Title: XWEB: Err Msg. Object Moved When Accessing Active Server	
Q182440, Title: XWEB: Err Msg: Unable to Render This View424Object Required	
Q175676, Title: OL97: Summary of Changes in Outlook 8.03	

Third-party information	Where found
MESA home page	http://www.mesa.com
Lotus cc:Mail Web site	http://www.ccmail.com
ComAxis Technology Web site	http://www.comaxis.com

Index

Numbers and Symbols

A

mspress.microsoft.com

Microsoft Press Online is your road map to the best available print and multimedia materials—resources that will help you maximize the effectiveness of Microsoft® software products. Our goal is making it easy and convenient for you to find exactly the Microsoft Press® book or interactive product you need, as well as bringing you the latest in training and certification materials from Microsoft Press.

Where do you want to go today?®

Microsoft Press has titles to help everyone— *from new users to seasoned developers—*

Step by Step Series
Self-paced tutorials for classroom instruction or individualized study

Starts Here™ Series
Interactive instruction on CD-ROM that helps students learn by doing

Field Guide Series
Concise, task-oriented A–Z references for quick, easy answers— anywhere

Official Series
Timely books on a wide variety of Internet topics geared for advanced users

All User Training   All User Reference

Quick Course® Series
Fast, to-the-point instruction for new users

At a Glance Series
Quick visual guides for task-oriented instruction

Running Series
A comprehensive curriculum alternative to standard documentation books

Have *best practices and techniques* at your fingertips *24 hours a day.*

U.S.A.	**$39.99**
U.K.	£34.99 [V.A.T. included]
Canada	$57.99
ISBN 0-7356-0528-9	

MANAGING AND MAINTAINING MICROSOFT® EXCHANGE SERVER 5.5 lets you leverage Microsoft Consulting Services (MCS) resources and make the most of Microsoft Exchange Server 5.5, the messaging and collaboration component of Microsoft BackOffice®. IT professionals, consultants, and technology integrators can learn about the issues and benefits of implementing Microsoft Exchange 5.5 and use this information to develop the most efficient messaging system possible. "How to" information derived from extensive field experience helps you set up and fine-tune procedures for administration, maintenance, disaster recovery, and other crucial system areas.

***Microsoft*®*Press**

MICROSOFT LICENSE AGREEMENT

(Deploying Microsoft® Exchange Server 5.5 - Book Companion CD)

IMPORTANT—READ CAREFULLY: This Microsoft End-User License Agreement ("EULA") is a legal agreement between you (either an individual or an entity) and Microsoft Corporation for the Microsoft product identified above, which includes computer software and may include associated media, printed materials, and "online" or electronic documentation ("SOFTWARE PRODUCT"). Any component included within the SOFTWARE PRODUCT that is accompanied by a separate End-User License Agreement shall be governed by such agreement and not the terms set forth below. By installing, copying or otherwise using the SOFTWARE PRODUCT, you agree to be bound by the terms of this EULA. If you do not agree to the terms of this EULA, you are not authorized to install, copy or otherwise use the SOFTWARE PRODUCT; you may, however, return the SOFTWARE PRODUCT, along with all printed materials and other items that form a part of the Microsoft product that includes the SOFT-WARE PRODUCT, to the place you obtained them for a full refund.

SOFTWARE PRODUCT LICENSE

The SOFTWARE PRODUCT is protected by United States copyright laws and international copyright treaties, as well as other intellectual property laws and treaties. The SOFTWARE PRODUCT is licensed, not sold.

1. **GRANT OF LICENSE.** This EULA grants you the following rights:

   a. **Software Product.** You may install and use one copy of the SOFTWARE PRODUCT on a single computer. The primary user of the computer on which the SOFTWARE PRODUCT is installed may make a second copy for his or her exclusive use on a portable computer.

   b. **Storage/Network Use.** You may also store or install a copy of the SOFTWARE PRODUCT on a storage device, such as a network server, used only to install or run the SOFTWARE PRODUCT on your other computers over an internal network; however, you must acquire and dedicate a license for each separate computer on which the SOFTWARE PRODUCT is installed or run from the storage device. A license for the SOFTWARE PRODUCT may not be shared or used concurrently on different computers.

   c. **License Pak.** If you have acquired this EULA in a Microsoft License Pak, you may make the number of additional copies of the computer software portion of the SOFTWARE PRODUCT authorized on the printed copy of this EULA, and you may use each copy in the manner specified above. You are also entitled to make a corresponding number of secondary copies for portable computer use as specified above.

   d. **Sample Code.** Solely with respect to portions, if any, of the SOFTWARE PRODUCT that are identified as sample code in the Readme file that forms a part of the SOFTWARE PRODUCT (the "SAMPLE CODE"):

      i. **Use and Modification.** Microsoft grants you the right to use and modify the source code version of the SAMPLE CODE, *provided* you comply with subsection (d)(iii) below. You may not distribute the SAMPLE CODE, or any modified version of the SAMPLE CODE, in source code form.

      ii. **Redistributable Files.** Provided you comply with subsection (d)(iii) below, Microsoft grants you a nonexclusive, royalty-free right to reproduce and distribute the object code version of the SAMPLE CODE and any modified version of the SAMPLE CODE, other than SAMPLE CODE, or any modified version thereof, designated as not redistributable in the Readme file that forms a part of the SOFT-WARE PRODUCT (the "Non-Redistributable Sample Code"). All SAMPLE CODE other than the Non-Redistributable Sample Code is collectively referred to as the "REDISTRIBUTABLES."

      iii. **Redistribution Requirements.** If you redistribute the REDISTRIBUTABLES, you agree to: (i) distribute the REDISTRIBUTABLES in object code form only in conjunction with and as a part of your software application product; (ii) not use Microsoft's name, logo, or trademarks to market your software application product; (iii) include a valid copyright notice on your software application product; (iv) indemnify, hold harmless, and defend Microsoft from and against any claims or lawsuits, including attorney's fees, that arise or result from the use or distribution of your software application product; and (v) not permit further distribution of the REDISTRIBUTABLES by your end user. Contact Microsoft for the applicable royalties due and other licensing terms for all other uses and/or distribution of the REDISTRIBUTABLES.

2. **DESCRIPTION OF OTHER RIGHTS AND LIMITATIONS.**

   - **Not For Resale Software.** If the SOFTWARE PRODUCT is labeled "Not For Resale" or "NFR," then, notwithstanding other sections of this EULA, you may not resell, or otherwise transfer for value, the SOFTWARE PRODUCT.

   - **Limitations on Reverse Engineering, Decompilation, and Disassembly.** You may not reverse engineer, decompile, or disassemble the SOFTWARE PRODUCT, except and only to the extent that such activity is expressly permitted by applicable law notwithstanding this limitation.

   - **Separation of Components.** The SOFTWARE PRODUCT is licensed as a single product. Its component parts may not be separated for use on more than one computer.

   - **Rental.** You may not rent, lease or lend the SOFTWARE PRODUCT.

- **Support Services.** Microsoft may, but is not obligated to, provide you with support services related to the SOFTWARE PRODUCT ("Support Services"). Use of Support Services is governed by the Microsoft policies and programs described in the user manual, in "on line" documentation and/or other Microsoft-provided materials. Any supplemental software code provided to you as part of the Support Services shall be considered part of the SOFTWARE PRODUCT and subject to the terms and conditions of this EULA. With respect to technical information you provide to Microsoft as part of the Support Services, Microsoft may use such information for its business purposes, including for product support and development. Microsoft will not utilize such technical information in a form that personally identifies you.

- **Software Transfer.** You may permanently transfer all of your rights under this EULA, provided you retain no copies, you transfer all of the SOFTWARE PRODUCT (including all component parts, the media and printed materials, any upgrades, this EULA, and, if applicable, the Certificate of Authenticity), **and** the recipient agrees to the terms of this EULA.

- **Termination.** Without prejudice to any other rights, Microsoft may terminate this EULA if you fail to comply with the terms and conditions of this EULA. In such event, you must destroy all copies of the SOFTWARE PRODUCT and all of its component parts.

3. **COPYRIGHT.** All title and copyrights in and to the SOFTWARE PRODUCT (including but not limited to any images, photographs, animations, video, audio, music, text, SAMPLE CODE, REDISTRIBUTABLES, and "applets" incorporated into the SOFTWARE PRODUCT), and any copies of the SOFTWARE PRODUCT are owned by Microsoft or its suppliers. The SOFTWARE PRODUCT is protected by copyright laws and international treaty provisions. Therefore, you must treat the SOFTWARE PRODUCT like any other copyrighted material **except** that you may install the SOFTWARE PRODUCT on a single computer provided you keep the original solely for backup or archival purposes. You may not copy the printed materials accompanying the SOFTWARE PRODUCT.

4. **U.S. GOVERNMENT RESTRICTED RIGHTS.** The SOFTWARE PRODUCT and documentation are provided with RESTRICTED RIGHTS. Use, duplication, or disclosure by the Government is subject to restrictions as set forth in subparagraph (c)(1)(ii) of the Rights in Technical Data and Computer Software clause at DFARS 252.227-7013 or subparagraphs (c)(1) and (2) of the Commercial Computer Software—Restricted Rights at 48 CFR 52.227-19, as applicable. Manufacturer is Microsoft Corporation/One Microsoft Way/Redmond, WA 98052-6399.

5. **EXPORT RESTRICTIONS.** You agree that you will not export or re-export the SOFTWARE PRODUCT, any part thereof, or any process or service that is the direct product of the SOFTWARE PRODUCT (the foregoing collectively referred to as the "Restricted Components"), to any country, person, entity or end user subject to U.S. export restrictions. You specifically agree not to export or re-export any of the Restricted Components (i) to any country to which the U.S. has embargoed or restricted the export of goods or services, which currently include, but are not necessarily limited to Cuba, Iran, Iraq, Libya, North Korea, Sudan and Syria, or to any national of any such country, wherever located, who intends to transmit or transport the Restricted Components back to such country; (ii) to any end-user who you know or have reason to know will utilize the Restricted Components in the design, development or production of nuclear, chemical or biological weapons; or (iii) to any end-user who has been prohibited from participating in U.S. export transactions by any federal agency of the U.S. government. You warrant and represent that neither the BXA nor any other U.S. federal agency has suspended, revoked or denied your export privileges.

DISCLAIMER OF WARRANTY

NO WARRANTIES OR CONDITIONS. MICROSOFT EXPRESSLY DISCLAIMS ANY WARRANTY OR CONDITION FOR THE SOFTWARE PRODUCT. THE SOFTWARE PRODUCT AND ANY RELATED DOCUMENTATION IS PROVIDED "AS IS" WITHOUT WARRANTY OR CONDITION OF ANY KIND, EITHER EXPRESS OR IMPLIED, INCLUDING, WITHOUT LIMITATION, THE IMPLIED WARRANTIES OF MERCHANTABILITY, FITNESS FOR A PARTICULAR PURPOSE, OR NONINFRINGEMENT. THE ENTIRE RISK ARISING OUT OF USE OR PERFORMANCE OF THE SOFTWARE PRODUCT REMAINS WITH YOU.

LIMITATION OF LIABILITY. TO THE MAXIMUM EXTENT PERMITTED BY APPLICABLE LAW, IN NO EVENT SHALL MICROSOFT OR ITS SUPPLIERS BE LIABLE FOR ANY SPECIAL, INCIDENTAL, INDIRECT, OR CONSEQUENTIAL DAMAGES WHATSOEVER (INCLUDING, WITHOUT LIMITATION, DAMAGES FOR LOSS OF BUSINESS PROFITS, BUSINESS INTERRUPTION, LOSS OF BUSINESS INFORMATION, OR ANY OTHER PECUNIARY LOSS) ARISING OUT OF THE USE OF OR INABILITY TO USE THE SOFTWARE PRODUCT OR THE PROVISION OF OR FAILURE TO PROVIDE SUPPORT SERVICES, EVEN IF MICROSOFT HAS BEEN ADVISED OF THE POSSIBILITY OF SUCH DAMAGES. IN ANY CASE, MICROSOFT'S ENTIRE LIABILITY UNDER ANY PROVISION OF THIS EULA SHALL BE LIMITED TO THE GREATER OF THE AMOUNT ACTUALLY PAID BY YOU FOR THE SOFTWARE PRODUCT OR US$5.00; PROVIDED, HOWEVER, IF YOU HAVE ENTERED INTO A MICROSOFT SUPPORT SERVICES AGREEMENT, MICROSOFT'S ENTIRE LIABILITY REGARDING SUPPORT SERVICES SHALL BE GOVERNED BY THE TERMS OF THAT AGREEMENT. BECAUSE SOME STATES AND JURISDICTIONS DO NOT ALLOW THE EXCLUSION OR LIMITATION OF LIABILITY, THE ABOVE LIMITATION MAY NOT APPLY TO YOU.

MISCELLANEOUS

This EULA is governed by the laws of the State of Washington USA, except and only to the extent that applicable law mandates governing law of a different jurisdiction.

Should you have any questions concerning this EULA, or if you desire to contact Microsoft for any reason, please contact the Microsoft subsidiary serving your country, or write: Microsoft Sales Information Center/One Microsoft Way/Redmond, WA 98052-6399.

Register Today!

Return this
Deploying Microsoft® Exchange Server 5.5
registration card for
a Microsoft Press® catalog

U.S. and Canada addresses only. Fill in information below and mail postage-free. Please mail only the bottom half of this page.

0-7356-0529-7   ***DEPLOYING MICROSOFT®***   ***Owner Registration Card***
EXCHANGE SERVER 5.5

NAME

INSTITUTION OR COMPANY NAME

ADDRESS

CITY   STATE   ZIP

Microsoft ®*Press*
Quality Computer Books

**For a free catalog of
Microsoft Press® products, call
1-800-MSPRESS**

BUSINESS REPLY MAIL
FIRST-CLASS MAIL   PERMIT NO. 53   BOTHELL, WA

POSTAGE WILL BE PAID BY ADDRESSEE

MICROSOFT PRESS REGISTRATION
DEPLOYING MICROSOFT®
EXCHANGE SERVER 5.5
PO BOX 3019
BOTHELL WA   98041-9946